PHILOSOPHY FOR AS

Philosophy for AS is the definitive textbook for students of the Advanced Subsidiary Level syllabus beginning in 2008. Structured closely around the examination specifications, it covers the two units of the AS level in an exceptionally clear and student-friendly style. As an 'invitation' to philosophy, the book encourages and enables students to engage philosophically with the following syllabus topics:

- Reason and experience
- Why should I be governed?
- Why should I be moral?
- The idea of God
- Persons
- Knowledge of the external world
- Tolerance
- The value of art
- God and the world
- The debate about free will and determinism

All the chapters are split into Introduction, which introduces the basic ideas, arguments and objections of the issue, and Development, which clarifies the previous section, introduces more complex ideas, and encourages students to link up ideas and draw new implications. To aid student learning and revision, each chapter includes:

- comprehension questions to test core knowledge
- discussion questions to deepen understanding
- 'going further' sections for advanced study
- cross-references to help students make connections
- helpful summaries and a glossary.

In addition, a chapter on exam preparation contains a wealth of helpful hints and tips on revision and exam techniques.

Written by an experienced philosopher and A level consultant, *Philosophy for AS* is an essential course book for all students of AS level philosophy.

Michael Lacewing is a Senior Lecturer in Philosophy at Heythrop College, University of London. He is founder of the company A Level Philosophy, and a consultant on philosophy at A Level for the British Philosophical Association.

PHILOSOPHY FOR AS

Michael Lacewing

Routledge
Taylor & Francis Group

LONDON AND NEW YORK

First published 2008
by Routledge
2 Park Square, Milton Park, Abingdon, Oxon, OX14 4RN

Simultaneously published in the USA and Canada
by Routledge
270 Madison Ave, New York, NY 10016

Reprinted 2009, 2010

Routledge is an imprint of the Taylor & Francis Group, an informa business

© 2008 Michael Lacewing

Typeset in Mixage by
Keystroke, 28 High Street, Tettenhall, Wolverhampton
Printed and bound in Great Britain by
the MPG Books Group

British Library Cataloguing in Publication Data
A catalogue record for this book is available from the British Library

Library of Congress Cataloging-in-Publication Data
Lacewing, Michael, 1971–
    Philosophy for AS / Michael Lacewing.
        p. cm.
    Includes indexes.
    ISBN 978–0–415–45821–4 (pbk. : alk. paper)
    1. Philosophy—Textbooks. I. Title.
    BD21.L17 2008
    107.6—dc22   2008016275

ISBN13: 978–0–415–45821–4
ISBN10: 0–415–45821–8

CONTENTS

ACKNOWLEDGEMENTS

Figure 6.2   Stockbyte, courtesy of Getty Images
Figure 6.4   Alex and Laila, courtesy of Getty Images
Figure 6.5   Benjamin Piggott

INTRODUCTION

An invitation to philosophy

The AQA AS Philosophy syllabus has been described by one of the senior examiners as an 'invitation' to philosophy rather than an 'introduction' to philosophy.[1] The emphasis is not primarily on *learning* philosophical *theories* but on *engaging* philosophically with a number of *issues*, the ten issues that make up the two units of the AS.

To help along the idea of an 'invitation', each chapter in this book is divided into two sections: 'Introduction' and 'Development'. The Introduction runs through the basic ideas, arguments and objections surrounding an issue. The aim is to get you, as a student, engaging in the argument. The discussion is provocative and leaves many lines of thought hanging. So, for instance, you might come up with new objections or replies that haven't yet been discussed. That's the idea.

If you haven't read philosophy before, you'll soon find that you have to read it in a very different way from reading anything else. Each paragraph is intended to be taken as a thought to be considered, re-read, reflected on. *Philosophy needs to be read slowly*; no one – even professional philosophers – just start at the beginning and keep reading until the end!

By the end of the Introduction, you should have got into the debate, and understand your way around. Then, in Development, we go deeper. We clarify and expand the ideas previously discussed, introduce more complex ideas, look at further objections and new replies, we link ideas and draw out new implications. In this section, as a result, things get a bit more theoretical. But the aim is still to provide you with ideas, arguments and objections that help you analyse, discuss and evaluate the issues. To follow the arguments, you may need to go back over the Introduction – but that is the idea. Philosophy needs to be read more than once to be understood.

How to use this book

Following the syllabus

Each of the ten issues is discussed in a separate chapter. Each chapter opens with a brief synopsis of what the chapter covers and what you should be able to do by the end of it, followed by the AQA syllabus for that issue. Within the Introduction and Development, the discussion follows the AQA syllabus very closely. Many headings and sub-headings from the syllabus are used to structure the discussion, and each section is further divided by the main ideas, arguments and objections. There is also an index of the syllabus on p. 405, which provides the page numbers on which each part of the syllabus is discussed.

Glossary

Philosophical terms are explained when they are first introduced, and there is a glossary providing definitions of the most important ones, so that wherever you start to read from, you can always look up the words you don't understand (words that appear in the glossary are in **bold**).

Marginal features

Alongside the text, there are a number of features in the margin. There are definitions of key terms; further thoughts; cross-references to other parts of the syllabus, for example, to the part of the A2 syllabus that looks at a particular point in more depth; references for quotations or to philosophical texts where the argument being discussed can be found; and questions that test your understanding. To get the most out of the book, stop and answer the questions – in your own words – as you go along.

Within Development, there are also additional questions that test your abilities to analyse and evaluate the arguments. These are the kinds of questions you'll find in the exam. To answer some of these questions, you'll need to draw on relevant material in the Introduction, not just the section you've just read.

Also in Development, there are 'Going Further' sections. These provide discussions of more difficult ideas or take the arguments further. So they will broaden your knowledge, and help you 'go further' in your evaluation of the theories and arguments.

At the end of each discussion, there is a list of 'Key Points', putting clearly the main issues the discussion has covered. And at the end of each chapter, there is a summary that outlines the main arguments and objections discussed.

Understanding is also about being able to make connections. So there are lots of CROSS-REFERENCES to other discussions, so that you can follow up the links and see how arguments and issues connect.

The final chapter provides advice on how to revise for the exam, and how to perform well on the day.

Companion website and further resources

You can find further resources, including book lists, helpful weblinks, PowerPoint presentations, and material on the philosophical skills you need to argue well, on the companion website www.routledge.com/alevel/philosophy.

The examination

Assessment objectives

The examiners mark your answers according to three principles, known as 'Assessment Objectives' (AOs). They are:

AO1: *Knowledge and understanding*: how well do you know and understand the central debates for a particular issue, the positions philosophers have defended, and the arguments they use to defend them?

AO2: *Interpretation and analysis*: how well do you interpret and analyse relevant philosophical positions and arguments? Are you able to select and apply relevant ideas, concepts, examples, and arguments to support your account of an issue? Do you understand how the argument works and what the implications of a position are?

AO3: *Assessment and evaluation*: how well do you assess and evaluate arguments and counter-arguments? Are you able to construct arguments in support of a particular position, and defend it against objections? Do you understand whether an argument succeeds or fails and why? How well do you compare arguments and counter-arguments to weigh up what the most plausible position is?

In addition, you will be marked on your writing. Do you write clearly and grammatically, so that the examiner can understand what you mean? Does the way you write reflect a proper philosophical engagement with the issue? Are your points made coherently?

The structure of the exams

There are two exams, one for each of Unit 1 and Unit 2. Each of the exams lasts for 90 minutes. Each exam has five questions to choose from, one from each of the five themes for that unit. On each exam you must answer two questions. For Unit 1, you *must* answer the question on Reason and experience, and then one other.

Each question has two parts. Here are two examples, from the Unit 1 specimen paper:

Theme: Reason and experience

1 (a) Explain what is meant by *a priori* and explain **one** reason why the *a priori* is philosophically significant. *(15 marks)*

(b) 'All ideas derive from the sense experiences which they copy.' Discuss. *(30 marks)*

Theme: Why should I be governed?

2 (a) Explain and illustrate what is meant by 'power' in political contexts. *(15 marks)*

(b) Consider the claim that political obligations are founded upon consent. *(30 marks)*

The marks

All 15 marks for part (a) are marks for AO1 (Knowledge and understanding). Of the 30 marks for part (b), 3 are for AO1, 18 are for AO2 (Interpretation and analysis), and 9 are for AO3 (Assessment and evaluation).

Acknowledgements

In preparing this book, I have drawn on two excellent reference works: the *Stanford Encyclopedia of Philosophy* (http://plato.stanford.edu/contents.html) and the *Routledge Encyclopedia of Philosophy* (http://www.rep.routledge.com). Thanks to Routledge for providing me with free access during this time.

In addition, the following books greatly informed my discussions in particular chapters: Peter Carruthers, *Human Knowledge and Human Nature* (Chapter 1), Catriona McKinnon, *Toleration* (Chapter 7), Graham McFee, *Free Will* (Chapter 10).

Thanks also to Gemma Dunn, Priyanka Pathak and Tony Bruce at Routledge for encouraging this project, and to my colleagues at Heythrop College for supporting my work with A level philosophy.

NOTE
1   Dave Rawlinson, London, 13 November 2007. The phrase 'invitation to philosophy' comes from the title of a book by Martin Hollis.

1

AN INTRODUCTION TO PHILOSOPHY 1

Section 1: Reason and experience

epistemology

epistemology is the study ('-ology') of knowledge ('episteme') and related concepts, including belief, justification and certainty. It looks at the possibility and sources of knowledge.

argument

an argument is a reasoned inference from one set of claims - the premises - to another claim - the conclusion.

How do we know what we know? This question is central to the branch of philosophy called epistemology. At its heart are two very important, very interesting questions about being human: How are human beings 'hooked up' to the world? And what 'faculties' do we have that enable us to gain knowledge? We will discuss two positions: that all of our ideas and concepts, and all of our knowledge, come from experience; and that we have ideas and knowledge that we have gained some other way, for example, through reason or innately. By the end of the chapter, you should be able to analyse and evaluate a number of **arguments** for and objections to both these views, and be familiar with important four pairs of concepts: **analytic/synthetic** (p. 8), **a priori/a posteriori** (p. 9), **deductive/inductive** (p. 18), and **necessary/contingent** (p. 38). In addition, you should be able to evaluate claims about what is 'certain' and about the relationship between experience and concepts.

SYLLABUS CHECKLIST

The AQA AS syllabus for this chapter is:

Mind as a tabula rasa

✔ The strengths and weaknesses of the view that all ideas are derived from sense experience.

✔ The strengths and weaknesses of the view that claims about what exists must be ultimately grounded in and justified by sense experience.

Innate knowledge

✔ The strengths and weaknesses of the view that the mind contains innate knowledge regarding the way the world is: the doctrine of innate ideas and its philosophical significance.

✔ The view that some fundamental claims about what exists can be grounded in and justified by a priori intuition and/or demonstration.

✔ Is 'certainty' confined to introspection and the tautological?

Conceptual schemes

✔ The idea that experience is only intelligible as it is because it presents sensation through a predetermined conceptual scheme or framework; and the philosophical implications of this view.

In covering these issues candidates will be expected to demonstrate their understanding of the contrasts and connections between necessary and contingent truths, analytic and synthetic propositions, deductive and inductive arguments, a priori and a posteriori knowledge.

INTRODUCTION

Introductory ideas

Knowledge and belief

There are different types of knowledge: acquaintance knowledge (I know Oxford well), ability knowledge (I know how to ride a bike) and propositional knowledge (I know that eagles are birds). The first two types of knowledge are very

proposition

a proposition is a declarative statement, or more accurately, what is expressed by a declarative statement, for example, 'eagles are birds'. Propositions can go after the phrases 'I believe that . . .' and 'I know that . . .'.

Some philosophers have thought that another difference between knowledge and belief is *certainty*. Knowledge must be certain; beliefs don't have to be. If a belief isn't certain, then it can't count as knowledge. Whether this is right, and what is meant by certainty will be discussed in Is CERTAINTY CONFINED TO INTROSPECTION AND THE TAUTOLOGICAL? (p. 37).

Outline and illustrate the difference between belief and knowledge.

Come up with three different examples of analytic propositions and three of synthetic propositions.

interesting, but we are concerned only with the third, what it is to know some **proposition**, 'p'.

We intuitively make a distinction between belief and knowledge. People can believe propositions that aren't true; but if you know that p, then p must be true. For example, if you claim that flamingos are grey, and you *think* you know this, you are mistaken. If flamingos are not grey, but pink, then you can't know they are grey. Of course, you believe that they are grey; but that's the difference – beliefs can be false. You can't know something false; if it is false, then you don't know it. You have made a mistake, believing it to be true when it is not.

There is another distinction between beliefs and knowledge. People can have true beliefs without having any *evidence* or *justification* for their beliefs. For example, someone on a jury might think that the person on trial is guilty just from the way they dress. Their belief, that the person is guilty, might be true; but how someone dresses isn't evidence for whether they are a criminal! So belief can be accidentally true, relative to the evidence the person has; if it is, it isn't knowledge. Someone can hold a belief that is, in fact, true, even when they have evidence to suggest it is false. For example, there is a lot of evidence that astrology does not make accurate predictions, and my horoscope has often been wrong. Suppose on one occasion, I read my horoscope and believe a prediction, although I know there is evidence against thinking it is right. And then this prediction turns out true! Did I *know* it was right? It looks more like my belief is irrational. I had no reason, no evidence, no justification, for believing that prediction was true. Knowledge, then, needs some kind of support, some reason for thinking that the proposition believed is true. Knowledge needs to be *justified*.

Two important contrasts

ANALYTIC/SYNTHETIC

The contrast between **analytic** and **synthetic** propositions is a contrast between *types of proposition*. A proposition is analytic if it is true or false just in virtue of the meanings of the words. Many analytic truths, such as 'squares have four sides', are obvious, but some are not, for example, 'In five days' time, it will have been a week since the day which was tomorrow three days ago' (think about it!). A proposition is synthetic if it is not analytic, that is, it is true or false not just in virtue of the meanings of the words, but in virtue of the way the world is, for example, 'ripe tomatoes are red'.

A PRIORI/A POSTERIORI

This contrast is, in the first instance, about how we know whether a proposition is true. **A priori** knowledge is knowledge of propositions that do not require (sense) experience to be known to be true. An example is 'Bachelors are unmarried'. If you understand what the proposition means, then you can see straight away that it must be true. You don't need to find bachelors and ask them if they are married or not. Propositions that can only be established through experience are **a posteriori**. An example is 'Snow is white'.

When applied to propositions, the a priori/a posteriori distinction is about how to check or establish knowledge. It is not a claim about how we acquire the concepts or words of the proposition. Babies are not born knowing that all bachelors are unmarried! Yet this is a truth that clearly doesn't need testing against experience; we know it is true just by knowing what it means. Of course, we first have to learn what it means, but that is a different issue from how we check if it is true.

However, we can also apply the distinction to concepts. An a priori concept is one that cannot be derived from experience. We will see examples discussed throughout the chapter (pp. 15, 30).

LINKING THE CONTRASTS

On first reflection, it might seem that the distinctions line up neatly: that a proposition that is analytic is also known a priori; and that a proposition that is synthetic is known a posteriori. 'Bachelors are unmarried' is not only known a priori, but is also analytic. 'You are reading this book' is synthetic and can only be known through sense experience. But is this alignment correct?

All analytic propositions are known a priori. Because they are true (or false) just in virtue of the meanings of the words, we don't need to check them against sense experience to know whether or not they are true. However, just because all analytic propositions are a priori does not mean that all a priori propositions are analytic. Perhaps there are some a priori propositions that are synthetic. So we must ask whether all synthetic propositions are known a posteriori. Or do we have some knowledge, apart from knowledge of analytic truths, that does not come from sense experience? That is the key question of this chapter, one that philosophers disagree over. The disagreement forms the debate between **rationalism** and **empiricism**.

> In your own words, explain and illustrate the distinction between a priori and a posteriori knowledge.

> Try to suggest some examples of synthetic a priori knowledge.

Defining rationalism and empiricism

The terms 'rationalism' and 'empiricism' have been used in different ways at different times, and sometimes quite misleadingly. They have been applied to theories of knowledge, theories of concept acquisition, theories of justification, and historical schools of thought. The main questions that divide them are 'What are the sources of knowledge? How do we acquire it?'. We can ask the question about our concepts as well – how do we get those? Rationalism gives an important role to reason, and empiricism to experience. But we may well wonder why we have to choose; in acquiring knowledge, don't we use both reason and experience?

However, there is a clear way of marking the difference between rationalism and empiricism, which has become common in philosophy. The distinctions we drew above help us: *Rationalism claims that we can have synthetic a priori knowledge of how the world is outside the mind. Empiricism denies this.*

In other words, rationalists argue that it is possible for us to know (some) synthetic propositions about the world outside our own minds, for example, about mathematics, morality, or even the physical world, without relying on sense experience. Empiricists argue that it is not.

(The clause 'how things are outside the mind' is necessary. Many propositions about my mental states are synthetic, for example, 'I feel sad' or 'I am thinking about unicorns'. But they don't require *sense* experience to be known; in fact, does knowing my own thoughts involve *experiencing* them at all? We don't need to worry about this. Rationalists and empiricists alike accept that we *just do* know that we have certain impressions and ideas, thoughts and feelings. The argument is about knowledge of things other than our own minds.)

As we will see, an obvious advantage of empiricism is that we can quickly understand the sources of knowledge. We gain knowledge through our senses by perceiving how the world is, which is a causal process. This is also how we form our concepts, from experience. Once we have acquired concepts, our understanding of them gives us analytic knowledge.

An important challenge to rationalism is: if we have knowledge which comes not from sense experience, and not just from the meanings of words, how do we gain this knowledge? Where does it come from? Rationalists argue either that we have a form of rational 'intuition' or 'insight' which enables us to grasp certain truths intellectually, or we know certain truths innately, as part of our rational nature, or both. They may also argue that some – or even all – of our concepts are innate or come from rational insight.

Try to think of some other source of knowledge.

Notice that most empiricists don't deny *all* a priori knowledge – you don't have to check whether all bachelors are unmarried to see if it is true! They simply claim that all a priori knowledge is of analytic propositions. If we don't know if a proposition is true or false just by the meaning of the words, we *have* to use sense experience to find out whether it is true or false.

Explain and illustrate the difference between rationalism and empiricism.

Key points • • •

- There are different types of knowledge: acquaintance, ability and propositional knowledge. Theories of knowledge discussed here are about propositional knowledge.
- Knowledge is not the same as belief. Beliefs can be mistaken, but no one can know what is false.
- Knowledge is not the same as true belief, either. True beliefs may not be justified, but can be believed without evidence. To be knowledge, a belief must be justified.
- Rationalism claims that we can have synthetic a priori knowledge of how things are outside the mind.
- Empiricism denies this. It claims that all a priori knowledge is only of analytic propositions.

Do all ideas derive from sense experience?

Locke on 'tabula rasa'

John Locke argues that all ideas are derived from sense experience. The mind is a 'tabula rasa', empty at birth. He begins his argument by attacking the opposite view – that some ideas are not derived from sense experience, but are '**innate**'. By 'innate idea', Locke means a concept or proposition which is part of the mind from birth. For an idea to be part of the mind, the mind (the person) must know or be conscious of it: 'No Proposition can be said to be in the Mind, which it never yet knew, which it was never yet conscious of'.

What is an 'idea'? There are many meanings of this word, and we need to fully understand what we are talking about. An idea can be a complete thought, taking the form of a proposition – 'He had the idea that *it would be fun to take the day off*'; or it can be a concept – the idea of 'yellow'. When Locke argues that there are no innate ideas, he talks about *both* concepts and 'truths'. Only a proposition can be a truth. So he is claiming both that all our *concepts* derive from sense experience; and that we have no *knowledge* prior to or independent of sense experience.

From Locke's definition of 'innate idea', it follows that everyone knows all innate ideas from birth. Assuming that our minds are alike in which innate ideas they have, if some truth were part of the mind from birth, every person would

'Tabula rasa' is Latin for 'blank slate'. The phrase recalls the time when children would have slates (or tablets (tabula)), like small blackboards, to write on. Until the teacher told them to write something, the slates would be blank.

An Essay Concerning Human Understanding, I.II.5

Discuss the different meanings of 'idea'.

know it. And here, of course, we must include children and 'idiots'; they have minds. But, Locke argues, there is no truth that every person, including children and idiots, assents to.

But perhaps innate ideas are ones that are known as soon as the person gains the use of *reason* – which children and idiots do not (yet) have. Locke replies that what is missing (in many cases) isn't the use of reason, but the *ideas*: a child can't know that $3 + 4 = 7$ before he can count to 7 and has the idea of EQUALITY. Once he has, then he can see that $3 + 4 = 7$. It is the same thing as knowing – as children do – that a cherry is not a stick. This isn't a development in reason; it is simply knowing what the ideas are. Everyone agrees that we must first acquire the concepts involved.

But if we must first acquire the concepts involved, this means the proposition can't be innate: if it were, why would we need to *acquire* anything? We should know it already. And so Locke argues that no *proposition* is innate unless the concepts used are also innate. But there are no concepts which the mind has from birth. All our concepts derive from sense experience; and so no truths (or concepts) can be innate.

A different definition of 'innate idea'

Locke defines an innate idea as a concept or proposition which the person knows or is conscious of, from birth. The view was popular at the time Locke was writing, but *no major philosopher has ever defended innate ideas using this definition*. His criticisms show just how hard it is to defend. So what is an innate idea, according to those who believe in them?

'Innate ideas' are obviously meant to contrast with ideas gained from experience. Rather than say that they are ideas had from birth, nativists maintain that they are ideas *the content of which cannot be gained from experience*. Nativist arguments, then, tend to focus on how a particular concept or item of knowledge could not have been acquired from experience, and how its use cannot be justified by experience. Now since we do not have the concept or knowledge (whatever it is) from birth, there is some point at which we first come to be aware of it. And so rationalists argue that experience *triggers our awareness* of the concept or truth (some add that it is innately determined, for example, genetically determined, that we will gain this knowledge at this time). But how does this idea of experience 'triggering' an idea differ from the view that we learn or derive ideas from experience?

When I am referring to a concept, I will put the word in capitals.

Explain and illustrate Locke's argument against innate ideas.

Nativism – the claim that we have certain concepts or knowledge innately – has certainly been historically associated with rationalism, and the syllabus understands nativism to be a form of rationalism. More recently, however, some philosophers have argued that nativism is compatible with the spirit of empiricism, and that rationalism should be restricted to the claim that we have substantive a priori knowledge through rational intuition and demonstration.

EXPERIENCE AS A 'TRIGGER'

The idea of triggering is often used in the study of animal behaviour. For example, in some species of bird, a baby bird need only hear a little bit of the bird song of its species before being able to sing itself. There has been far too little experience of hearing the song from other birds for it to learn from experience; rather the experience has triggered its innately given song.

The contemporary philosopher Peter Carruthers notes that there are many developments in our cognitive *capacities* that are genetically determined. For example, infants cannot see further than approximately 30 cm when first born. Within eight weeks, they can see much further. This development of the eye is genetically encoded. The ability to learn and speak a language develops around 18 months. Just as capacities develop, so why not *concepts* and *knowledge* as well (we will see examples on pp. 15 and 29)? At a certain point in development, a point that is genetically determined, children begin to use an idea for the first time, but that idea cannot be acquired from experience. This is not to say that experience has no role – a child must be exposed to the relevant stimuli for the knowledge to emerge, for example, children can't learn language unless people around them speak.

Here is a clear sense in which the idea is innate, but which differs from Locke's definition. With this redefinition, the idea of innate ideas is not as contradictory as Locke makes out. What shows that the idea is innate is that it cannot be derived from or justified by experience. But are there good reasons to think we actually have any innate ideas? To answer this question, we first need to look at the empiricist theory of how we gain concepts from experience.

Human Knowledge and Human Nature, p. 51

Genes always cause their effects through interaction with the environment. For example, there are genes for height, but this also depends on someone's diet. With language, the relevant environment is the social environment, not just the physical one.

Compare and contrast Locke's idea of innate ideas with the rationalist view of innate ideas.

Essay I.II.15

Empiricists on acquiring concepts

Locke summarises his view of how the mind acquires ideas thus:

> 'The Senses at first let in particular *Ideas*, and furnish the yet empty Cabinet: And the Mind by degrees growing familiar with some of them, they are lodged in the Memory, and Names got to them. Afterwards the Mind proceeding farther, abstracts them, and by Degrees learns the use of general Names. In this manner the Mind comes to be furnish'd with *Ideas* and Language, the Materials about which to exercise its discursive Faculty'.

As we come to remember particular experiences through repetition, we start to be able to label them. From there, we can abstract from the individual cases to talk about 'types' of experience, for example, we move from 'red', 'yellow', 'blue' and so on, to the idea of 'colour'.

But what does Locke mean when he says that the senses let in *ideas*? We often contrast an idea with a sensation: the *sensation* of yellow isn't the same thing as the *concept* YELLOW. When we see something yellow, this perceptual experience is quite different from the role YELLOW plays in the thought 'If it is yellow, it is coloured'. But Locke *doesn't* mark this distinction strongly, which is confusing.

Hume corrects this mistake (we will use his terminology from now on). Like Locke, Hume believes that we are immediately and directly aware of 'perceptions'. 'Perceptions' are divided into 'impressions' and 'ideas'. And both Locke and Hume divide impressions into impressions of 'sensation' and those of 'reflection'. Impressions of sensation derive from our senses, such as seeing a car; impressions of reflection derive from our experience of our mind, such as feeling emotions. (Locke also includes awareness of mental processes, such as reasoning, believing, willing and so on.)

Hume then argues that ideas are 'faint copies' of impressions. Think what it is like to see a scene or hear a tune; now what it is like to imagine or remember that scene or tune. The latter is weaker, fainter. And so there are ideas of sensation (for example, the idea of red) and ideas of reflection (for example, the idea of sadness). *Concepts* are a type of idea. So his theory of how we acquire ideas, viz. by copying them from impressions, is a theory of how we acquire concepts.

So Locke and Hume have slightly different versions of how we first acquire ideas with which we can think. We start with sense experiences of the physical world and experiences of our own minds; for Locke, this gives us ideas once we can employ our memories to reflect on the experiences; but this makes it sound as if the experiences, remembered, are the ideas with which we think. Hume corrects this: it is not sensory impressions themselves, but copies, that we remember and use in thinking.

An Enquiry concerning Human Understanding, § 2

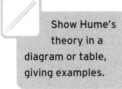
Show Hume's theory in a diagram or table, giving examples.

Simple and complex concepts

The basic building blocks of all thought and experience are simple impressions – single colours, single shapes, single smells and so on. And to each there is a corresponding idea. But we soon begin to unite these simple ideas in more complex ones, for example, we identify one and the same thing (a dog, say) as having a particular colour, shape, smell. So we can think of 'that thing', where the idea of 'that thing' is made up of many ideas of colour, shape, smell. This is a complex idea; in this case, it is a complex idea that has a kind of corresponding 'complex impression' in that we can, through our various senses acting together, experience this particular dog. We can also form complex ideas by abstraction, for example, the concept DOG doesn't correspond to any *one particular* set of impressions or any single dog. When we abstract, we ignore certain specific features and concentrate on others; so to develop the concept DOG, we ignore the different colours and different sizes dogs are, picking out other features, such as four legs, tail, bark, hairy.

> Outline and illustrate the empiricist theory of concept acquisition.

AN OBJECTION

The view that all ideas derive from sense experience is very appealing in many ways. The alternative – that some ideas do not derive from sense experience – raises the question of where these non-empirical ideas come from.

However, there are complex ideas that seem to correspond to nothing in our sense experience, for example, unicorns and God. (While many of us have seen a picture of a unicorn, *someone* had to invent the idea without seeing a picture.) So is it true that *all* ideas derive from sense experience?

Empiricists respond that all complex ideas are composed of simple ideas, and all simple ideas are copies of impressions. This is easy to see in the case of unicorns: we have experiences of horses and of horns and of whiteness; if we put them together, we get a unicorn.

Hume and Locke argue that in creating new complex ideas, we can only work with the materials that impressions provide. No idea, no matter how abstract or complex, is more than putting together, altering or abstracting from impressions. It is important to notice that there are many ways in which we do this; combination and abstraction are two of the most important.

> THE ORIGINS OF 'GOD' are discussed at length in Ch. 4, on p. 132 and p. 149, so we won't discuss it further in this chapter.

> Explain and illustrate the empiricist account of complex concepts.

Are there innate concepts?

We can challenge empiricists to give us their analysis of complex concepts such as NECESSITY, CAUSATION, SUBSTANCE or SELF. If they cannot give us a satisfactory analysis of how we derive these concepts from experience, that is a reason to think that the concepts derive from elsewhere – either they are innate, or they are reached using a priori reasoning.

Hume accepts that these four particular examples cannot be derived from experience. However, his response, for each of these examples, is that the concept – as we usually think of it – has no application. The concepts (and therefore our thoughts about necessity, causation, substance and the self) are confused; in their place, he suggests a clearer way of thinking, using concepts that can be derived from experience.

For example, we have no experience of our 'selves' – we only experience a continually changing array of thoughts and feelings. To come up with the idea of SELF (meaning each of us as one and the same thing over time), we've confused *similarity* (the similarity of our thoughts and feelings from one moment to the next) with identity (the identity of a 'thing' to which such mental states belong).

We do the same thing again with the idea of a physical object as a 'thing' or 'substance', meaning something that exists independently, in its own right. The concept of PHYSICAL OBJECT is of something independent of experience existing in three-dimensional space. But how can experience show us that something exists independently of experience? I see my desk; a few moments later, I see it again. If my two experiences are of one and the same desk, then the desk existed when I wasn't looking at it. But I can't know that my two experiences are of *one and the same* desk; I can only know that the two experiences are *very similar*. In coming up with the concept of a physical object that exists independently of my experiences, I have confused similarity with identity.

So, Hume concludes, the concepts SELF and PHYSICAL OBJECT (and SUBSTANCE) are confusions, they aren't coherent. But, we can object, this makes most of our common-sense idea of the world wrong. This is unacceptable. If an empiricist analysis makes such concepts 'illusory', we may feel empiricism is too challenging to accept. Our concepts are coherent. The fact that we cannot derive them from experience only shows that they are innate (or known through rational intuition). So the difficulty empiricists have in explaining our most abstract complex concepts is an argument that these concepts are not derived from experience.

But are they innate or arrived at by rational intuition? One reason to think they are innate is that children use these concepts early on in life. Rational intuition is likely to come later in life, when a person's rationality is better developed. So, rationalists accept Hume's argument that we can't derive these ideas from our sensory experience alone. Rather than reject or reinterpret the concept, they keep the concept, arguing that our experience *triggers* the concept, and we begin to conceptualise experience in terms of physical objects and selves.

Treatise on Human Nature

Explain Hume's analysis of the concept SELF. Is it possible that there are no 'selves', just thoughts and feelings?

Treatise on Human Nature

Discuss the concept PHYSICAL OBJECT. Can we derive it from experience?

Key points • • •

- Locke argues that the mind at birth is a 'tabula rasa' – there are no innate ideas, which Locke defines as ideas present in the mind from birth.
- Locke argues that there is no truth that everyone, including children and idiots, assents to – so no truth is innate.
- Rationalists define innate ideas as ideas (concepts or propositions) whose content can't be gained from experience, but which are triggered by experience.
- Locke and Hume argue that all concepts are derived from sense experience, from impressions of sensation or reflection.
- They claim that simple concepts are copies of impressions; complex concepts are created out of simple concepts by combining and abstracting from them.
- One argument for innate concepts is to challenge the empiricist to show how a particular complex or abstract concept, for example, PHYSICAL OBJECT, is supposed to be derived from experience. If it cannot be, and it is used by children, then this is a reason to think it is innate.

Are all claims about what exists ultimately grounded in and justified by sense experience?

We turn from looking at the origins of our concepts to claims about what exists. This should be taken in the broad sense, not restricted to the physical world, but referring to 'everything that is'. To talk about grounding and justifying claims is to talk about knowledge. So our question is this: does all our knowledge about what exists rest on sense experience?

Hume's 'fork'

Hume argues that we can have knowledge of just two sorts of thing: the relations between ideas and matters of fact. By relations of ideas, Hume means propositions such as 'All sons have fathers' (about the ideas 'son' and 'father') and 'If A is longer than B, and B is longer than C, then A is longer than C' (about the idea of length). His distinction was developed by later philosophers, and is now understood in terms of the two distinctions analytic/synthetic and a priori/a posteriori. In effect, Hume argued that all a priori knowledge (relations of ideas)

An Enquiry concerning Human Understanding, § 4, Part 1

For definition and discussion of these distinctions, see p. 8.

Explain and illustrate Hume's division of knowledge into two kinds.

Outline Hume's theory of our knowledge of matters of fact.

Another famous example of an inductive argument, induction through 'enumeration', is this:

Premise 1: This swan is white.
Premise 2: This other swan is white.
Premise 3: That third swan is white.
. . .
Premise 500: That swan is white as well.
Conclusion: All swans are white.

must be analytic, while all knowledge of synthetic propositions (matters of fact) is a posteriori. In other words, anything we know that is not true by definition, every 'matter of fact', we must learn and test through our senses.

'MATTERS OF FACT'

The foundation of knowledge of matters of fact, Hume argues, is what we *experience* here and now, or can remember. All our knowledge that goes beyond what is present to our senses or memory, he claims, rests on *causal inference*. If I receive a letter from a friend with a French postmark on it, I'll believe that my friend is in France – because I *infer* from the postmark to a place. I do this because I think that where something is posted causes it to have the postmark of that place; and if the letter was posted by my friend, then I believe that he is in France.

And how do I know all this? I rely on past *experience* – in the past, I have experienced letters being posted, I have seen different postmarks, I have found that postmarks relate to where you post something, and so on. I can't work out what causes what just by thinking about it. It is only our experience of effects following causes that brings us to infer from the existence or occurrence of some cause to its effect, or from some effect to its cause.

Does this give me complete *certainty*? Is this a *proof* that the letter was posted in France? No, says Hume: knowledge of matters of fact, beyond what we are experiencing here and now, relies on **induction** and reasoning about probability.

Induction and deduction

In INTRODUCTORY IDEAS (p. 8), we saw two important contrasts: analytic/synthetic and a priori/a posteriori. A third contrast relates to types of *argument* – **deductive** v. **inductive**. An inductive argument is an argument whose conclusion is supported by its premises, but is not logically entailed by them. That is, *if* the premises are true, the conclusion is *likely* to be true. A letter with a French postmark was *most likely* posted in France, because most letters (all so far?) with French postmarks were in fact posted in France. This is induction through 'inference to the best explanation'.

A deductive argument is an argument whose conclusion is logically entailed by its premises, that is, *if* its premises are true, the conclusion *cannot* be false. Here is a famous example:

Premise 1: Socrates is a man.
Premise 2: All men are mortal.
Conclusion: Socrates is mortal.

Using a priori intuition and demonstration to establish claims of what exists

Hume has argued that all matters of fact – which includes all claims about what exists – must be grounded on experience and the use of inductive reasoning. Rationalists challenge this claim, arguing that *some* claims about what exists can be grounded instead on a priori intuition and demonstration.

What is 'a priori intuition and demonstration'? 'Demonstration' is another word for 'deduction'. A priori demonstration is deduction that uses a priori premises. It doesn't start from premises derived from sense experience (or more often, the role of sense experience is very small).

What about 'intuition'? When you consider a deductive argument, such as the example in the margin, do you 'see', we say, how the conclusion follows the premises? Do you understand why, if the premises are true, then the conclusion must be true? (This is not to say that the premises are true!) In doing so, you use reason. But how is it that you can 'see' the conclusion follows? This takes us towards the idea of 'rational intuition', though it covers much more than deductive reasoning. At the heart of the idea of rational intuition, then, is the view that you can discover the truth of a claim just by thinking about it. It's easiest to understand through examples.

Descartes

Descartes argues that we can establish the existence of the mind, the physical world and God through a priori reasoning. He begins his investigation into what we can know, and how, by attacking sense experience. You can doubt even those sense experiences that seem most certain. Suppose all our sensory experiences are produced in us by an evil demon who wants to deceive us – everything you think you experience is false. In a modern version, replace the evil demon by a supercomputer: suppose you were plugged into the computer, as in the film *The Matrix*. Can you tell if you aren't, just from your sense experience? If, as Hume argues, sense experience is the foundation of knowledge about what exists, then we are in trouble, because we cannot know that our sense experience is a good guide to what exists.

Descartes then argues that there is one thing he can be completely sure of, even if the evil demon exists: that he thinks, and from this, that he exists. He

Rationalists have defended other types of knowledge using this method as well, but we will only be discussing claims about what exists. Claims about the existence of God, moral values, the mind, and even physical objects have been argued for this way. In this section, we will look at just the last two.

Descartes' theory is discussed at length in A2 Unit 4.4 Descartes *Meditations*.

Explain Descartes' argument and how this challenges Hume.

Meditation II

Explain Descartes' argument that the mind can exist without the body.

Meditation VI

Discuss Descartes' argument that we can know the physical world exists.

cannot doubt that he thinks, because doubting is a kind of thinking. If the demon were to make him doubt that he is thinking, that would only show that he is. Notice that he has got to this point by pure reasoning. And this truth is 'seen' by intuition – we recognise that it is true just by considering it.

Descartes then notices that even though he cannot doubt that he exists, he can continue to doubt whether he has a body; after all, he only believes he has a body as a result of his sense experiences, and so the demon could be deceiving him about this. So he knows he exists even though he doesn't know whether or not he has a body. From this Descartes concludes that it is possible for him to exist without a body. So Descartes believes he established another truth about what exists, just by a priori intuition and demonstration – that the mind can exist separately from the body.

But do bodies – do physical objects – exist? Of course, we might say they cause our experiences. But Descartes has argued that we don't yet know what causes our experiences – it could be a demon or supercomputer. Descartes later argues that there are only three options for what might cause these experiences: a real external world of physical objects, a demon, or God. If the cause was God, this would mean that God was a deceiver because He would have created us with a very strong tendency to believe something false (viz. that a physical world exists). And if it was a demon, then if God exists, God is as good as a deceiver, since God is allowing the demon to deceive us. However, Descartes argues, God is perfect by definition. Because we know that God is perfect, we know that God is not a deceiver. So if God exists, then there must really be an external world.

Descartes offers two arguments, both a priori, for the existence of God – one is the Trademark argument (THE IDEA OF GOD IS INNATE II, Ch. 4, p. 149) and the other is THE ONTOLOGICAL ARGUMENT (Ch. 4, p. 145). Since he believes he has demonstrated that God exists, he concludes that we know the external world of physical objects exists. Not because sense experience shows us that it does, but through a priori intuition and demonstration.

Key points • • •

- Hume argues that all a priori knowledge is of relations of ideas, and so analytic. All knowledge of synthetic propositions, matters of fact, is a posteriori. It depends either on present experience or causal inference, which relies on past experience.
- Our knowledge of matters of fact that relies on induction can only be probable, never proven.

- Some rationalists, for example, Descartes, try to show that we can use a priori intuition and deductive argument to demonstrate what exists.
- The core of the idea of rational intuition is that you can 'see' the truth of a claim just by thinking about it.
- Descartes argues that sense experience on its own cannot establish what exists – how can we know that all sense experience is not a deception, caused by an evil demon?
- He argues that he cannot doubt his own existence, and that the mind can exist without the body.
- Descartes argues for the existence of the physical world by first arguing for the existence of God. From God not being a deceiver, it follows that our sense experience – in general – can't be completely mistaken, so the physical world exists.

Conceptual schemes and their philosophical implications

Since the turn of the twentieth century, a number of thinkers have pointed out that human beings don't all have the *same* concepts. Instead, different cultures and different languages work with different sets of concepts or 'conceptual schemes'. How should we understand this?

Philosophers and anthropologists who were interested in the differences in the ways in which people think of the world argued that there are two distinguishable elements to our experience – the data of the senses and then the *interpretation* of this data by a set of concepts. (The data of the senses were sometimes thought of as purely physiological – the image on the retina, the vibrations of the ear drum, or the firings in the brain that these cause immediately.) On these data, different people would impose different conceptual schemes (usually thought of as cultural in some way).

It was then argued that these different conceptual schemes may be irreconcilable – that we can't translate from one into another. The strongest form of this 'conceptual relativism' claims that because their conceptual schemes are fundamental to how people experience and understand reality, people with different conceptual schemes have different 'realities'.

One famous version of this view is known as the Sapir–Whorf hypothesis, deriving from the linguist Edward Sapir and anthropologist Benjamin Whorf. They were struck by the difficulties in translating between languages. For example, Whorf worked with Hopi Indians, and argued that the way they talked

They object to Locke – our senses do not 'let in' ideas; rather, before we can form ideas, we must interpret what our senses tell us.

Whorf, *Language, Thought and Reality*, p. 55

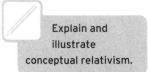

Explain the claim that there are a number of different conceptual schemes.

about time could not be expressed in English. But this isn't just a matter of language – their language is a reflection of how they think, of their concepts: 'We are inclined to think of language simply as a technique of expression, and not to realize that language first of all is a classification and arrangement of the stream of sensory experience which results in a certain world-order.' So their very experience of time was different from ours, or as some thinkers put it – time is different for them: 'We are thus introduced to a new principle of relativity, which holds that all observers are not led by the same physical evidence [that is, stream of sensory experience] to the same picture of the universe, unless their linguistic backgrounds are similar, or can in some way be calibrated.' So if people have different languages, different conceptual schemes, then they will end up with different pictures of the universe.

An implication: conceptual relativism

If there are different schemes, but we can translate between them, then Whorf is wrong – this doesn't lead to 'relativity'. However, the view that there are different conceptual schemes *and* that we cannot translate between them leads to the conclusion that truth is relative to conceptual schemes.

Some thinkers have gone so far as to claim that *reality* is relative to conceptual schemes, so that people with different conceptual schemes experience different worlds. But this is very difficult to defend, and it may not even make sense. First, it supposes that language somehow 'constructs' reality – but the world would still exist even if no one spoke any language. It existed before language, after all! Second, as the quotation from Whorf indicates, the theory is usually developed by contrasting something that is the 'same' (physical evidence, sensory experience) with the differing interpretations imposed by different conceptual schemes. So there is something that is 'real' which is 'outside' or 'before' or 'beyond' all interpretations.

The weaker claim, that truth is relative to conceptual schemes, says this: because there are conceptual schemes which cannot be translated into each other, a proposition in one scheme can be true without being something that the other scheme can express at all. So there is no one set of truths – or Truth – which describes how the world is. (Again, if we can translate between the schemes, then any true proposition in one scheme has an equivalent translation in another – so truth is not relative.)

Explain and illustrate conceptual relativism.

AN OBJECTION

Conceptual relativism looks like an empirical claim – we need to find out whether there are any conceptual schemes which are not translatable. But some philosophers have argued that the account of the relation between experience and conceptual schemes given above doesn't make sense. Whorf says that language (or the conceptual scheme embodied in a language) 'organises' or 'arranges' our experience of the world. You can only organise something if it has parts or contains objects – you can organise the clothes in a wardrobe, but you can't organise the wardrobe itself. If we claim that a conceptual scheme organises our 'experience', then we must think of experience as comprised of experiences. So here is something that different conceptual schemes all have in common – the set of experiences (that they organise differently). But in talking about these experiences, how do we pick them out? We can only do so in familiar ways – feeling cold, seeing a plant, smelling a rose. Any conceptual scheme which starts with *these* sorts of experiences will end up very similar to our own, and so we *will* be able to translate between the two schemes.

Of course, there may be *parts* of a scheme that cannot be translated. And perhaps this leads to a mild form of conceptual relativism. But it will be very mild. Because there are parts of the scheme that can be translated, we can use these to understand the parts that we cannot translate. We can then add these new thoughts into our conceptual scheme – we can expand our concepts. So we don't end up with the view that there is no one set of truths that describes reality; we end up with the view that we will need a very expanded conceptual scheme to provide the means for expressing these truths.

The metaphor of 'organising' should perhaps be rejected. But that doesn't mean we avoid conceptual relativism. The second part of the answer assumes that we can always combine different conceptual schemes. But this is questionable. A popular example is given by colour concepts. Different cultures, it seems, carve up the colour spectrum differently. Suppose that one culture uses just one concept in thinking about what we think of as two colours, blue and green. We cannot combine all three concepts in one scheme, since they conflict. In our scheme, we can say – truly – 'it is green but not blue'; in theirs, it is impossible to say this. Either you think of blue and green (as we would say) as two separate colours or as one colour.

However, it is misleading to say that 'truth is relative to conceptual schemes'. This would suggest that what is true according to one scheme is *false* in another. But what we have said is that what is true in one scheme *cannot be expressed* in another. In this situation, there is no *disagreement* over what is true – to

> Can conceptual schemes 'organise' experience differently in a way that leads to conceptual relativism?

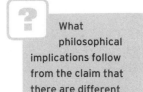

What philosophical implications follow from the claim that there are different conceptual schemes?

disagree, the two schemes would have to be able to express the same proposition (for example, 'it is green but not blue'). But this is what they cannot do.

We end up with the somewhat unsurprising position that in order to state something true, you must be able to state it. But what you can state depends on what concepts you have. However, we have not established *just how different* such conceptual schemes can be. In Development, we will look at an argument that there are a priori limits to conceptual schemes if people are to have experience of the world at all.

Key points • • •

- Thinkers who defend the idea of conceptual schemes often argue that there are two distinguishable elements to our experience – the data of the senses and then the interpretation of these data by a set of concepts.
- Some argue that human beings have formulated different conceptual schemes which are not translatable into each other. From the same sense experience, they form different views of the world.
- Because we must use concepts to formulate truths, we can argue that truths are relative to conceptual schemes. Or more accurately, some truths can only be stated in certain conceptual schemes and not others, and there is no one conceptual scheme which we can use to state all truths.

DEVELOPMENT

Do all ideas derive from sense experience? II

The empiricist theory assessed

COMPLEX CONCEPTS

The method of finding counterexamples is important in philosophy. If a theory claims to explain something, for example, the origin of concepts, generally, we only need to find a single instance it cannot explain to show that something is wrong with the theory. (Of course, we then have to find out *what* is wrong with it.)

In our previous discussion of the empiricist claim that all concepts derive from experience, we looked at an objection (p. 15) based on finding examples of complex concepts, such as SELF and PHYSICAL OBJECT, that were counterexamples. Hume argued that such concepts were confusions. However, we can rephrase the objection.

The empiricist theory has two claims: that complex ideas are built out of simple ideas, and that these are copied from experience. The previous objection looked at the problem of deriving a concept from experience. We could instead object that complex concepts cannot be built out of simple ones (leaving aside the question of experience): Hume challenges us to find an example of a complex idea that cannot be analysed into simple ideas; we can respond by suggesting one and challenging empiricists to provide an adequate analysis. For example, attempts to analyse philosophical concepts such as 'knowledge', 'truth' and 'beauty' into their simple constituents have all failed to produce agreement. Perhaps this is because they don't have this structure.

THE MISSING SHADE OF BLUE

Hume discusses a second objection: if someone has seen all shades of blue except one, and you present them with a spectrum of blue with this one shade missing, they will be able to form an idea of that shade, which they have nevertheless never seen. So here is an example of an idea which has not been copied from an impression.

If it is possible that we can form an idea of a shade of blue without deriving it from an impression, is it possible that we could form other ideas without preceding impressions? How can we allow for the missing shade of blue, but hold on to the view that all ideas are derived from experience? One solution is to say that all (coherent) ideas *can* be derived from experience. We can only create ideas that correspond to something we *can* experience. The idea of the missing shade of blue fits this perfectly, and the definition still ties ideas to experience.

A different solution maintains the stronger, original claim that all ideas *are* derived from impressions as a general principle, but explains both *why* the missing shade of blue is an exception and that exceptions to the rule must be *limited*. The explanation is this: the simple impressions of different shades of blue are not unrelated to each other, as they can be arranged in a sequence of resemblance. From the arrangement, we can form the idea of the missing shade, *drawing on other similar impressions we already have*. But if we have no relevantly similar impressions which strongly resemble the missing impression, we cannot form the missing idea.

Hume presents a separate argument to support this claim: someone who lacks a certain *type* of experience also lacks a certain *type* of idea – showing that the ideas derive from experience. Thus, a blind man does not know what colour is and a mild man cannot comprehend the motive of revenge. More generally, as human beings, we can have no ideas corresponding to the senses of aliens (if there are any). We are limited to thinking about what we can experience.

Try to give an analysis of any complex concept in terms of simpler ones. Do other people agree with your analysis?

Assess the two solutions to the missing shade of blue. Which is better?

Is Hume right to say that a mild man cannot understand revenge?

Going further: the impossibility of forming concepts from experience

Perhaps the most famous objection to the view that all ideas derive from sense experience is that this is impossible. Both Locke and Hume appear to assume that sense experience gives us discrete ideas directly. As first examples of simple ideas, Locke lists '*Yellow, White, Heat, Cold, Soft, Hard, Bitter, Sweet*'. He supposes that what makes all experiences of yellow into experiences of yellow is objective patterns of similarity between the experiences – yellow things all look 'the same'. For example, he says, 'In *Ideas* thus got [through sensation], the Mind discovers, That some agree, and others differ, probably as soon as it has any use of Memory; as soon as it is able, to retain and receive distinct *Ideas*'. This suggests that experiences are already 'packaged' into 'the same' and 'different'.

To stay with the example of colour, this just doesn't seem true. First, the colour spectrum is *not* divided into distinct parts of red, yellow and so on; it is continuous. Second, there are many shades of yellow; to call them all yellow is to abstract from their individual different shades. Putting these two points together, we realise that acquiring the concept 'yellow' is not a matter of copying *an* impression; no experience comes neatly packaged as an experience of 'yellow'. To learn the concept 'yellow' is to learn the *range and variety* of colours to which 'yellow' refers.

How is this done? In order to learn 'yellow', we have to pick out and unify our experiences of the very varied things that are yellow. But if all we have to go on are the many various experiences, how are we able to classify them in this way, distinguishing yellow from not yellow? Well, aren't all shades of yellow more similar to other shades of yellow than to shades of any other colour (say, orange)? All we need to do is read off, or copy, our concepts from experience.

Even if there are objective similarities and differences between experiences, we must still *notice and pick out* these similarities to form the concept. In order to do this, to know what is 'the same' or 'different', we must already be able to classify our experiences. The same or different *in what way*? Which similarity are you identifying? In what way are things that are a shade of yellow similar? – In being yellow! To pick out the common

Essay II.I.3

Essay I.II.15

Is the world already structured by relations of similarity and difference, quite independently of us? Some philosophers argue that no one way of classifying our experiences is forced on us by the experiences themselves. This is supported by the idea of different conceptual schemes (p. 21), and is discussed further in A2 Unit 3.3 Epistemology and Metaphysics, under OBJECTIVE KNOWLEDGE.

feature between different experiences, we must *already* possess the concept that unites them. (Of course, this is not to say that you have a *name* for the concept yet.)

To this, empiricists could say that we don't need to notice and pick out the similarities – they simply cause the concepts directly. However, if the objection is right, then all our concepts – or at least, all our simple concepts – must be innate. What this means is that the mind is innately set up to interpret and classify experience in particular ways.

Innate ideas assessed

We saw that defenders of the idea of innate ideas define them as ideas which we can't have derived from experience, but which experience 'triggers'. But can we make sense of this view, and are we right to think of such ideas as innate?

First, if experience is a necessary 'trigger', are nativists really just saying that to have an innate idea is just to have the *capacity* to come to know the idea? But this would reduce *all* ideas to innate ideas. We have the capacity to discover such empirical facts as the height of Mount Everest and the number of planets in the Solar System, but these are clearly not known innately, but derived from and justified by experience.

But this isn't what nativists claim. It is not just a *general capacity* to learn which is innate; empiricists have always allowed that these general capacities (memory, association and so on) are innate. Locke and Hume certainly thought the structure of our senses and our general abilities to learn were innate. However, as we specify the structure of our senses more and more, we come closer to saying that these capacities of the mind are innate forms of *information* about experience. And so the nativist claims that the idea we form has not been *learned* (inferred or derived or abstracted) from experience, but merely triggered by experience. This is specific to just those ideas that are innate, not all ideas.

But are we right to say that the idea is 'innate'? Or have we changed the meaning of the term? We can cite Carruthers' story, and say that the idea is innate in the sense of it being encoded genetically that we will develop that specific idea (not just a cognitive capacity) at a certain point or under certain conditions. Alternatively, we can defend a more general theory of human nature (as Descartes and Kant (see p. 41) did): Descartes thought that to speak of innate ideas is, roughly, to speak of dispositions we have as part of our nature

We can repeat the argument at a more general level: to be able to judge that two things are the same colour, we must already be able to pick that feature of the two objects – their colour – in virtue of which they are similar. But how do we do this? Vision picks up shape and size as well as colour. To pick things out by colour, we must already distinguish this feature from shape and size. But that means we already have the concept of colour. So we can't form concepts by classifying experiences.

Assess the claim that all concepts are derived from experience.

We saw some examples on p. 15, and consider others on pp. 30 and 41.

Compare and contrast Carruthers and Descartes. (Because he believes we can defend innate ideas using evolutionary theory, Carruthers says nativism is compatible with empiricism. Descartes offers a much more traditional rationalist explanation.)

Can the idea of innate ideas be defended?

Could claims about the origins of innate ideas be a weakness in the theory?

to form certain thoughts through reasoning and self-reflection. (In this, Descartes connects innate ideas to a priori knowledge through intuition and deduction.) This distinguishes the capacities (a priori reasoning and self-reflection) we have which deal with innate ideas from the capacities we have to learn a posteriori truths (the senses and a posteriori reasoning).

Locke objected that if an idea was innate, all children and idiots would know it. To this, we may reply that the children have not had the experience or reached the point in development when the idea comes to consciousness; and in idiots, cognitive capacities have not developed normally, and so neither has innate knowledge.

But if innate ideas do not derive from experience, just where do they come from? Carruthers suggests the cause is evolution, as what formed our genetic code. Descartes argued that our rational nature, including innate ideas, is implanted by God. Plato (p. 31) argues that they derive from a previous, non-physical existence.

Key points • • •

- One objection to the empiricist theory of the origin of concepts is that there are some complex concepts, for example, knowledge and beauty, that cannot be analysed in terms of simpler concepts.
- A second objection is that some simple ideas, for example, a particular shade of blue, don't have to be derived from sense impressions. Empiricists can respond in two ways: all ideas *could* be derived from sense experience; or some ideas are exceptions to the rule that all ideas are derived from sense experience, but these exceptions are derived from ideas that are derived from sense experience.
- Another objection is that it is not possible to derive any concepts from experience, because in order to form concepts, we must make judgements of similarity and difference to classify experiences. But we can only make these judgements if we already have the concepts.
- Defenders of innate ideas maintain that we innately have very specific capacities for forming particular ideas, and these ideas count as innate.
- Suggestions for the origin of innate ideas include evolution, God or a previous existence.

Are all claims about what exists ultimately grounded in and justified by sense experience? II

Rationalists claim that we have knowledge of synthetic propositions that does not depend upon sense experience (INTRODUCTORY IDEAS, p. 10). They argue that there are two key ways in which we gain such knowledge:

1   we know certain truths innately, for example, as part of our rational nature; and/or
2   we have a form of rational 'intuition' or 'insight' which enables us to grasp certain truths intellectually.

Many rationalists add that the synthetic a priori knowledge we gain through reason or innately cannot be arrived at in any other way. They may also argue that it is superior, for example, by being more certain, to the knowledge or beliefs we gain through the senses.

Innate knowledge

CHOMSKY: INNATE KNOWLEDGE OF LANGUAGE

We have looked so far at examples of innate concepts. But what about innate knowledge? The linguist and philosopher Noam Chomsky has argued that our knowledge of language or, more accurately, *grammar* is innate. A key part of grammatical knowledge is whether a sentence is 'allowed' in a language, for example, 'The sleepy cat is on the mat' is fine, but 'The sleepy cat look there on the mat' is not. To learn from experience, children would need to use memory, induction from examples, and inference to what grammatical rules best explained the examples of language they experience. Chomsky's central argument, called 'the poverty of stimulus' argument, is that children learn linguistic grammar accurately so fast, and from very poor information, that their knowledge of grammar can't have derived from experience. Children arrive at grammatical rules – not consciously, but in being able to construct and identify grammatically correct sentences: first, on the basis of far fewer examples than they can classify; second, many of these examples are ungrammatical – when speaking, we often say things like 'The cat . . . look there – on the mat', that is, we speak in incomplete, interrupted sentence phrases; and third, the mistakes children make are not often corrected. And so children cannot be learning

Syntactic Structures

Explain Chomsky's 'poverty of stimulus' argument.

Assess the nativist theory of experience triggering innate ideas.

grammar from their experience of language. Instead, exposure to language triggers their innate knowledge of grammar.

However, philosophers have objected that Chomsky hasn't identified a form of innate *knowledge*. The ability to classify and construct grammatically correct sentences, even if innate, isn't a type of knowledge. If it were knowledge, then children would have to have (non-conscious) *beliefs* about grammar. But this doesn't seem right. It is better to say they have an ability, and abilities aren't knowledge (they are know-how rather than know-that, propositional knowledge – see INTRODUCTORY IDEAS, p. 7).

However, we can reply that if the ability to classify grammatically correct sentences is innate, then this *generates* innate knowledge: the child's knowledge that 'the cat look there on the mat' is incorrect has not been learned from experience. So there is innate knowledge – not the ability, but the knowledge the ability enables.

PLATO: PHAEDO AND MENO

Many philosophers believe that, in the *Phaedo*, Plato defended the view that in judging that two sticks are of equal length, we are using an idea of EQUAL that we cannot have gained from experience. Nothing is *exactly* equal in experience, but only 'almost equal'. But the concept ALMOST EQUAL contains the concept EQUAL. So where does *it* come from? If we do not learn our concepts from experience, we must already know them. This knowledge must come from *before* birth. (The main aim of the *Phaedo* is to argue that the soul is immortal, and Plato uses the issue of innate concepts to support this claim.)

Plato takes concepts to be a type of knowledge, and so his argument for innate concepts is also an argument for innate knowledge. We are able to classify our experiences, for example, that two sticks are equal, by comparing them with our knowledge of what Plato calls the 'Forms'.

A Form is a perfect idea, which exists independently of us. Plato argues that all objects we experience through our senses are particular things. We don't ever sense anything 'abstract', but always some individual thing or other. For example, we only ever see this particular beautiful thing or that particular beautiful thing, but we never see 'beauty'. But, obviously, more than one thing can be beautiful. Beauty is a property that more than one thing can have. So, Plato claims, if many different things can be beautiful, then there is something they share in common, viz. beauty. So there must be something which is 'Beauty', even though we never experience beauty itself through our senses. The Form of Beauty manifests itself in all the different things, in all the different ways, we call 'beautiful'.

The Republic, Book V (476f.)

Properties and particular things are discussed further in UNIVERSALS AND PARTICULARS, A2 Unit 3.3 Epistemology and Metaphysics.

But why should we agree that just because many different things can be beautiful, there is some *thing* which is 'Beauty'? Because, Plato goes on to argue, Forms exist independently of particular things. All particular beautiful things could also be destroyed, yet that won't destroy beauty itself. So beauty must be a separate thing, existing in its own right. So, he concludes, particular things 'share' or 'participate' in the Forms, but these exist independently.

To have the concept EQUALITY is to know what equality is, and this is to know the Form of equality. This is the knowledge we gained before birth. It is because we know the Form of equality that we can have the concept EQUALITY, which in turn allows us to classify experiences of sticks as 'equal' or not. We *remember* or *recollect* our knowledge of the Forms in applying concepts.

Plato demonstrates this idea of recollection in a famous example in the *Meno*. Socrates talks to a slave boy about a theorem in geometry. The slave boy has not been taught geometry, and yet is able to discover the right answer in response to Socrates only asking questions. How is this possible? The boy didn't have experience of geometry, and wasn't taught it. It must be that Socrates' questions triggered the knowledge he had from before birth, but had forgotten.

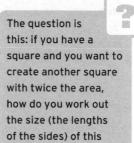

Explain Plato's idea of the Forms.

The question is this: if you have a square and you want to create another square with twice the area, how do you work out the size (the lengths of the sides) of this second square?

OBJECTIONS

An empiricist can reply that, in fact, the concept ALMOST EQUAL does *not* contain the concept EQUAL. Instead, ALMOST-EQUAL is a simple concept derived from sense experience of comparing objects. Plato is talking about equal length; we have experiences of two sticks not being the same length. They always differ by some (possibly tiny) amount. We form the concept EQUAL (as in equal length) by *abstracting* from the experience of differing lengths – two sticks are equal when they differ by no length.

To the slave boy example, we can respond that his knowledge was not innate, but gained through reasoning. However, an empiricist must add that this reasoning is working with analytic truths, otherwise one form of rationalism – nativism – is defeated only to be replaced by another, viz. the claim that we can acquire knowledge through reasoning alone.

Compare and contrast Hume's and Plato's theories of how we acquire abstract ideas.

On mathematical knowledge, see p. 35.

Knowledge through a priori intuition and demonstration

How do we come to have knowledge of the Forms? Obviously, it can't be through sense experience. So there must be some other faculty through which – if Plato was right – we could ground and justify claims about the existence and nature of the Forms. Plato thought this faculty was *nous*. Sense experience is about what is particular and concrete – *this* book, *this* rose. To know the Forms, we must turn towards what is abstract. Using pure reason, we move from one abstract idea to another, from one abstract truth to another.

But we can object that this is no explanation of *how* we come to know the Forms. We can explain how physical objects cause our sensory experiences through our five senses; we have no similar explanation of how abstract objects such as the Forms cause abstract thoughts. At this point, we should remember that Plato supplements his theory of *nous* by an appeal back to nativism; the truths we discover using a priori reasoning and insight depend on the triggering of concepts that are innate.

Nous seems obscure. But it isn't the only model of a priori reasoning. We earlier discussed an example from Descartes (p. 19). How this worked seemed clearer; Descartes analysed his ideas to see what it was impossible to doubt. But does Descartes' a priori reasoning lead to the results he wants? For now, we'll look just at his claims about the mind.

Descartes claims that 'I' am a thinking *thing*, a substance. Many philosophers have thought he means to show that I am the *same* thing from one moment in time to the next, a mind existing in time. The same 'I' persists from one thought to another. But how can Descartes be certain of this? All that we experience is *only a succession of thoughts* (this is why Hume rejected the concept SELF (p. 16)). Instead of 'I think', Descartes should have concluded 'There is thinking (going on)'.

> **Compare and contrast the ways in which sense experience and abstract reasoning might give us knowledge.**

> **Can Descartes know that he is a thinking thing? Why or why not?**

Going further: mind and body

Many philosophers also object to Descartes' claim to know that his mind exists independently of his body. Just because Descartes can *think* of his mind existing without his body, this doesn't mean that his mind *really can* exist without his body. Or again, just because he knows he exists, but doesn't know if his body exists, this doesn't mean he can exist without his body. Perhaps there is some connection between his mind and body that would make this impossible that Descartes doesn't know about. Descartes has used a test of what he knows and doesn't know as a test of what is possible. But this is not a good test, and so he hasn't shown that minds can exist independently of bodies.

What does this show about using a priori intuition and demonstration? Descartes has done his best to find what he thinks, using reasoning, is certain. His arguments are supposed to be inductive, and his premises established by rational intuition. But philosophers have still been able to point out unjustified assumptions and inferences. If intuition and demonstration do not give us knowledge, then rationalism is in trouble.

Before we become sceptical about intuition and demonstration, we should ask this: *how* have philosophers come up with objections to Descartes? It certainly isn't by using sense experience! So the objections themselves use the same *kind* of reasoning as Descartes. Only better reasoning, we hope. The objections cannot be objections to the way Descartes reasoned, only objections to the conclusions he drew.

Hume, however, argues that what can be established by a priori reasoning is very limited. Hume's fork (p. 17) claims that there are only two sorts of knowledge: what we confirm through the senses (a posteriori knowledge) and what reason can demonstrate (a priori knowledge). But, Hume argues, reason can only demonstrate *analytic* truths; there is no such thing as 'intuition' in how things are or what exists.

> What can a priori reasoning establish, if anything? Can we do philosophy without using it?

NIETZSCHE

Friedrich Nietzsche argues that Plato's theory of reason and the Forms is completely mistaken. Plato takes his a priori reasoning to be something that reveals the truth. In fact, argues Nietzsche, 'most of a philosopher's conscious thinking is secretly guided and channelled into particular tracks by his instincts. Behind all logic, too, and its apparent tyranny of movement there are value judgments, or to speak more clearly, physiological demands for the preservation of a particular kind of life.' Plato's entire metaphysical theory of the Forms is actually based on his desire to see good and bad as opposites: 'The metaphysicians' fundamental belief is *the belief in the opposition of values*.' This is why they construct a theory about a world beyond this 'lowly, deceptive' world, a world of purity and certainty. But if we reject this opposition as fictitious, as no more than a fantasy expressing a wish, all of Plato's reasoning will not be convincing.

> *Beyond Good and Evil*, § 3. Nietzsche is discussed in A2 Unit 4.5.

The same goes for any other attempt to establish truth without looking closely at experience and at the role our value judgements play in influencing what we think philosophically. Nietzsche agrees with Hume about the limitations of reason, but goes further when he argues that every great philosophy (including Hume's) is founded on the personal value judgements of the philosopher.

Ayer's verification principle

In the 1930s, an empiricist school of philosophy called logical positivism developed a modern, linguistic version of Hume's division of knowledge into two kinds. The 'principle of verification' states that a statement only has meaning if it is either analytic or empirically verifiable. A.J. Ayer explains: A statement is empirically verifiable if empirical evidence would go towards establishing that the statement is true or false. For example, if I say 'the moon is made of green cheese', we can check this by scientific investigation. If I say 'the universe has 600 trillion planets', we can't check this by scientific investigation in practice, but we can do so *in principle*. We know how to show whether it is true or false, so it is 'verifiable' even though we can't actually verify it. And like Hume, Ayer argued that empirical hypotheses are only *ever* more or less probable, never completely certain. So 'verification' does not mean 'proof'; it only requires that empirical evidence can raise or reduce the probability that a statement is true.

The principle is intended to be a criterion for meaningful statements, and it enabled logical positivists to reject as nonsense many traditional philosophical debates. Philosophy doesn't give us knowledge of a reality that transcends the investigations of science. It is not a source of speculative truth.

Language, Truth and Logic, Ch. 1

Going further: rejecting the verification principle

The verification principle has since been rejected by philosophers as an inadequate account of what it is for a statement to have meaning. The main difficulty is that according to the principle of verification, the principle of verification itself is meaningless! The statement that 'a statement only has meaning if it is analytic or can be verified empirically' is not analytic and cannot be verified empirically. But if the principle of verification is meaningless, then what it claims cannot be true. So it does not give us any reason to believe that the claims of ethics are meaningless.

Ayer claims that the principle is not intended as an empirical hypothesis about meaning, but a *definition*, though not an arbitrary one. In other words, it is intended to reflect upon and clarify our understanding of 'literal meaning'. He accepts that the verification principle isn't obviously an accurate criterion of 'literal meaning', but that is why he provides arguments in specific cases – ethics, religion, a priori knowledge – which support it.

But to this, we may respond by rejecting both his specific arguments and the verification principle. The verification principle is only as certain as the arguments that are intended to exemplify the consequences of its application. If we do not find those convincing, the principle provides no independent support.

Does the verification principle threaten rationalism? Why or why not?

Mathematical knowledge

Mathematical knowledge has often been held by rationalists as a good example of what we can know a priori through reasoning alone. It is difficult to argue that mathematical knowledge is a posteriori. If we say that $2 + 2 = 4$ is just a generalisation of our experience so far, then as Hume argued, this 'matter of fact' is not certain, but only probable: we are saying that one day, perhaps, $2 + 2$ will equal some other number. But this is unimaginable (2 apples in one hand, 2 apples in the other, but only 3 apples in total?? How?).

But empiricists can accept that mathematical knowledge is a priori, if they also argue (which they do) that it is analytic: all mathematical knowledge is reached by developing a series of definitions. But if this is true, how are mathematical 'discoveries' possible? How can we 'discover' something that is true *by definition*? Empiricists reply that analytic knowledge doesn't need to be obvious; mathematical truths are very complex, so it takes work to establish that they are true. But that doesn't mean they are not true by definition.

Discuss the claim that all mathematical propositions are analytic.

Going further: geometry

This reply can be difficult to believe. For example, truths of geometry don't seem to be true by definition. The fact that it takes at least three straight lines to enclose a space in two-dimensions seems to be a truth about the *nature* of space, rather than the *concept* of space. Yet it has mathematical certainty, and can be proved by mathematical geometry. How could such certainty come from sensory experience alone?

In fact, there is more than one geometry of space. It is in classical, or Euclidean, geometry that it takes three straight lines to enclose a two-dimensional space. But mathematicians have worked out perfectly good, consistent *non-Euclidean* geometries in which this and other 'truths' are not true (if you curve the two-dimensional plane, for example, the surface of the Earth, you can enclose a space with two straight lines). So, empiricists argue, geometry applied to the real world has two elements: a series of definitions, which are analytic truths; and then an *a posteriori* claim about which type of geometry applies to space. So there are geometrical truths about the nature of space, but they are not necessary – space could have been otherwise, for example, non-Euclidean. In fact, in some cases in advanced physics, Euclidean geometry does not describe space accurately.

In the twentieth century, empiricists such as Bertrand Russell argued that although mathematical truths were not analytic, they were nevertheless 'logical' truths. His argument depended on technical developments in logic and in mathematics. Philosophers still disagree about the success of Russell's attempt – and attempts by other philosophers since – to reduce mathematics to logical truths. It is fair to say that while some attempts are promising, no reduction has been completed.

1. Assess rationalism.
2. Assess empiricism.

Key points • • •

- Rationalists claim that we have synthetic a priori knowledge either innately or through rational intuition.
- Plato argues that many particular objects can have the same property, for example, beauty. These properties can exist independently of the particular objects, as shown by the fact if we destroy all beautiful things, we haven't destroyed beauty. These properties are instances of the Forms.
- Plato argues that innate concepts are our knowledge of the Forms from a previous existence. Unless we had such innate memories, we wouldn't be able to classify experience using concepts.

- Descartes argues he cannot doubt his existence. We can object that he cannot know he exists, only that thoughts exist.
- Descartes also argues that the mind can exist without the body. We can object that just because he can conceive that this is possible doesn't show that it is possible.
- Both these arguments and the objections use a priori reasoning. Hume objects that a priori reasoning can only establish analytic truths.
- Nietzsche argues that reasoning is not, in fact, something independent that reveals the truth, but is grounded on assumptions about value. Metaphysical theories are the result of attempts to defend a particular way of understanding the world, one that rests on the false assumption that good and bad are opposites.
- The verification principle claims that a statement only has meaning if it is either analytic or empirically verifiable. However, the principle itself is neither analytic nor empirically verifiable.
- Rationalists argue that mathematics is an example of synthetic a priori knowledge. Empiricists argue that mathematics is analytic.

Is certainty confined to introspection and the tautological?

Descartes understands knowledge in terms of what is 'completely certain and indubitable'. To establish this certainty, he seeks to test his beliefs by doubt. If we can doubt a belief, then it is not certain, and so it is not knowledge. However, Descartes takes 'certainty' to be a very high standard. He wants to find out what *cannot* be doubted, not just what it is reasonable to believe. When he says that he cannot doubt that he exists, or later that God exists, what he means is that when he considers these claims carefully, he is unable not to believe them. Using his best, most careful judgement, he judges that it is *impossible* that they should be false.

We said in INTRODUCTORY IDEAS (p. 8) that knowledge is more than true belief – it must be justified. Descartes argues that it must be certain. But we can object that this isn't necessary; we can have beliefs that are justified, for example, we have good evidence for them, but they aren't certain. So the question of this section – Is certainty confined to introspection and the tautological? – is not the question of whether *knowledge* is confined in this way. To say that it is, we must first argue that knowledge involves certainty. But we won't discuss it here, so we put aside the question of knowledge and concentrate on certainty.

Meditation I

How does Descartes understand the relation between doubt, certainty and knowledge?

What is certainty?

'Certainty' can have at least two different meanings, perhaps three:

1. It has a subjective, psychological meaning, as in 'I feel certain that . . .'. This is perhaps something like a feeling, a feeling of conviction.
2. It has a logical meaning, for example, the truth of a proposition can be certain because the proposition logically *must* be true.
3. And perhaps it has a third meaning somewhere between the two, viz. that a proposition cannot be doubted. This brings together the objectivity of the second meaning with the psychological nature of the first.

> **?** What is certainty? How is it relevant in debates about what we know?

Which of these senses is important for our discussion? The first seems irrelevant; we cannot discover what and how we know just from what people *feel* certain of. This is too subjective. But what we can and cannot doubt (the third meaning) is relevant. Now in many cases – but not all – we cannot doubt some proposition because it must be true (the second meaning).

To pursue the second definition further, we need to introduce one final distinction, one that plays a big role in the debate between rationalism and empiricism: **necessary** and **contingent** truth.

Necessary/contingent

A proposition is contingent if it *could* be true or false; of course, it will be either true or false, but the world could have been different. Many empirical facts are like this: it is true that you are reading this book; but you could have been doing something else. So it could have been false. There are more types of insect than there are of any other animal. This wasn't always true, and one day it might be false again.

> Of course, it is possible that the figure '2' could have been *used to mean* the number 3. But then '2 + 2' wouldn't mean 2 + 2; it would mean 3 + 3. To test whether a proposition is true or false, in all cases, you have to *keep the meanings of the words the same*. If '2' means 2, and '4' means 4, then 2 + 2 must equal 4.

A proposition is necessary, or necessarily true, if it not only *is* true, but *must* be true (it is necessarily false if it *couldn't* be true). Mathematics is usually thought to be necessary: 2 + 2 must equal 4; it is not possible (logically or perhaps mathematically possible) for 2 + 2 to equal any other number. Likewise, analytic truths are necessary: if a proposition is true by definition, then it *must* be true.

Historically, philosophers have also agreed that a priori knowledge is necessary and a posteriori knowledge is contingent. After all, a posteriori knowledge is knowledge of how the world is, and surely the world could always have been a different way – so all propositions about the world *could* have been true or false. Of a priori knowledge, empiricists thought it was necessary because it is analytic. Rationalists argued that the type of knowledge we gain through a priori reasoning is also necessary.

Certainty, introspection and tautology

A tautology is a statement that says the same thing twice in different words. In the context of epistemology, it is just another term for an analytic proposition. Because everyone agrees that analytic truths are necessary, then there is also no argument that they are certain. So what is tautological is certain.

But can any beliefs other than beliefs about analytic truths be certain? If certainty is restricted to necessary truths and these are all analytic, then the answer is no. But this is forgetting our third sense of 'certainty' – there may be beliefs that I cannot doubt, even though they are not necessarily true. The best examples are beliefs based on introspection, the observation of one's mental states and processes. Descartes and Hume both agreed that I cannot doubt my experiences themselves. I can doubt that I am seeing a table, but I cannot doubt that I *seem* to be seeing a table. Likewise, I may not know what is causing my pain, but I cannot be mistaken that I feel pain. The claims that I seem to see a table or that I am in pain are not necessarily true, but contingent. But they can still be certain. This must be the third sense of certainty – it is impossible, for the person who has the experiences, to doubt their truth.

These are the only two classes of certainty that empiricists have traditionally allowed. Hume argues that all a priori knowledge is analytic, while all knowledge of matters of fact, beyond my own mental states, involves induction, inference, and probability (see p. 17), and so cannot be certain. However, rationalists argue that there are synthetic a priori truths, and these are necessarily true, and so they are certain. So whether certainty is confined to introspection and analytic truths depends on whether rationalism can be defended.

> Explain and illustrate the distinction between necessary and contingent truth.

> Not all claims based on introspection are certain in this way, for example, I may think that what I feel is love but I am mistaken. Certainty is usually restricted to states of perception and sensation.

Key points • • •

- Descartes argues that what we can doubt is not certain enough to be knowledge. However, we can argue that certainty and justification are not the same thing, and that while knowledge needs to be justified, we need an argument to show that it must be certain.

- Certainty can refer to a subjective feeling, to a proposition being necessarily true or to the impossibility of doubting a proposition.
- Empiricists claim that analytic truth is the only kind of necessary truth. Rationalists argue that there are synthetic a priori truths that are also necessary.
- A necessary truth is certain. Claims about mental states, based on introspection, may also be certain for the person whose mental states they are.
- Whether any other claims are certain depends on whether there are necessary synthetic a priori truths.

Conceptual schemes and their philosophical implications II

Try to imagine what it would be like to have sensory experience but with no ability to *think* about it. Thinking about sensory experience requires concepts – at the most basic level, being able to distinguish what comes from the different senses (vision, hearing, etc.), and then being able to distinguish types of properties, for example, colour from shape. If we couldn't think about sensory experience, it would be completely unintelligible, no more than a confused 'buzz'. For instance and, very importantly, we couldn't tell that we were experiencing any*thing* – that is, *objects*. The idea of an object is the idea of something that is unified in some way – a colour, shape, position, and so on, going together; or even more fundamentally, something that exists in space and time.

A 'buzz' doesn't deserve the name 'experience'. Experience is experience *of* – experience of objects, in fact, experience of a world of objects, that is, objects that stand in organised relations (in space and time) to each other.

How is it that our experience is intelligible in this way? We take it for granted that we see desks, hear cars, smell roses. But we shouldn't take it for granted, and this leads to a, perhaps the, fundamental question in epistemology: how is it that we can make sense of reality, so that we have experience and not a buzz?

Immanuel Kant argued that intelligible experience – experience of a world of objects – presupposes and requires certain, very basic concepts, which he called categories. These concepts, taken together, form our fundamental conceptual scheme. Kant argued that sensation is completely meaningless to us unless and until it is brought under these basic concepts.

In our earlier discussion, we looked at the possibility of different conceptual schemes (p. 21). Kant thought that there was only one basic conceptual scheme that could provide experience as we know it. There can be no other set of

Discuss the difference between experience and an undifferentiated buzz of sensation.

Critique of Pure Reason

concepts which creatures like us could have. The conceptual scheme is *necessary* for experience at all; so any creature that we think has experience – intelligible experience of objects, not a confused buzz – must have these concepts.

Kant on the structure of experience

Knowledge is a *relation* between the mind and reality. Philosophers such as Descartes, Locke and Hume took this relation for granted, in the form of 'experience'. For example, Locke begins his account of how we acquire concepts by saying that 'The Senses at first let in particular Ideas' (see p. 13). This just takes it for granted that our minds are set up to represent the world as it really is. Kant's great insight was not to take this for granted, but to ask how this is possible. In Locke, there is no real *explanation* here of how we can know about the world through experience. Perhaps the senses are completely misguided. Descartes argues that we have the innate concept PHYSICAL OBJECT and that God, who is the source of innate concepts, guarantees that this concept applies to reality. But if his argument for God's existence fails (which Kant thought it did), then we are left with the possibility that our innate concepts are also misguided.

Essay Concerning Human Understanding I.II.15

The answer, Kant thought, lay in thinking further about experience. First, we know that intelligible experience is possible, because we have it. Intelligible experience is what we mean by 'experience', in the sense of a perceptual experience *of something*. Experience is of objects. So experience has a certain structure – it is structured by objects, and these objects exist in space and time. It is through experience that we gain knowledge. So what makes this structure of experience *possible*? If we could answer that, we would have shown why it is that we can know about reality.

Explain Kant's insight and why it is important.

CATEGORIES: AN EXAMPLE

We want to know what makes the structured experience of objects possible. Kant answers that it is the possession and application of certain basic concepts, each of which contribute to the concept of an 'object'. His argument for the (twelve) concepts he lists and no others is contentious, and many philosophers think it doesn't work. What has been more influential are his arguments for each concept in turn. One argument that has been thought particularly powerful is his argument for the concept CAUSALITY.

Critique of Pure Reason, B232-8

The argument is this. To experience the world in terms of objects involves distinguishing between the time in which our experiences occur – when we have them and in what order – from the time in which the objects exist. For example, I can, at two times, look at an object from two different angles, seeing different sides of it. My perception of the object changes, and one experience follows the other in time. But I don't say that the object has changed, or that there are two different objects, one of which follows the other in time – I say that the object has remained the same over time. Kant gives the example of looking around a house. I have a series of perceptions, changing in time, but the house remains unchanged. However, on another occasion, we say that the changes in our perceptions reflect changes in the object. Kant gives the example of watching a ship sailing down a river. In this case, it is not just that my perceptions change over time, the object itself is changing (in position). How is it possible that we can make the distinction between the sequence of changes in my perception and the sequence of changes in the object? Obviously, it is possible; but how?

Kant's answer is that in the case of looking around the house, we understand that the order of the perceptions can be changed, for example, we could have looked at the walls top to bottom instead of bottom to top, say, without the house itself changing. In other words, the order in which we have the experiences doesn't change *what* we experience. When the object doesn't change, the order of perceptions is not determined. In the case of the ship, the order of the perceptions cannot be different: we first see the ship upriver and then we see it downriver. If we saw the ship first downriver and then upriver, we would be seeing a different event – not a ship sailing *down* the river, but a ship sailing up the river. So when the objects change, we cannot change the order of the perceptions. The order of the perceptions is determined by the object changing.

This means that we have an idea of a 'necessary temporal order'. Without this idea we couldn't make the distinction between perceptions that change because the object does and perceptions that change when the object stays the same. This idea is that of CAUSALITY. Causality is the relation between cause and effect, and we think that effects *follow* causes; in fact, we think that effects *must* follow their causes. We say that an event c, for example, letting go of a pen, causes another event e, the pen falling to the floor, only when e regularly follows c. So CAUSALITY is precisely the concept that things happen in a certain, determined order. So Kant concludes that without the concept of CAUSALITY I cannot distinguish between an object changing and just my perceptions changing.

Finally, I need this distinction to be able to experience objects at all. So without CAUSALITY, I can't have intelligible experience. So CAUSALITY is necessary for experience to be possible.

Explain Kant's example of the house and the ship.

Explain Kant's argument that we cannot have experience without having the concept CAUSALITY.

Going further: comparing the two ideas of conceptual schemes

Kant argued that there were twelve concepts, including UNITY, SUBSTANCE, NECESSITY, CAUSALITY and others, that together were necessary for experience. Because they are necessary for experience, they are a priori – logically 'prior' to experience, rather than derived from experience. We do not have experience at all without them, so we cannot derive them from experience. Kant argued instead that they were part of the structure of the mind. They are each aspects of the 'pure thought of an object', and it is this that the mind brings to experience.

Critique of Pure Reason, B80

Our experience – every perceptual experience we have – is completely shot through by these concepts. It can be tempting to interpret Kant as saying that our experience is made up of two separate things: sensation and concepts. We apply the concepts to sensation to derive experience. This is the view of conceptual schemes discussed before (p. 21). But Kant would object: there is no such thing as pure sensation for us. We can't even talk about it meaningfully, because by definition such sensation is not something we can think about (as it comes 'before' the application of concepts). Consider: we *don't* have a confused buzz, we *only* have experience of objects. Experience, for Kant, is always conceptualised; and all experience is conceptualised (in the first instance) in the same way – as experience of objects. There is only one conceptual scheme, and it is necessary for all experience.

Explain how Kant's theory of the relation between our conceptual scheme and experience differs from the Sapir–Whorf hypothesis (p. 21).

If there is variation in conceptual schemes between cultures or languages, then, it cannot be very great. *All* conceptual schemes must use certain concepts for there to be experience at all. Kant argues that you need certain concepts in order to be able to state – or think or experience – anything at all. This isn't an empirical argument, for example, Kant doesn't do any psychological or anthropological investigation. It is an a priori argument, based on the nature of our experience.

Implications

What are the implications of Kant's theory? The most important regards the relation between the mind and the world. Experience, we have said, has a certain structure – it is experience of a world of objects; and this structure is made possible by certain key concepts which contribute to the ideas of an 'object' and of an objective world, including CAUSALITY, SUBSTANCE, UNITY and so on. These concepts can't be derived from experience, because they are what make experience possible in the first place. So they are a priori; Kant says they are part of the nature of the mind.

So we reach this conclusion: that the 'object'-ive nature of experience is a reflection of the nature of the mind. This means that our experience of and our thoughts about everyday objects – tables, plants, and so on – is not a straightforward presentation of what exists completely independently of the mind (what Kant calls 'things-in-themselves'). The idea of an object doesn't reflect the world, it reflects the mind. So everyday objects are *defined* by our structured experience of them.

So now if we try to think of how things are, how reality is, quite independent of these a priori concepts of ours, we find we cannot. We cannot know that reality is completely independent of how we think about reality – which is in terms of objects. And yet we clearly don't want to say that reality depends entirely on our minds – something exists independently of our minds, the something that produces experiences. But *we cannot know anything about this 'something'* – we have to think using our a priori conceptual scheme.

This doesn't mean that the world of experience – the world of objects – isn't real. Of course it is real; indeed, it is by definition 'objective'. However, it is defined by the contribution our mind makes as well as the (unknown) contribution made by whatever is completely independent of our minds.

> This explains synthetic a priori knowledge: we can have a priori knowledge of synthetic propositions about physical objects, for example, that they exist, because our a priori conceptual scheme defines what it is to be an object we can experience.

> Evaluate the claim that experience is only intelligible because it presents sensation through a predetermined conceptual scheme.

Going further: the conditions of the possibility of experience

We saw that Kant starts from the objection to empiricism and rationalism that they cannot explain the relation between the mind and the world that is necessary for knowledge. The empiricists assume that the senses 'let in' the world as it really is; rationalists assume that our innate concepts match it. Both assumptions are unjustified. Perhaps the way we experience or conceptualise the world is completely different from how the world is. But has Kant left us in the same position?

He would argue that he hasn't. He has shown how we can know about the world – the world of physical objects that we experience with the senses; we can know about it because the world as we know it is *structured* by our a priori concepts. How things are is given by these concepts, so there is no question of a 'match' between our minds and how things are.

But then what about how things are independent of our minds? About this we can know absolutely nothing; we cannot even coherently think about it. But this is not an objection for Kant, because there is no meaningful way in which we *could* know about it. If Kant had argued just that our experience *is* a certain way, we could object that our concepts were a limitation to our knowledge – we weren't able to experience the world as it really is. But Kant has argued that our experience *must be* the way it is – there is no alternative to experiencing the world as a world of objects, so there is no alternative way of experiencing 'the world as it is'. Any alternative wouldn't be 'experience' at all.

This makes our experience properly objective, the basis of knowledge of how things are. What we don't know – how the world is completely independently of our minds – is what it is impossible to know. So there is nothing here we *could* know but don't.

For example, the distinction between the temporal order of experience and the temporal order of objects is not just what makes experience of objects possible. It is also *necessary* if we are to be able to talk about experience of objects. The distinction between the temporal order of experience and the temporal order of objects is part of the general distinction between experience and the world which we experience. Without this distinction, 'experience' would not be 'experience of' anything.

Key points • • •

- Kant argues that experience is of objects, and asks how it is possible for experience to be intelligible in this way, not a confused buzz.
- He answers that what makes experience possible are certain concepts, which he calls categories. These categories together express the 'pure thought of an object'.
- One such category is CAUSALITY. This enables us to distinguish the temporal order of our perceptions from the temporal order of objects.
- Kant argues that to talk of concepts interpreting sensation is misleading. Our sensory experience is always already conceptualised as experience of objects.
- Two implications of Kant's theory are that the structure of the everyday world of objects is defined by our a priori concepts; and that we cannot know anything about how reality is completely independent of how we think of it.

SUMMARY

In this chapter, we have looked at two answers to the question of how and what we can know:

1. Empiricism: which claims that our knowledge is limited to what can be derived from sense experience and analytic truths.

2. Rationalism: which claims there is, in addition, synthetic a priori knowledge that we have innately or by the use of a priori reasoning.

In our discussion and evaluation of these theories, we have looked at the following issues:

1. What is the difference between knowledge and belief?

2. What is the distinction between analytic and synthetic propositions? Between a priori and a posteriori knowledge? Between deductive and inductive argument? Between necessary and contingent truths?

3. How are the different distinctions linked to each other?

4. What is an innate idea? Are there any innate concepts?

5. How, according to empiricists, are all concepts derived from experience? Do certain complex concepts present counterexamples? Can any concepts be derived from experience?

6. Is there any innate knowledge?

7. How does Plato argue that we have innate knowledge of the Forms?

8. What is a priori intuition and demonstration? Can we use it to gain knowledge?

9. How does Descartes use a priori intuition and demonstration to argue for the existence of his mind and of the physical world? Does his argument succeed?

10. Does the verification principle define what we can know?

11. What is certainty? What can we know for certain?

12. What is a conceptual scheme? How does it relate to experience?

13. What is conceptual relativism? Is it defensible?

AN INTRODUCTION TO PHILOSOPHY 1

2

Section 2: Why should I be governed?

If we are to answer the question 'Why should we be governed?', we need to consider three issues. First, why should we think that being governed at all is a good idea? What would life be like without a government, without laws? Second, is it only right to be governed if we have agreed to it? Is a government only 'legitimate' if the people have approved it? Third, if we are governed, must we always obey the law, or may we disobey it, for example, if we think it should be changed? By the end of the chapter, you should be able to discuss these questions, explaining and evaluating different answers to each of them, and the reasons supporting each answer.

SYLLABUS CHECKLIST ✔

The AQA AS syllabus for this chapter is:

The state of nature

✔ Different views of the condition of mankind in a 'state of nature': a war of all against all in which life is 'nasty, brutish and short' (Hobbes); a state in which men live together according to reason, in perfect freedom and equality without superiors to judge them (Locke).

✔   The benefits of political organisation: why it may be rational for individuals to submit to some form of authority which regulates conduct.

Political obligation and consent

✔   Consent as the basis of obligation: the legitimate political obligations of individuals are grounded in a considered, voluntary and binding act of consent. The concepts of hypothetical consent and tacit consent.
✔   The concepts of power, authority and legitimacy and the relationship between them. Whether legitimacy requires popular approval.

Disobedience and dissent

✔   The view that we can only be said to possess obligations if we have a guaranteed right of dissent: just grounds for dissent.
✔   Civil disobedience and direct action: the use of unlawful public conduct for political ends. The aims, methods and targets of civil disobedience and direct action. How either might be justified.

INTRODUCTION

I. The state of nature

The idea of a 'state of nature' is the idea of life without government, without a state or laws. To imagine a state of nature, we imagine away government, law, police, and see what we are left with. The idea has a long history in political philosophy, because it can help us answer the question – why do we, or why should we, live under the rule of law? In everyday life, we take it for granted that we do – that there are things we are not allowed to do, laws we should not break, that if we do, we will be punished, and that these matters are decided by other people. Why accept this? If we want to see what living under a state does for us, it is helpful to imagine being without it.

In imagining what it would be like to be without a state, we also imagine what it would take for us to create a state. Philosophers have used the idea of a state of nature to argue that the state is based on an *agreement* between people to live together under laws. So the idea of a state of nature helps answer another question – it tells us a story about how a group of individuals who are free become obligated to obey the laws of a state.

The story, however, is not meant to be factual. Perhaps human beings have never lived without group rules and submission to someone who has the power to enforce them. Nevertheless, we can come to understand what *justifies* this situation – why it is a good thing (if it is) and why we should accept it (if we should) – by imagining what it would be like to live without the state.

> What is the 'state of nature'? What is the point of thinking about it?

Hobbes: the state of nature as a state of war

Thomas Hobbes argued that to understand political society, we first need to understand its components – people. We then need to understand the agreements that form society, and from these agreements we will understand the form and status of the state. Imagining a state of nature, said Hobbes, helps us understand what human beings are like simply as human beings.

'Self-preservation' is our most fundamental desire; and if there is no law or authority to override our acting on this desire, no one can tell us how or how not we may try to stay alive. So Hobbes argues that in a state of nature, we have the right to use our power however we choose in order to stay alive.

> Hobbes' argument about the state of nature can be found in *Leviathan*, esp. Ch. 10-14.

However, second, our 'natural right' conflicts with other people's natural right. Usually, if I have a right, someone else has a duty. For example, if I have the right to life, everyone has the duty not to kill me; if I have the right to what I own, everyone has the duty not to steal from me. But because in the state of nature, no one has the authority to say how or how not to exercise the right to stay alive, if someone judges that in order to stay alive, they will kill someone else or steal from them, then they have a 'right' to do this, and each person judges individually how best to do this. They have no duty not to kill or steal. So each person's right to self-preservation conflicts with everyone else's.

Third, each person must eventually rely just on themselves, on their strength and intelligence. This will lead to a state of war, not in the sense that people will always be fighting each other, but that everyone will be disposed or ready to fight if they need to, and will live in a state of 'continuall feare, and danger of violent death'.

> Explain Hobbes' claim that we have a natural right to self-preservation. Explain the implications of this right in a state of nature.

Leviathan, Ch. 14

Under these conditions, people will not work or study or create: 'In such condition, there is no place for Industry; because the fruit thereof is uncertain: and consequently no Culture of the Earth . . . no Knowledge of the face of the Earth; no account of Time; no Arts; no Letters'. And so, as a result, our lives will be 'solitary, poore, nasty, brutish, and short'.

The causes of war

How does Hobbes get from everyone having the right to self-preservation to war? The answer, he says, lies in human psychology and the conditions of the state of nature.

First, we desire power. By 'power' Hobbes means the means to obtain what we want. Or, more accurately, to have power is to now possess the means to get what you want *in the future*. That we want power follows from the fact that we want anything – whatever we want, in order to get it, we need the means. There are many things that give us power, including how other people see us. For example, if people like us or if they are afraid of us, then they may give us what we want.

Second, our desires are never-ending. Once we have fulfilled one desire, there will be another. And so we do not try just to satisfy our desires now, we also try to make sure we can satisfy our desires in the future.

In the state of nature, first, we are roughly equal; no one is so strong that they can dominate others and overpower all resistance. Any difference of physical strength can be matched by the other person finding people to help, or by their intelligence, or by their experience. Second, there is scarcity. Not everyone can have everything they want – especially when what they want includes the power to get what they want in the future. Third, we are vulnerable – other people can cause us to fail to achieve the power we need to satisfy our desires.

All this leads to a vicious circle. We might not be inclined to attack other people, but we know that some of them may attack us. The best form of defence, the best way to get what we want, is to attack first. Furthermore, the only way to have enough power is to have more power than other people. So even people who are not violent have reason to become violent if they fear losing what they want. We will fight for gain, to get what we need; we will fight for security, to get what we need in the future; and, says Hobbes, we will fight for 'glory' – the reputation of being powerful, either because we simply enjoy it or

Outline and illustrate Hobbes' three conditions in the state of nature.

because it is a kind of power in its own right (people tend to be compliant towards people who are known to be powerful).

Locke on the state of nature

John Locke agrees with Hobbes that the state of nature is a state of perfect freedom and equality. But he understands both these terms differently. For Hobbes, equality is about our ability to gain power and satisfy our desires, and liberty just means that we each have the natural right to do *whatever* we think is necessary to secure self-preservation. Locke argues for a *moral* interpretation of each term. Equality means no one has the right to hold power over anyone else. And while we have the right to self-preservation, there are limitations on what we may do, given by what Locke calls the Law of Nature. The Law of Nature says that no person may subordinate another, harm his life, health, liberty or possessions (except in self-defence), and furthermore, that we should help each other when this does not harm ourselves. And so, Locke says, the state of nature is a state of liberty but not a state of 'licence', because it still falls under a law, viz. the Law of Nature.

But laws are usually made by states, and there is no state in the state of nature. So where does this Law of Nature come from? Ultimately, Locke argues, it comes from God, and it is because we are created by God that we have the duty to preserve and not to harm life, both our own and other people's. However, if we do not want to appeal to God, Locke also argues that the Law of Nature is discoverable by reason.

We may object, on Hobbes' behalf, that the existence of a Law of Nature is not enough for the state of nature to be peaceful – in addition, people have to obey it. But Hobbes has argued that we need power and we act out of the fear created by the conditions of the state of nature. So even if we *should* obey the Law of Nature, we won't.

Locke, however, disagrees with Hobbes about scarcity, one of the conditions that leads to war. In the state of nature, there is plenty of land for each person to have some for themselves, which they can cultivate and so provide themselves with food and shelter. And most people will prefer to do this than try to attack someone else to steal what they have grown, so it is possible that we live together peacefully. In fact, we can argue that we have a right to own land, because ownership is the most efficient and effective way of securing what we need to live. As long as there is enough land for other

> Explain why, according to Hobbes, the state of nature will be a state of war.

> *Second Treatise of Government*, Ch. 2–5

> Hobbes also argues for a Law of Nature, but again, he understands this differently to Locke (p. 69).

> Explain the differences between Hobbes' and Locke's understandings of equality and liberty.

> Discuss whether, in the absence of scarcity, the state of nature would be peaceful, with people living freely and as equals.

people as well, then taking land for ourselves is no violation of the Law of Nature.

The benefits of political organisation

Leviathan, Ch. 17

Hobbes argues that the main benefit of a state is that it can defend us from being harmed by other people. Given his emphasis on violence and the threat of violence in the state of nature, this is a very considerable benefit. We will look at his and Locke's views in more detail in Development (p. 68f.).

A Treatise of Human Nature, Book III, Part II, § 2

David Hume presents a different and much broader argument for the benefits of society. It is a two-stage argument. The first stage emphasises, in contrast to Hobbes, what *co-operation* in the state of nature has to offer. Human beings, Hume says, are unusual among animals in needing a great deal but having few resources to provide for themselves. We can lack the power to get what we want or need, we can lack the ability, and we can lose what we have through misfortune. Grouping together with other people remedies all three: together we have greater power; by a division of labour and then exchange of goods, we obtain what we don't have the ability to do for ourselves; and through mutual support, we are less vulnerable to misfortune.

Explain and illustrate the advantages of cooperation in the state of nature.

However, just as society makes life better in these ways, the threat of having our goods stolen from us increases as well. Our self-interest can tempt us to try to become better off quickly by robbing others. A society that lived under the laws of justice would remove this threat, increasing peace, stability and the enjoyment of what we own. In the long term, living in a just society, which involves submitting to the laws that justice requires, is better for everyone. However, self-interest is not always long-sighted in this way.

This leads to the second stage of the argument: we have a conflict between short-term gain (through theft and other injustices) and long-term self-interest (peace and stability). But no motivation is as strong as self-interest, Hume argues. What we need is a way to make acting justly in our *short-term* interest as well as our long-term interest. And this is precisely what the law does – the threat of punishment means that it is better to obey the law than break it. And so we get the added benefits of peace, stability and private property. Because doing what is in our interests is rational, it is rational to submit to an authority that administers the laws of justice.

What are the benefits society can offer? Is it rational to agree to live under the law? Why or why not?

Although they disagree about what exactly the benefits of the state are, Locke and Hobbes agree with Hume that living in a state is in our self-interest, so they agree with Hume that it is rational to submit to an authority.

Key points • • •

- The state of nature is the idea of living without government or laws.
- Hobbes argues that in the state of nature human beings have the 'natural right' to do whatever they consider necessary for self-preservation.
- He argues that we desire power – the present means to satisfy our future desires; and that in the state of nature, there is equality, scarcity and vulnerability. Together, these conditions and human psychology produce a state of war.
- Locke argues that in the state of nature, there is a Law of Nature (given by God, but discovered by reason) that no one may subordinate or harm anyone else, and that we should help others when this does not harm us.
- He argues that there is no scarcity, and that the state of nature will be largely peaceful.
- Hume argues that society brings the benefits of cooperation – gains in power, ability and protection against misfortune. However, it also increases the threat of injustice, including losing our possessions.
- He argues that the law turns justice, which is in our long-term interests, into our short-term interests, and so secures peace, stability and private property.
- It is rational to do what is in our self-interest. The benefits of living in a law-governed society make it rational to agree to do so.

II. Political obligation and consent

Consent as the basis of obligation

Political obligation is the obligation to obey the law because it is the law, rather than because there is some independent moral justification for doing what this or that law requires. For example, we could argue that we shouldn't drive recklessly, because it endangers the lives of other people. This cites a specific moral reason to obey this specific law. It is different from arguing that we shouldn't drive recklessly because it is against the law. And it only gives us an obligation to obey this law, not other laws.

If this is the only kind of answer that can be given to 'Why obey the law?' – specific moral reasons for specific laws – then there is no political obligation. The

Outline and illustrate the question of political obligation.

question of political obligation is whether we have a *general* obligation to obey the law, not just an obligation to obey this law or that law? And second, if we do, *why* do we have this obligation?

We have just looked at the question of whether it is rational – in the sense of in one's self-interest – to submit to some form of authority. If it is, then, if we act rationally, we ought to submit to that authority. Hume argued that laws and the state are the most efficient means of securing peace and stability. He went on to argue that we should explain why we *feel* we ought to obey the law in these terms; and argue that our feeling is right – the benefits we receive give us an obligation to obey.

But philosophers have objected that the fact that it is rational for us to obey the law is not enough for us to have an obligation to do so. An obligation is a duty, it is to be bound (from the Latin, *ligare*) to do something. The question of obligation goes beyond the question of what it is rational to do, because we can ask whether we have an *obligation* to act rationally. People can be held to their obligations. But should I be forced to do what is in my self-interest?

Why is there an issue here? Because we take individuals to be free and equal. The law, however, coerces people to act in specific ways. If you break the law, you are punished. If you have an obligation to obey the law, this is just. But how can it be right to coerce people who are free and equal? One tradition in political philosophy suggests that the answer must be, can only be, that somehow the individual has *agreed* to obey the laws of the state.

Giving consent is certainly the way we acquire many other obligations. For example, if I make a promise, I am agreeing to acting in a way that keeps my promise. So perhaps political obligation also comes from consent.

Discuss whether the fact that it is rational to obey the law means that we are obliged to obey the law.

Explicit consent

The strongest form of this answer claims that individuals must explicitly consent to the rule of the state for them to have an obligation to obey it. This argument appears in Locke's story of how the state comes to exist:

> Men being . . . by nature all free, equal and independent, no one can be put out of this estate and subjected to the political power of another without his own consent, which is done by agreeing with other men, to join and unite into a community for their comfortable, safe and peaceable living . . . they have thereby made that community one body, with a power to act as one

body, which is only the will and determination of the majority . . . And thus every man, by consenting with others to make one body politic under one government, puts himself under an obligation to everyone of that society to submit to the determination of the majority.

Second Treatise §§ 95f.

As Locke himself realised, however, if this ever actually happened, which seems very unlikely, it only happened for the first generation of that society. For everyone born into an established society, there is no such procedure. People alive today have never explicitly consented to be ruled – we were never offered the choice. If explicit consent were the basis of obligation, then we (at least most of us) would have no obligation to obey the law of the society in which we live.

Explain why it is difficult to base political obligation on explicit consent.

VOTING

Perhaps this is too quick. If it is an act of consent we are seeking, then voting appears to be the place to look. This is certainly the closest we come to saying that we agree to be governed.

But is this what voting expresses? For voting to be the basis of political obligation, it must be an act of consent – to what? To obey whatever laws the elected government passes? The view that voting is consent must claim that people who vote for the opposition are just as much giving their consent to obey the rules of the successful party. Does it make sense to say that I express my consent to live by laws I am trying – by voting – to prevent?

We shall examine other ideas of consent in Development, p. 75f.

With explicit consent, if I say that I do not consent to the state, then you cannot say that in fact I do. By definition, I do not explicitly consent to something until I say I do. So if I do not intend my vote to be consent to obey the laws passed by whatever government is elected, then the mere fact that I voted cannot be taken as an expression of consent.

Is voting an expression of explicit consent to the state?

The concepts of power, authority and legitimacy

Power

Power, in the context of politics, can be defined as the ability to get others to do things even when they might not want to. Power can operate through persuasion, so that people cooperate willingly and freely, on the basis of reasons they accept (which may include incentives that are offered for cooperation); or through coercion – the use of threats, sanctions and force.

What is political power?

States have power, in the end, because they can make laws. And laws are enforced by the police, again in the end, by the use of force. If you don't obey the law, at some point, you will be fined or jailed or worse. However, we want to be able to make a distinction between cases in which it is *right* that the state has power, and cases in which it is wrong or objectionable in some way. To make this distinction, we need the concepts of 'authority' and 'legitimacy'.

Authority

Authority is a much more complex concept, and we need to make distinctions between several different ideas of authority.

A first sense of authority is *theoretical authority* or expertise. This is the sense in which a person can be 'an authority', an expert, on a particular topic. We ask the advice of theoretical experts, as they can give us reasons for what to believe – for instance, whether whales are fish – but also for what to do – for example, an engineer knows how to build a bridge that won't collapse.

What is the difference between theoretical and practical authority?

Our interest is in the second sense of authority, *practical authority*. This is the sense in which a person can be an 'authority figure'. An authority can get us to act in particular ways, because they have power. However, just having power is not enough for also having authority.

There are two senses of practical authority. In the *descriptive* sense of practical authority, a state has authority if it maintains public order and makes laws that are generally obeyed by its citizens. It has the power to make and impose laws successfully. Authority goes beyond power because it can secure public order, which depends in part, on people respecting the law. Contrast with this a state in which many people break the law, but the state still has a police force that punishes some of the law-breakers. In this case, in which citizens and the state are in conflict, the state no longer has authority.

In the **normative** sense, a state has practical authority if its authority in the descriptive sense is legitimate.

Some philosophers, such as Hobbes, argue that any state that has authority in the descriptive sense is legitimate; so there is no real distinction. On the other hand, some philosophers think the descriptive definition of practical authority is too weak, and doesn't distinguish enough between mere power and genuine authority. They argue that the state only has authority of any kind (and not just power) if the citizens generally obey the laws because many or most of them believe it has authority in the normative sense. A state in which citizens obey the

normative

'normative' means relating to 'norms', rules or reasons for conduct. In this case, it means that the practical authority is right, justified, supported by good reasons.

law simply because they are too scared to break it does not have authority, only power. Adding this condition still makes a distinction between descriptive and normative authority – for descriptive authority, the citizens must *believe* the state is legitimate; for normative authority, the state must *be* legitimate.

Legitimacy

So in addition to whether a state has authority, in the sense that people obey its laws, we can ask whether it has *legitimacy*. The term *legitimate* comes from the Latin for 'lawful'. In the most basic sense, a state is legitimate if it exists and operates according to the law. But this definition is too shallow: if a country has no laws about how a government can come to power, then no matter how the government came to power, it will be legitimate. Or again, if a government is elected lawfully, but then changes the laws to create a police state ruled by a dictatorship, the dictatorship will be legitimate. But this is not what we mean by a legitimate government.

If a government is legitimate, then in some way, the fact that it has power is right or justified. If it is right it has power, then we can argue that we ought to obey it. If it is objectionable that it has power, then we don't have an obligation to obey it. Many philosophers have argued that people only have a political obligation if the government has legitimate authority. So what makes a state legitimate?

Whether legitimacy requires popular approval

Following arguments that we gave in previous sections, we could suggest that a state is legitimate if it delivers important benefits; or that it is legitimate if its citizens consent to it. Both of these views support or complement the view that legitimacy requires popular approval.

Neither consent nor benefits is the same as approval. However, it is unlikely that people would consent to something that they don't approve of. So if a state has its citizens' consent, it will also have their approval. Likewise, if a state secures important benefits, it will probably receive general approval. People are more likely to disapprove of a state if it starts to fail to provide security, justice and the other goods discussed.

So we can argue that even if consent is not necessary, there is still something peculiar in suggesting an authority could be legitimate *irrespective* of how those

> Explain normative authority. What does it add to authority in the descriptive sense?

> We make this more precise in Development, p. 76.

> Discuss the relations between power, authority and legitimacy.

> But it is worth noting that a state may have approval without consent, for example, a popular dictatorship.

under the authority felt about it. Legitimacy emerges when those under the authority believe or are *shown* that it is beneficial or rational to obey the authority, and we can tell if they have this belief by their approval of the state.

Plato's objection

Republic, esp. 487–94.

However, there is an old but important challenge to this line of thought, from Plato. He argues that legitimate practical authority is founded on theoretical authority, not on consent or even giving people what they want. He makes a comparison between politics and skills. If you want to build a bridge, you don't ask just anyone how to do it – you listen to an expert. If you are ill, you consult a qualified doctor. A state, likewise, is legitimate only if those in power have knowledge of how to rule and skill in ruling. Popular approval has nothing to do with either of these.

Plato argues that democracy is based on the freedom to do what you want. But if you don't know what is good for you, then this kind of freedom is harmful. He illustrates his point with an analogy. He compares people in a democracy to a powerful beast, and their rulers to the animal's tamer. The rulers govern by giving people what they want (otherwise they will be voted out of government). But this misses the question of what is *good* for the state. The tamer (politicians) 'would not really know which of the creature's tastes and desires was admirable or shameful, good or bad, right or wrong; he would simply use the terms on the basis of its reactions, calling what pleased it good, what annoyed it bad' (494b–c). So democracy is really rule by ignorance, because neither the politicians nor the people who elect them know what is good for the state as a whole.

Explain Plato's analogy of the beast.

Consider: people are so often incompetent and irrational. In general elections, the way people vote is swayed by all sorts of desires and prejudices; thinking hard about what might be good for everyone is very rare, despite the fact that there is information available. How many people even bother to read party manifestos, let alone research the possible impact of different policies? Good politicians need many skills, knowledge and insightful judgement; they need to understand economics, psychology and motivation; they need intelligence, an enormous capacity for work, a good memory, attention to detail and excellent people skills. We won't get the best politicians by letting incompetent and irrational people vote. We'll get politicians who are willing to give the people what they want. But people don't *know* much about what is good for society as a whole. And people *care* most – perhaps only – about getting the things *they* want for *themselves*. So if politicians give people what they want, they won't be governing by what is best for the state.

Discuss Plato's objection to the view that legitimacy depends upon popular approval.

Key points • • •

- Political obligation is the obligation to obey the law because it is the law. Philosophers have argued that free and equal people do not have an obligation to obey an authority unless they have consented to do so. So political obligation must be based on consent.
- However, we have never explicitly consented to be ruled by a state and obey its laws.
- It can be argued that voting expresses consent to the state. But unless this is what a voter intends by his or her vote, it cannot count as genuine consent.
- Power is the ability to get others to do things.
- Practical political authority in the descriptive sense is the power of the state to make and enforce laws that are generally obeyed by citizens. It may also require the citizens' belief that this power is legitimate.
- Normative political authority is legitimate practical authority.
- A state is legitimate if it is right or justified that those in power hold power.
- Many philosophers argue that legitimacy depends on popular approval – perhaps as a response to benefits, perhaps expressed as consent.
- Plato objects that legitimate practical authority depends on theoretical authority. In the case of the state, this involves those in power having knowledge of what is good for the state and the skill to rule it. A state based on popular approval will not get such leaders.

III. Disobedience and dissent

Obligation and the right of dissent

In our discussion of consent (p. 53), we noted that giving consent is one way in which we acquire obligations. For example, if I freely promise to do something, I then have an obligation to do it. It is important, however, that my promise is *free*. If I am forced to promise, for example, by threats, then we would not usually think that I have to keep the promise. So we can argue that for obligations

If we understand obligation just to mean 'duty', then not all obligations are acquired by consent. We have many moral obligations or duties without having a say over them, for example, the obligation not to murder. The question of political obligation is how free and equal individuals could have an obligation to obey an authority, and we have seen that some philosophers have argued that this is not a moral duty unless the individuals have given their consent.

Explain why obligation requires the right to dissent.

acquired by consent, the consent must be given freely. For me to consent freely, there must be an alternative – I must be able to refuse to consent, that is, I must be able to dissent.

The reason, we said, consent is needed for obligations not given by morality is that individuals are free and equal. But coercion does not respect the freedom and equality of the individual. So consent is meaningless if it is coerced. Consent without the right to dissent is not consent at all. So we can see that unless I have the right to dissent to something asked of me, I cannot become obliged to do it.

The implications of dissent for political obligation

If political obligation rests on consent, then we could argue that people who dissent have no political obligation. They have not agreed to obey the law, so they have no duty to obey the law. On this understanding, dissent abolishes (or prevents) political obligation. We discuss this further in TACIT CONSENT, p. 75.

A weaker implication is that we cannot have political obligation unless we have the *right* to dissent, but dissent does not free one from political obligation. We could argue that political obligation depends upon having the right to political participation, and this right includes the right to dissent, within certain limits. The law must protect our right to dissent and express our dissent.

Before going further, we should note that we can talk of dissent from a particular law or laws; and also dissent from the government or state as a whole. We consider both in what follows.

In liberal democracies, there are legal ways in which we can express our dissent. We can vote against the government that made the law, we can take part in protests and we can join pressure groups that try to change the law. To dissent in a stronger sense is to say 'I refuse to obey the law', that is, it involves illegal action. This can take the form of conscientious objection or civil disobedience. Whether our right to dissent covers civil disobedience is contentious, and is discussed in JUSTIFYING CIVIL DISOBEDIENCE (p. 81).

The most famous case of conscientious objection is refusing to fight for one's country because one is a pacifist, but it describes any personal refusal to obey a law that one thinks it is morally wrong to obey. Conscientious objectors do not usually try to change the law, but simply dissent from it personally. For example, they may believe that while they themselves may not fight, it is not necessarily wrong that others do. When it is a legal requirement to join the armed forces, this is breaking the law. If they break the law, they can be imprisoned – and many will not resist this as they do not disrespect or dissent from the authority of the law generally.

The most fundamental dissent is to the state as a whole, expressed in revolution. In a revolution, not only are the rulers replaced, but the structure and institutions of the state are also changed. If we acquire political obligation, as Hobbes and Locke argued, by consenting to be ruled, then we must also retain the right to dissent from being ruled – or at least, from being ruled by the state as it is. We shall look at their arguments in the next section.

Just grounds for dissent

Where dissent is expressed within the law, then there is no need to justify it. On whatever matter someone disagrees with the law, he or she has the right to express that disagreement legally. This right is guaranteed by the right to political participation, and no further grounds for dissent are needed.

Where dissent involves disobeying the law, then it needs to be justified. Conscientious objection can be justified in two ways. First, case-by-case, objectors justify their actions by appealing to the moral value they believe the law conflicts with. The social consequences of an individual act of conscientious objection tend to be minimal, and so there is little need to look for additional justification of the individual's actions at a social or political level. But, second, we can offer a defence of the value of conscientious objection in general to society. To force an individual to obey a law they hold to be morally wrong would be a violation of their moral integrity, which could harm the individual. Furthermore, at present they do not disrespect the law or dissent from its authority generally, nor do they encourage others to break the law. Forcing them to act against their conscience could lead to both these adverse consequences. It is far better, therefore, to treat their dissent leniently. Given that it involves breaking the law, some punishment or other requirement needs to be enforced (or conscientious objection will, in practice, become legal). So it is best to apply either a light sentence or, for example, require productive work in lieu of armed service.

We will look at How CIVIL DISOBEDIENCE MIGHT BE JUSTIFIED later (p. 66), so we shall focus here on the more fundamental case of dissent from the state as a whole.

Hobbes argues that the main purpose of the state, and the reason we consent to it, is to protect us against violence and the threat of violence. Our

In many countries, conscientious objection is legal, but the objector may be required to perform some other, non-violent task for the state as a substitute for fighting. When conscientious objection is legal, then the objector is not dissenting from the law, only from fighting for their country.

Outline and illustrate different forms dissent takes.

How can conscientious objection be justified?

Leviathan, Ch. 21

obligation to the state, therefore, lasts 'as long and no longer' than the ability of the state to protect us. If it fails to deliver protection, we have the right to cease to obey its laws. Second, Hobbes argues that in the state of nature, we have a 'natural right' to do what we need to do to stay alive (p. 49). We retain this right in a weakened form in the state. Any law or command that threatens our self-preservation, we have a right to dissent from and disobey. Again, since the purpose of the state is to protect us, any such law goes against the purpose of the state and our reasons for consenting to it; so we have the right to dissent. However, these are the *only* grounds on which we can justly disobey the law or revolt against the state.

Second Treatise, Ch. 19

This is discussed in BENEFITS OF POLITICAL ORGANISATION II, p. 70f.

Compare and contrast Hobbes and Locke on the right to revolution.

Which forms of dissent do we have a right to?

Locke similarly argued that what makes a state legitimate is also what gives citizens the right to rebellion. A state is made legitimate by the consent of the citizens, and for the purpose of enforcing the Law of Nature. The government can lose its legitimacy by failing in its purpose or, in general, by losing the support of the citizens. At this point, the citizens no longer have an obligation to obey the government, as it is not a legitimate authority. If those in power try to retain power, then, in a sense, it is they who are 'rebelling' against the people. The people therefore have the right to respond to this assertion of power by people who are no longer a legitimate authority and to overthrow them.

Both Hobbes and Locke agree, then, that we are justified in dissenting from the state when it ceases to perform the main function that it serves. They have different accounts of what this is – protecting us against violence or enforcing the Law of Nature. The state fails to be legitimate when it fails to deliver the benefits it is supposed to. If we think consent is also an important part of legitimacy, we can add that we are justified in dissenting from the state when it fails to command the consent of its citizens.

Civil disobedience and direct action

The term 'direct action' is very broad. It refers to the use of demonstrations, strikes, boycotts and other public protests, rather than negotiation or voting, in order to achieve one's goals. Direct action may be legal (as in organised demonstrations, agreed with the police in advance) or illegal (such as breaking into a laboratory and releasing the animals). It may be directed against the state or it may be aimed at employers or institutions. It may be violent or non-violent. It may try to achieve its aims by raising the public awareness of an issue or simply by intimidation. The syllabus glosses direct action and civil disobedience as 'the use of unlawful public conduct for political ends'. So we shall not discuss legal direct action further.

The definition of 'civil disobedience' is narrower, but also more contentious. We will concentrate on developing this definition, and return to the relation between direct action and civil disobedience at the end of this section.

Defining civil disobedience

To define civil disobedience as any deliberate violation of the law, motivated by a sense of morality and pursuing a social or political end is too broad. An assassination could fulfil these conditions. So we start with a much narrower definition by the philosopher John Rawls, and will then discuss each element of the definition: 'I shall begin by defining civil disobedience as a public, non-violent, conscientious yet political act contrary to law usually done with the aim of bringing about a change in the law or policies of the government. By acting in this way one addresses the sense of justice of the majority of the community.'

A Theory of Justice,
p. 363

CONTRARY TO LAW
Civil disobedience always involves doing something illegal. However, in most democratic countries, civil disobedience is not itself a crime. If arrested and prosecuted, protestors are charged with breaking whatever law was broken by the act of civil disobedience (blocking a public highway, trespassing, etc.).

CONSCIENTIOUS YET POLITICAL . . . DONE WITH THE AIM OF BRINGING ABOUT A CHANGE IN THE LAW OR POLICIES OF THE GOVERNMENT
Ordinary violations of the law do not have the aim of changing the law nor demonstrate opposition to a government policy. They do not seek to make a statement or communicate a message to society. People break the law for many reasons, apart from the usual ones of greed, self-interest and emotion that motivate criminals. For instance, they may break the speed limit without thinking they are doing anything particularly wrong, because they feel there is no strong moral reason to obey the speed limit. Or they may break the law because it conflicts with a personal moral conviction. This may be because they rank some other moral duty, for example, to protect a friend, higher than the duty to obey the law; or it can be a case of conscientious objection.

Like conscientious objection, civil disobedience is motivated by sincere, serious views about what is morally right. Protestors are also often concerned

? What is the difference between conscientious objection and civil disobedience?

about what is in the best interests of society. They think that the law or policy they are protesting against is immoral or damaging to society. However, conscientious objectors usually do not try to change the law, but simply seek to 'opt out', while civil disobedience always aims to change some law or policy. Conscientious objectors do not necessarily try to publicise their actions, and their reasons for breaking the law. Civil disobedience always has this political aim.

Some famous instances of civil disobedience have succeeded in changing the moral ideas of society. The suffragette movement of the early twentieth century secured the right of women to vote; Mahatma Gandhi in India secured the end of the British Raj and self-government for Indians; in the USA, Martin Luther King and others secured equal civil rights for non-whites; and student protests contributed to the end of the Vietnam War. Contemporary civil disobedience campaigns include anti-abortion campaigns that trespass on abortion clinics; in the animal rights movement, the releasing of animals from laboratories; and many of the actions of Greenpeace, for example, against whaling, and other environmental organisations in protest at developments that destroy nature or lead to pollution.

Must all civil disobedience aim at changing the laws or policies of the government? What about protests against companies or universities? An example would be protests against companies that rear animals for experimentation. Some protests aim to get a legal ban on the institutions' practices, and so fall under Rawls' definition. But we could argue that there are more social authorities than the state. Action that aims at changing the rules or policies of a social authority that is not the state shouldn't be ruled out as civil disobedience just for that reason.

Discuss the ways in which civil disobedience is 'political'.

ADDRESSES THE SENSE OF JUSTICE OF THE MAJORITY OF THE COMMUNITY

This condition is too narrow. Civil disobedience always makes some moral appeal, but it can attempt to *change* society's sense of justice, or it may not appeal to *justice*, but to other moral concerns, such as the right to privacy, or issues of security, or the issue of how we treat animals.

Appealing to society's sense of justice is also not the only means civil disobedience uses to change the law. Many acts of civil disobedience also aim to make it more difficult to implement a policy, for example, chaining oneself to a tree to prevent a wood from being cut down. The hope is that the costs of putting the policy into practice will be so high, the government will change its mind.

NON-VIOLENT

It may be that using violence in protest against a law is not *justified* (see p. 66f.), but that doesn't mean that all violent acts of protest fail to *count* as civil disobedience. We need to make this distinction, because we should not assume that all acts of civil disobedience are justified. If the violence is widespread and unfocused, then the protest will not be civil disobedience, but a riot or revolutionary action. However, limited violence, focused very specifically, may form part of an action designed to highlight a serious moral wrong.

PUBLIC

Civil disobedience must be public, but what does this mean? First, civil disobedience aims to communicate to society the protestors' condemnation of the law and their desire for the law to be changed. This message can only be communicated if the act of civil disobedience is announced. But does the act itself need to take place publicly? If this was always done, some acts would become impossible, because they would be prevented. The example above of releasing animals from laboratories is such a case.

Second, the public nature of civil disobedience relates to the protestors showing that they respect and submit to the law. By allowing themselves to be identified and arrested, they show that by *breaking* the law, they are nevertheless not seeking to *undermine* the law. However, we can again question whether this is part of the definition of civil disobedience, or part of its justification. Many animal rights protestors who release animals from laboratories *do not* give themselves up. And in a tyranny, it may be life-threatening to do so. Furthermore, under such an unjust government, the protestors may lack respect for the law. To rule out acts that would otherwise count as civil disobedience just because the protestors do not submit to the law may be too restrictive.

A continuum of cases

We saw that direct action covers a very wide range of cases – legal or illegal, directed at the state or institutions, violent or non-violent, working through moral appeal or just intimidation. Civil disobedience covers far fewer cases, but exactly how many depends on how restrictive the definition is. At its core, civil disobedience is always illegal, done for moral reasons, aiming at a change in the rules of a social authority, and public, because it attempts to appeal to and

> Some philosophers have argued that civil disobedience must be 'civil' in its methods and tactics, and therefore non-violent. But this is just a pun on 'civil', which relates to the state not to behaving 'civilly'.

> Must civil disobedience be non-violent and appeal to considerations of justice?

> What does it mean to say that civil disobedience is 'public'?

communicate with society's sense of morality. Civil disobedience, then, is clearly a type of direct action.

It is probably more useful to find the rough borders of civil disobedience than an exact definition. At one end, there is direct action that is legal, for example, boycotts and protest rallies. Then there is civil disobedience – first, cases that comply with Rawls' restrictive definition and then cases that don't. Then there are cases that are on the border between civil disobedience and revolution, which aim not at changing this or that law, but the whole structure of the state, such as Gandhi's protest against the British Raj. Then, at the other end of the spectrum, there are cases of direct action and revolutionary action that do not aim to bring about change by persuasion, but by violence and intimidation.

> Outline and illustrate the spectrum of expressions of dissent.

Justifying civil disobedience

Because civil disobedience involves breaking the law, many philosophers have argued that it needs special justification. However, we can argue that this only applies when we have an obligation to obey the law. If, for example, the state is not legitimate or is very unjust, then perhaps we don't have political obligation. If we aren't obliged to obey the law, we do not need a special justification for breaking it. This doesn't automatically mean civil disobedience would always be justified, but that justifying it is no different from justifying other actions.

The background assumption in most discussions, and in what follows, is that the state is 'reasonably' just, enough to give us political obligation. The fact that we are breaking the law itself counts as a reason against civil disobedience if there is political obligation. In addition, of course, many laws are supported by independent moral reasons. To justify civil disobedience, we also need to provide a justification that outweighs these moral reasons as well.

In Plato's *Crito*, Socrates argues that it is never right to break the law, even if the law treats you wrongly. He argues that we have an obligation to keep the law in return for all the benefits the state provides, and suggests that by living under the state, we have agreed to abide by its laws.

But we can respond that it can sometimes be right to break an obligation for the sake of some greater moral value. Rawls argues that if the aims of an act of civil disobedience are important enough, then the act can be justified on certain conditions. One of these is that all *legal* attempts to change the law have failed. Civil disobedience must be a 'last resort'. Second, civil disobedience must be non-violent. The most important interest that the law protects is our safety.

To threaten this is to act unjustifiably, says Rawls, because the aim of civil disobedience cannot be more important than the protection against violence. Furthermore, if we compare the consequences of violent and non-violent action, we see how the consequences of non-violence are better than violence. Non-violence doesn't encourage the use of violence in other situations in which it would be wrong. Non-violence does not antagonise those opposed to the civil disobedience as much as violence, so it is less divisive of society.

We can object to both conditions. They may help, but are they *always* necessary? In an emergency, when there is no time to wait for legal means to fail, perhaps civil disobedience could be used straight away. Or, a different objection, how is the judgement that legal means have been exhausted to be made? One can always go on campaigning. Regarding violence, we may argue that the issue should not be violence v. non-violence, but whether the consequences of the action are justified by its aim. Sometimes the consequences of non-violence can be just as bad as violence, for example, ambulance drivers going on strike. And sometimes, it may be that limited, directed violence can make a point where non-violence would not succeed, for example, when the civil disobedience occurs in an unjust state.

> Explain Rawls' justification of civil disobedience.

> Discuss whether civil disobedience must be non-violent to be justified.

Key points • • •

- We can only give consent meaningfully if we consent freely. Consent therefore requires the right to dissent. If political obligation rests on consent, then we must have the right to dissent to have political obligation.
- Dissent can be expressed legally, or more strongly through violations of the law, as in civil disobedience, and in the extreme case, through revolution.
- Hobbes argues that dissent is justified when the state threatens one's life or fails to protect it.
- Locke argues that revolution is justified when the state ceases to be legitimate and the rulers refuse to leave office. The state can become illegitimate either through failing to enforce the Law of Nature or in failing to command the general support of the citizens.
- Rawls defines civil disobedience as 'a public, non-violent, conscientious yet political act contrary to law usually done with the aim of bringing about a change in the law or policies of the government . . . [and that] addresses the sense of justice of the majority of the community'.
- Philosophers have objected that civil disobedience does not by definition

have to address society's sense of justice (although it must appeal to its sense of morality) and that, likewise, it is not by definition non-violent.

- Protestors usually submit to the law by not resisting arrest or punishment. We may object, however, that this is not part of the definition of civil disobedience, although it demonstrates that protestors are not objecting to the authority of the law as such, only to specific laws.

- Civil disobedience may be justified when the aim is important enough to override our obligation to obey the law, and certain other conditions are met. Rawls argues that it must be a 'last resort' and non-violent. But if we justify civil disobedience by its consequences, it may be that using violence or turning to civil disobedience before legal protest has been seen to fail could be justified in special cases.

DEVELOPMENT

I. The state of nature

We said (p. 48) that the function of the idea of the state of nature was to help us understand, first, why we do or should live in a state, under a rule of law, and, second, what it takes to create a state. However, some philosophers object that the idea of the state of nature cannot answer these questions, because we are not just imagining something false, but something that goes against human nature. We *naturally* live together under laws, or something like them. Social and political organisation is natural for us. To imagine living without it will not tell us anything helpful about ourselves or why we have the state. Furthermore, we don't need to justify the state – we haven't 'given up' natural freedom for obedience.

For example, it is an important fact that we start off as children. This has many implications – that we won't survive at all unless looked after by someone else, that to produce children requires two people, and to raise them often requires at least this couple or a wider group. Hobbes seems to think that we can imagine people as individuals prior to any social interaction at all. But we are part of a social group of some kind from birth, and must be to survive.

If human beings are social by nature, the state of nature must take account of this fact and its implications for our psychology. Perhaps the state will develop *naturally*, not through consent.

> **?**
>
> What difference to the state of nature does the social nature of human beings make?

Hobbes on the Laws of Nature

We noted (p. 51) an important difference between Hobbes and Locke on their interpretations of liberty and equality, viz. that Locke gave these concepts a *moral* meaning, backed up by the idea of a Law of Nature. This may form an objection to Hobbes, viz. that he has no place for morality in the state of nature.

In one sense, this is true. He declares that there are no rights (apart from the natural right to do whatever one chooses as a means to self-preservation) and no justice, since both depend upon laws. However, he also has a theory of the Laws of Nature. He differs from Locke in presenting the Laws of Nature as purely rational, rather than moral – what people should do, rationally speaking, in pursuit of self-preservation.

Because the main threat to our self-preservation is violence, the fundamental Law of Nature is 'That every man, ought to endeavour Peace, as farre as he has hope of obtaining it; and when he cannot obtain it, that he may seek, and use, all helps, and advantages of Warre.' However, this is not enough to lead to peace. For example, if we agree with someone not to attack one another, the question arises whether we can trust them. If they are prepared to break the agreement, then it is not safe for us not to guard against them. So it is possible to follow the Law of Nature, but still be violent or be prepared to be violent.

Leviathan, Ch. 14

Furthermore, we can't trust people to be rational and seek peace in the first place. Some people, Hobbes thought, will be irrationally moved by their desires and emotions, taking more than they need, taking pleasure in their power. Feelings of honour or pride or revenge may motivate them. Other people may simply be short-sighted, and not see the long-term benefits of keeping an agreement when it involves short-term costs. Look at how suspicious we are of other people even when we do live in the state – we hide our valuables, we lock our houses, we take precautions against being attacked. If we can feel this way when there is law and order, think how much worse our fear and suspicion will be when there is no law.

> Explain and illustrate two ways in which people can act irrationally.

Because we cannot be sure that other people will keep their agreements to seek peace, then we all have a reason to fall back on acting violently if we think it is necessary. And this is the basis of Hobbes' objection to Locke (p. 51). Even if there is a Law of Nature, and even if many people – seeking peace where possible – may prefer to cultivate their own field than attack and rob others, we cannot be sure that *someone* won't come along and do this. Attack may be foolish, it may be risky, but it is also less work than growing crops! And so we are back in a situation in which we live in fear of having the 'fruits of our labour'

> Compare and contrast Hobbes and Locke on the Law of Nature.

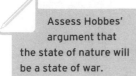

Assess Hobbes'
argument that
the state of nature will
be a state of war.

stolen from us – it will become pointless to try to cultivate land if, as soon as we have harvested, we are robbed.

The benefits of political organisation II

Locke on punishment

Locke accepts that people may break the Law of Nature, and so it needs to be enforced. But we have no state, no police, and we are all equal, with no one having more authority than anyone else. But for exactly this reason, says Locke, we *all* have the right to punish those who break the Law of Nature. Those who break the Law are a threat to everyone, and so everyone has the right to punish them, to exact reparation for the harm the person caused, and to deter them and others from breaking the Law again.

Second Treatise, § 12

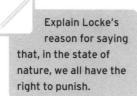

Explain Locke's
reason for saying
that, in the state of
nature, we all have the
right to punish.

We may have the *right* to punish, but is this enough? If we punish someone who robs us of our crops, that person may band together with other thieves, and return for revenge. The only way that punishment becomes effective is if someone is so powerful that it is impossible, or at least pointless, to resist them. But this would be the end of the state of nature and the beginning of the state.

At first, Locke maintains, offences against the Law of Nature will be few, given the abundance of land. However, with the invention of money, we can sell and buy – and so people can hoard up money, buy land, pay people to work. In this way, land can become scarce, and more violations of the Law of Nature will occur. With more violations, we need the system of punishment to work well.

Second Treatise, Ch. 9, §§ 124-7

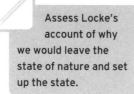

Assess Locke's
account of why
we would leave the
state of nature and set
up the state.

But it doesn't. First, we will disagree on whether someone has broken the law – and this disagreement could continue unresolved, causing tension. Second, when we punish, we are likely to be biased rather than objective, confusing punishment with revenge and being too severe. Third, we will often lack the ability to administer the punishment – so there will be no incentive for people not to break it. On this view, the primary benefit of living in a state is that there is a single, common interpretation of the law, that it is administered fairly, and that it is enforced.

Is it rational to submit to authority?

To judge whether it is rational to submit to an authority, we need to consider whether doing this is *better* than the alternative of being in a state of nature. So what do we lose by submitting to authority? For Locke, we give up the right to punish offences as we see fit, but we gain an objective system of punishment. Submitting to authority isn't a risk, since the Law of Nature and our moral equality place constraints on the state, and Locke argues that the state must be some form of democracy.

For Hobbes, we give up much more. We submit our *wills* and our *judgement* to the state. But he argues that this is necessary; for the state to be able to defend us adequately, it needs to have absolute power. Unless the state can create whatever law it thinks is necessary and lay down the correct interpretation of the law, then once again conflict could break out between different people on what the law should be or how it should be applied and enforced. This leads logically, Hobbes says, to a single person or political body on whom there are no restraints of law, an 'absolute sovereign'.

Put another way, the Law of Nature requires us to seek peace and so forth only if other people are doing the same. But we can only be sure that they will do this if they can be forced to. The advantage of the state is that we can now follow the Laws of Nature together, because it is reasonable to expect other people to keep their word and avoid violence.

> Compare Hobbes and Locke on the type of state we should submit to.

Going further: an absolute sovereign?

Locke argued that it was not rational to prefer Hobbes' absolute sovereign to the state of nature. The risk to our lives is *greater* under an absolute sovereign than in the state of nature, given the amount of power the sovereign has, while the rough equality of a state of nature will deter violence.

Hobbes replies that the sovereign is very unlikely to be a ruthless tyrant who would threaten the lives of his subjects. It is in the self-interest of the sovereign to treat his subjects well (or risk provoking rebellion). Furthermore, the sovereign still falls under the Law of Nature – which requires that he

> *Second Treatise*, Ch. 7, § 93

seeks peace when others do; and given that he has absolute power, others will seek peace! But we can respond that sovereigns are as prone as anyone to acting irrationally from desires, emotions and short-sightededness.

Unless we agree with Hobbes that *any* society is better than the state of nature, we may argue that it is only rational, only in our self-interest, to submit to some kinds of authorities – some could make things worse. In particular, Locke and other philosophers have been concerned that we – the citizens – retain some form of power over the authority, for example, through elections.

Leviathan, Ch. 21

Assess the claim that any state is better than no state at all.

Two reasons to submit to authority

In acting in accordance with the law, sometimes we see and act on the reasons for behaving in a certain way, for example, not driving when drunk because it is dangerous. But we can't always do this. Relying on authority can be a type of 'short cut'; we obey the law because it's the law, even though we don't know all the reasons for why the law is exactly as it is. We accept that there are reasons to do what the law recommends, even though we don't know them. And so we treat the law as an authority.

So one way authority works is by replacing reasons for action that people had *anyway*. Quite independently of the law, as Hume argued, we have reasons to help others and contribute to the common good. The law assists in this.

Second, as an important example of this, an authority solves the problem of cooperation, as Hobbes, Locke and Hume all argue. It is clear that we are better off if we coordinate how we behave with other people, working together to secure things we need to live our lives individually. But if we all individually made our judgements of how to act, it would be difficult for this cooperation to come about. It makes sense, then, for us to agree to obey an authority, that is, a body that decides how we are to act cooperatively, that is, that makes laws.

Explain and assess two reasons why we should submit to authority.

AN OBJECTION FROM ANARCHISM

Anarchism is the view that there is no political obligation, and that the state has no legitimate authority over us. Anarchists object that submitting to authority, rather than doing what one thinks one should do on the basis of considered reasons, will undermine moral judgement. Authoritarianism prevents people

In a famous experiment by the psychologist Stanley Milgram, a

continued

from thinking for themselves about what is right and wrong, as they simply accept whatever the authority says. First, this can lead to people doing what is morally wrong just because they are told to. Second, authority replaces moral thinking with self-interested thinking. The reason the person acts is to avoid getting into trouble, and not for moral reasons.

Because it is not rational to undermine our ability to make and act upon moral judgements, and because this will also lead to the bad consequence of more morally wrong actions being performed, anarchists argue it is not rational to submit to an authority.

Going further: authority, autonomy and community

In submitting to an authority, we obey the authority just because it is the authority. Some philosophers have argued that this is inconsistent with autonomy, the idea of acting on rules that one gives oneself. They add that morality requires us to act autonomously; we must always do what we judge we ought to do. Making these judgements is an exercise in freedom and in reason, and it is always wrong to hand over responsibility for such judgements to someone else. Not only is it wrong, it is not rational to agree not to use one's rationality (to make these judgements).

If we do act in submission to an authority, this must only be because we freely consent to do so on this occasion. We should not consent to act in submission to it in the future – this violates our autonomy in the future. But then we are not, in fact, submitting to an authority at all, but deciding, on each occasion, whether or not to act in accordance with its laws.

Two responses can make authority and autonomy more compatible. First, we can argue that the authority must respect the individual's autonomy, for example, by upholding rights that protect the ability of the individual to act as they see fit in many cases. The only justification, argues John Stuart Mill, for the law is preventing harm to others. It should otherwise leave them alone. The authority should also respect individuals' views by taking them into account, for example, through elections, when making laws.

A second response challenges this view of individuals and autonomy. Human beings are not individuals on their own, but always – from birth

person was strapped to an electric chair, and volunteers were told to deliver electric shocks when the person got an answer wrong. The voltage of the shock went up for each wrong answer. The volunteers were told the experiment was about learning. In fact, the chair was not wired up, the person in the chair was an actor, and the experiment was about how far the volunteers would go in giving electric shocks when told to do so by the 'authority figure', the scientist. Many delivered shocks of such high voltage it would cause extreme pain, and some even delivered shocks high enough to kill the person in the chair. This is clearly morally wrong. Milgram concluded that people are more willing to do morally wrong actions if told to by an authority.

On Liberty, Ch. 1. Mill is studied in A2 Unit 4.3.

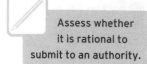

Discuss whether we can be autonomous and submit to an authority.

Assess whether it is rational to submit to an authority.

onwards – in relationship with each other (p. 68). To live together at all, we must submit to communal views about how to act. But this is no violation of autonomy, because who we are is defined in part by belonging to a community. Our judgements about how to act are made not individually, but together. There is no need to oppose the community (in the form of the authority) and the individual.

Key points • • •

- An account of the state of nature and the beginnings of the state needs to take into account that human beings are naturally social and perhaps naturally live together under laws.

- Hobbes argues there are Laws of Nature which say what we should rationally do. The fundamental Law is to seek peace; but if we cannot obtain it, to use war if necessary for self-preservation.

- Because we cannot trust people to act rationally, for example, in keeping agreements to act peacefully, the Law of Nature will not lead to peace in the state of nature.

- Locke argues that in the state of nature we all have the right to punish those who break the Law of Nature. However, we will be biased and subjective in administering punishment, and the first benefit of the state is to provide an objective system of punishment.

- Hobbes argues that we must submit our will and judgement to the state, because only a state with absolute power can avoid the violence of the state of nature. Locke argues this is irrational, as there is a greater risk to our lives from an absolute power, and the people need to retain power over the state, for example, through democracy.

- There are two further reasons to submit to authority: in doing so, we will do what we had reasons to do anyway, but didn't know it; and it solves the problem of cooperation.

- Anarchism objects that obeying authority undermines moral judgement, and that it is incompatible with our autonomy. We can respond that if the authority respects individual autonomy, it is not incompatible. Furthermore, individuals are part of a community and exercise moral judgement within the community.

II. Political obligation and consent

Tacit consent

In our earlier discussion, we looked at objections to the view that political obligation is grounded in explicit consent (p. 54). Knowing that explicit consent was hard to secure, Locke developed a theory of 'tacit' consent, that is, consent which is not actually spoken, but may be understood to have been given: 'every man that hath any possession or enjoyment of any part of the dominions of any government doth hereby give his tacit consent . . . whether this his possession be of land to him and his heirs for ever . . . or whether it be barely travelling freely on the highway'.

Second Treatise, Ch. 8, § 119

We can object that this leaves no room at all for dissent – except to leave the country. Consent is only meaningful if dissent is possible; you can only meaningfully consent if you have a choice in the matter (see p. 59f.). Hume pointed out the flaw: 'such an implied consent can only have place where a man imagines that the matter depends on his choice . . . Can we seriously say that a poor peasant or artisan has a free choice to leave his country, when he knows no foreign language or manners, and lives, from day to day, by the small wages which he acquires?'

'Of the Original Contract' in *Essays Moral, Political and Literary*

A second objection is that it is difficult to see how just walking on a road could express consent to obey all the various laws a government has passed (rather than, say, just traffic regulations). Consent is meaningless unless it is understood as consent by the person consenting.

Voting and tacit consent

We may argue that to vote is to voluntarily take part in a system of governance, so it expresses tacit consent to that system. You are taking part in a social institution that has certain rules; just in taking part, you are agreeing to abide by the rules – rather like playing a game. One of those rules is that you accept the result of the vote.

This may true for many people. But what if I cast my vote for a party that promised revolution? I am explicitly advocating the abolition of the state; is this consistent with saying that I consent to its continuation? To ignore or discount the voter's intention as expressed by their vote – by saying that to vote at all expresses consent to the existing system of government – makes their vote meaningless as a form of consent.

Assess the view that political obligation is based on tacit consent.

Second, if voting is consent, then I cannot express dissent from the current political system through voting for a revolutionary party. We could reply that I can express dissent by *not* voting or by deliberating ruining my ballot paper.

But then, third, what about people who simply don't *bother* to vote? If we say that they give tacit consent, as they have the *opportunity* to vote, this makes it impossible to dissent once more, since everyone has this opportunity.

Hypothetical consent

Perhaps actual consent, whether explicit or tacit, is not needed for political obligation. Is it enough that consent would be rational or is deserved? As we have seen (pp. 52 and 70f.), philosophers have argued that were we in a state of nature, we would find it rational to create the state and obey its laws. If this is right, then we can say that we *would* consent if rational; this is 'hypothetical' consent.

But there are three problems with basing political obligation on hypothetical consent. First, the fact that it would be rational for me to consent does not mean that I do consent; and part of what it is to respect the free equality of individuals is to respect their choices even when we believe they are irrational (see p. 53). Second, that I would consent in a state of nature does not mean it is rational for me to consent now any more than the fact that it would be rational of me to request a glass of water if I were thirsty implies that I should request one now. We need to show that consent is rational under current circumstances. And this depends on what type of state I live under and what the *real* alternatives to this state are. Third, if by 'rational' we mean to appeal to the individual's self-interest, we will not establish a secure and stable society. For people will withdraw their consent as soon as it becomes in their interests to do so. We need people to believe that they have a *duty* to obey the state, not just that it is a good idea.

Explain and assess the view that political obligation is based on hypothetical consent.

Legitimacy and popular approval

> #### Going further: what is 'legitimate authority'?
>
> What is it for the state to be a legitimate authority? Is it enough that it is capable of keeping public order and is morally justified in coercing people

to keep public order? We can object that this definition does not require that the people over which the government has authority *willingly* obey it. A state could have legitimate authority in this sense without those under its rule recognising its authority as legitimate. Second, it does not claim that the people have a duty to obey the state. It only requires that the exercise of power is morally justified.

If we add these conditions, we can say that the state is legitimate if it can impose duties on the people under it. To impose a duty is not the same as forcing someone to do something. To impose a duty is to put them in a position where they have an obligation to do something, in this case, to obey the law.

The definition does not specify who the imposed duties are owed to. There are two possible answers: we owe it to the state to obey the law, or we owe it to our fellow citizens. Which is the better answer? If we consider the state of nature story, at the point at which we consent to obey the law, who do we agree this *with*? Not with the state, because the state doesn't exist yet. The state is created through our agreement. So we agree it with other people. Our obligation to obey the law is therefore owed to other citizens. This reflects the idea that we are equal; our obligation is not *to* something that has power over us, but to other people, and it is all of us - not the state - that will benefit from the agreement.

Discuss what it is for the state to be a legitimate authority.

The question of popular approval

In our previous discussion (p. 58), we saw the objection from Plato that legitimacy does not rest on popular approval, but on ability to govern, which is a type of knowledge. Legitimacy rests on theoretical authority.

In presenting this objection, Plato makes two important assumptions. First, he assumes that politics is about the common good, not about what people want. Second, he thinks there can be knowledge about what this common good is and how to bring it about – but that the rulers in a democracy don't have this knowledge.

If Plato is right about these two assumptions, his objection is forceful. Legitimacy is determined by what is good and just, and not by consent (or benefits, if this is thought of as what people want to receive). Since people don't know what is good for them, consent can only tell us what they want, not what is good. Choice, freedom, consent in the absence of knowing what is truly good is not valuable. What is valuable is to choose what is good. And to choose what is good, we first need to know what the true good is.

We can object that even if there is some truth to Plato's argument, he might not be right to reject democracy in favour of some alternative form of government. Winston Churchill said that 'Democracy is the worst form of Government except all those other forms that have been tried from time to time.' And one reason for this is that other forms of government are prone to corruption. Needing to gain popular approval, as in democracy, guards against this.

There are two stronger objections to Plato. First, Hume would reject Plato's view that there is such a distinction between what people want – or to rephrase it, what people find useful – and what is good. People want what is beneficial, and what is beneficial is good. If this is right, then knowledge of what is good for society *just is* knowledge of what people want. However, Plato might argue that people are often confused about what is *really* beneficial, and legitimacy rests on this, not what on people think is beneficial. But already the two views are not so far apart.

Second, basing legitimacy on popular approval defends the values of individual freedom and equality. If we think that freedom and equality are the most important values, then the only way to secure what is good for society is to protect them – and this can only be done if people are not forced to obey the state when they have not consented to do so.

> Plato, in fact, makes this point in *The Statesman.*

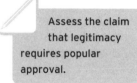

> Assess the claim that legitimacy requires popular approval.

Key points • • •

- Locke argued that political obligation is based on tacit consent, which can be given by enjoying any of the benefits of the state. We can object that this leaves no room for dissent.
- However, voting may express tacit consent to abide by the result of the vote. But this is difficult to argue for those people who vote for a revolutionary party. And what can we say about people who don't bother to vote?
- Philosophers have argued that it is rational to submit to the authority of the state; so we can say we have consented hypothetically. But hypothetical consent is not real consent at all. It does not respect people's freedom and the argument that it is rational to submit to the state compared the state to the state of nature – which is not a comparison we face now.

- A legitimate authority, we can argue, involves the ability to impose the duty to obey the law. This duty can be owed either to the state itself, or to our fellow citizens. The latter answer reflects our equality better.
- Plato's argument that legitimacy does not depend on popular approval assumes that politics is about what is truly good, so should be left to experts. But perhaps people do want what is good, or perhaps what is good is freedom and equality. In either case, democracy can secure what is good. Even if not, it protects us from corrupt governments.

III. Disobedience and dissent

Dissent and obligation

If political obligation rests on consent, and consent is expressed through voting, does a person's dissent or failure to vote mean that they do *not* have an obligation to obey the law?

If we say 'yes', we have a problem: only those people who vote, or perhaps only those people who vote for a political party that accepts the current political system, have an obligation to obey the law. That means that the government is not justified in enforcing the law against those who dissent or don't vote.

If we say 'no' – people who express dissent still have a political obligation – does this rob their dissent of meaning? Their dissent has had no affect on their relation to the state.

We can respond that this is too simplistic. In our previous discussion, we said political obligation required the *right* to dissent (p. 59f.). There are many forms of legitimate democratic activity that can express dissent, apart from voting, such as joining pressure groups. Dissent remains meaningful when these ways of influencing the government are available.

However, there are two objections to this. First, the point of basing political obligation on consent was to protect freedom and equality. Appealing to pressure groups and other forms of influence only protects equality if individuals have equal influence; and it is clear that they do not. So this answer may secure political obligation, but sacrifices equality.

Second, appealing to influence means that consent is no longer the basis for political obligation. It may be that political obligation is based on the opportunity to engage in legitimate democratic activity. *But this opportunity isn't equivalent to consent*.

> Discuss the relation between obligation, the right to dissent, and consent.

Just grounds for dissent: assessing Locke

In our earlier discussion (p. 61), we saw that Hobbes and Locke argued that we are justified in dissenting from the state when it ceases to be legitimate. As Locke's theory is very close to contemporary theories, it is worth discussing further.

Locke argues that when creating the state, people hand over the right to punish offences of the Law of Nature. Enforcing the Law of Nature is the purpose of the state. So if a government either fails to do this, or acts in a way that violates the Law of Nature, then rebellion is justified. Second, a government is only legitimate if it has the consent of the citizens. For Locke, this is not explicit consent, but TACIT CONSENT (p. 75), which he also refers to as an attitude of trust. The loss of this trust is also a ground for rebellion.

How do these two conditions relate? Suppose that a government breaks the first condition and, in some way, it doesn't do what it ought to do. However, it does not lose the trust of its citizens, or at least the majority of its citizens. Perhaps it hides the truth about what it has done, or the citizens are not upset enough to object. Is dissent justified? What if we reverse the situation: the government has not failed in any way, but it does lose the trust of its citizens? Is dissent justified then?

Locke appears to think that the grounds go together. In other words, he assumes citizens as *informed* and *rational* – they withdraw consent when and only when the government acts wrongly. But what if his assumptions are wrong?

We can argue that, for Locke at least, consent is fundamental. A government without consent cannot be legitimate. By contrast, justifying dissent against a government that retains consent leads back to the 'inconveniences' of the state of nature (p. 70), with each person using their own judgement about what is right. It was so that we could have a common, established position that the state was set up.

This leads to a second question: does the *individual* have a right to rebellion (or at least, the attempt to resist the state), or is the right to rebellion something which only the majority of people, together, can have? To give the right of rebellion to the individual would again return us to the inconveniences of the state of nature, each person deciding individually when to dissent from obedience to the law. We give up this right to the community as a whole when setting up the state. It is only when the majority withdraws its consent that the government becomes illegitimate, and rebellion is justified.

> The Law of Nature states that no person may subordinate another, harm his life, health, liberty or possessions (except in self-defence).

> ?
>
> What is more important for legitimacy – retaining consent or upholding the Law of Nature?

But this answer faces an objection: what shall we say when the state violates the rights to life, health, liberty or possessions of *some* of its citizens, but the majority are not moved to withdraw their consent? If only the majority have the right to dissent, then the victims will not be justified to dissent. But this seems unacceptable. Surely a minority can be justified in disobeying the law, or even in rebellion, if the state violates their rights.

On what grounds may we justly rebel against the state?

Justifying civil disobedience II

Going further: a right to civil disobedience?

Some philosophers argue that we have a *right* to civil disobedience as part of our democratic rights. For example, Ronald Dworkin argues that whenever the law wrongly violates one's rights, then one has a right to civil disobedience. This right, he argues, is entailed by our other rights, the ones the law has violated. The conditions Rawls lists – conscientious, public, non-violent, addressing the sense of justice – could count as a description of the type of illegal action we have the right to do when we consider the law unjust. On the other hand, any action which does *not* have these features will not count as civil disobedience, and we will not have the right to do it.

Why might we think we have a right to civil disobedience?

But do we have a right to civil disobedience? Certainly, we have a right to political participation; and we have argued that if political obligation rests on consent, then we must also have a right to dissent for consent to be meaningful (p. 59). But it is not obvious that a right to express one's dissent guarantees a right to civil disobedience. It may only give us the right to legal protest.

The arguments from Locke in the previous section suggest that the right to disobey the law can only be held and exercised by 'the people', the majority, not by individuals. We can argue, then, that when we have political obligation, for example, in a liberal or just state that protects the right to dissent legally and perhaps also the right of conscientious objection, then there is no right to civil disobedience as well.

This doesn't mean that civil disobedience cannot be justified. It means that its justification must be 'exceptional'. A right gives a standard, regular,

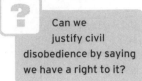

Can we justify civil disobedience by saying we have a right to it?

well-defined ground for justification (the right to non-violent, public action, but not to violence, etc.). Justifying civil disobedience, by contrast, will have no 'normal' form, but will need to be very sensitive to the individual circumstances of the action we are trying to justify.

To justify civil disobedience, we need to look at the nature of the action, its consequences and the motivation of the protestor. As we looked at two features of action previously – that civil disobedience must be a last resort and it must be non-violent – we will focus here on consequences and motivation.

Consequences

Civil disobedience exposes society to harm – it can be divisive, it may encourage disrespect for the law, it could increase political instability and, in serious cases, it may even lead to reprisals on people who do not support the aims of the protestors. To undertake it without a good chance of gaining the desired change in the law or policy would be irresponsible. The aim can only help justify the action if it has a *realistic chance* of being achieved.

However, a number of the features of civil disobedience help mitigate these dangers. The willingness to submit to punishment makes clear the protestors' general respect for the authority of the law, and so will minimise any encouragement of unjustified disobedience or general disrespect for the law. It also indicates the protestors' strength of feeling and the fact that they are not acting for personal gain – both these will diminish the antagonism and resentment that others feel if they disagree with the protestors.

Of course, these are empirical claims, and we can argue over whether a particular act of civil disobedience really does carry the risks of bad consequences listed above. This will make a difference to whether we think it is justified or not.

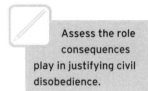

Assess the role consequences play in justifying civil disobedience.

Motivation

It is part of the definition of civil disobedience that it is motivated by a genuine sense of the law being morally wrong. However, this may not be enough. Rawls argues that protestors must seek to address society's sense of *justice* specifically.

This is because he argues that justice is the most important and fundamental value in political society. People may legitimately disagree about other moral values, and so these cannot be the basis for laws or changing laws. Laws should be based on justice, and arguments about laws should therefore refer to justice. Many philosophers disagree with Rawls, and argue that politics can be about other values as well. If so, then civil disobedience does not need to be motivated by or appeal to a sense of justice alone.

Rawls also argues that what motivates civil disobedience must be a *clear* and *substantial* injustice, as only such a serious wrong could justify the serious act of breaking the law. However, we can respond that the issue is really one of making sure the means is proportional to the end. If a group of parents illegally block a street as part of a campaign to have a crossing installed for their children, is this obviously unjustified, since the issue is not socially 'substantial'? A small protest for a small aim is not obviously wrong.

Generalising the point, we may argue that the protestors must have given careful thought to the appropriateness of the action. And this depends on a sensitivity to the social and political context. How unjust is the government generally? How unjust is the law? How much protest can society take? These questions cannot be answered in general.

Mill argued that instead of becoming annoyed with people who contest an accepted view, we should be grateful to them. They help open our minds, and they are doing what we should be doing – thinking for ourselves and aiming to get at the truth. We can argue a similar case for justified civil disobedience, that instead of looking at it as an irritant and being disruptive to the smooth running of society, it is essential for the political health of the state and therefore a demonstration of good citizenship by the protestors.

Justifying direct action

We said that direct action can be legal – in which case, it needs no special justification; or it can take the form of civil disobedience – which we have discussed. But what about direct action that is neither of these? Is it possible to justify direct action that is covert, or in which the protestors do not submit to arrest and punishment, or which works through violence?

Most people hold the view that you cannot justify violence that is directed against people who are innocent. Even in war, targeting non-combatants is not (usually) justified. Some people disagree – if the end is important enough, it is

Theories of JUSTICE, including Rawls', are discussed in A2 Unit 3.2 Political Philosophy.

Assess the view that, to be justified, civil disobedience must aim to change a substantial injustice.

Can civil disobedience be justified? If so, how?

We are not here discussing revolutionary action that seeks to overthrow the state, only discussing direct action that aims at some change in law or policy.

justifiable to kill people who do not cause the injustice one is protesting against. At this point, though, direct action comes very close to, or even a form of, terrorism.

Most people engaged in violent and covert direct action want to distance themselves from this accusation. They argue that direct action is justifiable if it attacks only people who are involved in causing the injustice. Two significant recent examples involve the use and threat of violence against people who carry out abortions and against people who carry out experimental research on animals. In both cases, part of the defence is that what these people are doing itself involves violence and death – death of the foetuses and of the animals. If anything can justify violence, it is the prevention of violence against creatures that have done nothing wrong.

These debates raise complicated moral issues which we cannot resolve here. From a political point of view, they are a reminder of the point of law and the state – to provide a way that we can live together peacefully even though we disagree about what is right and wrong. According to Hobbes and Locke, the most important value that the state protects is security. Therefore, to violate this value by using violence when one disagrees with the law is to challenge the very foundations of the state, to take back the right to decide for oneself individually, rather than together with society as a whole, when violence is justified. And so such a decision will be very hard to justify politically.

> These issues are discussed in MORAL DECISIONS, A2 Unit 3.4 Moral philosophy.

> Assess the claim that violent direct action that goes beyond civil disobedience cannot be justified.

Key points • • •

- If people who dissent have no political obligation, then the government is not justified in enforcing the law against them. If, on the other hand, they are still obliged to obey the law, what difference has dissent made? We may argue that it remains a way to influence the government. However, because influence is not consent, this answer does not base political obligation on consent.
- Locke argues that rebellion against the government is justified if it breaks the Law of Nature or loses the trust of the people. But we may question whether one without the other is enough to justify rebellion.
- Locke could answer that it is not enough for the *individual* to judge that the government has broken the Law of Nature. The right to rebellion belongs to the people as a whole. We can object that this denies that an oppressed minority may justly rebel.

- If we have a right to civil disobedience, then it will be justified. But our right to dissent, in a just state, may give us no more than a right to legal protest. However, an act of civil disobedience may still be justifiable, depending on the nature of the action, its consequences and its motivation.
- Civil disobedience can have negative consequences for society. These are mitigated by the respect for the law shown by the protestors.
- Rawls argues that civil disobedience must aim to correct a clear and substantial injustice; nothing else could justify breaking the law. We can reply that it can be justified as long as the protest is proportional and appropriate to the end.
- Direct action that goes beyond civil disobedience in being covert and violent is more difficult to justify. By judging that violence is justified, without the agreement of society, such protestors challenge the most important value the state protects, security.

SUMMARY

In this chapter, we have looked at three questions:

1. What is the state of nature, and how does it help us understand the benefits of submitting to an authority?

2. Is political obligation based on consent?

3. Can we justify disobeying the law, and if so, how?

In our discussion of these questions, we have looked at the following issues:

1. Is the state of nature a state of war, as Hobbes argues, or a state of freedom and equality, as Locke argues?

2. What benefits does living under an authority that enforces the law bring us?

3. Is it rational to agree to obey an authority? Does this depend on the nature of the authority?

4. Do we have an obligation to obey the law because it is the law? How did we acquire this obligation?

5. If this obligation is based on our consenting to obey the law, what form does this consent take? Is it explicit, tacit or hypothetical? Is it given through voting?

6. What is the difference between power, authority and legitimacy? What is legitimate authority?

7. Is the basis of legitimacy popular approval? Or does practical authority depend upon theoretical authority?

8. Do we have a right to dissent? If so, what kinds of dissent do we have a right to, and on what grounds?

9. What is civil disobedience?

10. How can we justify civil disobedience?

11. Is it possible to justify direct action that goes beyond civil disobedience?

AN INTRODUCTION TO PHILOSOPHY 1

3

Section 3: Why should I be moral?

In this chapter, we look at three answers to the question 'Why should I be moral?'. The first two argue that acting morally is in our self-interest, but understand this differently. The first view thinks of morality as a rational agreement we make with others, so we each individually get what we want. The second argues that acting morally helps define what our self-interest is. The third view rejects the connection between morality and self-interest, arguing that we should be moral for quite different reasons. By the end of this chapter, you should be able to demonstrate a good understanding of each of these three answers and be able to analyse and evaluate several arguments for and against each one.

SYLLABUS CHECKLIST ✔

The AQA AS syllabus for this chapter is:

Morality as a social contract

✔ It is reasonable to conform to the expectations of morality because morality is a conventional agreement for our mutual advantage. Exactly what kind of agreement could it be?

✔ Can we articulate our self-interest independently of morality?

Morality as constitutive of self-interest

✔   It is reasonable to conform to the expectations of morality because self-interest can only be realised in the context of a moral life.
✔   Are self-interested reasons compatible with an understanding of morality?

Morality as overcoming self-interest

✔   It is reasonable to conform to the expectations of morality and these expectations disregard self-interest as morally relevant.
✔   Does eschewing self-interest leave us without any motivating reasons to act altruistically? Is moral motivation a reflection of natural dispositions (for example, Humean 'sympathy') and, if so, what might be the implications for ethics?

INTRODUCTION

'It is reasonable to conform to the expectations of morality'

Why does the question 'Why should I be moral?' arise? First, we may want to know why people are moral. How does a concern for morality arise and how does being told 'that's wrong' or 'that's what you ought to do' get people to actually do things? This is an investigation in *moral psychology*. Second, we may want to know whether we *should* act morally, whether it is rational to be moral, and if it is, what the reasons are. This is an attempt to *justify* morality, and our focus in this chapter.

Why should we think that we need to 'justify' morality? A clue is in the phrase in the syllabus 'it is reasonable to conform'. Morality is something that *constrains* our actions. We have moral *obligations*, actions that we ought to perform, whether we want to or not. We all, at times, feel a conflict between what we want to do, and what we know we ought to do.

Sometimes we can acquire an obligation by agreeing to it, for example, if I promise to do something, then I am obliged to do it because I have agreed to. But what about killing, stealing, lying? We haven't ever *agreed* not to do these things, but we ought not to. If we expect people to act in certain ways whether they want to or not, and they haven't agreed or promised to do so, then how is our expectation 'reasonable'? This is what we need to show.

Why might we think we need to 'justify' morality?

Morality

Just as we can distinguish between why people are moral and why they should be moral, we can also distinguish between two senses of 'morality'. In a *descriptive* sense, 'morality' just refers to whatever set of rules and expectations a particular society or culture (or perhaps even just an individual) has at a particular time. So we talk about the 'moral code' of this society or that person. In a *normative* sense, 'morality' means that set of rules and expectations that is 'objectively correct'. For instance, we might say that the moral code of eighteenth-century England permitted owning slaves. But this was nevertheless morally wrong.

Explain and illustrate the distinction between the descriptive and normative senses of 'morality'.

   Throughout this chapter, we are concerned with morality in the normative sense. Our question is not 'Why should I conform to my society's moral code?' but 'Why should I conform to what is morally right and good?' (If there is no objective morality, then perhaps the distinction between two questions collapses – what is moral is what my society says it is.)

I. Morality as a social contract

Morality is a conventional agreement for our mutual advantage

If we expect people to be moral, we need to have some idea of *why* they would be moral. So we need to know why people do things. One obvious answer is 'self-interest' – people will do what they think will benefit them in some ways. So one answer to the question 'Why should I be moral?' is that, in some way, being moral is in my self-interest. In other words, I will benefit from being a moral person and acting morally. We can develop this answer to argue that morality is, in fact, an agreement about how to behave, an agreement that people have reached because they realise that certain ways of behaving, which we call moral, are in their self-interest.

   This view understands morality as a means to an end; the end, for each person, is doing what is best for themselves. However, if you ask people 'Why did you do that?', they don't always cite some benefit to themselves. They may give some other reason, for example, 'I thought it would help him'. This raises the questions – what reasons *do* we act on and what reasons *should* we act on?

Philosophers have given different theories of reasons, some arguing that rationality is just a matter of pursuing your self-interest intelligently, others arguing that we have reasons to act in ways that aren't about self-interest. We look at the first view here, and will return to the second in later discussion.

Self-interest and rational egoism

The answer, that one should be moral because it is in one's self-interest, has the advantage of simplicity. First, it is obvious that individuals are motivated by their self-interest. Second, this doesn't need justifying: it would be strange to ask the question 'Why should I do what is in my self-interest?'. The basic desires to stay alive and stay free of pain and the more complex desire for happiness are part of human nature.

Morality can require that, at times, we give up something we want for ourselves for the sake of someone else. But we cannot assume that people are interested – or *as* interested – in other people's well-being as they are in their own. Perhaps we would help each other when it is no cost to ourselves; but if there is a competition between getting what one wants and helping others, we cannot assume that people will sacrifice their self-interest and be altruistic.

What is 'reasonable' here? There is a particular view of what it is rational to do, usually adopted in economics and politics when trying to predict what people will do. If people are motivated by self-interest, then it is rational for them to do what benefits themselves. A rational person is someone who selects the *means* to their *end* of self-interest. They will consider what they need to do to get what will benefit themselves, and then, if they can, do it. A simple example: I'm thirsty, I want a drink (my end). I know where to find water, so I go there (my means) and get the water.

This ability to work out the right means to that end defines what rationality is, on this view. People are 'rational egoists'.

Explain the theory of rational egoism.

Towards an agreement

Being rational, we can see that it is very much in our self-interest that other people do not harm us – physically, or emotionally, or financially – when pursuing their self-interest. It would be good if there were constraints on what other people did, constraints that they followed. On the other hand, it looks like it is *not* such a good thing to be constrained oneself. If by stealing people's wallets I could get rich without much work, this looks like a good means to benefiting myself. But if I am constrained not to steal, then this easy path to wealth is no longer an option. So perhaps I ended up poorer, which is not in my self-interest.

We can see how this problem could be solved: we need to agree *not* to do things that would harm other people in exchange for them not doing things that harm us. While that means that my self-interest will suffer a little, it would be much worse for me if other people harmed me.

Another example: suppose I want a house to live in, but I can't build one on my own. I need the cooperation of other people to help. It would be a very good thing if I could trust other people to cooperate if they say they will. Perhaps someone agrees to help me build my house if I first help him build his. Despite the extra work for me, I decide it is worth it – after all, having a house is better than having no house, even if I have to build two houses – his and mine – to get my house. But can I trust him to help me build my house when we have finished his? From his point of view, it is a lot of work to help me build mine, and he gains nothing because he already has his house! I might decide that, because he is self-interested, I shouldn't trust him. So I don't help him build his house. So we both end up without houses.

Again, we can see how to overcome this: we need to be able to trust other people to keep their word, so that we cooperate together on projects that will benefit us both.

Outline the argument that it is rational to agree to constraints on what one does if other people agree the same.

Explain and illustrate the importance of trust for self-interest.

Morality as an agreement

Agreeing to live by the rules of morality – and then actually doing so! – solves the problems that acting on rational self-interest raises. Knowing that someone else will act morally means that we do not need to fear them harming us or breaking their word. The benefits this brings are very large, but the costs of signing up to the agreement ourselves are, by comparison, relatively small. There are certain ways in which we can no longer pursue our self-interest, but we are protected from harm and able to achieve more benefits for ourselves through cooperation than we could achieve alone.

Of course, it is only worth signing up to if it does in fact produce cooperation. But people will only cooperate (willingly) if they feel that the agreement is fair. Being self-interested, no one wants to sign up to an agreement which

This is discussed in a different context in Ch. 2, THE BENEFITS OF POLITICAL ORGANISATION, pp. 52 and 70.

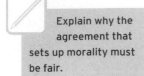

Explain why the agreement that sets up morality must be fair.

benefits other people more than it benefits them – because then they will be at a relative disadvantage. So the agreement must be fair – not because otherwise it would be immoral, but because otherwise it wouldn't *work*.

Can we articulate our self-interest independently of morality?

The argument so far has assumed that we know what self-interest is. Or if not what it is exactly, that at least it makes sense to talk about someone's self-interest without mentioning morality. The assumption is that people can think about and pursue their self-interest without thinking about what is morally good or bad, right or wrong. They then realise that an agreement about ways to behave will help them achieve what is in their self-interest. Their self-interest is independent of this agreement, and the agreement is just a means to the end of self-interest which they already had.

But is this assumption right? If we try to say what is in our self-interest, can we do so without either explicitly or implicitly drawing on ideas about what is morally good? Suppose we say, for example, that your self-interest is being happy. Then this is open to the objection that sometimes, getting what makes you happy is not actually good for you, that it is possible to be made happy by things which will harm you.

For example, someone might think that he is happy getting good marks without much work by copying essays off the internet. He feels happy, but later, he realises that he has not learned as much as he would have if he had worked out his own thoughts. So he starts doing this, and he feels a 'truer' happiness of real achievement.

We can argue that only 'true' happiness is in one's self-interest. But how can we make a distinction between a superficial feeling of happiness and 'true' happiness? In the case above, we mentioned the *value* 'achievement'. Perhaps you are only truly happy when there is something of real value in your life. Self-interest, then, is getting what is truly valuable.

If this is right, then we can't talk about self-interest without talking about what is truly valuable. Some values will be moral values, for example, the value of achievement involves the moral value of honesty – cheating doesn't lead to achievement. So we cannot say what is in someone's self-interest without knowing what is morally good.

In that case, morality can't be an agreement we would make for the sake

Is there a distinction between 'superficial' and 'true' happiness?

of self-interest, because self-interest is not something we can meaningfully specify independently of or prior to what is morally good.

Key points • • •

- The question 'Why should I be moral?' asks for a justification of morality. One answer is 'because it is in your self-interest'.
- People naturally act on self-interest. To act rationally, according to one view, is to take the best means to one's end.
- We can argue that an agreement with other people to act morally is in one's self-interest. Morality protects us from harm and enables trust. Although it constrains what we do in pursuing our self-interest, the benefits outweigh the costs.
- The argument describes morality as a means to the end of self-interest. It therefore assumes that what is in our self-interest can be described independently of what is morally good.
- This assumption can be challenged. For example, if what is in one's self-interest is getting what is truly valuable, we cannot know what self-interest is without relying on ideas of moral goodness.

II. Morality as constitutive of self-interest

Self-interest can only be realised in the context of a moral life

In the previous section, we saw the objection that when we start to reflect on what is really in our self-interest, it becomes difficult to describe what this is without referring to what is morally good. There are a number of ways in which this claim can be developed and defended. We'll look at one here, and discuss alternative arguments in Development (p. 109f.).

Plato's argument: the moral soul

The most famous defence of this position is given by Plato. He is discussing justice, but his argument applies to being a morally good person generally. His

> Explain the objection that we cannot explain self-interest independently of ideas of moral goodness.

> *Republic*, Bk. 1, 2, 4. Plato's argument is studied in more depth in A2 Unit 4.2.

argument is psychological: if you act immorally, your mind (or 'soul') will not be at peace, but at war with itself.

Plato wants to answer this challenge: suppose that morality is an agreement between people each out to get the best for themselves. Then people who are in a better bargaining position will bias the agreement to favour themselves. If this is 'unfair' or 'unjust', so what? If they can get away with it, there is no reason for them not to. Acting 'unjustly', in the sense of disregarding the interests of other people while pursuing one's own, will make one happy.

Of course, you have to get away with it. If you can force people to live according to rules that suit you, or if you can get away with breaking the rules of morality, great; if you can't, if you break the rules and get caught and punished, then you won't be happy. The point is, you have no reason to act morally, if you can get more for yourself by acting immorally. No one who is rational and self-interested would act morally if they can get away with cheating.

THE VIRTUOUS SOUL

Plato responds that this argument ignores the state of the soul of the person who would act in this way. Plato notes that we commonly experience internal, mental conflict, and we can think of this as different 'parts' of the soul pulling us in different directions. A common conflict is between what we instinctively want to do and what we think, on reflection, it would be best to do. So our souls have a 'desiring' part and a 'rational' part.

We are happier when there is no conflict between these two parts. This can only happen, Plato says, when reason is in charge. Our desires can get us into all sorts of trouble, they have no idea what is good for us. A happy soul is one in which desires are restrained, and happy to accept the rule of reason.

The desires of someone who is immoral are out of control. Each desire pushes for its own fulfilment, whether or not this is what the person needs. They aim for more and more or some desires, particularly forceful or 'lawless' ones, may outgrow others. The person may not recognise their situation. When ruled by desire, how we conceive of what is good is skewed – which is why we think that getting whatever we want will be better than acting morally. But this is simply a mistake.

By contrast, in a virtuous person, reason is in charge. This has three effects. First, they know what is morally right and good. (Plato believes that morality is objective, and known through reason.) Second, with reason in charge, they are motivated to act morally and not immorally. But third, and this is the crucial point for our argument, with reason in charge, *they are happier*, because a life without

> Explain the view that acting immorally, when you can, is in your self-interest.

> Outline and illustrate Plato's picture of what it is like to be ruled by desires.

inner conflict is a happier life than one in which parts of the soul fight each other for supremacy. Rule by desires, therefore, cannot provide happiness as securely as rule by reason.

OBJECTIONS

Plato's argument makes several assumptions that we can challenge.

First, he thinks that desires are unable to regulate themselves, that they are in some way 'blind' to what is good. Is this right? This description seems to fit bodily desires and obsessions (for example, with money) better than others (for example, those involved in friendship). Do desires necessarily get out of control? Plato can respond that desires, by their nature, do not involve consideration for the person *as a whole*. This kind of reflection is part of reason.

Second, we can object that the kind of reason needed is prudential, not moral. An immoral person needs to think about how to act in their self-interest, and this can involve reasoning. But why think this reasoning will lead them to act morally? Plato assumes that having reason in control automatically means acting morally. This is because he believes that if we reason well, we will realise that acting morally is truly good. But that still doesn't mean it is in my self-interest. As the argument stands, a *prudential* immoral person could be happiest.

Third, Plato argues that only the rule of reason can secure the absence of inner conflict that is the mark of true happiness. We could reply that a little conflict could be worth it in order to satisfy certain desires.

Finally, the answer to why we should *act* morally is that we achieve a moral and happy *soul*. But does acting morally always produce a moral soul? Does acting immorally always produce an immoral soul? Suppose that acting morally does not make my soul better – I remain in conflict and I resent having to act morally. Since I am not being made happy, then perhaps I would be better off *not* conforming to the expectations of morality. I may not be as happy as someone with a moral soul, but I will be as happy as *I* can be. In this case, it is still an open question why I should behave morally, rather than get away with immoral acts which promote my self-interest if I can.

> **? Why does Plato think being moral will make us happy?**

> **? What is the difference between prudence and morality?**

> **✎ Assess Plato's argument that self-interest can only be realised in the context of a moral life.**

Are self-interested reasons compatible with an understanding of morality?

We've considered two answers to the question 'Why should I be moral?'. According to the first, this is the best means to getting what is in your

We will challenge this interpretation of the second answer in Development, p. 109.

? Is morality based on recognising that other people matter?

Explain and illustrate the argument that morality is not based on self-interest.

self-interest. According to the second, being moral constitutes your self-interest. Both answers try to show a connection between acting morally and acting in a way that benefits oneself, or again, between being a moral person and being happy. So it looks like both answers say you should be moral because it is good *for you*.

But, intuitively, this is a peculiar and inappropriate answer to give. First, it seems to miss the heart or point of morality, which is about caring for and respecting other people *because other people matter*. Acting morally is a matter of recognising the importance and value of other people. And so, second, the answer doesn't describe how morally good people think or feel. Behaving in a morally good way in order to get the best for oneself doesn't make you a morally good person – you don't really care about other people at all, only about yourself.

Third, it doesn't explain the importance of morality. Suppose I know that if I exercise a bit more and eat a bit less, I'll be healthier and feel better for it – so this is in my self-interest. But I don't really want to do this, I like what I eat, and I don't mind that I'm not all that healthy. This isn't very important. Now suppose that I could be kinder and more thoughtful to other people, and I'd be a slightly happier person for it, but I can't really be bothered, and I enjoy insulting them. This seems a more serious flaw, one for which I can rightly be criticised by other people. But if morality is just about self-interest, what's the difference between the two cases?

Another way of putting this whole objection is that basing morality on self-interest doesn't explain the moral 'ought'. 'You ought not to steal' doesn't (seem to) mean 'if you were completely rational, you would not steal' or even 'you would live a better life if you don't steal'. 'You ought not to steal' doesn't depend, we think, on what you want or what you would gain from stealing or not stealing. If we knew someone thought this way about what they ought to do, we would find it difficult to trust them, because in deciding what to do, they are not taking *other people* into consideration in the right kind of way.

Key points • • •

- Plato presents himself the challenge that acting immorally, when one can get away with it, is in one's self-interest.
- He argues that this view overlooks the state of the soul of the immoral person, who is ruled by desires in conflict with reason, which leads to unhappiness.

- Happiness is having a harmonious soul, which means that reason must be in charge and desire restrained. But reason recognises what is morally good and pursues it.
- We can object that the kind of reason needed for a harmonious soul is prudential, a careful consideration of how best to satisfy one's desires. This may not be the same as acting morally.
- We can also object that the happiness of satisfying one's desires outweighs the happiness of a harmonious soul.
- Finally, we can object that acting morally may not lead to a happy soul. In this case, we have no reason not to act immorally if that will make us happier.
- We can also object that we should not be moral because it is in our self-interest, but because other people matter. Only this answer can explain why acting immorally is important, while acting against our own self-interest may not be.

III. Morality as overcoming self-interest

Disregarding self-interest

If acting morally is in our self-interest, we have a straightforward answer to why it is reasonable to conform to the expectations of morality. However, it is peculiar to argue that we should be moral because it benefits us. Being moral, we can argue, is about caring for and respecting other people because they are valuable in some way. This may benefit us or it may not – that question is irrelevant.

But if our self-interest is irrelevant, what reason do we have to act morally? So far, we have taken reason to be defined in terms of self-interest – it figures out the means to our ends, and it helps us judge what is really in our self-interest. So to argue that it can be reasonable to be moral when this involves disregarding self-interest as irrelevant, it seems that we need a different conception of what is 'reasonable'.

Kant: morality is based on reason

Immanuel Kant argued that self-interest is irrelevant to both what we morally ought to do and why we ought to do it. He argued that morality was based on

Critique of Practical Reason, Ch. 1

Kant's theory is discussed in MORAL DECISIONS, A2 Unit 3.4 Moral philosophy.

Explain Kant's argument that morality can't be about happiness.

Can young children make free choices in the same sense that adults can?

Explain the three features of reason that connect it to morality.

reason alone, and once we understood this, we would see that acting morally *is the same as* acting rationally.

Kant argued that morality, by definition, must help us decide what to do. When we are choosing how to act, we know that our self-interest or happiness influences our choices. However, happiness can't be the basis of morality. First, what makes people happy differs. If morality depended on happiness, then what it was right to do would change from one situation to the next. But, he argues, morality is the *same for everyone*. Second, sometimes happiness is morally bad. For instance, if someone enjoys hurting other people, the happiness they get from this is morally bad. It is bad to hurt someone; it is even worse to hurt someone and enjoy it. But if morality was about producing happiness, we would have to say 'if you're going to hurt someone, it is better to enjoy it – at least that way, someone is happy'. Which just seems wrong.

So if morality is not based on happiness, but it can help us decide what to do, then there must be something else that is capable of influencing our choices apart from happiness. And Kant argues there is – reason. We are able to think about and reflect on different actions, and decide between them. We are not 'forced' by our desires to act this way or that, we have a power of will that is distinct from desire and the pull of happiness.

So what is the connection between reason and morality? First, this capacity to choose freely is necessary for morality – animals and young children simply act on their desires, and so we don't think they are capable of acting morally. Yes, their actions can have good or bad consequences, but because they don't make choices in the right sense, we don't really praise or blame them in the same way we do adults.

Second, says Kant, reason works in a way that is independent of our desires. This is easy to see when doing maths or science. For example, you have £20, and there's a book and a CD you really want to get. But the CD is £13.99 and the book is £7.99. Despite the fact that you *want* £20 to be enough for both, it isn't and you know this. The same is true, Kant argues, for reasoning about what we ought to do. Morality is independent of what we want.

Third, it is rational for everyone to believe that £20 is not enough for both the CD and the book. What it is rational to believe is 'universal' – the same for everyone. This 'universality' is just a feature of reason; reason doesn't vary from one person to the next. So when it comes to what it is rational to do, this is also the same for everyone. It is only rational to do what everyone can do. Morality is also the same for everyone.

This last point leads Kant to a moral test for our choices. When I choose to do something, my choice may depend on other people behaving differently. For instance, if I want to steal something, I can only do this – by definition – if someone else owns it. However, if *everyone* stole whatever they wanted whenever they wanted it, then the system of ownership would break down. (Imagine everyone walking into shops and simply leaving with what they wanted.) But if no one owned anything, then it would be impossible to steal from them! So I can only steal if other people don't steal.

This must go against reason, Kant argues, because acting rationally means acting in a way everyone can act. This test of reason is also the test of morality: you should act on only those choices that everyone else could also act on.

Kant's theory provides an answer to our question 'Why should I be moral?': being immoral is being irrational. It is reasonable to conform to the expectations of morality even though morality disregards self-interest as irrelevant because morality is based on reason and shows us what it is rational to do.

Motivating reasons and morality

Kant's theory has two parts: that reason can tell us what to do, and that reason can *motivate* us to do it. He asserts that it is not only happiness and desire that can influence our choices, but also reason. But is this true? If it isn't, if reason cannot motivate action, then to act morally I would have to *want* to. Telling me that I ought to be moral or that it is rational to be moral will not motivate me.

But in answering the question 'Why should I be moral?', we are looking for an answer that will *motivate* us, a motivating reason. Kant's answer will only motivate us if he is right about reason being able to bring about action separately from what we want.

When we are trying to give people motivating reasons for doing something, we can argue, we appeal to what they want and what they care about. Appealing to something they don't care about will make no difference to their decision. Whenever we make a choice, we always do so on the basis of something we want or care about. For example, unless I *want* not to steal, the argument that it is irrational to steal will make no difference to me.

In response, we can point out that when we say to someone 'but stealing is wrong', this *is* a consideration that will influence their decision. Arguments about what we morally ought to do motivate us, even when we want to do something that is morally wrong. So isn't Kant right?

> In *Groundwork to a Metaphysic of Morals*, Kant expresses the test, called the Categorical Imperative, like this: 'Act only on that maxim through which you can at the same time will that it should become a universal law'. (A 'maxim' describes the choice you make, for example, 'to steal when I want something', 'to have fun'.)

> Explain Kant's argument that acting morally is acting rationally.

> So far, we have assumed that Kant is right that reason can tell us what morality requires. We'll look at objections to this claim in Development, p. 114.

Explain and illustrate the argument that reason cannot motivate us without appealing to what we want.

Not necessarily. Perhaps thinking about what we morally ought to do influences us *because we care about what is morally right*. Someone who doesn't care about morality will not be influenced by our saying 'but stealing is wrong'. Reason on its own doesn't motivate us.

Is moral motivation a reflection of natural dispositions?

If reason cannot motivate us, does this mean that morality must be based on self-interest? Only if self-interest is the only thing that motivates us. But we don't have to accept this. Just because we are only motivated by what we want, this doesn't mean that all we want is some benefit for ourselves. Most people (everyone?) also care for other people and their happiness, they want to help, or at least not to harm, other people. It is these desires that motivate us to act morally.

Hume on sympathy

Enquiry concerning the Principles of Morals

David Hume argues that at the heart of morality are feelings of approval and disapproval. To say something is morally wrong is to disapprove of it; to say it is right is to approve of it. Why do we have these feelings?

Well, let us start with the question of what kinds of thing we approve or disapprove of. Hume argues that we approve of what someone does, or of their character, if we find it pleasant or useful to other people. We approve of what helps people and what makes them happy.

Explain and illustrate Hume's argument that self-interest is not the basis of moral approval.

We could think, then, that this is because it is in our self-interest for other people to behave like this. I approve of what you do because it helps me or makes me happy. But, Hume argues, this can't be right. First, we approve and disapprove of actions that have absolutely no effect on us personally, for example, events we read about in the papers happening on the other side of the world. Second, we can distinguish between what is morally right and what is in our self-interest. So we don't always disapprove of something that harms us, for example, if you and I apply for a job, and I don't get it, you do, I don't *disapprove* of your success. Or again, if I need some money, and you get it for me by stealing it from someone else, I don't approve of what you've done. Third, we don't try to persuade people to feel approval or disapproval for a particular action by considering how it affects them, but, for example, how it hurt or helped someone else.

The origin of our feelings of approval and disapproval, says Hume, is *sympathy*. It is just a fact – a fact of human nature – that we feel pleasure at other people's pleasure and pain at their pain. Would you, could you, deliberately tread on someone's toes for no reason? Can you look at someone in pain and be completely unmoved? Sympathy is the root of approval and disapproval, and the root of moral motivation. We conform to the expectations of morality because we care about other people. We don't have to justify that care any more than we have to justify self-interest; it is just as natural to care about other people as it is to care about ourselves.

Of course, sympathy can come into conflict with self-interest, and on many occasions, self-interest will win. But that's a different point – it doesn't show that we don't feel sympathy. In fact, it shows that we must, or there would be no conflict!

> Outline Hume's argument that moral motivation is based on sympathy.

Key points • • •

- If self-interest is irrelevant to morality, to argue that it is reasonable to be moral, we need to develop a theory of reason that is independent of self-interest. One such theory is Kant's.

- Kant argues that morality cannot be based on happiness. People are made happy by different things, but morality is the same for everyone. And happiness can sometimes be morally bad.

- We are able to make choices, Kant argues, that are not 'caused' by our desires. We only praise or blame creatures that have this power of the will.

- Reasoning about what to believe works independently of our desires and is 'universal' (the same for everyone). Reasoning about what we ought to do – morality – has the same properties.

- Kant concludes that it is irrational to act on a choice that not everyone could act on. He makes this test the standard of what is morally right or wrong as well.

- We can object that even if reason can tell us what is morally right, it can't motivate us to act morally. Unless we want to act morally, we won't.

- Hume argues that morality is based on sympathy, which grounds our feelings of approval and disapproval and motivates us to act morally.

DEVELOPMENT

I. Morality as a social contract

Morality is a conventional agreement for our mutual advantage II

The Prisoner's Dilemma

The Prisoner's Dilemma is a fictional scenario invented in the 1950s. Any situation which has the same structure of costs and rewards, such as the example of house-building (p. 91), is called a Prisoner's Dilemma after the original.

If everyone acts on their self-interest, it may seem that we will each do the best for ourselves. But we can show that this is false, and that one great advantage of morality, for everybody, is that it creates trust and cooperation. Suppose two men, Adam and Barry, are arrested for a crime, and held in separate rooms for interrogation. The prosecutor only has enough evidence to charge them with illegally possessing a gun, but if he can get one of them to confess, he can charge them with armed robbery. Adam is told this: 'If you confess, your sentence will be reduced because you have helped the prosecution. In fact, if you confess and Barry doesn't, we'll let you go free, but Barry will serve ten years in prison for armed robbery. If Barry confesses and you don't, you will serve ten years in prison, and he'll go free. If you both confess, you'll get a lighter sentence of seven years each. If neither of you confess, then you'll be charged with illegally possessing a gun, and you'll both get two years in prison.' Barry is given the same deal.

So there are four options, which we can display in a table:

	Barry confesses	Barry doesn't confess
Adam confesses	Both get seven years	Adam is free, Barry gets ten years
Adam doesn't confess	Adam gets ten years, Barry is free	Both get two years

Explain the Prisoner's Dilemma, using your own example.

What should Adam do? If Barry confesses, then it is better that Adam confesses as well (he'll get seven years rather than ten). If Barry doesn't confess, then once again it is better that Adam confesses (he'll go free rather than get two years). So, from a purely self-interested point of view, Adam should confess.

Barry is thinking the same thing. So Barry also confesses. Because they both confess, they get seven years. But it would have been better for them both not to confess, and only get two years each. If both of them act rationally from a self-interested point of view, the result is *worse* than if they had trusted each other to act in a way that benefited them both!

This clearly shows that acting only in one's self-interest can lead to worse consequences for oneself than cooperating with others, even when there is a cost to cooperation. For Adam and Barry, not confessing meant giving up the possibility of freedom. But if they could trust each other to do this, they would both be better off (getting two years) than they are in a situation in which they cannot trust each other and they both confess (getting seven years).

Explain how
the Prisoner's
Dilemma shows that
acting in self-interest
does not always lead to
the best consequences
for oneself.

The 'free rider' problem

The Prisoner's Dilemma shows that cooperating can be better than everyone acting out of self-interest. Suppose that, realising the benefits of morality, we agree with each other to act morally. Now we know that, by and large, we can trust each other.

Suppose now that Barry doesn't confess, trusting that Adam won't confess either. Adam suspects that Barry trusts him not to confess – so now the options Adam has to choose between are either not confessing, and getting two years, or confessing and walking free. This means that if Adam has good reason to think that Barry trusts him, he is better off acting self-interestedly.

Everyone acting morally is better than everyone acting self-interestedly. But if everyone *else* is acting morally, it is *even better* to act self-interestedly – at least if you can get away with it. This is called the 'free rider' problem – someone who does this gets the benefits of morality (other people trust him, do things for him), but he doesn't bear the costs of acting morally, because he cheats people.

We discussed Plato's
version of this
argument on p. 93f.

It turns out that whether I have reason to conform to the expectations of morality depends on whether I can get away with acting immorally when other people are acting morally. If I can, then I have *more* reason to act immorally than to act morally.

Morality as an agreement is in everyone's self-interest, collectively, to set up. But once it is set up, it is in each person's self-interest, individually, to get away with breaking the agreement, if they can avoid punishment. Is there some way we could describe morality as an agreement that will help solve the free rider problem? This is one of the questions we discuss in the next section.

Explain why
the free rider
problem is an objection
to the view that acting
morally is in one's
self-interest.

Exactly what kind of agreement could it be?

It may seem beside the point to talk about morality as an agreement – it clearly isn't. We have never agreed to be moral, and nobody ever asked us.

A tacit agreement

Some philosophers respond that morality can be understood as a *tacit* – an unspoken – agreement. This view is defended by people who want to explain morality in the descriptive sense (see p. 89), that is, why we have the particular moral practices we do. So, for example, why has there been a 'double standard' about sex? In many societies, it is seen as morally bad for a woman to sleep with many men, but more acceptable for a man to sleep with many women. This seems very unfair. We can explain it if we think of our moral code as a tacit agreement *between people who had or have power*, in this case, men.

> Explain the view that morality is a tacit agreement. Does this view tell us why we should be moral?

If morality is this kind of agreement based on power, then it is not an agreement for the *mutual* advantage of everyone. So you only have reason to be moral if you are one of the powerful people morality benefits. So if we take a realist approach to morality being an agreement, it may turn out that we don't have reason to be moral.

A hypothetical agreement

We want to show why it is *rational* to be moral, where being moral is mutually advantageous. To show that it is rational, we don't need to show that morality is an actual agreement, only that *if we could make such an agreement*, we should. Morality is a 'hypothetical' agreement, an agreement we would or should make because it is rational to do so. The point of looking at it this way is not to explain our moral code as it is, but to justify morality.

GAUTHIER

To show that it is rational to conform to the expectations of morality, David Gauthier argues that the situation without morality is like the Prisoner's Dilemma – even if we try to cooperate with each other, because we are self-interested and can't trust them, we will both end up in a situation which isn't as good as it could be. This will motivate us to agree to morality.

To argue that it is rational for *me* to be moral, I need to imagine *me* in that situation; and the same for you. But we know that people are very different in power and ability – perhaps it would be more rational for powerful people to agree among themselves to enforce a morality that isn't equally in everyone's interests. However, Gauthier argues, this situation will be unstable – the people who are not treated equally could threaten to upset the agreement. A stable agreement must be one in which no one feels coerced or cheated.

For the argument to work, individuals must be the best judges of what is in their self-interest and how to achieve this. Suppose that I thought I always made bad decisions – I might, then, feel it was rational for me to ask other people to decide what I should do. I could choose to submit to morality for this reason. But this isn't how Gauthier understands the agreement – each person agrees because they think it will be the best for them.

WHAT DO WE AGREE TO?

We saw earlier (p. 103) that thinking of the agreement to be moral in terms of the Prisoner's Dilemma leads to the free rider objection. If I am motivated by self-interest to agree to morality, then presumably I am still self-interested after making the agreement. But my self-interest will then lead me to be immoral when this is in my self-interest and I can get away with it. Realising this, will we really trust other people? And if we don't, then we haven't got an agreement to be moral at all.

Gauthier argues that we can solve this problem if what we agree to is not simply to act morally, but *to change what motivates us*. We agree to adopt a new *disposition*, the disposition to be moral. In other words, we agree to become people who will not act on self-interest when this conflicts with acting morally.

We can still object, however, that if our motivation to be moral rests ultimately on self-interest, it will not be strong enough to get us to act morally when this conflicts with self-interest. Human psychology doesn't respond as well to these arguments about justification as it does to immediate self-interest. If this is right, then Gauthier's story about why we ought to be moral cannot tell us why we are moral.

> Why is it not in my self-interest to try to enforce an agreement biased towards my self-interest?

> Outline Gauthier's argument that it is in our self-interest to agree to morality.

> Perhaps it makes little sense to talk about *choosing* a motivation. But Gauthier is not trying to tell a realistic story, but justify morality. What he argues is that it is *rational* to have this disposition to be moral.

> Assess the free rider objection to the view that morality is an agreement for our mutual advantage.

Two objections

Who's in?

A further objection to the view that morality is an agreement for mutual advantage is that it is only rational to make this agreement with people from whom you can benefit. This is in danger of leaving out some people, for example, people with disabilities. If the cost of treating them morally is greater than the benefits that result from their cooperation, then it is not in our self-interest to include them in the agreement. But then we have no reason to treat people with disabilities well.

One possible response is that including them in the agreement is a kind of insurance – I could become disabled, and then the cost of being left outside the agreement would be very high. So I have reason to make sure the disabled are covered by the agreement to act morally, since I might be disabled one day.

This reply won't work for other cases, though. Does morality cover how we treat animals or the environment? We cannot make an agreement with animals or the environment. We can, of course, make an agreement with other people to treat animals and the environment in certain ways. But why would we? What do *I* gain from how people treat animals? What do *I* gain from people not exploiting or polluting the environment (as long as it isn't near me)?

> **Discuss whether understanding morality as an agreement can account for the extent of our moral duties.**

> ### Going further: morality before the agreement
>
> If morality is the agreement we make, then there are no moral rules for making the agreement. Gauthier agrees with this – the only reason the agreement needs to treat people equally is that it is more likely to break down if it doesn't. Is this right? Life goes on despite a great deal of unfairness. If I think that I will do better ignoring morality when it suits me, it is not obvious that I am wrong.
>
> Rather than arguing that the agreement is based just on self-interest, we could say that the agreement is itself a *moral* agreement. It expresses what morality is about, and signing up to the agreement is an expression of our commitment to morality, not an expression of self-interest.
>
> This view is defended by Thomas Scanlon. He uses the idea of agreement to explain what morality is: 'An act is wrong if its performance under the

> *What We Owe to Each Other*, p. 153

circumstances would be disallowed by any set of principles for the general regulation of behaviour that no one could reasonably reject as a basis for informed, unforced, general agreement.' If I behave immorally, I am acting in a way that I cannot reasonably expect other people to accept. The motivation for being moral, then, is not self-interest, but wanting to be able to *justify* our behaviour to each other.

Why would we want to do this? We have reason, says Scanlon, to want to live with others on terms that they accept (or at least, that they would accept if they were being reasonable). We could argue that this is in our self-interest, or that we have a natural desire to live together with other people, or we could argue that reason demonstrates that we have a duty to live this way (as Kant would argue). Whichever answer we give, on this view, morality doesn't depend on self-interest alone. Rather, what is in our self-interest can only be understood in terms of what is morally right.

> Explain the difference between Scanlon's and Gauthier's theory of morality as an agreement.

> Discuss the challenges facing the claim that morality is an agreement in our self-interest.

Can we articulate our self-interest independently of morality?

Rationality and self-interest

In our earlier discussion (p. 92), we argued that only 'true' happiness was in one's self-interest, and that we cannot understand what this is without appealing to moral values. A similar point was made in the previous section – that we have reason to live together with others on terms they reasonably accept, and that this is itself a moral value.

The defender of rational egoism can reject these claims. Let us focus on 'true' happiness again. Yes, it is true that we cannot say that self-interest is getting whatever makes you happy. We must be able to *evaluate* our desires into 'good' (contributing to self-interest) and 'bad' (harmful to self-interest). But we can do this without using moral evaluation. Instead, we need to beef up our idea of *rationality*.

We said earlier that rationality just helps discover the means to our ends (p. 90). It can be more than this. Rather than talk about what is 'truly valuable', we should say this: what is in my self-interest is *getting what I would want if I were completely rational*. Being 'completely rational' means knowing all the relevant facts about my desires and their consequences in the real world, and selecting the

Explain and illustrate the claim that self-interest is getting what you would want if you were completely rational.

Assess the claim that we can articulate our self-interest independently of morality.

Assess the view that morality is a conventional agreement for our mutual benefit.

best means to fulfil my desires. This definition doesn't refer to any moral values, only to my desires. However, it provides a standard for evaluating my desires as 'good' or 'bad', viz. whether I would act on this desire if I were fully rational. So it is possible to articulate self-interest independently of any moral considerations.

TWO RESPONSES

Is this a good definition of self-interest? Suppose someone feels very depressed. What they want, above all, is for the pain to stop. What would they want if they were completely rational? Would they continue to want to die or would they want to live? Can we answer this question without appealing to what is 'good', for example, without saying that life is good, so it is more rational to want to live? Or again, suppose someone is obsessed with collecting every European stamp, and they sacrifice even friendships to pursue their hobby. Is this irrational? Is it in their self-interest? Or would it be better *for them* if they preferred friendship to stamps?

Second, is the account of self-interest complete? Scanlon argues that part of our self-interest lies in *being treated morally*. Having other people respect you, having the right to expect other people to be able to justify their behaviour to you – these are valuable. But we cannot explain their value in terms of some *other* benefit, such as getting what you want. It is in our nature as rational creatures to justify our behaviour to each other. It is in our self-interest, then, to have this capacity respected, for people to behave towards us in ways that we cannot reasonably reject.

Key points • • •

- The Prisoner's Dilemma is a fictional case set up to show the difficulties of always acting on self-interest.
- Basing morality on self-interest faces the problem of the free rider – someone who takes advantage of other people being moral. If it is rational to act on self-interest, then it is rational to be a free rider when one can rather than be moral.
- If morality is a real, but tacit, agreement, this may explain some aspects of our moral practices. However, a real agreement may favour the powerful over the powerless, and so may not justify morality.
- Gauthier argues that morality is a hypothetical agreement – an agreement we would make, if we had the choice, because it is rational to do so.

- He argues the situation without morality is like a Prisoner's Dilemma, that the agreement must be fair in order to be stable, and that individuals are best able to judge their own self-interest.
- He argues that, to solve the free rider problem, we must agree to change our motivation, but we can argue that if self-interest is the reason for the agreement, self-interest will always be a stronger motivation than a disposition to be moral.
- We can object that morality as an agreement for mutual advantage will leave out disabled people, animals and the environment.
- Scanlon argues that it is better to understand morality as an agreement based on the value of justifying our behaviour to other people.
- Rational egoism can argue that self-interest is getting what you would want if you were completely rational. This defines self-interest independently of morality.
- We can object that the definition fails, because people could still want what is bad for them; and that it is incomplete, because being treated morally is part of self-interest.

II. Morality as constitutive of self-interest

Self-interest can only be realised in the context of a moral life II

In our earlier discussion (p. 93), we saw Plato's argument that being moral is good for an individual's soul. A different argument says that people are *essentially social*. On this view, what is good for me is defined, in part, by how I relate to other people, and a good relationship is good for both me and others. And so I can only achieve what is good for me by acting in ways that are necessarily beneficial to other people as well.

Aristotle on living in accordance with reason

Aristotle agreed with Plato that being a morally good person is the best way (for oneself) to be. He argued that it is the fullest realisation of what it is to be a human being. But in making this argument, Aristotle appealed to the social nature of human beings much more than Plato did.

Nicomachean Ethics

Explain and illustrate Aristotle's claim that in order to know what is best for us, we first need to know our nature.

We are all aiming, says Aristotle, to lead the best life we can. But in order to understand what the best life for us is, we need to understand more about our nature. Think of a tiger and a sheep. The best life for a sheep is quite different from the best life for a tiger. Sheep live together, tigers – mostly – live alone. A sheep on its own will be less happy, and tigers together will fight.

Aristotle argues that what is distinctive about us is our capacity to reason. So the best life for a human being will be one lived 'in accordance with reason'. As Plato argued, our *state of mind* is very important. In particular, a life in accordance with reason will be one in which our desires, emotions and choices are reasonable.

Anyone who doesn't want or need other people is either a beast or a god, says Aristotle. So we need to consider carefully how our desires and emotions fit in with living with other people.

Nicomachean Ethics, Book II, Ch. 6

There is no quick answer, he says, and he goes on to consider a wide range of desires and emotions, arguing that there is a reasonable and an unreasonable form of each. Take, for example, anger. First, this is natural and necessary – anger is a legitimate response to being put down or badly treated, and it can help us stand up for ourselves. But to feel anger 'well' or 'reasonably', we should only get angry when we really have been treated badly, so we need to know when this is. Then again, we need to direct our anger at people who deserve it, not sound off at people who don't. And so on. So, Aristotle says, we need to feel anger 'at the right times, with reference to the right objects, towards the right people, with the right motive, and in the right way'.

Explain Aristotle's argument that living a morally good life is living the best life for oneself.

If we can do this with each desire and emotion we have, then we will be a morally good person, and our relations with other people will be as good as they can be. We will also be living in accordance with reason. And so we will be living the best life for ourselves.

Beyond Good and Evil, discussed in A2 Unit 4.5.

Going further: are we all social?

Friedrich Nietzsche would object to the idea that there is one account of human nature, applicable to everyone, and morality is defined relative to this. People are unequal. Only the 'highest' or 'most noble' can hope to achieve the best human life possible. The need they have for relations with other people is limited to their equals. But most people are 'common' and the 'higher' types are very rare indeed, and will in any case seek solitude. How they treat people 'below' them is irrelevant. They will view most people with contempt and are willing to use them in whatever way is necessary for their own self-interest.

Second, this is not simply a matter of fact, it is entirely right, Nietzsche argues, an expression of the noble person's love of life and power. Life necessarily involves predation, while the desire to be pleasing to others, to be part of a community, is a 'herd instinct'. Morality, as it has developed in Europe over the last 2,000 years, is an expression of this herd instinct. The best individuals break away from it. Of course, if someone is not 'exceptional' – and by definition, very few of us are – then the best life we can achieve is through the community. But this is not the best life for everyone.

It is as though, for Nietzsche, there are human beings that are sheep, so need a sheep's life; and there are human beings that are tigers, and so need quite a different life, one that he describes as 'beyond good and evil'. It is a life in which we sheep will be treated in ways which we would call 'immoral'. But there is no reason why such people shouldn't be immoral.

Beyond Good and Evil, § 259

Explain Nietzsche's objection to the view that the best life is one involving equality, respect and other 'good relations' with other people.

Self-interest and morality

In our earlier discussion (p. 95), we objected that being moral for self-interested reasons doesn't take into account the way that other people matter. Can we make the same objection to Aristotle?

It is true that in answer to 'Why should I be moral?', Aristotle answers 'because that will be the best life for you' – but it is important to understand what he means by this. To live this best life, you must treat people in certain, morally good ways. Self-interest and morality are intertwined – it is not possible to use morality as mere means to self-interest.

We can illustrate this with friendship. It is a very important part of leading a good, happy life that one has friends. But someone who is a friend just out of self-interest is not a real friend. He will miss out on the good things – the feelings, the character, the state of mind – that come from being a real friend. On the other hand, someone who does not find friendship a beneficial and important part of their life – who is a friend without feeling that they gain from it – is also missing out on what is important in friendship.

Discuss how friendship involves and yet goes beyond self-interest.

We can answer 'Why should I be moral?' in a similar way. If we consider our relationships with other people just in terms of the benefits for us, we won't gain the real benefits of those relationships. On the other hand, if we do not find relating to other people in morally good ways part of the good life for us, then we are missing out on the real value of those relationships.

In our earlier discussion, we gave three objections to basing morality on self-interest: that it doesn't recognise that other people matter; that it doesn't describe how morally good people think; and that it doesn't explain the importance of morality. We can now answer these objections.

Being a morally good person, for example, being just or generous, involves recognising that other people matter. Failing to do so means that our relationships with them will not be as good as they could be. Second, while morally good people think about what is good for other people, they also believe that being morally good is good for themselves. Doing what is morally good without seeing how it is part of the best life for you, is a dry and unattractive way to live. Third, morality is important because the quality of our relationships with other people is at the heart of the good life for us. Where there is a conflict between self-interest and morality, we will find that we cannot properly enjoy or benefit from acting on self-interest if this means acting immorally.

> Assess Aristotle's account of how self-interest and the morally good life are intertwined.

> Discuss whether self-interested reasons for being moral are compatible with an understanding of the nature of morality.

Going further: Nietzsche on moral motivation

Beyond Good and Evil, § 260

To Nietzsche, these arguments are all disingenuous. There are, he argues, two kinds of morality – a 'master morality' and a 'slave morality'. The assumption that everyone is equal, has equal rights and deserves to be treated well is part of 'slave morality'. A master morality aims at what is 'best', 'noble', at the exercise of power in the fullest way, and does not care about the consequences, least of all the effects on 'common' people. Common people simply do not matter. Slave morality – which is what we have inherited – is concerned with suffering, with approval and justifying ourselves to other people. And it is motivated, above all, *by fear*. In such a morality, 'love' of one's neighbour or 'respect' for others is a smokescreen for fear of one's neighbour. What is strong and individual is dangerous, what is conforming and beneficial to society is good.

Beyond Good and Evil, § 201

At heart, Nietzsche argues, morality has no rational basis. It is an expression of instinct. Most people have a strong need to obey, to be ruled; some individuals are more honest in their 'will to power', their desire to assert and develop themselves as individuals. From Socrates onwards, philosophers have tried to rationalise morality, to make it seem reasonable, to provide arguments for it. But this is hypocrisy.

Nietzsche's view comes closest to the first answer to 'Why be moral?' – because, given one's own weakness, fear of asserting one's own power, inability to take responsibility for both weakness and fear, it is a good idea to agree with others to live according to rules. But even this is a rationalisation – it is not reason that provides the motivation, it is a basic need to obey someone else.

> **?** Is being concerned for others' suffering an expression of love or fear?

> **✎** Assess Nietzsche's view that trying to justify morality is hypocrisy.

Key points • • •

- On the view that people are essentially social, my self-interest involves good relations with others, and these relations are good for both myself and other people.
- Aristotle argues that to understand the best life for us, we need to understand human nature.
- What is distinctive about us is our capacity to reason. So the best life for ourselves is one lived in accordance with reason.
- This involves having desires and emotions, and making choices, that are reasonable. If we do, we will also have good relations with other people.
- Nietzsche objects that people are unequal, and it is right that 'higher' types treat 'common' people however they see fit. Morality is an expression of a herd instinct, and not part of the very best life for the most noble people.
- Aristotle can argue that morality can properly involve self-interest. Just as a real friend both cares for his friend and benefits from the friendship, a morally good person cares for others and understands that the moral life is best for them.
- Nietzsche objects that morality (as we know it) is motivated by fear. Furthermore, it is an expression of instincts, and so trying to give it a rational basis is hypocritical.

III. Morality as overcoming self-interest

On what is reasonable

In our earlier discussion (p. 97), we argued that if it is reasonable to conform to the expectations of morality, but morality is not based on self-interest, we need to find some other sense in which morality is 'reasonable'. We noted that Kant's theory that morality was based on reason alone has two parts: that reason can tell us what to do, and that reason can *motivate* us to do it. We discussed the objection that reason cannot motivate us without relying on what we want. But can it even recommend what to do on its own?

What reason recommends

Suppose someone has no desires at all, there is nothing they want. However, they are rational. Will there be certain actions that they should do, and others they should avoid, just because they are rational? We can argue that there are not. If you have no ends, nothing you are seeking to achieve, then reason has nothing 'to work with'. Whether an action is rational or not depends on what one is trying to achieve (is the action a good means to the end?), and on whether this end is 'helpful' or 'harmful' to other ends one has.

For example, why should I eat? Because I am hungry – I want food; or, if I have lost my appetite, because I want to stay alive. Suppose I don't want to stay alive – should I eat? Well, we can still ask why I don't want to stay alive, for example, because my life is painful – and then we can ask whether dying is the best means to my end of ceasing to feel pain, especially in relation to other ends I might have, for example, being happy.

The same kind of considerations apply to moral actions. Why should I not steal? Because I want to avoid prison, because I do not enjoy other people getting angry with me, because I feel guilty if I do, or perhaps simply because I care about other people. In any case, we need some answer like this, one that cites a particular end I have, to decide what it is rational to do. Without citing any particular end, we cannot say whether an action is rational or not.

Kant's reply is that it is only rational to do what everyone can do. And there are constraints on this, so reason can say what we should do without referring to what we want. But why think that we must all behave in the same way in order to be rational? Because 'universality' is the nature of reason. What is rational is rational for all, not relative to one person or another.

We can agree that this is true about what it is rational to believe, as we saw above, but disagree that it is true about what it is rational to do. Acting irrationally, we may respond to Kant, is doing something that defeats what you want to achieve. So it is relative to what you want.

Alternative accounts of reason

Kant's theory is not the only theory of how morality could be 'reasonable' without being based on self-interest. We discussed one example earlier (p. 106f.): Scanlon argues that it is wrong to act in a way that other people could reasonably reject. Because we are rational, we expect other people to justify themselves to us, and we recognise that they deserve the same respect. Another argument, following John Stuart Mill, is this: we want to be happy, and we recognise that other people want to be happy. Using reason, we can understand that there is nothing 'special' about ourselves and our desire for happiness, but that we are all equal. So we should act in a way that promotes everyone's happiness, not just our own.

Both of these views, like Kant's, involve two claims: that other people – their happiness or their nature as rational beings – gives us a reason to act morally towards them; and that this can motivate us to curb our self-interest and actually act morally. We should be moral, then, because it is reasonable, because other people deserve it from us. In this way, whether being moral is in our self-interest is not the central concern.

Reason, motivation and self-interest

Going further: reason before desire?

Is it possible to motivate people to act morally without appealing to what they already want?

One argument is this: we can always ask *why* someone desires something. For instance, suppose you want to do well in your studies – why? Presumably because you think that success will be good, better than failure.

> This argument allows that Kant could be right that *morality* involves behaving in a way that everyone could follow. But it claims that acting morally is not equivalent to acting rationally.

> *On Utilitarianism*

> Explain the different ways in which acting morally may be 'reasonable'.

What We Owe to Each Other, p. 23

? Do we decide how to get what we want or decide what we have most reason to do?

✏ Outline and illustrate the argument that desires are based on reasons.

Beyond Good and Evil, § 3

? Can we motivate people to act morally without appealing to what they want?

There are different answers to how or why success is good – you might think it will help you go to university, and this will help you get a better job. Or you might think knowledge is valuable for its own sake. You might simply enjoy it. Whatever your further thoughts on success, your desire to succeed is backed by a *belief* about what is good. This belief about what is good provides your *reason* for your desire.

This insight provides a theory about what it is to be rational (a theory that is quite different from Kant's). When deciding what to do, our attitudes to each option is informed by reasoning. Scanlon argues that we have 'the capacity to recognize, assess, and be moved by reasons . . . every action that we take with even a minimum of deliberation about what to do reflects a judgment that a certain reason is worth acting on'.

To have a desire, to want to do something, is not simply an 'urge'. If we think carefully about our desires, we can distinguish an urge to act, a feeling of unpleasantness, but also a sense that what our desire is for is *good* in some way. Imagine someone who has an urge to read philosophy but can't see *anything* good in it. This would be very unusual, and it would be strange to say that they *want* to read philosophy.

This shows that our desires respond to reasons. So if you can show someone the reason for being moral, for example, that other people deserve to be treated well, then they can acquire the desire to act in this way. If this is right, we can motivate people to act morally without appealing to what they already want, but by appealing to reasons.

But suppose a self-interested person does not see any reason to be moral – can we argue that he is insensitive to reason? There are many motivations that we share with the selfish man, and we will appeal to these to try to demonstrate that there are reasons to be unselfish. But this is all we can do – appeal to desires and emotions that we share.

Nietzsche goes further and argues that, on the whole, reasoning and giving reasons is a reflection on one's instincts and desires, nothing more: 'most of a philosopher's conscious thinking is secretly guided and channelled into particular tracks by his instincts . . . demands for the preservation of a particular kind of life'. Our values, our commitments, do not rest on reasoning; reasoning is an attempt, often a falsifying, deceiving attempt, to justify our values when they have and can have no justification as they are simply expressions of instincts.

Psychological egoism

Any view that justifies morality in terms of reasons that are not to do with our self-interest faces a general challenge: that human beings only ever act in ways that promote their own self-interest, a view called 'psychological egoism'. If psychological egoism is right, there is no point in appealing to anything apart from self-interest in order to get people to act morally – it can have no effect on them.

Psychological egoism argues that whatever action you look at, you will find something that the agent has gained – or thought he would gain – from doing that action. It doesn't matter how altruistic the action seems to be – giving money to charity, spending time comforting people who are in distress, etc. – there will always be something 'in it' for the person, and this is *really* why they do it. Any action will reveal an underlying self-interested motive.

Why should we believe this? Psychological egoists point to two things. First, when someone does an altruistic action, such as giving money to charity, they are doing what they *want* to do. And so they are getting what they want, they are satisfying their desires. Second, they get pleasure from what they do, a sense of satisfaction, that buzz that comes from 'doing a good deed'. Alternatively, they may do what they do in order to avoid feeling guilty. In either case, they do what they do because it brings them pleasure or helps them avoid pain – and this is what motivates them.

> Explain psychological egoism and the arguments that support it.

However, we can object that people *don't* always do what they want – they sometimes do what they feel they *ought* to do, even when this conflicts with what they want to do. The psychological egoist can reply that they *must* be doing what they want to do; after all, no one is forcing them, for example, to give money to charity.

This reply shows that the egoist is saying that acting voluntarily and doing what you want are the same thing. But this *assumes* what needs to be proven, viz. that only our desires can motivate us, and reason can't. If reason can motivate us, then sometimes when people act voluntarily, they are doing what they believe is reasonable, not what they want to do.

Second, we can object that even when we do what we want, this doesn't mean that we are acting on self-interest. Altruism – unselfishness – is the desire to help other people, even at a cost to oneself. Even if people always do what they want, this doesn't show that what they want is always something *for themselves*. We can want good things for other people, and can choose to give up good things for ourselves in order to help other people get something good. This is what Hume argued for with his theory of sympathy (p. 100).

> Discuss the implications of the claim that we only ever do what we want.

Going further: pleasure and desire

Suppose the psychological egoist is right that we always have a feeling of pleasure, or avoid guilt, when acting unselfishly. This doesn't mean that *the reason why* we act unselfishly is in order to get this feeling. If you ask someone who is giving money to charity why they are doing so, they will probably say 'in order to help other people'.

The psychological egoist claims this answer is false – that the real answer is 'in order to feel good about myself'. But this is a confusion. Just because the person gets pleasure from the action doesn't mean that what they really wanted – what they were motivated by – was the pleasure they would get. To desire pleasure is a particular desire; just as desiring pleasure is distinct from desiring knowledge, it is also distinct from desiring to help other people. If the psychological egoist is right, we only have one kind of desire – the desire for pleasure – and so there is really no distinction between wanting pleasure, wanting knowledge, wanting to help. But we say that helping someone in order to feel good about yourself and helping someone because they really need it are quite different.

> Assess the view that we always act on self-interest.

Moral motivation as a reflection of natural dispositions: implications for ethics

If Nietzsche's theory of how morality is based on natural dispositions is right, then the implications for ethics are considerable. First, he argues that there are no objective values – that values are invented, as expressions of instincts. Second, he argues that we are not by nature equal. The best human beings must go 'beyond good and evil' in their lives. So morality (as we think of it normally) does not have the importance or authority we thought it did. Third, a morality of equality is an attempt to deceive us about our natural inequality. Moral values and 'moral' motivations are mostly deceptions, weakness trying to masquerade as reason, and (normal) morality is an attempt to control those who are naturally stronger and better.

> Outline the implications of Nietzsche's view that morality is an expression of instincts.

If morality is based on sympathy, as Hume argues (p. 100), what implications does this have? We will spend longer on this question.

Sympathy and self-interest

If sympathy is the basis of morality, can it be strong enough to counter self-interest when the two come into conflict? Sympathy, says Hume, 'is much fainter than our concern for ourselves'. But, he argues, sympathy is not in fundamental conflict with self-interest. Helping others gives us pleasure, both at the time and in memory. If you could choose to be either self-interested or sympathetic to others, if you are wise, you will chose sympathy. Hume echoes the argument from Aristotle, that the quality of our relations to others is central to our personal happiness (p. 109).

> *Enquiry concerning the Principles of Morals*, § V, Part II

> Discuss whether sympathy and self-interest can be in conflict.

Sympathy as the foundation of morality

Nevertheless, we may think that making sympathy the foundation of morality will lead to biased action. After all, we feel sympathy much more for people we know and love than people we don't. Surely Kant was right to think that morality requires that we treat people equally in certain ways, whether we are close to them or not.

Hume agrees, and so he supplements his account of sympathy. When we are making moral judgements, we should put aside our personal connections to the people involved 'and render our sentiments more public and social'. Notice that there is a distinction between sympathy and like or dislike. We can think that someone we dislike is still a morally good person; and that someone we like behaves badly. This shows that we can distinguish our feelings of sympathy, which is about people in general, from our personal feelings. But to do so, says Hume, 'in order to pave the way for such a sentiment, and give a proper discernment of its object, it is often necessary, we find, that much reasoning should precede'.

> *Enquiry concerning the Principles of Morals*, § I

What reason does here is not create sympathy where there was none. But it can appeal to our feeling of sympathy and redirect it. For instance, we can reason that there is no difference between a child starving in some distant country and a child starving in our street. And this can motivate us to give to charity, even though we don't personally know about the people the charity helps.

> Discuss the objection that sympathy is biased, so it cannot be the basis for moral motivation.

Sympathy and argument

If morality is based on reason, then someone who acts immorally is acting unreasonably. But if morality is based on sympathy, it seems that we cannot necessarily say this. It is not *rationally* obligatory to be moral, it seems. If we say to someone 'you must do this' or 'you mustn't do that', is this legitimate? Don't we have to say 'if you want to be sympathetic, you must do this'? – in which case, the person could say 'I don't care about sympathy'.

But how serious is this objection? While we can't say that this person is irrational, we can still say that they are immoral, cruel, selfish, or whatever. Is it a stronger criticism that someone acts irrationally than that they act selfishly?

However, it is true that we cannot *argue* someone into morality. If appealing to their sympathy, and then also to their self-interest (since the two are connected), doesn't work, then nothing will. But there will be very few people for whom this doesn't work. Somebody who is completely without sympathy will be a sociopath; and we don't reason with sociopaths, we either lock them up or treat them as mentally ill! To lack sympathy is to cease to be fully human in some way.

> **(How) Can we reason about morality if moral motivation reflects a natural disposition?**

Does all morality stem from sympathy?

Sympathy disposes us to approve of what is pleasurable and useful, and to disapprove of what is painful and useless. So, if morality is based on sympathy, then what is morally good must either be useful or pleasurable. But many people have thought that morality includes commitments that are neither. For example, within religious moralities, there is often an element of self-denial, the idea that in ourselves we are sinful, and it is only through God's love and forgiveness that we have value. These thoughts, and the life of penitence and self-sacrifice that they can motivate, seem neither pleasurable nor useful, and do not seem to express sympathy. And so Hume rejects them – they should be no part of morality.

But is this too quick? Religious people can have great integrity and wisdom, and through their self-sacrifice can contribute a great deal to the happiness of others. But, they would argue, it is not possible to keep the integrity, wisdom and self-sacrifice (since they are useful) and simply get rid of the idea of self-denial. The connections run too deep.

The point can be made more generally. We sometimes value things as morally good quite independently of the pleasure or use they bring. For example, we might say that someone has led a 'worthwhile' life in fighting for a cause they really believe in (for example, saving the rainforests) – even if the battle causes them stress and in the end they don't succeed. If this is right, then Hume's view that morality should always aim at the useful and pleasurable seems too narrow.

> Is there more to morality than what sympathy leads us to approve of?

> Discuss the implications for ethics of the view that moral motivation rests on natural dispositions.

Key points • • •

- Kant argues that reason on its own can tell us what we ought to do, because it is only rational to act on a choice that everyone can act on.
- We can object that acting irrationally is to defeat what you want to achieve, so reason must appeal to what someone wants to recommend how to act.
- Scanlon argues that we have reason to justify ourselves to other people, while Mill argues that we have reason to promote everyone's happiness. Both views argue that it is reasonable to act morally, independent of our self-interest.
- Scanlon argues that desires rest on reasons, what is good about what we want. We can object that in giving reasons, we are really still appealing to desires. If someone sees no reason to act morally, we can only appeal to their desires and emotions. Nietzsche argues that reasoning is just an expression of our instincts, not a justification.
- Psychological egoism claims that we only ever act on self-interest. We can object that we don't always do what we want; even if we did, we don't only want our self-interest; and finally, if we get pleasure from acting unselfishly, this does not make our pleasure the reason we act unselfishly.
- If Nietzsche is right, moral values are not objective, but invented; morality should not constrain 'higher' people; and morality deceives us about our natural inequality.
- Hume argues that sympathy and self-interest are not in tension, so the fact that self-interest is stronger than sympathy should not worry us. However, we need to correct the bias in our feelings of sympathy so that we feel sympathetic towards people we don't know as well as people we do.
- If moral motivation reflects natural dispositions, rather than reason, we cannot argue someone into being moral. However, we can still criticise someone immoral for being immoral.
- We can object that sympathy is too narrow to encompass all morality, as it only motivates us towards what is pleasurable and useful, and morality can include commitments which are neither.

SUMMARY

In this chapter, we have looked at three answers to the question 'Why should I be moral?':

1. It is reasonable to conform to the expectations of morality because it is in one's self-interest, as morality is an agreement for mutual advantage.

2. You should be moral because the moral life is the best (most beneficial) life for you.

3. It is reasonable to conform to the expectations of morality because morality is based on or an expression of what is reasonable.

In our discussion and evaluation of these answers, we have looked at the following issues:

1. Is it (always) rational to do what is in one's self-interest?

2. Is morality a hypothetical agreement that it is in one's self-interest to make?

3. If so, is it rational to keep to the agreement or to act immorally when one can get away with it?

4. Can self-interest be defined as getting what one would want if one were completely rational?

5. Is it possible to say what is in one's self-interest without referring to what is morally good?

6. Is leading a morally good life in one's self-interest because it leads to a harmonious and happy soul?

7. Is leading a morally good life in one's self-interest because it expresses one's nature as a rational and social being?

8. Is trying to show how morality benefits oneself to miss the point and importance of morality?

9. Is morality the expression of a 'herd instinct', which certain 'noble' people rise above?

10. Can morality be justified by reason without appeal to what we want? Can reason alone then motivate us to act morally?

11. Do we only ever act on self-interest?

12. Are we motivated to act morally because we have the natural disposition of sympathy?

13. Can sympathy be the foundation of morality?

4

AN INTRODUCTION TO PHILOSOPHY 1

Section 4: The idea of God

There are three central issues in philosophy of religion relating to the idea of God. First, just what is the idea of God an idea of? Can we make sense of it? Second, there is a philosophical argument, called the ontological argument, that claims to prove that God exists just by unpacking our understanding of the idea of God. Third, where does the idea come from? Did we (humanity) invent it? Did we 'imagine' God? Or does the idea derive from God, did we 'discover' God? By the end of the chapter, you should be able to analyse and raise objections to the idea of God, to evaluate a number of arguments about the origins of the idea, and to argue for and against the ontological 'proof' of God's existence.

SYLLABUS CHECKLIST ✔

The AQA AS syllabus for this chapter is:

The divine attributes

✔   God has been described as possessing omnipotence, omniscience and supreme goodness. He is said to be transcendent and immanent and His existence has no beginning or end, being either eternal or everlasting. What are we to understand by these attributes and how do they apply?

✔   Are these divine attributes singularly or mutually coherent?

The ontological argument

✔ Attempts to demonstrate a priori that if God's existence is conceivable then God must exist – God's being is necessary.
✔ Strengths and weaknesses of 'ontological arguments' for God's existence.

The origins of 'God'

✔ The claim that the idea of 'God' is innate within all of us and the difficulties surrounding that claim.
✔ Attempts to explain how the idea of 'God' is merely a human construction and projection that emerges from mundane social or psychological processes.

INTRODUCTION

I. The divine attributes

At the heart of philosophy of religion is the idea of God. There are many ideas of God around the world, and different religions have different views on the nature of God. However, almost all agree that God is 'maximally great' – that nothing could be greater than God. This is the conception of God we will start with. But our scope will become more narrow, and the properties of God we will discuss are those which Judaism, Christianity and Islam have thought central. But, even more selectively, we will only look at how the debate over God's attributes has been understood and developed in the Western Christian tradition.

We are starting with the thought that nothing could be greater than God. Another way this thought has been expressed is that God is perfect. Augustine says that to think of God is to 'attempt to conceive something than which nothing more excellent or sublime exists'. Some philosophers claim that God is the most perfect being that *could* (not just does) exist.

A note on referring to God: I have adopted the traditional personal pronoun 'he' in referring to God. There are two reasons for this. First, the conception of God that is discussed in the syllabus is personal, so the impersonal 'it' sounds awkward. Second, English unfortunately has only two personal pronouns, 'he' and 'she', both gendered. If God exists, I don't believe that God is gendered in either way. My use of 'he' is purely to avoid the awkwardness of alternating 'he' and 'she' and of using 's/he'.

God as personal

Some philosophers argue that to lack either intellect or will is to lack perfections – things without either intellect or will are not as great as things with intellect and will. Certainly we prize these abilities very highly. So to be perfect, God must have both intellect and will, that is, be personal.

Before turning to the properties of God listed in the syllabus, we may ask why these properties have been thought to belong to God. Part of the answer is that many religions and philosophers have thought that God is personal. Properties that essentially characterise a person include intellect and will. The intellect is characterised by rationality and knowledge, the will by morality, freedom and the ability to act.

Intellect and will are properties of mind. If God is a person, he is so in virtue of being a mind. Being perfect, if God is a mind, then he is an ideal mind. He will have perfect intellect and perfect will. Perfect intellect involves perfect wisdom, perfect rationality and perfect knowledge (omniscience). Perfect will involves perfect goodness and perfect power (omnipotence).

However, if God were a person, he would be very unusual. As the most perfect possible being, God cannot become more perfect; nor can God become less perfect, as then he would not be the most perfect being possible, and so not God. So unlike other persons, God cannot change. Persons also usually have bodies. But the most perfect being can't have a body, at least literally. Anything made of matter changes over time, but God can't change. And anything made of matter must have parts. God cannot have parts, because whatever has parts depends on them for its existence. So God can't be material. For these reasons, philosophers have said God is *personal* rather than a *person*, that is, God has attributes essentially associated with being a person, but God is not a person, because he does not change and does not have a body.

Explain, in your own words, the difference between God's being personal and our being persons.

Omnipotence

As perfect, God will have perfect power, or the most power possible. Power is the ability to do things. The most obvious definition of omnipotence is 'the power to do anything'. But does 'anything' include the logically impossible? For instance, could God make 2 + 2 = 5? Could God create a married bachelor?

Some pious philosophers have wanted to say yes – logic is no limit on God's power. However, there is simply no way we can meaningfully say this.

What is logically impossible is not anything at all. Any description of a logically impossible state of affairs or power is not a meaningful description, because it contains a contradiction. The *limits* of the logically possible are not *limitations*. So almost all philosophers have restricted omnipotence to 'the power to do anything that is logically possible'. Even if God can't do the logically impossible, there is still nothing that God can't do.

Is logic a limitation on God's power? Why or why not?

Omniscience

Perfect knowledge is usually taken to mean 'omniscience'. The most obvious definition of omniscience is 'knowing everything', but we need to remember that God is the most perfect *possible* being, and perhaps it is impossible to know *everything*. For example, if human beings have free will, then perhaps it is not possible to know what they will do in the future. So being omniscient, God knows all the truths that it is possible to know. What we think it is possible for God to know will depend on other attributes of God, for example, whether we think God exists outside time (so there is no 'future' for God).

Omniscience is not just a matter of *what* God knows, but also of *how* God knows. Aquinas argues that God knows everything that he knows 'directly' and 'immediately', rather than through inference or through understanding a system of representation (such as language or thinking in terms of **propositions**). Other philosophers disagree, and argue that if we say that God doesn't know all true propositions, then there is something that God doesn't know; so God does have propositional knowledge as well as direct and immediate knowledge.

Can God know everything? What does this mean?

Perfect goodness

There are two ways of understanding perfect goodness. If goodness just is perfection, then saying God is perfectly good is just to say that God is perfectly perfect – or the most perfect possible being. There is more than one way to be perfect (including, as we've seen, perfect power and perfect knowledge), and God is perfect in all ways. This is a metaphysical sense of 'goodness'. The other sense of 'goodness' is the moral sense. In this sense, 'God is perfectly good' means that God's will is always in accordance with moral values.

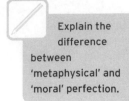

Explain the difference between 'metaphysical' and 'moral' perfection.

Plato and Augustine connect the two understandings of perfect goodness. What is perfect includes what is morally good; evil is a type of 'lack', a 'falling short' of goodness. If evil is a 'lack' or 'failure', what is morally good is more perfect than what is not.

Transcendence and immanence

The idea of transcendence marks the way God is very different from creation. First, God is 'outside' or 'goes beyond' the universe. Since God is self-sufficient and the creator of the universe, clearly God is not reducible to the universe. Second, God is not spatial as the universe is, and many philosophers argue that God also transcends time in the sense that God is timeless, rather than existing in time (see below). Third, while God is personal, he has intellect and will in quite a different way from persons.

However, emphasising God's transcendence can make it seem that God is very remote from us, no part of our lives. The claim that God is immanent marks the close connection between God's existence and the existence of everything else. For example, it is said that God is omnipresent, that is, that he exists everywhere – in everything that exists, God is 'there'. In being everywhere, God knows everything from the 'inside'. Some thinkers also argue that God is immanent in time and so in human history, giving a sense that we work alongside God in producing what is morally good.

Immanence without transcendence, the view that God is wholly immanent, would lead to 'pantheism' – that God and the universe are the same thing. It would also lead to a denial of God being personal – since the universe isn't. So transcendence is necessary for the traditional conception of God; immanence is necessary to prevent that God being impossibly remote from us.

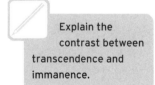

Explain the contrast between transcendence and immanence.

Existence without beginning or end

Being perfect, God is self-sufficient, dependent on nothing else for existence. If there was something that brought God into existence, God would be dependent on that thing to exist. If there were something that could end God's existence, then God is equally dependent on that thing (not exercising its power) to continue to exist. If God is the ultimate reality and depends on nothing else, then nothing can bring God into existence or end God's existence. And so (if God exists) God's existence has no beginning or end.

There are two ways in which this can be expressed, related to transcendence and immanence. If we think that God exists in time, then we say that God's existence is *everlasting* – God exists throughout all time. If we think that God exists outside time, then we say that God's existence is eternal – God is timeless. In this case, God has no beginning or end because the ideas of beginning and end only make sense in time – something can only start or stop existing in time. God is not in time, so God cannot start or stop existing.

Key points • • •

- Traditional conceptions of God stem from the idea that God is the most perfect possible being.
- *Personal*: God has traits similar to those of a person, in particular intellect and will.
- *Omniscience*: God knows everything it is possible to know. At least much of what God knows, he knows directly and immediately.
- *Omnipotence*: God has the power to do anything it is possible to do.
- *Perfect goodness*: God is the most perfect possible being, and because moral goodness is a perfection, God's will is in accordance with moral values.
- *Transcendence and immanence*: God is more than the universe, being outside space and perhaps also outside time. Yet God also exists throughout everything that exists.
- *Existing without beginning or end*: if God exists in time, then God is ever-lasting; if God exists outside time, then God is eternal.

II. The ontological argument

St Anselm's version of the ontological argument

ontological
The word 'ontological' comes from **ontology**, the study (-ology) of what exists or 'being' (ont).

St Anselm and Descartes both famously presented an ontological argument for the existence of God. Their versions of the argument are slightly different, but they both argue that we can deduce the existence of God from the idea of God. Just from thinking about what God is, we can conclude that God must exist. Because it doesn't depend on experience in any way, the ontological argument is a priori. We will look at St Anselm's version here, and Descartes' version later (p. 145).

An a priori argument is one that doesn't depend on sense experience at any point, in particular, in its premises.

Anselm's argument relies on 'conceivability':

1. By definition, God is a being greater than which cannot be conceived.
2. I can conceive of such a being.
3. It is greater to exist than not to exist.
4. Therefore, God must exist.

In THE DIVINE ATTRIBUTES (p. 125), we saw that the idea of God as the most perfect possible being has a long history. And perfection has also been connected to reality: what is perfect is more real than what is not (see p. 128). Anselm's argument makes use of both these ideas.

Anselm starts from a definition of God – if we could think of something that was greater than the being we called God, then surely this greater thing would in fact be God. But this is nonsense – God being greater than God. The first being isn't God at all. We cannot conceive of anything being greater than God – if we think we can, we're not thinking of God. The second premise says that this idea – a being greater than which we cannot conceive – is coherent. Now, if we think of two beings, one that exists and one that doesn't, the one that actually exists is greater – being real is greater than being fictional! So if God didn't exist, we could think of a greater being than God. But we've said that's impossible; so God exists.

Objections

GAUNILO AND THE PERFECT ISLAND

Anselm received an immediate reply from a monk named Gaunilo: you could prove anything perfect must exist by this argument! I can conceive of the perfect island, greater than which cannot be conceived. And so such an island must exist, because it would be less great if it didn't. But this is ridiculous, so the ontological argument must be flawed. You can't infer the existence of something, Gaunilo argues, from the idea of its being perfect.

Anselm replied that the ontological argument works *only* for God, because the relation between God and greatness or perfection is unique. An island wouldn't cease to be what it is – an *island* – if it wasn't perfect; of course, it wouldn't then be a perfect island. But islands aren't perfect by definition; perfection is something an island can have or not have. It is an 'accidental' not an 'essential' property of islands. It's perfectly coherent to think of an island that isn't perfect.

Explain this claim in your own words.

Explain Anselm's version of the ontological argument.

An essential property is one that something must have to be the thing that it is. Islands must be areas of land surrounded by water. Can we say that 'perfect islands' are islands that are essentially perfect? Not convincingly, because perfect islands aren't a different *kind* of thing from islands, but a *type* of island. So they are still only essentially islands, and accidentally perfect.

By contrast, God, argues Anselm, *must* be the greatest conceivable being – God *wouldn't be God* if there was some being even greater than God – it's incoherent to think of God as imperfect. Being the greatest conceivable being is an essential property of God. But then because it is better to exist than not, existence is an essential property of God. So to be the greatest conceivable being, God *must* exist.

HUME ON NECESSARY EXISTENCE

Notice that this conclusion is more than 'God does exist'; it claims God must exist – God's existence is **necessary**. That isn't true of you or me or islands – we can exist or not, we come into existence and cease to exist. Our existence is **contingent**. The ontological argument only works for God, says Anselm, because only God's existence could be necessary.

Hume argued that the idea of 'necessary existence' was meaningless. To understand his claim, we need to understand what Hume thought about knowledge (this is discussed in more detail in Ch. 1, ARE ALL CLAIMS ABOUT WHAT EXISTS ULTIMATELY GROUNDED IN AND JUSTIFIED BY SENSE EXPERIENCE?, p. 17f.). Hume argues that we can have knowledge of just two sorts of thing: the relations between ideas and matters of fact. His distinction was developed by later philosophers, and is now understood in terms of two distinctions: **analytic/synthetic** and **a priori/a posteriori**.

Matters of fact we establish through sense experience, and are a matter of evidence and probability. The ontological argument doesn't rely on sense experience, but on pure reasoning. So the argument, and its conclusion that God exists, are a priori. But the only claims that can be known a priori are 'relations of ideas'. These are 'demonstrable', that is, provable, not a matter of probability, but certain. Take the claim 'all vixens are female'. What is a vixen? By definition, it is a female fox. So 'all vixens are female' means 'all female foxes are female'. To deny this is to contradict oneself; if not all female foxes are female, then some female foxes are not female. But how can a female fox not be female?!

If 'God exists' is a priori, then we shouldn't be able to deny it without contradicting ourselves: 'Nothing is demonstrable, unless the contrary is a contradiction', Hume says. But, he goes on, 'Whatever we conceive as existent, we can also conceive as non-existent. There is no being, therefore, whose non-existence implies a contradiction. Consequently there is no Being whose existence is demonstrable.'

So Hume argues that God does not possess existence essentially – it is possible to conceive of God not existing (and still be thinking of God). So God

Outline and illustrate the debate between Gaunilo and St Anselm.

There are definitions of 'necessary' and 'contingent' truth in Ch. 1, p. 30. The existence of a being is contingent if it could be true or false that that being exists, for example, it could now exist, but later cease to exist. The existence of a being is necessary if it cannot come into or go out of existence; it is necessarily true that it exists (or doesn't).

See Ch. 1, INTRODUCTORY IDEAS, p. 8 for definitions and discussion of these distinctions

Dialogues on Natural Religion, § IX

Hume assumes that all demonstrable truths must be analytic. Rationalists would argue that there are synthetic a priori truths (see Ch. 1, p. 10) that are demonstrable as well, and the claim that 'God exists' could be one of these.

Explain Hume's claim that 'Whatever we conceive as existent, we can also conceive as non-existent'.

does not exist necessarily. And so the ontological argument for God's existence fails.

Key points • • •

- The ontological argument is a priori; it works from an analysis of the idea of God, not from any fact of experience.
- St Anselm's ontological argument takes for granted the idea that God is the greatest conceivable being.
- The conclusion of the ontological argument is that God necessarily exists. Everything else only exists contingently.
- Hume objects that it is not a contradiction to deny that God exists, so God does not exist necessarily, and the ontological argument fails.

III. The origins of 'God'

In what follows, I'll refer to the idea of God and the concept of God interchangeably. I mean the same thing by idea and concept here. I refer to the concept/idea as GOD (all capital letters).

The idea of God is innate

Outline and illustrate the three types of ideas Descartes says there are.

See Ch. 1, Do all ideas derive from sense experience?, p. 12 for further discussion of what 'innate' means.

Descartes argues that the concept GOD is one that we have innately. In his argument, he says there are three possible sources for a concept: that we have invented it (it is 'fictitious'), that it derives from something outside the mind (it is 'adventitious'), or that it is innate. By 'innate', he doesn't mean we have it from birth in the sense that a baby can think using this concept. It would be very strange if babies could think about God but didn't yet have a concept of power or reality or love! Innate ideas are ideas that the mind has certain capacities to use, and which can't be explained by our experience.

Arguments that an idea is innate are usually arguments that can't be anything else, that is, they can't have been invented or derived from experience. Descartes' argument is like this, and we'll look at the details in Development (p. 149). But let's start with the alternative explanations to see whether they are persuasive first.

The idea of God is derived from experience

The syllabus is misleading in suggesting that the only alternative to GOD being innate is that we invented it. There is the possibility that, like so many other concepts we have – such as apple, yellow and pain – we acquired the concept through experience, in this case, through experience of God. We will only look at this briefly, since the syllabus concentrates more on the theories that say we invented the concept GOD.

There is a standard philosophical account of how experience can be the origin of concepts. If we have experiences of God, then this could be an explanation of where the concept GOD comes from. However, we immediately run into a problem: are experiences of God *sense* experiences? Do we have any good reason to think anyone has *literally* seen or heard God? If God has the attributes we discussed earlier (THE DIVINE ATTRIBUTES, p. 125f.), then no one can literally see or hear God as God has no body, so has no physical parts with which to reflect light or generate sound waves. Of course, God could directly create an experience in someone's mind of seeing or hearing – but because this experience doesn't come from the sense organs, then it isn't literally seeing or hearing. It is more like hallucinating: an experience just like a sense experience, but not caused by the sense organs responding to something in the real world.

But are experiences of God like sense perception at all? Some philosophers have argued that (at least some) experiences of God are importantly similar to perception, an immediate awareness of something other than oneself that is real; instead of physical objects, the 'something other' is God. They are quite unlike trying to *think* about God or imagine God.

But to this we can object that sense experience is much richer in detail than experiences of God – think how long it would take to describe a view of a garden, but people find it difficult to say much at all about experiences of God. So perhaps they are not like sense perception.

Another objection to the claim that GOD is derived from experience is that we all have the concept GOD, but religious experiences are very uncommon. But we can reply that many concepts originate with the experiences of only a few people, for example, ELECTRON. They then explain it to others, and so on, until it becomes common.

We can also object that concepts of God differ greatly from one religion and time to another, which again suggests the concept GOD doesn't come from just one type of experience. One reply here is that the concept GOD originates with religious experience, but people add much more to that concept (perhaps

You can study religious experience as the basis of an argument for the existence of God in more depth in A2 Unit 3.5 Philosophy of Religion.

See Ch. 1, DO ALL IDEAS DERIVE FROM SENSE EXPERIENCE?, p. 14.

Things in hallucinations do not exist. So for us to explain GOD as deriving from experience, experiences of God need to be like sense experiences, like perception, rather than hallucinations. If experiences of God were hallucinations, then the concept GOD would derive from imagination rather than experience.

for all sorts of reasons, some of which we discuss below in the other accounts of where GOD might come from). Differences in beliefs about God come from an elaboration of the concept, but the concept still originates in religious experiences.

Explaining the idea of 'God' as a human construction and projection

If we don't have any direct experience of God, and the idea GOD isn't innate, then in some way, we have invented it. But even if we have, that doesn't mean that God doesn't exist, that is, that the concept doesn't refer to anything. It is possible that we need the concept GOD, which we have come up with, to explain what we do experience or to explain the existence of the world, or something like that; and that these explanations are right. However, perhaps we invented the idea of God for reasons other than true explanation, for example, because we really want there to be a powerful being to watch over and care for us.

Invention as explanation

In science, we often invent concepts, which we think refer to things – such as the concepts GENE or ELECTRON – which we haven't experienced. Both these concepts were invented in order to explain what scientists saw. No one had seen a gene or properly identified its structure when the concept was created – as a hypothesis – to explain what happens in heredity. And no one can see electrons (with their eyes at least) at all! Just because we invented the concepts doesn't mean that they don't apply to the real world. If genes and electrons exist, then we were right to invent the concepts, that is, the explanations we gave which used these concepts, and how we define GENE and ELECTRON, are the right explanations and definitions; this is how the world is.

What is important here is that we invented the concepts because, in some way, explanations using them are true. So the reason for the concept is to describe the world truly. But we can object that unlike scientific concepts – at least the ones we still use – explanations in terms of God are *not* true, or at least we have no reason to think they are true. We have other, better explanations now, so we can discard the idea of God. For example, perhaps people invented the idea of a God to explain the unpredictable forces of nature, such as lightning or tidal waves. But we can explain these scientifically; so we have no reason to use the concept GOD any more.

Invention and projection

Over time, the idea of God has changed. For example, the ancient Greeks thought there were many gods, related to different parts of nature (sea, fire, sun, sky, etc.), that they fought and loved each other, that they appeared in many forms to human beings, and could even have children with them. This is very different from the traditional, Christian philosophical concept of God described in THE DIVINE ATTRIBUTES (p. 125f.)! Do we have any reason to think this was a process of 'discovery' of the true nature of God, or is it better to think that the idea of God is *no more* than part of the human response to the world? Perhaps we should say this to explain the origins of GOD: we wanted to explain mysterious events and forces that we didn't understand, and there is some psychological or social need that is fulfilled by the idea of God. If this story is right, then perhaps GOD is a 'mere' invention, it doesn't refer to anything real.

But in that case, we want to know why many people have thought that God is real. How can we get mere invention and reality mixed up? This is the view that the idea of God is 'projected' from our minds onto the world. Projection happens when what is only in our minds we mistakenly think is part of the world. It can happen with many ideas. For example, some forms of REPRESENTATIVE REALISM (Ch. 6, p. 204) argue that colour is projected onto the world; colour actually only exists in our minds, in our sense experiences, but we mistakenly think that material objects are themselves coloured (this was Hume's view).

But it is easy to understand why we would think that physical objects are coloured; it is less obvious why people would come to believe in God without experiencing God – or something like God – directly. We need an explanation of the psychology of belief in God.

So we have a number of different explanations of the origin of 'God':

1. The idea of God is innate.
2. The idea of God comes from (religious) experience.
3. The idea of God is invented, but in order to explain reality.
4. The idea of God is invented for reasons other than truth, and is projected onto reality.

Is there anything in the world, or in our experience, that only the idea of God can explain?

It doesn't *show* that God doesn't exist; but the existence of the concept is no evidence that God does exist; and it would seem strange that a concept we invented in this way turned out to apply to the world – a bit like discovering that Santa Claus really does live at the North Pole!

Explain the claim that God is a projection.

In the rest of this chapter, we will concentrate in greater length on (1) and (4), following the syllabus. In discussing (4), we will also look again at (3). There are two questions we are trying to answer in the discussion: 'Where did the concept of God come from?' and 'If it came from us, *how* and *why* did we come up with it?'.

Key points • • •

- Descartes argues that there are three possible sources for any concept: it derives from experience or imagination, or it is innate.
- One possibility is that the idea of God is derived from experiences of God. Religious experiences are sometimes described in similar terms to sense perception. But sense perceptions are rich in detail, while religious experiences are usually very hard to describe.
- If we invented the concept of God, this may have been an attempt to explain experience. We accept scientific concepts, such as GENE and ELECTRON, because when we test them, they make good sense of our experience. However, perhaps we have better, scientific explanations of the phenomena GOD was invented to explain.
- GOD may be a *mere* invention, something we invented for psychological reasons as well as an attempt to explain the world. In this case, we have projected it onto the world, believing it corresponds to something real when it does not. But then we need an explanation of why and how we invented the concept.

DEVELOPMENT

I. The divine attributes

We saw that at the heart of the idea of God is the view that God is perfection – a greater being cannot be conceived. The idea of perfection has often been linked to the idea of reality – so another aspect of the idea of God is that God is the ultimate reality – the ground or basis for everything that exists. The view is that what is perfect is more real than what is not. (This idea is developed, for example, in A2 Unit 4.2 PLATO'S *REPUBLIC*.) Perfection has also been thought to involve complete self-sufficiency, that is, not to be dependent on anything; and not to lack anything. Again, this connects with being the ultimate reality: that which is not the ultimate reality will depend on that which is, and so not be perfect.

Are the divine attributes singularly or mutually coherent?

If God is the most perfect possible being, then each of the perfections attributed to God must be possible, and the combination of the perfections must also be possible. Both of these requirements lead to difficulties. For example, it is unclear what it means to say that 'God knows everything it is possible to know'. And the attributes can appear incompatible with each other. For example, can God will evil? Omnipotence suggests 'yes', perfect goodness suggests 'no'. In the light of this, some philosophers say that God has the perfections he does to the greatest possible *degree* that is *compatible* with his having all perfections.

Omniscience

Everlasting v. eternal

What is it to know everything it is possible to know? If God is everlasting, that is, exists in time, then does God know what will happen in the future? If not, for example, because we have free will and so God does not know what we will do, then it seems that there is something God does not know. Furthermore, as the future unfolds, God would gain new knowledge. But as the most perfect possible being, God is unchanging. Doesn't his gaining knowledge mean his 'omniscience' increases? But if God gains knowledge, he wasn't previously omniscient.

We may reply that if God does not know the future, this may not be a *restriction* on or *lack* in God's knowledge. If it is *impossible* to know the future, for example, because of the existence of free will, God not knowing the future is no failure; God still knows everything it is possible to know *at any given time*. And God's gaining knowledge as time passes is consistent with God being omniscient: God always knows everything it is possible to know. It is just that *what* it is possible to know changes over time.

If God exists outside time, the problem doesn't seem to arise. God never gains new knowledge, and God already knows what happens in the (our) future.

> We will discuss a number of these issues, though there are others. A different kind of tension arises when we look not just as the idea of God on its own, but in the context of the world as we know it, a world in which evil exists. If evil exists, then being good, wouldn't God want to prevent it, and being omnipotent, wouldn't God be able to? So why does evil exist, unless God is either not perfectly good or not omnipotent? This is discussed in The problem of evil (Ch. 9, p. 320).

> Can we coherently say that God is both everlasting and omniscient?

KNOWING WHAT GOD DOESN'T

If omniscience is knowing everything it is possible to know, then God should surely know everything that we know. However, some of what we know derives from *sense experience*, such as how red looks or how coffee tastes. God does not have sense organs, so could God know things like this?

We might argue that God does not know this, but that is no lack in knowledge, because only an *imperfect* being has this type of knowledge, since it relies on having a body. But we need to rephrase omniscience as 'knowing everything it is possible for a perfect being to know'.

Alternatively, we could argue that God does know these things. God knows everything that exists directly and immediately; how red looks and so on are real properties, and so God has direct knowledge of these properties, even though God doesn't have sense organs.

> **?**
>
> What is the best understanding of 'knowing everything it is possible to know'?

> Free will and prediction are discussed further in Ch. 10, esp. DETERMINISM DISTINGUISHED FROM PREDICTABILITY, p. 356 and FREE WILL AS COMPATIBLE WITH DETERMINISM, p. 380.

Going further: omniscience, transcendence and perfect goodness

Transcendence (of time) coheres well with omniscience, it seems, but it conflicts with God's perfect goodness in this way: free will is thought to be a good thing (it's an essential attribute of being a person), and as perfectly good, God wants the best for us. But can we have free will if God already knows all of our decisions in advance?

Simply being able to *predict* what someone is going to do is not enough to undermine free will. For example, you can predict that a friend of yours will help this old lady across the street, because he is a kind person, in a good mood and has just said that this is what he will do. But it is different if we could predict an action with total certainty: the prediction is not simply reliable, but *infallible*. Furthermore, knowing someone's character enables knowledge of the general shape of their choices and actions, but not every minute detail.

Both these points cause problems in the case of God's knowledge. If God knows now what I will be doing on 23 May 2022, this can't simply be because he knows my character well! For a start, God must know whether I will be alive then, and could only know that if the future is fixed in some way, for example, by physical determinism. Second, God's (perfect) knowledge is surely infallible, not just reliable. For instance, much of God's knowledge is direct and immediate, not inferential. And if God is 'outside' time, then surely he knows all moments in time *in the same way*. Past, present and future are all the same to God. It is hard for us to understand how God can know the future in the same way as the past unless the future is fixed just as the past is. But if the future is fixed, do we have free will?

Perhaps we don't have free will – then there is no problem with God's being transcendent and omniscient. But then a different problem arises: if we don't have free will, is this compatible with God being perfectly good? The argument here is that free will is a great good that allows us to do good or evil and to willingly enter into a relationship with God or not. Without free will, if we couldn't choose how to live or what kind of person to be, how would our lives be meaningful or morally significant? As perfectly good, God would want our lives to be morally significant and meaningful, so he would wish us to have this ability. But this returns us to the problem above: can we have free will if God is outside time and knows everything that will happen?

Physical determinism is the view that all physical events are determined by previous physical conditions plus the laws of nature. It is discussed in WHAT IS DETERMINISM, p. 351f.

Assess the claim that if God is transcendent, free will is impossible.

'God cannot be omniscient and perfectly good.' Discuss.

Omnipotence

OMNIPOTENCE AND THE STONE PARADOX

Can God create a stone that he can't lift? If he can, then he will not be able to lift the stone. But otherwise, he can't create such a stone. Either way, it seems, there is something God cannot do. If there is something God can't do, then God isn't omnipotent.

This famous paradox makes an assumption we should question: it pre-supposes the possibility of something logically impossible. 'The power to create a stone an omnipotent being can't lift' is logically incoherent, so it's not a possible power. If God lacks it, God still doesn't lack any possible power. Alternatively, we may allow that God could create such a stone, but in that case, the stone is, *by definition*, impossible to lift (clearly it will not be the stone's *weight* that prevents its being lifted by God, so it must be some other, essential attribute). If God lacks the power to lift a stone it is logically impossible to lift, there is still no power God lacks.

What is the best solution (if any) to the stone paradox?

DOING WHAT GOD CAN'T

How should we understand 'omnipotence'? Is it 'the power to do whatever it is logically possible to do'? I can go jogging, which shows it is a logically possible act, but God can't. So perhaps omnipotence is 'the power to do whatever it is possible for a perfect being (or the greatest possible being) to do'. One interpretation of this is 'maximal power' – it is not possible for any being to have more power overall than an omnipotent being.

A different response says that God possesses every power it is logically possible to possess. We need to take care in how we should identify and individuate powers. The power to go jogging isn't a distinct power. It is a combination of free will and the power to move my body in accordance with that free will, but subject to laws of nature. But this is not a power God lacks. God can't go jogging because God doesn't have a body. But this is not a lack of *power*. God has free will and God can move bodies, including my body, in accordance with his will. God can even move bodies without regard to the laws of nature. So there is no logically possible power I have that God lacks.

Is omnipotence a coherent idea?

Omnipotence and perfect goodness

THE FIRST PUZZLE

Can God commit evil? If God is perfectly good, then God cannot commit evil. But is this a lack of *power*? 'I could never do that' we sometimes say, faced with the option of something horrendous. This is not because we lack the power, but because we don't will it, or can't bring ourselves to will it. What does it mean for God not to be able to will something? If God is 'morally incapable' of doing evil, is this a lack of power, or because God doesn't will it? But if God is perfectly good, should we say that God *can't* will it? Is God's will being different a logically impossible state of affairs? If it is *logically* impossible for God to will evil, how is God's will free?

Explain the objection that if God is perfectly good, he cannot be omnipotent.

There are three possible solutions:

1. There is a distinction between powers and acts of will. God has the power to commit evil, and he can will it, but simply chooses not to.

2. There is no distinct 'power to commit evil', because 'evil' doesn't name a distinct act. To commit evil, God would have to do something, for example, hurt someone unjustifiably. God has all the powers to bring this about –

there is no power he lacks to do whatever the evil act would be – but chooses not to act in that way.

3. There is no distinct 'power to commit evil', because evil is not a 'something', but an absence of good. Asking whether God can commit evil is like asking whether God can fail. Being 'able' to fail is not a power; failing demonstrates the lack of power to succeed. There is no 'power to commit evil' as committing evil is the result of the lack of power to do good. As God does not lack the power to do good, God cannot commit evil.

THE SECOND PUZZLE

Can God make right be wrong? For example, could God make murdering babies morally right? Does God conform his will to what is morally good, which is independent of what God wills; or is what is morally good whatever God wills it to be? Put another way: is morality whatever God wills or commands or is it something independent of God's will? If morality is whatever God wills, then if God wills what is (now) morally wrong, then what is wrong will become right – if God commands us to murder babies, then murdering babies would be morally right. But if morality is independent of what God wills, then God cannot make what is wrong be right – murdering babies is wrong whatever God commands. But then, to be good, God must conform his will to something independent of him. Isn't this a *constraint* on God?

THE EUTHYPHRO DILEMMA   In his dialogue *Euthyphro*, Plato considered the question 'what is piety?': is piety doing whatever the gods want or do the gods want what is pious? Plato argued that both answers seem unsatisfactory, creating a dilemma. Our version substitutes 'morally good' (or 'morally right') for 'pious'.

If we say that morality exists independently of God's will, then we must explain why morality is not a constraint on God. For instance, if God is perfectly good, but morality is independent of God, then God cannot will anything (only what is good). This would mean that God is not omnipotent. Since God is omnipotent, morality is not a restriction on God's will, but dependent on it. Or again, if God exists and is good, then everything that is morally valuable must relate back to God as the ultimate reality. What is moral must depend on God.

On the other hand, saying that moral goodness is whatever God wills faces two powerful objections.

Discuss the claim that God cannot do evil.

Explain the dilemma created by asking whether morality depends on God's will.

We have just seen a different solution to these problems. If evil is nothing except an absence of good, then there is no power God lacks. However, we can still ask whether 'good' names whatever God wills or some independent standard.

IS 'GOD IS GOOD' A TAUTOLOGY? If good is whatever God wills, then 'God is good' doesn't say anything substantial about God. *Whatever* God wills is by definition good. This empties the claim 'God is good' of meaning. Here are three responses (a fourth appears in the 'Going Further' box below):

1. 'God is good' means 'God is good to us', that is, God loves us and wants what is best for us. And what is best for us can be understood in a way that is not dependent on whatever God wills. But if this is so, what is best for us does not depend on what God wills, which leads to (2).

2. Not *all* of morality depends on God's will, only our moral duties. Now if morality includes not only duties, but also what is morally *good* and moral *virtues*, then this answer allows that moral goodness and virtue do not depend on God, and this leads to problems. First, there is something that is ultimately real that does not depend on God. Second, as God is perfectly good, what God wills is dependent on something independent of God, which seems to be a constraint on what God can will. Third, if what God commands is based on what is morally good, then do we need to refer to God's commands to say what our moral duties are? Why not say that our moral duties are given directly by what is morally good, that is, the *reasons* for God's commands, not God's commands themselves?

3. 'God is good' should be understood *metaphysically*, not morally: 'God is good' just means that God has all perfections. But then what is the connection between the metaphysical sense of 'good' and the moral sense of 'good'? Does God being perfect entail that God is *morally* good? If so, then 'God is (morally) good' still has not meaning. But if not, then is morality independent of metaphysical perfection?

What does 'God is good' mean?

MORALITY IS ARBITRARY Another objection to saying that what is good is whatever God wills is that it makes morality arbitrary. There is no answer to *why* God wills what he wills. God doesn't will what he wills because there is some moral reason or value he is responding to. God *invents* morality. But if God has no reasons to will what he does, this means that there is no rational structure to morality. Furthermore, it entails that it would be right to murder babies if God willed it. This doesn't seem right!

There must be some standard we are implicitly relying on to say that what God wills is, in fact, morally good. So we might argue that it is only right to do what God wills if what God wills is good. But how can we tell whether this is true unless we have some independent standard of goodness? But then morality is independent of God.

We may reply that although God's will does not respond to anything independent of it, it is not arbitrary. For example, we can appeal to God's other attributes, such as love.

But then aren't we judging God's will to be the standard of love? If so, morality is still independent of God. But this is a misunderstanding: the claim is not that the basis of morality is love, but that it is *God's* love.

There is, however, still no further basis to morality than God's (loving) will. But is this a problem? Suppose morality didn't depend on God's will, but some set of 'ultimate' moral values or judgements, such as 'unnecessary suffering is bad' or 'rationality should always be treated as an end in itself'. Are these any less arbitrary than God's will, especially if we claim that God is ultimate reality? It seems not.

> Explain the argument that morality must be independent of God's will.

> 'The foundation and origin of morality is God's loving will.' Discuss.

Going further: good is the same property as what God wills

A fourth solution to the *Euthyphro* dilemma is to say that 'God is good' is not an **analytic** truth, because 'God' and 'morally good' are different concepts. However, goodness is the same property as what God wills. This is what 'God is good' states; it is similar to 'water is H_2O'. It is informative, because it provides an account of what 'good' refers to, viz. God's will.

'Water' and 'H_2O' are different concepts, and before the discovery of hydrogen and oxygen, people knew about water. They had the concept of water, but didn't know that water is H_2O – so 'water is H_2O' is not analytically true. However, water and H_2O are one and the same thing – the two concepts refer to just one thing in the world. Once we know that water is H_2O, we also know that anything that isn't H_2O *can't be* water. Water is *identical* to H_2O; it is one and the same thing, so water is necessarily H_2O.

The same account can be given of 'good' and 'what God wills' – they are different concepts, and people can have and understand one concept without the other. However, what is good is the same thing as what God wills, in fact it *can't be* anything other than what God wills. So it is dependent on what God wills.

> **analytic**
> an analytic truth is a proposition that is true by definition – see Ch. 1, p. 8 for discussion.

> Explain and illustrate the claim that what is good is identical with what God wills.

But still, how can we judge that God's will and what is good are the same thing unless we have an *independent* standard of goodness? We may argue that this is a question of how we *know* what is good, not what goodness turns out to *be*. We can only judge that water is H_2O if we have some independent idea of what water is. But that doesn't mean water is not H_2O. Likewise, to judge that what is good is what God wills, we need, *at least initially*, an independent conception of what is good and of what God wills. Which is fine, since we do form these concepts in distinct ways. Furthermore, once we think water is H_2O, we will say that whatever is H_2O is water. So once we come to believe that what is good is what God wills, we may use what we believe God's will to be to start judging what is good. God's will, we may argue, is our best source of knowledge about what is, in fact, good.

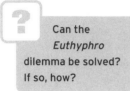
Can the *Euthyphro* dilemma be solved? If so, how?

Transcendence, immanence and the personal

A final puzzle: we have said that if God were wholly immanent, then God could not be personal (p. 128). On the other hand, if God were wholly transcendent, God would be very remote and different from us and creation. But is it possible for God to be both transcendent and immanent?

A particular example of the tension: one personal attribute is a free and rational will. We exercise our wills, make choices, in time. If God transcends time, how is God active *in* time? How can God bring things about, for example, miracles, at a particular time? From God's timeless perspective, all times are 'simultaneous'. Furthermore, God's will doesn't undergo changes but is constant, so there is no time at which God makes a choice.

If, however, we say that God is immanent in time, then if God acts, God seems to undergo change, choosing to bring about *this* at this time, *that* at another time. God becomes much more like a person – is this compatible with God being transcendent?

One suggestion is that God doesn't make choices in time, even though what he chooses to happen occurs in time. Or better, God's actions aren't in time; but what is *brought about* by his actions can be in time. If God cured someone of cancer in 2003, they were cured in 2003, but God didn't choose or act in 2003.

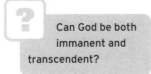
Can God be both immanent and transcendent?

Key points • • •

- We face difficulties in saying coherently what God's individual attributes
  are, and in our attempts to combine them. Some important debates are:

  - Is omniscience knowing everything it is possible to know? Or is it
    knowing everything it is possible for a perfect being to know?
  - Is it possible for God's knowledge to increase over time?
  - Is God's omniscience compatible with human free will, as a gift from a
    good God?
  - Can God create a stone that he can't lift?
  - Is omnipotence having the power to do everything it is possible to do?
    Or having the power to do everything it is possible for a perfect being
    to do? Or having as much power as it is possible to have?
  - Can God commit evil? If not, is God omnipotent?
  - Is morality independent of God or created by God's will? If the former,
    is God omnipotent? If the latter, is morality arbitrary?
  - Can God be both transcendent and immanent? For example, can God
    act in time if God is outside time?

II. The ontological argument

Descartes and perfection

We saw that St Anselm's version of the ontological argument relied on the
inconceivability of anything greater than God (p. 129). Descartes' version of the
argument relies on perfection alone, not conceivability:

> It is certain that I . . . find the idea of a God in my consciousness, that is the
> idea of a being supremely perfect; and I know with . . . clearness and
> distinctness that an [actual and] eternal existence pertains to his nature
> . . . existence can no more be separated from the essence of God, than the
> idea of a mountain from that of a valley . . . it is not less impossible
> to conceive a God, that is, a being supremely perfect, to whom existence
> is wanting, or who is devoid of a certain perfection, than to conceive a
> mountain without a valley.

Meditation V

Descartes' argument is this:

1. I have the idea of God;
2. God is a supremely perfect being;
3. Existence is a perfection; therefore,
4. God must exist.

We can object that there is a gap between the idea that God exists eternally and God actually existing eternally. Descartes is aware of this, and objects to himself:

> just as it does not follow that there is any mountain in the world merely because I conceive a mountain with a valley, so likewise, though I conceive God as existing, it does not seem to follow on that account that God exists.

But, he replies,

> the cases are not analogous . . . it does not follow that there is any mountain or valley in existence, but simply that the mountain or valley, whether they do or do not exist, are inseparable from each other; whereas, on the other hand, because I cannot conceive God unless as existing, it follows that existence is inseparable from him, and therefore that he really exists.

Descartes is arguing that the analogy is not between mountains and existence and God and existence; but between mountains and *valleys* and God and existence. The idea of existence is no part of the idea of a mountain. But just as the idea of a valley is implied by the idea of a mountain, so the idea of existence is part of the idea of God. And so, as he says, I can't think of God without thinking that God exists.

But what does this show? Just because I can't think of God not existing, does that have any relevance to whether or not God exists? Absolutely. The bounds of our thought are, at least on some occasions, indications of what is possible (just when thought can be trusted to reveal what is true for Descartes is discussed is A2 Unit 4.4 Descartes' *Meditations*). This isn't because our thought creates or influences reality, but because thought reveals reality. And so, Descartes argues, the necessary connection between God and existence isn't something I've come up with, it is something I discover:

Everyone agrees the problem lies with (3). What is a 'perfection'? It's a property that it is better to have than not have. So is existence this kind of property? Descartes and Anselm are supposing that it is – that something that 'has' existence is greater than something that doesn't.

Explain Descartes' analogy – both the similarities and the differences – between God existing and mountains having valleys.

the necessity which lies in the thing itself, that is, the necessity of the existence of God, determines me to think in this way: for it is not in my power to conceive a God without existence.

There is a conceptual connection between the concept of God and God's existence, and this entails that God must exist.

Objections to Descartes

Gassendi objects that existence is *not* part of the idea of God as a supremely perfect being. Can't I form the idea of a God who does not exist? (This is similar to Hume's objection, p. 130.) Descartes replies by claiming, with St Thomas Aquinas, that divine perfections all entail each other. Because our minds are finite, we normally think of the divine perfections – omnipotence, omniscience, necessary existence, etc. – separately and 'hence may not immediately notice the necessity of their being joined together'. But if we reflect carefully, we shall discover that we cannot conceive any one of the other attributes while excluding necessary existence from it. For example, in order for God to be omnipotent, God must not depend on anything else, and so must not depend on anything else to exist.

However, Aquinas *didn't* think that existence is a perfection. He objects, and Johannes Caterus put the point to Descartes, that the ontological argument doesn't demonstrate that God really exists. It only shows that the *concept* of existence is inseparable from the *concept* of God. Descartes' argument is only convincing for the claim that *if* God exists, God exists necessarily.

Descartes accepts that what he has shown is that necessary existence is part of the concept of God. But this, he responds, is enough: *necessary* existence entails actual existence. That God must exist to be God means that God exists. But Caterus says this isn't enough: the question is whether the *concept* of necessary existence entails actual existence.

KANT

Immanuel Kant develops the objection. The ontological argument wrongly assumes that existence is a property (premise 3 of Descartes' argument). But things don't 'have' existence in the same way that they 'have' other properties. Consider whether 'God exists' is an analytic or synthetic judgement. According to Descartes, it must be analytic: his argument is that 'God does not exist' is a

> Explain and illustrate how what it is possible or impossible to think can demonstrate what is or is not possible.

> Is God's existence entailed by his other properties?

> Assess Caterus' objection to Descartes' ontological argument.

> *Critique of Pure Reason*, Book II, Ch. 3, § 4

'Analytic' and 'synthetic' are defined and discussed on p. 8.

Assess Descartes' ontological argument.

contradiction in terms, for the concept GOD contains the idea of existence (necessary existence belongs to God's essence). But, Kant claims, this is a mistake. Existence does not add anything to, or define, a concept itself; to say something exists is to say that some object corresponds to the concept. To say something exists is always a synthetic judgement, not an analytic one.

When we list the essential properties of something, we describe our concept of that thing. For instance, a dog is a mammal. But now if I tell you that the dog asleep in the corner is a mammal and it exists, I seem to have said two very different sorts of things. To say that it exists is only to say that there is something real that corresponds to the concept 'dog'. It is not to say anything about the dog as a dog.

Existence, Kant argues, is not part of any concept, even in the case of God. To say that 'God exists' is quite different from saying that 'God is omnipotent'. So it is not true to say that 'God exists' must be true.

Necessary and contingent truths are defined and discussed on p. 38.

Explain the difference between God having necessary existence and it being necessarily true that God exists.

Going further: necessary existence

If existence isn't a property that something 'has', then it can't be a property that God has necessarily! And yet it seems plausible to think that *if* God exists, God exists necessarily. God cannot be a contingent being. If God's existence were not necessary, God would depend on something else that could cause God to come into or go out of existence. If Kant were right, then not only can existence not be a property, necessary existence – as a type of existence – can't be a property. So God can't exist necessarily, even if God exists.

In fact, this doesn't follow. There is still a sense in which God can exist necessarily, if God exists. Rather than saying 'God has necessary existence', which suggests existence is a property, we should say that 'it is necessarily true that God exists'. The 'necessity' applies to the claim: 'God exists' must be true. Of course, we need an argument to support the claim, but at least it makes sense.

The ontological argument seems to say that because, according to the concept of God, God exists 'necessarily', that is, not contingently, without dependence on anything else, then 'God exists' must be true. But this doesn't follow; it confuses two meanings of 'necessarily'.

Key points • • •

- Descartes argues that it is impossible to think of God, as a supremely perfect being, lacking existence. What it is not possible to think, in this case, shows us what is not possible, viz. God not existing.
- Gassendi objects that existence is not part of the idea of God. Descartes replies that it is entailed by God's other perfections.
- Caterus objects that Descartes at best demonstrates a necessary connection between the concept of God and the concept of existence, but this has no implications for whether God really exists.
- Kant's objection claims that the argument is wrong to think that existence is a property of something. To say something exists is only to say that something corresponds to a concept we have; it is not to say anything further about that concept. So existence can't be an 'essential property'.

III. The origins of 'God'

The idea of God is innate II

In an argument known as the 'Trademark argument', Descartes tries to prove that God exists just from the fact that we have an idea of God. This idea is like the 'trademark' our creator has stamped on our minds. Our interest here is in Descartes' argument that the idea of God must be innate.

As we saw earlier (p. 132), Descartes says that every idea must have a cause, and argues that ideas can have any of three sources: they can be 'adventitious' (caused by something external to the mind), fictitious (caused by the mind), or innate. Like many arguments for innate ideas, Descartes' argument that the idea GOD is innate is an argument that it cannot be derived from experience or imagination. He tries to show that it cannot be either fictitious or adventitious.

His argument is difficult to summarise without talking about medieval metaphysics, but we'll just give the gist of it here. The idea GOD, he argues, is very special. As minds, we can come up with all sorts of ideas. However, we are imperfect and finite minds, for example, we do not have perfect knowledge. As imperfect and finite, we could not have come up with the idea of something perfect and infinite. And GOD is just such an idea, as God is perfect and infinite.

Meditation III

See Ch. 1, Do ALL IDEAS DERIVE FROM SENSE EXPERIENCE?, p. 15, for other examples.

Is there a difference between 'infinite' and 'not finite' or between 'perfect' and 'not imperfect'?

Descartes, pp. 138–9

This seems puzzling, and Descartes responds to the obvious objection immediately. As imperfect and finite, I could be the cause of an idea of something that is '*not finite*' and '*not imperfect*'. Could I not come up with the idea GOD by simply thinking away all limitations? No, claims Descartes, because this *negative* conception of infinity and perfection is not the idea of God. The idea of God requires a *positive* conception of these properties – not the absence of limits, but something for which there could be no limits.

Descartes' view can be made a little clearer by analogy with a common-sense example, given by Bernard Williams: if we discover a picture of a sophisticated machine, we automatically think it must have been the product of an advanced society or a highly fertile imagination, even though it's just a picture. If we actually found the machine, working as it should, this would be even more impressive. The moral is that the effect (the picture, the machine) should be matched by the cause. On this basis, the only possible cause of GOD, for Descartes, is God.

Could this idea have come from experience? Not generally: we *all* have the idea GOD, but most of us have no direct experience of God. It is also unclear what kind of experience could be an *experience* of something perfect and infinite. Nor could we have derived the idea from our more usual experience of the world; Descartes says there is nothing in the physical world that is remotely like God.

So the idea GOD is neither fictitious nor adventitious; so it must innate, placed in our minds by God.

Outline Descartes' argument that the idea of God is innate.

Objection

See Ch. 1, Do all ideas derive from sense experience?, p. 13.

Explain the importance of Descartes' claim that our idea of God as perfect and infinite is positive, not negative.

As an empiricist, Hume claims that all ideas are created from experience one way or another. We have formed the idea of God from experience by abstraction and negation: we are familiar with things being finite and imperfect, so we can form an idea of something that is not finite (infinite) and not imperfect (perfect). So Descartes' argument turns on his claim that our ideas of the infinity and perfection of God are not negative ideas, 'not imperfect' and 'not finite', but positive. In fact, Descartes argues that the idea of imperfection or lack depends upon an idea of perfection; we can't recognise that we are imperfect *unless* we have the idea of God, of perfection, with which to compare ourselves. Is this persuasive?

Going further: positive and negative concepts

The claim that we must have the positive concept before the negative might work in some cases, for example, REAL and REALITY. It is intuitively plausible that our concept REAL is not an abstraction from NOT UNREAL – how could we first have experiences of what is unreal on which UNREAL is based? Our experiences are fundamentally of what is real, so REAL is the primary concept.

Does this work for perfection and infinity? It is much harder to argue that it does. PERFECTION and INFINITY are arguably challenging and unclear concepts. But Descartes is claiming that we have a very powerful – clear and distinct – positive idea of God of perfect and infinite, and not some hazy notion of something indefinitely great. But this requirement conflicts with Descartes' *own claim* that as finite minds, we cannot form a *clear* idea of God's infinity. So he wants to say the idea of God is not clear, but it is clearly and distinctly positive rather than negative. This sounds like a contradiction. Yet Descartes must insist that the idea of God is positive; if we do only have a negative idea of God, because we are finite, then it becomes possible that we are the cause of that idea.

In ARE ALL CLAIMS ABOUT WHAT EXISTS ULTIMATELY GROUNDED IN AND JUSTIFIED BY SENSE DATA? II (p. 29), we saw an argument for Plato that would support Descartes' position. The concept IMPERFECT contains the concept PERFECT (this doesn't work for FINITE and INFINITE, because FINITE does not seem to be NOT INFINITE, but vice-versa: INFINITE is NOT FINITE). Plato would agree with Descartes that we must have the concept of perfection in order to know imperfection, and Plato uses this claim, like Descartes, to argue for innate knowledge. I won't repeat the discussion here – see p. 29.

> Assess Descartes' argument that the idea of God is innate.

> Do Plato's arguments for innate knowledge support the view that the idea of God is innate?

Explaining the idea of 'God' as a human construction and projection II

God of the gaps

We saw earlier (p. 134) that if the origin of GOD is neither innate nor religious experience, it could be a concept that arises from our attempts to explain the

There are some arguments for the existence of God that suggest God is still the best explanation for certain aspects of the world. THE ARGUMENT FROM DESIGN (p. 331) is one, and you can study others in A2 Unit 3.5 Philosophy of Religion, including the arguments that God is the best explanation for how the universe began, for religious experiences, and for miracles.

Critically discuss the claim that the only use of GOD is to explain what we don't understand.

world we experience. In other words, it could be a *theoretical* concept, like many scientific concepts are. And certainly historically, people explained lightning and storms, wars and famine as God's actions. Perhaps the need to explain the world is where the idea of God comes from. And one question that perhaps suggests the concept GOD most universally among human cultures is 'Where did the world come from?'. Every culture has a creation story, and in very many, God plays a part.

There are two types of objection we can raise to this account, the first about whether, if it is right, we should continue to use the concept GOD; the second is whether this view – that God is a theoretical explanation – is enough on its own.

The first objection isn't actually about the *origin* of the concept of God; it is about the *validity* of the concept, that is, should we keep using it? If the account above is right, then if we are going to be justified in continuing to use the concept, we have to think that God is the *best* explanation for that aspect of the world which we want to explain. And this is certainly not true in many cases. Scientists and historians don't usually appeal to God now to explain lightning, wars, and so on. What about how life began? Or how consciousness is possible? Well, our knowledge is advancing all the time, so if we do succeed in answering these questions, there will be no need to refer to God. This theory – that God is used to explain what we can't yet explain scientifically – is often called the 'God of the gaps' theory. God fills in the gaps; the more we know, the less we need to appeal to God.

The second objection is that our desire to explain natural events and so on isn't enough to explain why we came up with the concept GOD. We should also note that we based the explanation on what we were familiar with. What created the world? Well, something *like us* in having a plan and a purpose and so on, but hugely more powerful. Ancient Greek myths, like the myths of many cultures in human history, make God or the gods sound very human. But why think that what created the world is *anything like* human beings? We need to appeal to other factors, for example, the tendency of human beings to think the world is somehow arranged for them, or that human lives form part of the meaning of the existence of the world. GOD then is not a *purely* theoretical concept, such as scientific concepts, but one that depends on human psychology as well.

Freud: a psychological explanation

The Future of an Illusion

Sigmund Freud presents a psychological explanation of the origins of beliefs in God. He suggests that these beliefs could originate not in an attempt to *explain* the world, but in a very deep unconscious wish that human beings have. This wish goes back in history to the emergence of the human race, and in each individual, to their earliest infancy. The wish is for consolation and reassurance.

In the face of the uncontrollable forces of nature, we feel vulnerable, afraid and frustrated that there is so little we can do. We want to rob life of its terrors. Likewise, when we are infants, we are completely helpless and dependent and need protection. Both motives come together in the thought that there is a God, a protector, a means by which we can control nature (for early religions) or feel safe in the face of danger and uncertainty. Our relationship to God takes on the intimacy and intensity of our relationship to our parents (Freud thought the father gives protection and security, so we think of God as more of a father than a mother).

Religious beliefs are 'fulfilments of the oldest, strongest and most urgent wishes of mankind. The secret of their strength lies in the strength of those wishes.' Isn't it remarkable, he says, that religion describes the universe 'exactly as we are bound to wish it to be'? A belief that is based on a wish, rather than on evidence, Freud calls an 'illusion'. It isn't necessarily false; it's just that it isn't based on seeking the truth.

The Future of an Illusion, p. 30.

(Just as religious beliefs are based on wishes, so religious experiences are as well. Freud argues that dreams are caused by deep desires we are unaware of, and he argues that religious experiences are similarly caused. They are hallucinations that happen when we are awake, caused by the wish for security and meaning, for things to 'be OK'.)

Outline Freud's argument that the idea of God emerges from psychological processes.

Discussion

It would be wrong to think that the conclusion of Freud's argument is that God doesn't exist (though it suggests that the mere fact of religious belief is not good evidence for God's existence). Freud's argument, and our concern here, is about the *origin* of the idea GOD, not about whether God exists or not. It is not enough to know how a belief is arrived at to know whether it is true.

At the heart of Freud's account is the claim that the type of thinking that produces the concept GOD is not directed towards truth or reality. But let us suppose, for the sake of argument, that God does exist. If God exists and human beings need a relationship with God to be fulfilled, then we would of course have a strong wish for such a relationship. Our wish for contact with God would be realistic – if we are made by God, then a relationship with God would be one of our deepest desires. In other words, the wish Freud identifies may not be the result *only* of our vulnerability in the face of nature and as infants; it could be a response to our needy spiritual nature. This alternative account situates the origin of GOD in human psychology, but explains human psychology in terms of creation by God.

Freud can reply that this doesn't do justice to the difference between the kind of thinking that aims at discovering the truth about the world and the wish-fulfilling nature of religious belief. But to this, we might say that religious belief is not obviously the fantasy Freud says that it is. Belief in God can be very demanding in how it requires one to act. For example, if one takes the life of Jesus as a model of a relationship with God, one could argue that there is a great deal of engagement with the world, with poverty and oppression, which involves a *rejection* of the fantasy that God will 'make everything alright'. Again, many religious believers do not seem to exhibit a kind of neurotic need for a father figure; many can be examples of psychological maturity. Of course, they take comfort from their religious beliefs, but this is not enough to make Freud's case.

> Analyse and evaluate the claim that the idea of God is a projection based on human psychology.

Social explanations

Popular alternative explanations of religious belief, and the concept GOD, are sociological and/or evolutionary. For example, in a recent book, the biologist and anthropologist D.S. Wilson argues that 'Many features of religion, such as the nature of supernatural agents and their relationships with humans can be explained as adaptations designed to enable human groups to function as adaptive units'. At the level of society (or at least the groups of human beings that existed in the evolutionary past), religious belief promotes cooperation, mutual respect and solidarity, and these features help the group to survive. As with Freud's explanation, this theory claims that what produces religious beliefs are not processes aiming at discovering the truth. In this case, the processes are aiming at evolutionary survival.

> *Darwin's Cathedral: Evolution, Religion and the Nature of Society,* p. 51

The line of thought that religion is socially valuable is also put forward by the 'founding father' of sociology, Emile Durkheim. Durkheim emphasises the way in which religion secures solidarity and a sense of identity for individuals in the society, but most importantly, it provides the basis for a collective morality

> *The Elementary Forms of the Religious Life*

and for authority in the society. Durkheim thought of religion positively, as an expression of being social, which is what makes us human.

Karl Marx, however, was more cynical about religion and the collective morality and authority it supported. He argued that what created the need for religion was tension *within* the society, in particular between those who had power – especially economic power – and those who did not. Those who do not have power, he argued, are 'alienated' from their own lives (he thought that working for a fixed wage, and not getting a full share in the *profits* generated by what one does, was a central example of alienation – in this case, alienation from one's labour, even more so if the job is boring and unfulfilling).

Marx is not completely clear on *how* alienation creates religion, but one element is that, as Durkheim says, we need a sense of communal identity. Religion creates this sense, but it is a *false* sense of a community in which we are all equal in the eyes of God. The idea of religion – and its support of authority – actually works in favour of those who have power, because, with its false idea of equality, it undermines the motivation of the powerless to try to change society. And so Marx said that 'Religion is the opiate of the people' (opium calms people down, saps them of energy and creates a sense of lethargy).

DISCUSSION

As with Freud's account of religious belief, the fact that religious belief has some positive effect on human beings, in this case on human society, does not demonstrate that the beliefs are false.

However, there is an additional point to make here. As it stands, this is not an explanation of the origin of the concept GOD. Explaining the origins of religious practices and beliefs is not yet to explain the origins of GOD, because even if human societies work better with religious belief, this is not to say that the concept or belief in God must be part of that religious belief, and Durkheim recognised this. Some religions don't believe in God, for example, Buddhism. Some societies, noticed Durkheim, don't even believe in the supernatural.

To make the explanations offered work as an account of the origin of the concept GOD, what we need is either an account of how possession of the concept GOD itself, rather than religion in general, leads to group success, or a separate, supplementary account of how and why some religious beliefs and practices came to develop the concept GOD.

It may be that the concept evolved over time. There is no need for our explanation to say that the concept – characterised by all the divine attributes discussed in this chapter – emerged all at once. For example – a purely

---

Explain one version of the claim that religious belief is socially useful.

'Contribution to Hegel's Philosophy of Right, Introduction'

Durkheim rejected Marx's derivation of religion from economic life. In primitive societies, he argued, religion permeates life; it is the first expression of society and communal identity. If Marx were right, religion ought to emerge later in the development of society, as a response to particular economic conditions.

Explain the difference between the concept of God and religious belief and practice.

speculative story – it could be that at first people worshipped their ancestors and exceptional human beings. Those who had power in life were thought to retain it after their death. And so the idea of a spirit emerges as well as the connection of being a spirit and having power. Then the forces Durkheim mentions shape this idea, so that the group comes to identify with one particularly powerful spirit as 'theirs' communally. And so there are different tribes, each with their own 'god'. In this way, human beings create an idea of 'god' that reflects themselves, their ideas of power, and their community.

But do we have enough evidence to assert that this story is in fact true? This is not a question we can answer as philosophers. What we can require of any answer is that it gives us a clearer, more detailed story of how people might move from a conception of human power and values to an idea of God.

> Assess the claim the concept GOD originates in social needs and organisation.

> *Beyond Good and Evil*, §§ 1-9. This text is studied in depth in A2 Unit 4.5.

> *On the Genealogy of Morals*, Essay 1

Going further: Nietzsche

Friedrich Nietzsche accepted the connection between religious belief and morality that Durkheim noticed. All gods, he argued, are no more than reflections of what people value. We project our values on to the world (on projection, see p. 135), but claim that our interpretation of the world is objective. The idea of a god that embodies these values is part of this projection. God is a personification and objectification of what we value. To continue to believe in God is to lack the courage to recognise that values originate with us and have no external source or confirmation.

Part of Nietzsche's argument for this view is a historical one. We can see, he said, that societies with different values have different ideas of God. We can even see how changes in the idea of God are part of an attempt to change the system of values. The most significant shift was the shift from pagan gods to the Christian idea of God.

Any system of value, Nietzsche argued, will favour some people over others. The first set of values that European societies had reflected were powerful people's idea of what was good. This class of people called themselves and the traits of character they valued 'good', in contrast to the sorts of people who were in lower classes. The Greek and Roman gods reflected these values. Some of the values involve self-control and self-denial (particularly important in military situations). But these were given a new interpretation by people who were not in power – that self-denial is intrinsically valuable, because our animal nature is bad. This life is not valuable, but the suffering we go through has a meaning – that it will be redeemed by another life, the afterlife. In the afterlife, we no longer have our animal nature.

The new idea of God that emerged – as pure thought, caring for human suffering, beyond emotion – was a projection of this new value system. (This life-negating idea of God Nietzsche thinks is found in most religions.) It emerged as an attempt by weak people to turn the tables on powerful people; in particular, Nietzsche thought it was promoted by the priests, who were weak people who wanted power, but couldn't get it by competition with people who were powerful. An important part of the new idea of God is that God *judges* us, and will reward or punish us in the afterlife. The priests know what it is that we must do to be judged favourably. So the new value system gives them power, and makes the lives of powerful people appear 'wrong'.

Nietzsche indicates the kind of evidence we should look for in arguments that the origins of GOD lie in human society, and gives us a historical argument regarding the concept as we now have it. But we may challenge him with two questions. First, is his story historically accurate? Second, is his view of Christianity fair? As both of these are empirical questions, and very large questions at that, we will not pursue them further here.

> Critically assess the claim that the origin of GOD rests in morality.

Key points • • •

- Descartes argues that the idea of God is innate, and could only have been caused by God, because as imperfect and finite beings, we could not come up with the idea of something infinite and perfect.
- We can object, with Hume, that we can come up with the idea of God. 'Infinite and perfect' is just 'Not finite and not imperfect' and we have experience of finite, imperfect things.
- Descartes responds that this negative idea of infinity and perfection is not the idea we have of God.
- The idea of God could be a theoretical concept, used to explain facts we cannot otherwise explain, for example, the creation of the world.

- We can object that science has replaced many explanations that previously referred to God. We can also object that saying God is a theoretical concept doesn't explain the attributes of God, for example, that God is personal.
- Freud argues that religious beliefs are caused by a very deep wish for security and meaning in an uncertain world. The concept GOD has its origins in how we want the world to be.
- We can object that, if God does exist, human beings would *reasonably* have a desire for God, as a relationship with God would be our deepest purpose.
- We can also object that many revered religious believers seem to demonstrate maturity, not wishful thinking, in their lives.
- Some thinkers have argued that GOD originates in social needs. Durkheim argues that religious belief helps society cohere and gives people a sense of communal identity. Marx argued that this was necessary as a fiction which covered the truth that we are not all equal, and supported those in power.
- However, an account of the social importance of religious belief is not yet an account of the origin of GOD, as there is a difference between religion and the concept GOD.
- Nietzsche argues that GOD is part of a projection of our values onto the world. He gives a historical argument that as values change, so the idea of GOD changes as well.

SUMMARY

In this chapter, we have considered three aspects of the idea of God:

1. What the idea of God is an idea of, that is, what are the attributes of God.

2. Whether we can use the idea of God to argue to the existence of God (the ontological argument).

3. The origins of the idea of God.

In our discussion and evaluation of these issues, we have looked at the following claims and arguments:

1. How should we best understand the attributes of omnipotence, omniscience, perfect goodness, transcendence, immanence and existence without beginning or end?

2. Do these attributes make sense, for example, can God know everything it is possible to know even though God has no body? Can God do everything it is possible to do?

3. Can these attributes be combined without incoherence, for example, can God be omnipotent (for example, God can will anything) and perfectly good (God only wills what is morally right)? Can God be both transcendent and immanent?

4. How do Anselm and Descartes try to prove the existence of God from the idea of God alone?

5. Is the ontological argument defeated by objections, for example, that nothing exists necessarily or that existence is not a predicate?

6. Does Descartes' argument that the idea of God is innate succeed?

7. Can the idea of God be derived from religious experience?

8. Is the idea of God a theoretical concept intended to explain experience?

9. Is the idea of God a human invention and projection that originates in our wish for reassurance? Alternatively, is it a projection of our values?

10. Does the idea of God serve a social function, such as providing a sense of community and a source of moral authority? If so, does this fact serve to explain the origin of the idea of God?

5

UNIT 1 AN INTRODUCTION TO PHILOSOPHY 1

Section 5: Persons

In this chapter, we discuss three questions. First, what is it to be a person? What characterises persons and distinguishes them from things and creatures that are not persons? Second, what is it that is a person? Are all humans persons? Are any non-humans persons? Third, what is it to be the *same* person over time? By the end of this chapter, you should be able to discuss these questions, explaining and evaluating different answers to each of them, and the reasons supporting each answer.

SYLLABUS CHECKLIST

The AQA AS syllabus for this chapter is:

What are the characteristics of personhood?

✔ The characteristics associated with personhood, such as: rationality, being reflective about one's experiences, feelings and motives as well as those of others; possessing a network of beliefs; self-awareness and awareness of oneself as a continuing subject of experience; creativity, autonomy and/or individuality, one who shapes themselves through choices, goals, actions and reactions and is responsible, accountable and possesses rights in virtue of this; one who is embodied, one to whom we ascribe mental and physical characteristics; a language user, able to communicate meanings; a social being, one whose sense of self emerges in and is created through relationships with others.

✔ The concept of a person as a natural phenomenon and as primitive. We generally identify persons before applying the above criteria. Yet these characteristics are possessed as a matter of degree: we have the concepts of complex and diminished persons; potential and ex-persons.

What is a person?

✔ The notion that not all humans are persons and, perhaps, that some non-humans are persons.

✔ To what extent do some non-human animals and some machines possess at least some characteristics associated with personhood and to a sufficient degree for personhood?

What secures our personal identity through time?

✔ Whether either physical or psychological continuity through time are necessary or sufficient conditions of identity.

✔ Whether our survival, rather than identity, through time is a more appropriate concept; the implications of cloning, brain damage, body alterations etc.

INTRODUCTION

I. What are the characteristics of personhood?

The characteristics associated with personhood

The syllabus lists eight characteristics associated with personhood. I have arranged them, roughly, from the simplest to the most complex – in other words, the later characteristics usually depend on the earlier ones.

There is one traditionally very important characteristic that the syllabus does not mention, viz. *possessing a soul*. It is a traditional Christian doctrine that the fundamental difference between human beings and everything else (for example, animals and machines), and what makes human beings persons, is that they have a soul, and nothing else does.

But if we don't have souls, would that mean that we aren't persons? No – we are persons whether or not it is true that we have souls. So we can talk about what *characterises* being a person without referring to souls.

> The idea of a 'soul' has had many religious and philosophical interpretations. The central idea, for our purposes, is that the soul is something that can exist separately from the body, for example, it can continue living after the body dies.

One who is embodied, one to whom we ascribe mental and physical characteristics

A person is not just a body, they also have a mind. Rocks and plants aren't persons because they have no mental characteristics – they don't think and they aren't conscious. Persons feel pain, they have beliefs about the world.

We intuitively think that each consciousness is individual; for example, each experiences the world from a particular 'perspective', and no two perspectives are the same. First, no two conscious creatures are in exactly the same place at the same time, so one can see what the other can't, and so on. They literally experience the world from different (spatial) perspectives. Second, we each have our own 'take' on or interpretation of what we experience. We have different beliefs, desires, values and plans, which gives us each a unique 'perspective' on the world in a metaphorical sense.

> This argument is discussed further in THE CONCEPT OF A PERSON AS A NATURAL PHENOMENON AND AS PRIMITIVE (p. 179).

Could something that didn't have a body be a person? For example, if we have souls, and our souls can exist without our bodies, then we might think that being a person doesn't mean being embodied, but having a soul. However, we standardly attribute physical properties to persons. For example, how heavy are you? If you are a soul, the answer is that you don't weigh anything (your body weighs . . .)! Do you have eyes? Not if you are a soul. There are also many activities that persons engage in which, again, they couldn't if they were souls. For example, writing a cheque – this involves both thought (about words and numbers) and physical movements.

> **?**   What does it mean to say a person is 'one to whom we ascribe mental and physical characteristics'?

Possessing a network of beliefs

Having a perspective involves experiencing the world in a particular way, for example, from where one is located. Beliefs represent how the world is. (Or at least, that is their purpose; false beliefs fail in this way, and true beliefs succeed.) In having a belief, we believe the world is one way rather than some other way.

We don't form or have beliefs individually, but in 'networks'. Once you are able to form one belief, then there are many others you are able to form as well. For example, if you believe 'there is food', then you have other beliefs about what counts as 'food' and what does not.

Some philosophers have thought that a creature can possess mental characteristics without being able to form beliefs. For example, if a creature's experience of the world is very simple, perhaps we just say that it reacts to stimuli. We reason with beliefs. If a creature doesn't reason, but just reacts, perhaps talk of 'beliefs' is misleading.

> What is it to possess a network of beliefs?

Rationality

BASIC RATIONALITY

One of the most basic forms of reasoning is drawing inferences between beliefs. If you believe that mashed potato is food, and that this (in front of you) is mashed potato, then you will believe that this is food. An even simpler case: you believe this is red; so you believe that it is not yellow. There is a close connection between having beliefs and being able to reason with them – what it is to have a particular belief is partly defined by the other beliefs that you infer from it.

Means-end reasoning uses beliefs and desires, and is expressed in action. You want something, for example, you are thirsty, so you want water (your end). You have beliefs about the world, for example, about where to find water. You put the two together, so now you want to go where the water is. You have other beliefs about where you are now, and how to get to the water from here. So you work out a route – this is your means to your end.

A STRONGER SENSE OF RATIONALITY

A stronger sense of rationality involves being able to *evaluate* our beliefs and desires. For this, we need to have the ability to imagine having different beliefs and desires from the ones we have. For example, if we wonder whether a belief is false, and set about testing it, we must be able to imagine having a different,

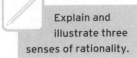

Explain and illustrate three senses of rationality.

true belief. When evaluating desires, we weigh that desire against others, we wonder what we *really* want and what we *should* want.

A social being, one whose sense of self emerges in and is created through relationships with others

We might call a 'self' any creature with a perspective on the world, particularly if it is able to bring together beliefs and desires to act in specific ways. But having a perspective isn't enough for a *sense* of self. After all, what one experiences is *the world*, not oneself. To have a sense of self involves being aware of the distinction between the world and oneself. The most basic expression of this is being aware that one's body is distinct from anything else, a merely biological sense of oneself.

What is the difference between having a perspective and having a sense of oneself?

A stronger, social sense of oneself emerges in relation to others who are also selves. This sense of oneself is not just a sense of one's body, but a sense of having certain relationships with particular others. For example, many social creatures have a 'leader', who is dominant and to whom others submit. Or again, many social creatures form special bonds with their family members. These relationships are the basis for a sense the individual may have of being the particular being it is, expressed in the way it interacts with others in the group.

Self-awareness can be expressed in the ability to identify one's body in a mirror, which involves the thought 'that [in the mirror] is me'. This thought requires the ability to put together the subjective sense of oneself 'from the inside' – me – with a 'public' idea of oneself 'from the outside' – that [in the mirror].

Self-awareness and awareness of oneself as a continuing subject of experience

The sense of self just discussed is a 'weak' sense of self. It is unclear whether it is a genuine form of awareness of oneself as a *self*. This requires more. First, it requires some conception of one's experience as experience. Second, it requires a sense of having a past and a future. Looking forward to a pleasant experience and fearing pain both express the idea that one might have certain experiences in the future. In this anticipation of experiences, there is the minimal sense of having an awareness of the continuation of experiences through time.

However, this ability to have some conception of one's experience is not yet an ability to think about one*self* as the subject of experiences. The term 'self-awareness' captures this. In self-awareness, a creature is aware of itself as a self. It is able to think about itself as something that has experiences.

Developing self-awareness requires a sense of other selves that are distinct from oneself. It is an awareness of having a *particular* perspective on the world, and that there are others. You must have the concept of a self, a subject of experience, of which oneself is just one example. In self-awareness, one also becomes aware of the fact that each self is individual.

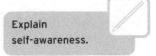

Explain self-awareness.

A language user, able to communicate meanings

Many people think that animals can have beliefs and desires. For example, a dog, seeing its master pick up its leash, runs to the front door excitedly and starts barking. It believes it is going for a walk. Again, the dog wanders over to the cupboard where its food is and whines. It wants food.

However, some beliefs are only possible if the believer can use language. For example, a dog can't believe that its master will take it for a walk next Thursday. Days of the week only make sense if we have a language with the concept of days of the week. So fewer creatures are language users than are believers.

A language requires a community of language users. Only social creatures can have a language. However, not all social creatures have language, and we can argue that babies start to develop a sense of self before they acquire language. So fewer creatures are language users than are social beings.

Some non-human animals communicate by the use of signs – does this ever amount to a language? Many philosophers argue it does not. The hallmark of a language is that the signs – words (or, in sign language, gestures) – are *conventional*. The link between the sign, for example, the word 'dog', and what it is a sign for, a dog, is completely arbitrary. Shouting out in pain is, by contrast, a natural sign that something hurts. Most of the gestures, facial expressions and sounds used by animals to communicate are natural signs, so they wouldn't count as a language.

We could argue, however, that they do communicate meanings, such as 'danger', 'food', 'stay away'. Of course, we have to use language to say what these meanings are!

The use of a language makes a *huge* difference to the type of life a creature leads and to its mental characteristics. Language greatly extends our ability to reason and our ability to think about the past, the future, and anything we aren't experiencing now. It completely changes our lives with others, as we are able to communicate about a much wider range of topics. If we didn't have language,

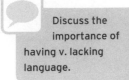

Discuss the importance of having v. lacking language.

we could at best express our immediate desires and beliefs – what we want now and how we believe the world is now.

A creature with a language is a very different kind of self than a creature without language, which is why possessing a language has been thought to be a distinguishing characteristic of being a person.

Being reflective about one's experiences, feelings and motives as well as those of others

Reflection involves more than just a preference of one type of experience to another. Dogs get restless, and when they do, they prefer exercise – this is not reflection. Part of being reflective about one's experiences involves being able to identify them and to imagine having different ones. And this involves self-awareness as discussed above. It almost certainly also requires language. Without language, picking out and identifying, comparing, and evaluating one's experiences is not possible.

This is all the more certain for motives. Thinking about motives is more than just being able to anticipate what a creature will do. Lions can anticipate that antelope will run when chased, but they can't think that they run from fear or in order to save their lives. In coming to the idea of *why* a creature does something, we form some idea of a *pattern* in its life. Even the simplest motive, such as hunger, can express itself in many different actions. Without language, thinking about motives at all is unlikely to be possible.

Our ability to identify our own experiences, feelings and motives is not separate from our ability to identify others'. In the case of experiences, 'joint attention' is very important. A baby learns that it is looking at a table by being told by an adult; the baby can see that the adult is looking at the table. They are both looking at the same thing, which the adult calls the table. So in learning to identify its experience – seeing a table – the baby also learns to identify the adult's experience.

Feelings have an 'inner' and an 'outer' aspect. Learning what it is one feels involves coordinating the two, for example, the feeling of anger and the behaviour that expresses anger. Without an adult to identify the feeling from the behaviour, the child would not grasp the concept of anger and use it to identify its feelings.

Explain and illustrate how being reflective about one's experiences, feelings and motives as well as those of others involves self-awareness and language.

Creativity, autonomy and/or individuality, one who shapes themselves through choices, goals, actions and reactions

This characteristic takes the idea of reflectiveness further. Once we can imagine having different feelings and motives, we are able to imagine different futures and different ways to be. In other words, we can start to make choices about the kind of self, or person, we want to be. We can adopt goals to aim for and choose the actions that will help us reach those goals.

The way in which one evaluates one's experiences, feelings and motives expresses not just preferences, but alters and shapes oneself, so that one becomes a particular sort of person. This process of self-development is a creative one; because we can imagine different ways to be, we have a certain freedom in developing one way or another.

Autonomy is the idea of acting on 'rules' one gives oneself. We adopt goals and ways of behaving, including moral goals and behaviour. When one does this not according to the expectations and values of others, but as an expression of one's own values, this expresses one's individuality all the more.

> The syllabus joins this and the next characteristic, but they are worth separating. The first part emphasises psychological capacities, the second part emphasises the moral implications of having such capacities.

> 'Autonomy' comes from the Latin for self-rule: 'auto' means self and 'nomos' means rule or law.

One who is responsible, accountable and possesses rights in virtue of this

A creature that can't imagine having alternative motives will simply act on the motives it has. There is nothing else it can do, and so it cannot be praised or blamed. Autonomous creatures can make choices according to their values, and so are responsible for their choices. Because they are self-aware, they understand that they would do things differently if they chose to.

Our choices can affect other people in good or bad ways. Because we are responsible for what we choose to do, we are accountable to other people for the effects of our actions on them. Accountability is the idea that we cannot treat other people any way we choose, but that we should be able to *justify* what we do to them. If we cannot, then we can be blamed.

Being autonomous is of great importance to an autonomous creature; it is how it shapes itself. But autonomy can be undermined or diminished by how one is treated, for example, through coercion. Autonomy, then, needs to be protected against interference by other people. A right gives this protection, but also leads to accountability, as others have rights too.

> **?** How does the ability to reflect lead to the ability to make moral choices?

> Explain and illustrate the moral significance of autonomy.

Key points • • •

- The syllabus lists eight characteristics associated with personhood, which we discussed in order of simplicity (and divided the eighth into two):

  - One to whom we ascribe mental and physical characteristics, which we developed as the idea of having a perspective.
  - Possessing a network of beliefs.
  - Rationality, of which we identified three varieties – inference, means-end reasoning and evaluation.
  - A sense of self created through relationships with others, which we distinguished from merely having a perspective and from a purely biological sense of self.
  - Self-awareness, which involves not just a conception of one's experiences, but of oneself as the subject of experiences.
  - A language user, which greatly changes the kind of self one is.
  - Being reflective, which requires self-awareness and probably language.
  - Autonomy, the ability to give oneself 'rules' and shape oneself through choices, values and goals.
  - One who is responsible, accountable and possesses rights.

II. What is a person?

The moral importance of personhood is discussed in MORAL DECISIONS in A2 Unit 3.3 Moral Philosophy.

At the end of the last section, it was suggested that persons have special rights. So the question of what qualifies as a person is an important ethical question. However, we will not look at the ethical implications of this question here. It is important to separate the discussion of what counts as a person and how we should treat persons and non-persons.

Are all humans persons?

We will discuss three responses to this claim in ARE ALL HUMANS PERSONS? II, p. 183.

To be a human being is to belong to the species *Homo sapiens*, which we can specify in terms of having a particular genetic code. On this definition, a human being exists from the moment of conception.

By any of the characteristics of persons we have discussed, not all human beings are persons. Every characteristic involves having mental characteristics.

But these are not present from conception. For instance, the most primitive form of consciousness that we know of is consciousness of sensation, pleasure and pain, called *sentience*. But as far as we know, this does not appear in the foetus until around the twentieth week of pregnancy. So for twenty weeks, the foetus is human but not a person.

The capacity for consciousness is not something that every human being has even after this stage. Two examples: some babies – called anencephalic – are born with much of their brain missing, including the part that supports consciousness. They may be capable of some reflex actions, such as breathing and responding to sound, but these are not thought to be conscious responses. Second, people can suffer terrible brain damage, for example, as a result of an accident. Their body may perform regulatory functions (breathing, the heart beating, etc.) or it may need a life support machine. They may still show reflex responses, but again, there are medical reasons to think these aren't accompanied by consciousness. Without any mental characteristics, they don't qualify as persons. (Note that this is not a *value* judgement, but a judgement about the application of the term 'person'.)

> Explain why someone might argue that not all humans are persons. Can you think of a response?

Non-human animals, machines and the characteristics of personhood

Do any non-human animals or machines – computers in particular – show the characteristics of personhood? We can expect to find the simpler characteristics more widespread and the more complex characteristics more restricted.

Non-human animals

Clearly a wide range of animals have some form of consciousness, as this is one of the distinguishing features of animals as compared to plants. We can talk of animals as having a 'perspective' on the world, as experiencing the world from a particular point of view.

BELIEF AND RATIONALITY

Do some animals have a network of beliefs? While we noted that it is intuitive to say that they do, some philosophers have debated this. First, 'belief' connects to the idea of truth. We arrive at beliefs by making *judgements* about what is true. For this, we need the concept of truth, and the ability to contrast truth and falsehood. Unless a creature can judge what is true, can it really have beliefs?

Second, belief connects to inference. Inference involves making a judgement on the basis of understanding the connection between two beliefs. Making logical connections depends upon having concepts and, in particular, upon having *linguistic* concepts. Suppose a creature can only form the kinds of concepts that go with basic recognition. It can recognise, say, cat food. And it can recognise other forms of food, for example, cream, dead birds. Can it draw the inference that because cream is food and this is cream, this is food? It seems impossible to express this sequence of thought without language.

So what about the dog which gets excited when it sees its master pick up its lead? Picking up the lead that *caused* the dog to anticipate the walk, but it didn't *infer* this. We can describe animal behaviour in terms of the ability to recognise and respond appropriately to many objects and situations. But this is not enough to say that they have beliefs.

We can object that this is a very restrictive use of the term 'belief'. We can, instead, emphasise the connection of belief to action. Animals certainly seem to have desires, and many show some sense of selecting the means to get what they want. They demonstrate means-end reasoning, and this requires beliefs.

Do any animals evaluate their beliefs and desires? As far as I know, they do not. Some animals can refrain from *acting* on their desires, for example, for the promise of a future reward or from fear. But this is not the same as thinking that one's beliefs are false or one's desires *should* not be acted on.

SOCIAL BEINGS AND SELF-AWARENESS

Many 'higher' animals live in groups with very specific social structures. They interact with different members of the group differently, depending on their relationship to them and their place in the structure. So they appear to have a social sense of themselves and of others as *particular* individuals.

But do any animals have a conception of having a point of view, or being a continuing subject of experience? Many mammals have a sense of what they *will* experience in the future, shown in anticipation and fear. Some animals can also display memories of how they have been treated by other individual animals in the past.

An experiment in the 1960s placed a rhesus monkey in a cage and taught it to get food by pulling a chain when a light came on. A second monkey was then placed in another cage, which was wired up to the chain, so that when the first monkey pulled the chain, the second monkey received an electric shock. The

> Explain one argument for the view that animals don't have beliefs.

> A second objection is this: unless we could have beliefs without language, we could never learn a language. A baby needs to believe that when an adult says 'table', it is talking about the particular object in front of them both.

first monkey could see the second, but not vice-versa. Repeatedly, the first monkey would go without food for long periods of time, rather than cause a shock to the second monkey. This suggests that some animals are capable of understanding other animals as subjects of experience in their own right. This adds another layer of complexity, because it suggests the idea of *different* perspectives on the world. But we can argue that it doesn't demonstrate full self-awareness, because it is not yet an ability to *think* about oneself as a subject.

A famous experiment by Gordon Gallup in 1977 shows that chimps are able to identify themselves in a mirror after a few days. Once they had, Gallup put the chimps under general anaesthetic and put a mark over one eyebrow and the opposite ear. After waking up, when seeing the marks in the mirrors, the chimps would explore the marks on themselves. By contrast, chimps that hadn't been exposed to mirrors before being marked did not explore the marks on themselves. Nor did monkeys, even when they had been exposed to mirrors for a long time. Gallup concluded that chimps have or can acquire a sense of self-awareness, which monkeys do not have.

However, how strong is this sense of self-awareness? First, it seemed to develop only in response to a specific situation and is not something chimpanzees naturally develop on their own. Second, it is closely tied to the situation of the mirrors; the chimps do not start displaying other kinds of self-aware behaviour.

> Discuss whether the two experiments show that some animals have self-awareness.

LANGUAGE, REFLECTION, AUTONOMY

Once we make the distinction between communication and language, then it is clear that no non-human animal that we know of has a natural language. However, apes can learn sign-language to a degree from human beings. (Sign-language is a genuine language as the signs are conventional, not natural.) The chimpanzee Washoe learned around 250 signs. At first, she was trained by being rewarded when she acquired a sign. But later she could learn new signs from other people signing around her without being rewarded. She was able to combine signs in a new way and even taught her son some signs. However, attempts to produce similar results with other chimpanzees did not work as well. As a result, scientists and philosophers disagree about whether any non-human animals can be language users.

Without self-awareness and language, animals can't become reflective about their experiences, feelings and motives in the way we can. Nor can they be autonomous. However, drawing on conversations with them in sign language, the Great Ape Project has argued that chimpanzees, bonobos, gorillas and chimpanzees possess enough self-awareness and rationality to have rights.

> Research the Great Ape Project and explain the reasons why it thinks apes should be given rights.

Machines: computers

The development of the computer led to a revolution in psychology and the rise of 'cognitive science', which uses the idea of computation as a model for understanding thought. However, many scientists and philosophers have made a stronger claim. Computers don't just provide a model for thought; if they are sophisticated enough, *they can think*.

Can computers think? Do they have beliefs, about which they can reason and draw inferences? Can they use language? They are clearly not social beings, but could computers in the future come to have a sense of self-awareness?

What do we mean by 'thinking'? Philosophers who argue that computers can think defend the view that thinking can be understood computationally – from an input, following certain specified rules, reaching an output. When we think mathematically, this seems to be what we do. Of course, not all our thinking resembles thinking about maths, for example, thinking in a language. But, they argue, this is just at the level of *consciousness*. Underlying what we experience consciously is a sub-conscious process that occurs in the brain, and this process can be described in terms of the transformation of symbols (for example, meanings of words) in terms of rules (for example, the rules of grammar). The essence of thinking is the ability to manipulate or process symbols, following rules.

We can object that this can't be right. Imagine a man locked in a room. In the room are symbols in Chinese, but the man doesn't understand Chinese. Through a slot in the wall, someone passes in a symbol. There is a rulebook in the room that says when a particular symbol comes in, then pass another particular symbol out. The man follows the rules – Chinese symbols come in, Chinese symbols go out. To someone outside the room who understands Chinese, this exchange makes sense. The symbols going in are questions, the symbols coming out are answers. The man is processing symbols, following rules – *but he doesn't understand Chinese*. Computers, likewise, are just following rules; they don't understand the *meaning* of the symbols they manipulate, so they are not thinking.

If they do not understand meanings, then computers do not have beliefs. The computer doesn't have a perspective in the sense we identified as basic to having mental characteristics. And when they process in accordance with the rules of the program, going from one symbol to the next, they are not making inferences or reasoning. They make no judgements, but just go through a series of states, each one causing the next. If these arguments are right, we should say that computers can *simulate* thinking, but what they do is not actually thinking (just as the Chinese Room simulates a person who knows Chinese).

These arguments are contentious. Can the brain be anything other than a very sophisticated machine? Brain cells don't understand anything, and yet when they work together, the person can understand. If computers become as sophisticated as the brain, why should we deny that they really can think? Perhaps, ultimately, there is no difference between simulating thinking and really thinking when the simulation becomes good enough. This idea is the basis for many works of science fiction.

If this is right, then computers have some of the characteristics of personhood. They have beliefs, they can reason, they can use language. Perhaps they can even have self-awareness if they have some kind of 'self-scanning' program. With self-awareness and a sophisticated program, they could reflect on their programs and the ends their programs have given them and decide whether to rewrite their programs and pursue other ends. In this case, they would achieve autonomy as well.

> Discuss whether computers can think (if they become sophisticated enough), and if they can, whether they are persons.

Key points • • •

- To be a human being is to have a particular genetic code and belong to the species *Homo sapiens*. A human being exists from conception.
- Humans do not acquire mental characteristics until around twenty weeks after conception. Some humans, for example, anencephalic infants, never acquire them. Some humans lose them, for example, after brain damage. So not all humans are persons.
- Non-human animals display a wide variety of the characteristics associated with personhood, with some apes even displaying a form of self-awareness. Whether any non-human animals are genuine language users is debated. However, some people argue that the great apes display enough self-awareness and rationality to qualify as persons and deserve rights.
- Computers manipulate symbols in accordance with rules. The Chinese Room example argues that this is not sufficient to count as genuine thinking.
- Philosophers respond that the brain also manipulates symbols according to rules, so if computers can become sophisticated enough, they will be able to think. If they can, then they have beliefs, can reason and use language, and may even develop self-awareness.

III. What secures our personal identity through time?

Physical and psychological continuity

A first distinction

In order to understand what is at issue in personal identity, it is important to distinguish between *numerical* identity and *qualitative* identity. Throughout life, we change what we are like as people. In common speech, we often say things such as 'he was a different person after the cancer scare'. This use of 'different person' picks out a qualitative change. But it presupposes that there is just one person here, before and after the cancer scare – otherwise, who does 'he' refer to? Persons can persist through qualitative change. What it is for a person to persist through time is the question of numerical identity – what does it take for someone to be the *same* person in this sense?

> Explain and illustrate the difference between qualitative identity and numerical identity.

Necessary and sufficient conditions

The syllabus talks about 'necessary and sufficient conditions' for being numerically the same person over time. What does this mean?

Necessary and **sufficient conditions** can be understood in terms of 'if . . . then . . .' statements (called '**conditionals**'). Such statements relate the truth of two **propositions**, for example, 'it is raining' and 'I am getting wet', as in 'If it is raining, I am getting wet'. The conditional asserts that if the first statement (known as the antecedent) is true, then the second statement (the consequent) is also true.

Suppose the conditional is true: *if* it is raining, I am getting wet. Notice that this does *not* say that it *is* raining and I am getting wet. Instead, it says that there is a relationship between it raining and my getting wet. Another example: if the planet Mercury didn't exist, the Earth would be the second planet from the Sun. This obviously does not say that Mercury doesn't exist!

Here are two conditionals about personal identity:

1. 'If I am the same person at times t_1 and t_2, then . . .'
2. 'If . . . , then I am the same person at times t_1 and t_2.'

> One way to fill in the blanks, that we'll discuss below, is 'I remember at t_2 what I did at t_1'. So:
>
> 1. 'If I am the same person at times t_1 and t_2, then I remember at t_2 what I did at t_1.'
> 2. 'If I remember at t_2 what I did at t_1, then I am the same person at times t_1 and t_2.'
>
> Is this always true? That's what we'll discuss.

Philosophers want to find out what goes in each of the blanks, so that the conditional *always* turns out true. If we could do that, we will have discovered something important about personal identity. Why?

Filling in (1) will give a necessary condition: for me to be the same person, something else – the consequent – *must* be true, for example, I remember the earlier event. Just by knowing I'm the same person, we will know something else about me. So we give an analysis of personal identity.

Filling in (2) will give a sufficient condition: for me to be the same person, it is *enough* that the antecedent is true. If we know the antecedent is true, we know that I must be the same person.

It might be that the same statement fills the blanks in (1) and (2). The statement is then both necessary and sufficient for personal identity. In that case we have a complete analysis of personal identity.

> Explain and illustrate the concept of necessary and sufficient conditions.

Psychological theories of personal identity

LOCKE'S MEMORY THEORY

John Locke singled out memory as central to personal identity. If I remember doing something, then I am the same person that did that thing. He identifies the self as 'that conscious thinking thing . . . which is . . . capable of happiness or misery, and so is concerned for *itself* as far as that consciousness extends. . . . *Person* is the name for this *self* . . . This personality extends it *self* beyond present existence to what is past only by consciousness'. Memory is the 'extension' of consciousness to the past. It is only by consciousness that we are able to be persons at all, for example, to reason and to reflect on ourselves. And our consciousness distinguishes us from other persons. So it is through our consciousness that we remain the same person over time: 'as far as this consciousness can be extended backwards to any past action or thought, so far reaches the identity of that *person*'.

> *An Essay on Human Understanding*, Bk II, Ch. 27, § 17, § 26

> *Essay* Bk II, Ch. 27, § 9

Thomas Reid objected that I can't remember everything I've ever done in my life, and what I can remember changes over time. He gave this example: suppose an old general has forgotten the time when he was a child when he was punished for stealing apples, but he can remember when he was a soldier and given a medal for bravery in battle. By Locke's theory, he is the same person as the soldier who received the medal, but not the same person as the boy. But now suppose that when he received the medal, he *could* remember being punished for stealing apples as a boy. This means that the person who received the medal is the same person who was punished. This leads to a contradiction: the general is the same person as the soldier who received the medal (he remembers it); the soldier who received the medal is the same person as the boy who was punished (he remembers); but the general *isn't* the same person as the boy who was punished (he doesn't remember it)!

This is impossible. Identity is 'transitive', that is, if A = B, and B = C, then A = C. So if the general is the soldier and the soldier is the boy, then the general *must* be the boy. But because memory changes over time (we forget things), it doesn't give this result. So personal identity must be something other than memory.

> Explain Reid's objection to Locke's theory of personal identity.

REVISING LOCKE'S THEORY

Rather than say that you are the same person as the person who did the things you can now remember, we need to be more subtle, and not rely just on *current* memories. Instead, let us use the transitivity of identity to say this: since the general remembers being the soldier, he is the same person as the soldier; since the soldier remembers being the boy, he is the same person as the boy; so the general is the same person as the boy – not because he now remembers being the boy, but because he now remembers being the person (the soldier) who *could at that time* remember being the boy. It is *overlapping chains* of memory that comprise personal identity.

Personal identity is like a rope – no strand of memory must directly connect all parts of the rope; it is enough for any part of the rope to be connected to some other part, which is connected to some other part, and so on. Rather than direct connections, we can appeal to continuity.

We can also challenge Locke's emphasis on memory. Certainly memory is important, but is it everything that makes a person who they are? What about beliefs, desires, character traits? We don't need to rely on just memories, but can invoke the many types of psychological state that persist through time and have a causal influence on our future psychological states. *Personal identity is psychological connectedness and continuity*.

> Outline and illustrate the view that personal identity is psychological continuity.

Is psychological continuity sufficient for personal identity?

In the 1960s TV science-fiction series *Star Trek*, people 'teletransport' from the spaceship *USS Enterprise* onto the surface of a planet and back again. The teletransporter 'reads' all the information off a person's body – every cell, every neural connection – destroys that body, and then creates a body in a different location with exactly the same information. So if my psychological properties depend on my brain, say, when a brain with *exactly* the same neurological properties is created, it has all my memories, emotions, beliefs, and so on. So, according to the psychological theory, that new person is me.

Suppose, however, the teletransporter malfunctioned. Instead of 'erasing' the captain, Kirk, onboard the ship, it didn't erase him, but it also recreated him on the planet's surface. Which one of these two identical Kirk's would be the 'real' one? If psychological continuity is *all* that personal identity consists in, are they *both* Kirk?

This is logically impossible – one person cannot become two persons, even if the two persons are qualitatively identical with the one person. This is because identity consists in numerical identity – and one thing is never two things! So we should say that the two people are *duplicates* of Kirk, but not Kirk himself.

This is meant to show that psychological continuity is *not sufficient* for personal identity. If something (a duplicate of me) can have complete psychological continuity with me, but without being me, then psychological continuity is not enough for personal identity. Personal identity must involve something else.

> Explain one argument for the claim that psychological continuity is not sufficient for personal identity.

Physical continuity theories of personal identity

THE ANIMAL THEORY

There are two famous versions of physical continuity theories. The first says that being the same person consists in being the same human animal. After all, this is the way we usually re-identify people over time. This doesn't mean that I can't lose a limb or even several; but I need to be fundamentally the *same living organism*. Of course, at any point in time, my body is a little bit different from how it was before. Over a long period of time, it is made of completely different matter. But it is still the same body, the same organism, because there is physical continuity.

But consider a case in which your brain is transplanted into my body, and my brain is transplanted into your body. Which body are you now 'in', the one with my brain or the one with your brain? If all your memories, beliefs, desires, etc. depend primarily on your brain, then our intuition will be that you 'go' with your brain. You have had a 'body transplant'. But according to the animal theory, we have each had a brain transplant: like a liver or heart transplant, the organ is new, the body remains the same animal. So the animal theory says you now have

Discuss whether, if you and I swap brains, we have had a brain transplant or a body transplant.

my brain (with all my memories, desires, emotions, etc.) and vice-versa. This doesn't sound right; it makes more sense to say I have your body than to say that I have your memories.

The objection argues that being the same animal is not necessary – I can become another animal by having my brain transplanted into another body.

THE BRAIN THEORY

The second physical continuity theory says that being the same person is a matter of having the same brain. In fact, not even the whole brain. People already undergo surgery in which a significant part of their brain is removed. The remaining brain is often able to 'pick up' what the lost part used to do and carry on. So, you need enough of the brain to support those mental characteristics that are important to personhood.

Explain why the case of the reprogrammed brain is an objection to the brain theory of personal identity.

But now consider another thought experiment: your brain and mine are both erased of all psychological properties and then 'reprogrammed' so that your brain has all the psychological properties that mine had, and mine has all the psychological properties that yours had. If I 'go' with my psychological properties, as the psychological continuity theory says, I now have what was your brain (and body), while you have mine. The brain theory says I have your memories.

This objection argues that the continuity of the brain is neither necessary nor sufficient. It's not necessary, because I am still me although I don't have the same brain; and it is not sufficient, since what was my brain has continued to exist, but it is no longer me.

Compare and contrast the brain theory and the psychological continuity theory of personal identity.

We can reply that I *don't* go with my psychological properties in this case. We could say the continuity of my brain is sufficient – I am the person with the same brain as before, but completely new memories, traits, etc. Alternatively, we could say the continuity of my brain is necessary, but not sufficient. Personal identity requires psychological continuity *as well*. In this case, I no longer exist; no person after the reprogramming has *both* physical and psychological continuity (one has what was 'my' brain, but with new psychological properties; another has 'my' psychological continuity, but a new brain).

Key points • • •

* Numerical identity is distinct from qualitative identity. Persons change, and do not retain qualitative identity over time. The question of personal identity is a question of numerical identity.

- A necessary condition of personal identity is whatever fills the gap in 'If I am the same person at times t_1 and t_2, then . . .'.
- A sufficient condition of personal identity is whatever fills the gap in 'If . . . , then I am the same person at times t_1 and t_2'.
- Locke argued that memory is a necessary and sufficient condition of personal identity. Reid objected that identity is transitive, but I remember different events at different times in my life.
- The psychological continuity theory says that psychological continuity – overlapping chains of connected mental states – is a necessary and sufficient condition of personal identity.
- However, as in the case of the malfunctioning teletransporter, two persons could be psychologically continuous with me. This is impossible, so psychological continuity cannot be sufficient.
- The animal theory says that being the same animal is a necessary and sufficient condition of personal identity.
- We objected that if two people's brains were swapped, each person would be identical with the person who had their brain, not their body. In this case, the person has become another animal, so being the same animal is not a necessary condition.
- The brain theory says that the physical continuity of enough of the brain to support the mental characteristics needed to be a person is a necessary and sufficient condition of personal identity.
- We objected that, if my brain were reprogrammed with your psychological states, I would not continue to be me – so the physical continuity of the brain is insufficient. If, at the same time, your brain were reprogrammed with my psychological states, if I would continue to exist, now with your brain, then having the same brain is also unnecessary.

DEVELOPMENT

I. What are the characteristics of personhood?

The concept of a person as a natural phenomenon and as primitive

The first characteristic of a person we discussed (p. 162) was that of having ascribed both mental and physical characteristics. We talked as if persons were minds (or consciousness or souls) with bodies (or bodies with minds). But understanding a person in this way faces a serious objection: Why do we ascribe mental characteristics to the very same thing, a person, as physical characteristics? If a person is mind + body, we shouldn't. We should ascribe the mental characteristics to the mind, and the physical characteristics to the body.

Peter Strawson,
Individuals, Ch. 3

Going further: the concept of a person as primitive

Of course, your experiences depend on your body, for example, what you experience depends on where *this* body is in space (the basis of our earlier idea of having a perspective, p. 161); or again, the experience of being touched depends on *this* body being touched. But this is only a causal dependency; and the experience is a characteristic of the mind and the spatial location or being touched are characteristics of the body.

This can't be, says Strawson. First, notice that, in the discussion of reflecting on one's experiences, feelings and motives (p. 166), we argued that we cannot identify, or ascribe to ourselves, our own mental states without also being able to ascribe mental states to other people. To identify one's experiences is only possible through learning at the same time what it means to ascribe experiences to other people. Any mental characteristic can be ascribed to other people, as well as myself. To understand the mental characteristic, for example, 'pain', I have to be able to say of other people 'he is in pain'.

But if mental characteristics are attributed to minds, while all physical characteristics are attributed to bodies, how can we identify other minds so as to ascribe mental characteristics to them? We have no experience of 'minds' on their own. So we have to ascribe mental characteristics to *something that also has physical characteristics*. Mental and physical characteristics have to be attributed to the same thing for us to ascribe mental characteristics to anything at all.

This means that we have to have the concept of something with mental and physical characteristics - the concept of a person - *before* we can have the concept of something with *just* mental characteristics. So we can't explain what a person is by saying a mind + a body; we don't know what a mind is unless we already know what a person is. We can only understand the idea of a mind (or soul or consciousness) by abstracting from the idea of a person. The idea of a person, as something that has both physical and mental characteristics, is primitive. (Persons are not embodied souls; rather, souls, if they exist, are disembodied persons.)

'Primitive' here doesn't mean 'backward' or 'not civilised', but *logically primary*. It comes first in order of explanation.

The concept of a person as natural

Explain the claim that the concept of a person is 'primitive'.

The concept of a person picks out a 'natural' category. Just as there are rocks, plants, animals and so on, there are also 'persons'. Persons, creatures who have both mental and physical characteristics, are a natural kind of thing. From the very first, our experience of the world involves experience of persons. As we come to think of ourselves as having mental characteristics, we understand that there are other physical creatures that do as well.

If persons were mind + body, a person would not be a natural thing, but a combination of two things which are, in essence, separate. We would not be able to satisfactorily explain why we naturally think in terms of persons as single unities, rather than always thinking in terms of souls and bodies. As we noted before, very many of the characteristics we ascribe to persons, such as writing a cheque, reading a book, etc. depend on one and the same thing having both mental and physical characteristics.

Can we explain the concept of a person in terms of mind + body?

A matter of degree?

In our earlier discussion of the characteristics associated with personhood (p. 161f.), we noted that some creatures can have some of the characteristics but not others, for example, many more creatures have physical and mental characteristics than have autonomy. We also noted that a number of the characteristics, such as rationality and a sense of self, come in degrees.

Does this mean that creatures can be 'more or less' persons, or that a creature can be less of a person at one time and more of a person at another time? We can argue that the answer is no. Although there are a variety of characteristics *associated* with personhood, it may be that just one is necessary and sufficient for actually *being* a person.

Explain the difference between a characteristic being associated with personhood and being necessary and sufficient for personhood.

This claim is argued for in ARE NON-HUMAN ANIMALS OR MACHINES PERSONS? (p. 185f.), where the view is that to be a person, a creature must be self-aware in a particular way. This form of self-awareness is much less a matter of degree than other characteristics (although it is still fuzzy around the edges) – so in most cases, a creature either has it or doesn't have it.

POTENTIAL AND EX-PERSONS

A 'potential person' is a creature that will, or at least could, become a person. An 'ex-person' is a creature that was a person, but isn't any longer. Human foetuses and babies are sometimes called 'potential persons'. If personhood requires self-awareness, since foetuses and babies don't yet have this characteristic, they are not persons. However, they are the *kind of creature* – human beings – who will, naturally and normally, become persons in time, that is, gain self-awareness. Likewise, there are human beings who have lost all forms of self-awareness, for example, after terrible brain damage. They are no longer persons, but ex-persons.

COMPLEX AND DIMINISHED PERSONS

The characteristics of reflectiveness, creativity, autonomy and individuality can be possessed as a matter of degree. The range of someone's concerns, what they love and with what passion, the originality of their thought or expression, the extent to which they have shaped themselves, these can all vary between one person and the next – contributing to how complex or superficial they are 'as persons'. Or again, these characteristics can vary from one time in someone's life to another. For instance, if something very bad happens, a severe psychological blow, we can talk of a person being 'diminished' or 'destroyed'.

However, these differences do not make someone more or less a person; someone is still a person even if they are superficial or their life feels empty of meaning. Personhood is not something that comes in a quantity that can increase or decrease. When we talk of 'diminished' or 'complex' persons, we are referring to their *personalities*, not to whether they are persons.

> This view is compatible with the idea that concept of a person is primitive. In our discussion of self-awareness, we argued that one cannot be aware of oneself as a self without having the idea that there are other selves. But we couldn't ascribe self-awareness to persons unless they also have physical characteristics. Furthermore, we can explain self-awareness in terms of persons. What is the self that self-awareness is an awareness of? The person.

> None of this shows that the concept of a person is not primitive. In explaining what potential persons and ex-persons are, we have to take the concept of a person for granted.

Key points • • •

- Strawson argues that the concept of a person is 'primitive', not analysable as mind + body. To understand a person as mind + body makes it impossible to say how we ascribe mental characteristics to other persons. We do not have experience of 'minds' alone. We must therefore ascribe mental characteristics to one and the same thing that also has physical characteristics, viz. a person.

- We experience persons in this sense naturally, and can think of them as a natural category.
- While many characteristics associated with personhood are a matter of degree, this does not imply that being a person is also a matter of degree. It is possible that one characteristic, for example, self-awareness, is necessary and sufficient for personhood.
- The view that the concept of a person is primitive is not undermined by talk of potential or ex-persons, complex or diminished persons. Potential and ex-persons are defined in terms of what it takes to be a person; being complex or diminished are attributes of persons.

II. What is a person?

Are all humans persons? II

Our previous discussion (p. 168) suggested that the answer is that not all humans are persons. There are several ways in which we may resist this conclusion.

Souls

First, it is a traditional religious doctrine that we acquire our souls at conception. If to be a person is simply to have a soul, then even anencephalic babies and people with brain death could still be persons if they have souls. However, they exhibit none of the *characteristics* of persons. If personhood depends on possession of a soul *only*, then the characteristics we have discussed are secondary to the definition of a person. We may not even be able to tell whether something is a person or not.

'Individuals'

One dictionary definition of 'person' is 'a human being regarded as an individual'. Do foetuses and brain-damaged adults count as individuals? Or do individuals

New Oxford Dictionary of English

need 'individuality', 'personality'? Without a mind, it is hard to see how a human being will be a particular individual in this sense. A human being that displays only reflex actions does not display any personality. He or she is only an individual human being by being an individual human body, not by being a person.

Extending the term 'person'

We can say that something is a person:

1.   If it qualifies as a person according to the characteristics of personhood.
2.   If it has the potential to develop these characteristics under normal conditions.
3.   If it has qualified as a person under condition 1) in the past.

This is a peculiar use of a concept. An acorn is not an oak tree, although it will become an oak tree under 'normal' conditions. And firewood is not an oak tree, although it was in the past. Why should we accept anything different for 'person'?

The reason for extending personhood in this way is usually ethical, for example, that we should accord potential and ex-persons with the same sorts of rights that we accord persons. However, it is perhaps better to make this argument separately, rather than extend the concept of a person. For example, we might argue that personhood is so important that the potential to be a person or the fact of having been a person gives a being the same rights as persons. This does not say that such creatures are, presently, persons.

2) extends personhood to foetuses before they acquire sentience; 3) extends personhood to human beings with brain damage. However, those human beings, such as anencephalic infants, that do not have the potential to develop into persons under 1) are not persons at all.

Assess the claim that all humans are persons.

Are some non-humans persons?

In our ordinary speech, we only use the term 'person' to refer to human beings (as the dictionary definition indicates). But as a philosophical concept, this restriction needs to be justified. Even if we do only think of humans as persons, it is not as obvious that we apply the concept of a person to *all* human beings. So the concept distinguishes between those human beings who are persons and those who are not. But then, we can ask, what are the differences between these two sorts of human? *Whatever* we answer, we could then argue that some non-humans have some of the features that distinguish persons from those humans who are not persons. If these non-humans are more similar to persons than to humans who are not persons, we can say that *in consistency* we *should* apply the concept 'person' to those non-humans as well.

This depends, of course, on what we think it takes to be a person.

Souls again

If persons are souls, and only humans have souls, then no non-humans are persons.

There is no religion that claims that computers have souls. Given that people created computers, then it would be odd if they had souls – for then it would seem that we have created souls!

However, religions disagree on whether animals have souls. Traditional Christian doctrine is that they do not, that the possession of a soul is restricted to human beings. So even if some animals (or computers) displayed those characteristics of personhood, they wouldn't be persons because they don't have souls.

Religions that claim animals do have souls, for example, Hinduism, often also believe in reincarnation. The same soul can be either an animal or a human being in different lives. Does this mean that the same soul can be a person in one life and not in a different life? If so, then having a soul is irrelevant to being a person. We need some other criterion for whether there are non-human persons or not. But if all souls are persons, then *all* animals count as persons, just because they have souls. In which case there are non-human persons.

> Reincarnation is the existence of the same soul in different 'lives' or bodies over time.

> **?**
> If to be a person is to have a soul, does this mean that only humans are persons?

Are non-human animals or machines persons?

Our earlier discussion (p. 169f.) identified the extent to which some animals and computers display characteristics associated with personhood. However, to say that they are persons is to say more than this. Which of the characteristics must a creature have in order to be a person?

Lynne Rudder Baker argues that answer is self-awareness. A person, she argues, essentially has the capacity for a first-person perspective, 'a perspective from which one thinks of oneself as an individual facing a world, as a subject distinct from everything else'.

> *Persons and Bodies*, Ch. 3

First-person perspective

Having a first-person perspective is more than just having a perspective. A dog has beliefs and desires and can reason about what it wants, so it has a perspective. But it doesn't think of itself as anything, nor does it have a conception of its own perspective as unique and different from other possible perspectives. To have a first-person perspective is to be able to think of oneself and others as subjects of thought, and to think of one's thoughts and experiences *as one's own*.

Baker argues that first-person perspective explains the importance of being a person. A creature with this perspective is fundamentally different from one without it, and the concept of a person marks the difference. The first-person perspective is the ground and origin of both what matters about us and what matters to us. It enables us to be rational in the strong sense of evaluating our beliefs and desires. It enables us to be reflective about our experiences, feelings and motives and those of others. We have a conception of our own futures and we attempt to shape them creatively through our autonomous choices. It enables us to be responsible, because we know what we are doing, and choose to do what we do. We understand that we, personally, have done things, and would have done different things with different desires and beliefs. The first-person perspective, then, is the ground of our rationality and our moral agency.

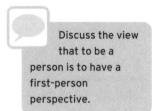

Discuss the view that to be a person is to have a first-person perspective.

Animals, machines and first-person perspective

If Baker is right, to decide whether there are any non-human persons, we need to consider whether either animals or computers have a first-person perspective. In our earlier discussion (p. 170), we considered the chimpanzees who could identify themselves in the mirror as a possible example of self-awareness. However, we noted that the self-awareness displayed was tied closely to the situation with the mirror, and that the chimps did not go on to display other behaviour that expressed a first-person perspective on themselves. On the other hand, the use of sign language by apes has led a number of thinkers, as in the Great Ape Project, to argue that they do have a sufficient first-person perspective to be considered persons.

Computers do not currently display any form of self-awareness. There would need to be significant advances in the ways in which computers work for us to take this suggestion seriously. And even then, there are strong philosophical arguments (p. 172) to suggest that they could do no more than simulate self-awareness.

Are any non-humans persons?

Key points • • •

- We can argue that potential and ex-persons count as persons. However, some humans will still not qualify as persons.
- We can argue that all humans and no non-humans are persons because to be a person is to have a soul, and only and all humans have souls.
- Some religions think that a soul can be a human or an animal, in different lives. If animals aren't persons, then having a soul is not relevant to being a person. Alternatively, all animals (that have souls) are persons.
- Baker argues that to be a person is to have a first-person perspective, which involves the ability to think of one's experiences as one's own.
- She argues that this view explains the importance of being a person, underlying our ability to reflect, to evaluate, and to be autonomous and responsible.
- Philosophers disagree over whether any animals have a first-person perspective, or whether computers could in the future.

III. What secures our personal identity through time?

Physical and psychological continuity II

In Are non-human animals or machines persons? (p. 185), we argued that to be a person is to have a first-person perspective, a form of self-awareness. We could therefore argue that to be the same person over time is to have the same first-person perspective. But the question would still arise: what secures the 'same' first-person perspective? What counts as the same 'self' in self-awareness? The self could be the animal, or it could be constituted by relations of psychological continuity, or we could relate it to the functioning brain.

However, all three theories of personal identity faced objections. We might argue, then, that there is no helpful answer – the self is the person, and the fact of whether a person is the same person is 'simple', it can't be explained in any other way. The idea that the self is the soul is often understood as a version of this last answer.

A second version is discussed on p. 192.

Persons are souls

If persons are souls, then we can say that the continued existence of the soul is what personal identity consists in. In other words, having the same soul is necessary and sufficient for being the same person. There are three arguments we could give for this view. First, that no other theory works (see p. 192). Second, religious doctrine – which we shan't discuss. We turn to the third argument, from Descartes, now.

DESCARTES' ARGUMENT

Let us assume that you and I and Descartes are persons. What is it for each of us to exist? Which properties, if I lost them, would mean I would no longer be what I am? Suppose I didn't have a body. For example, suppose that I am a disembodied mind that is telepathically being fed false experiences of having a body. Does this make sense? Would I be me? Yes, says Descartes. I can doubt whether I have a body. But I can't doubt whether I exist. So even if I didn't have a body, that wouldn't show I didn't exist. So having a body isn't essential to continuing to exist as me.

What is? Well, just as I cannot doubt that I exist, I cannot doubt that I think. If I were to doubt whether I existed, that would prove that I do exist – as something that thinks! Suppose I completely ceased to think – Descartes means 'think' in the broadest sense, to cover any experience, imagining, willing, feeling or thought. Would I exist? In what sense? We can conclude that to be a person is to be something that thinks, something that can exist without a body – a soul.

LOCKE'S OBJECTION

Many philosophers think that Descartes has not managed to show that souls can exist independently of the body. We won't worry about that now (see p. 31 for objections). Our concern is, if there are souls, whether persons are souls.

John Locke argued that personal identity is comprised by our memories (see p. 175), not by the continued existence of my soul. Souls are distinct from thoughts; souls have thoughts, but they are not the same thing as thoughts. So suppose all my memories were swapped with those of another soul. Suppose, Locke says, the memories (but not the bodies or souls) of a prince and a pauper (a poor person) were swapped. It would make more sense to say that the prince wakes up in the body of the pauper rather than saying the pauper now remembers everything in the life of the prince and nothing in his own life. What makes me me is not having a particular soul, but the memories (or after we've

The argument that follows is discussed in more detail in USING A PRIORI INTUITION AND DEMONSTRATION TO ESTABLISH CLAIMS OF WHAT EXISTS, Ch. 1, p. 19. It is adapted from *Meditation* II, studied in A2 Unit 4.4.

Explain Descartes' argument for thinking that we are souls.

corrected Locke's theory (p. 175), the overlapping chain of psychological states) which my soul has had and has now.

REINCARNATION

If reincarnation occurs, the physical theory of personal identity must be wrong – having the same body, or even brain, is not necessary. But does it support the soul theory? Not necessarily. On the psychological theory, to be reincarnated is for another creature or soul to be psychologically continuous with you. This continuity is rarely a matter of memory – most of us have no memories of previous lives. It is usually considered a matter of your psychological characteristics and experiences being the result of the psychological characteristics, experiences and choices made in a previous life (this relation of cause and effect is known as karma). Having the same soul, or any soul at all, isn't necessary. Only psychological continuity matters.

Is psychological continuity necessary or sufficient for personal identity?

> ### Going further: on connectedness
>
> We saw an objection from Reid to Locke's memory theory of personal identity (p. 175). He had a second. What is a memory? A memory resembles the original experience, and it is caused by it. But suppose we could copy a memory from my brain of a holiday in Italy and put it in your brain. You 'remember' the holiday (from my perspective) – is it really a memory of yours? No, because you are not the person who had the experience. In other words, for a mental state to count as a genuine memory, the person who remembers must be the same person who experienced. To explain memory, we have to assume personal identity. That means that we can't explain personal identity in terms of memory, or we go around in a circle. You cannot say that memory constitutes personal identity, because a mental state is only a *memory* if the person who has the memory is the *same person* as the person who had the experience.
>
> There is a general problem for the psychological continuity theory here. How do we identify the mental states that are related to each other by

Explains Locke's objection to the soul theory of personal identity.

Assess the claim that personal identity consists in having the same soul.

Explain and illustrate the claim that memory presupposes personal identity.

connectedness and continuity? Our usual way is to identify *the person* whose states they are. What if we don't? Well, your mental states and my mental states are connected. For example, if I say what I think and you hear it – we now both have memories based on my thought. So *which* connections make up personal identity? We can't say 'connections between the same person's mental states', since 'same person' is what we are trying to explain.

One response is that the 'same person' is just that person who has the *most number* of connections between its mental states. If two people have mental states that are psychologically continuous with some previous person's, the one who is the 'best candidate' is the very same person as the previous person. You have far fewer connections to my previous mental states than I do.

We can object that what unites psychological properties into a bundle is not *more* connections, but a different *kind* of connection. What makes a memory mine is not that I have many other related memories.

An alternative response, defended by Hume, is that *there is no personal identity over time. All* there is are connections of causal dependence and resemblance. There is no 'self', just a sequence of mental states connected in these ways. At any point in time, the mental states in the sequence are not identical with the mental states in the sequence at any other point in time. So there is no real identity, only psychological continuity. We are right to point out that psychological continuity is not enough for personal identity, but we are wrong to think that this is an *objection*. Personal *identity* is an illusion created by connectedness; it does not exist.

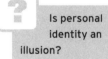

Discuss the 'best candidate' theory of personal identity.

A Treatise on Human Nature, Part IV, Ch. 6

Is personal identity an illusion?

TELETRANSPORTATION AGAIN: THE PROBLEM OF DUPLICATION

Using the case of the malfunctioning teletransporter, we objected that psychological continuity is not sufficient (p. 176). The person on the spaceship and the person on the planet are both psychologically continuous with Captain Kirk. We can summarise the objection like this: identity does not logically allow for duplication; psychological continuity does logically allow for duplication; therefore psychological continuity cannot be identity. If we think Kirk after teletransportation is the same person as Kirk beforehand, we are confusing *qualitative* identity with *numerical* identity.

This isn't only a problem if the teletransporter duplicates Kirk. Even if it works fine, so there is just one Kirk, now standing on the planet's surface, this person can't be the same person as the one that was onboard ship before teletransporting. Why? Well, we've argued that he wouldn't be that person if another Kirk was created by the teletransporter malfunctioning. But whether the person on the planet is the same person as the person who was onboard ship cannot depend on *someone else* existing or not. We can't say 'he is Kirk if the teletransporter didn't malfunction' but 'he isn't Kirk if the teletransporter did malfunction'. Either he is or he isn't Kirk, whatever else exists.

This is the idea that identity is 'intrinsic', that is, whether something at a time (a person, an animal, a rock) is identical (over time) with something previous to it depends only on the relations between the two things. It doesn't depend on anything else.

> Explain the claim that personal identity is intrinsic, and why this is an objection to the psychological continuity theory.

SOLVING THE DUPLICATION PROBLEM

The claim that persons are souls doesn't face the duplication problem. If the soul of Kirk attaches to 'his' body in its new location, then the person in the new location is Kirk. But if it does not, for example, if teletransportation severs the link between body and soul, the new person is, at best, a duplicate of Kirk.

Physical continuity theories (p. 177) also solve the duplication problem. The Kirk on the planet is *not* the same person as the person who was onboard ship because his body is not continuous with that person's body; it has been newly created.

For him to be the same person, teletransportation would have to involve physical continuity. Suppose the teletransporter, instead of destroying Kirk's body and building a new one, turns Kirk's body into energy, beams *that energy* to the new location, and rebuilds his body from the energy. In this way, teletransportation involves not just psychological continuity, but *physical* continuity as well.

> In this case, the teletransporter can't malfunction in the way described above – it can't create *two* bodies out of the energy of just *one* body. To build a second body would require new energy; but then we can say, whichever body was created out of new energy is not Kirk, but a duplicate of him.

Physical and psychological continuity together are necessary and sufficient

Our discussion so far has suggested that not only are psychological properties alone not enough (teletransportation), but also that brain continuity alone is not enough (brain erasing, discussed on p. 178). If we combine both conditions, we solve the objections raised. Perhaps personal identity requires both psychological and physical continuity.

However, there is a problem facing any theory that invokes brain continuity. Suppose members of an alien race exhibited all THE CHARACTERISTICS ASSOCIATED

> Explain how both the soul theory and the physical continuity theories can solve the duplication problem.

WITH PERSONHOOD (p. 161f.). However, they don't have brains. In fact, they don't have *any* single bodily organ that performs the functions of brains. Surely this doesn't matter to whether they are persons. Yet according to our theory, they aren't persons.

There is also a problem facing any theory that invokes psychological continuity. If psychological continuity is necessary for personal identity, then I am not identical with the new-born baby whose body became my body, because that baby did not have a mind that is psychologically continuous with me. Once the baby has memories, forms beliefs, desires and emotions that last over time, then psychological continuity can slowly get going. But before it has psychological properties there is no psychological continuity, so there is no person.

The animal theory solves both these problems. I am, obviously, the same animal as that baby. And the aliens are persons since they are animals, even if they don't have brains. However, we objected to the animal theory (p. 177) that if my brain was transplanted to another body, I would continue to exist in the new body, even though I would be a different animal.

PERSONAL IDENTITY IS SIMPLE

All theories that analyse personal identity in terms of physical or psychological continuity, then, face objections. We can argue that this shows that *there are no (independent) necessary and sufficient conditions* for being the same person. Personal identity is 'simple' – it cannot be equated to or derived from any other facts that are independent of the idea of a person.

The view that persons are souls is a version of this view. That persons are souls is not an *informative* or separate criterion. You can't use the claim that persons are souls to discover whether someone is the same person or not. But this is a strength of the theory, its defenders claim. What our discussion has shown, they claim, is that all the *evidence* of whether some creature is a person or the same person – its psychological characteristics or its continuity over time – is fallible. So personhood is not something that can be established on the basis of this kind of evidence. It must be independent of it – as souls are.

But the soul theory faces objections as well, viz. that we attribute physical characteristics to persons, not just mental ones (p. 180); and that if two souls swapped psychological characteristics, it is not clear that we should say the soul is the person (p.188).

Another option is the one suggested by the idea that to be a person is to have a first-person perspective. This is uninformative – we cannot judge that a first-person perspective is the *same* first-perspective as some previous one

---

Review the brain erasing and teletransportation cases, using the theory that personal identity is brain and psychological continuity together.

Assess the theory that brain and psychological continuity are necessary and sufficient conditions for personal identity.

The claim that persons are souls is only as strong as the arguments for the view that souls actually exist. These arguments are discussed in SUBSTANCE DUALISM, A2 Unit 3.1 Philosophy of Mind.

without judging whether it is the same person we are talking about. We return to the idea that the concept of a person is primitive and so personal identity cannot be analysed into independent necessary and sufficient conditions.

Assess the claim that personal identity is unanalysable.

Is our survival, rather than identity through time, more important?

Derek Parfit defends the 'best candidate' theory of personal identity (p.190). As long as there is just one person who is *most* psychologically continuous with me, that person is me. This leads to a surprising conclusion.

Reasons and Persons, Ch. 12–13

We noted earlier (p. 178) that if someone has brain damage, the rest of the brain can pick up some of the functions of the damaged part. Now suppose I face a brain operation – half my brain (call it A) will be transplanted into another body, and will continue to support my mental states. The other half (B) is destroyed. The person with A – on the best candidate theory – continues to exist as me. But now suppose that instead of the second half being destroyed, it is also transplanted into another body and continues to support my mental states as well. Which of the two people is the same person as me before the operation? Well, neither, because there are two 'best' candidates. I have ceased to exist, and two people, with equal psychological continuity to me, have come into existence.

However, whether the brain half B is destroyed or not, a person (the person with brain half A) exists who is psychologically continuous to me. So in thinking about the two options – having both halves transplanted or having half destroyed – it shouldn't make a difference to me which occurs. For example, it would be irrational for me to try to ensure that only one half of my brain was transplanted and the other half was destroyed. Yet only if B is destroyed do I continue to exist. If both halves are transplanted, I cease to exist.

Parfit concludes that personal identity *doesn't matter*. What matters is psychological continuity, which he calls 'survival'. My concern for my future is not for someone *identical* to me to exist, but for someone psychologically continuous with me to exist. Obviously, in everyday life, the only way to make sure that someone exists who is psychologically continuous with me is to make sure that *I* continue to exist. But in the split brain transplant case (and in the malfunctioning teletransporter case), this is no longer true. As long as I am replaced by someone psychologically continuous with me, I have nothing to worry about.

Explain Parfit's claim that identity doesn't matter, survival does.

We can object that our concern for ourselves and for other people is a concern for us/them as individuals. Parfit's suggestion is that we/they could be replaced by *other* people who are psychologically continuous, and we would be as happy. But someone who is a psychologically continuous replacement isn't the same person – and this matters to us. Yet his argument shows that we cannot both hold the best candidate theory of personal identity and think that personal identity, rather than psychological continuity, is what matters.

However, we can reject the best candidate theory of personal identity. Our objection (p. 191) to this was that identity is intrinsic. If Kirk is not Kirk when the teletransporter malfunctions, then he is not Kirk when it works normally. So teletransportation is not a form of transport – it is death followed by replacement by someone else who is psychologically continuous. In the case of the brain transplant, whether I continue to exist as me can't depend on whether some other person comes into existence. So I don't continue to exist even in the case when brain half A is transplanted and brain half B is destroyed.

But are we making the right judgements here? If we are not, then Parfit may be right that it is psychological continuity, not identity, that matters.

Assess the claim that personal identity is not important.

The implications of cloning, brain damage, body alterations etc.

At the beginning of this section WHAT SECURES OUR PERSONAL IDENTITY THROUGH TIME? (p. 187), we noted a connection between the view that to be a person is to have a first-person perspective, a form of self-awareness, and views of personal identity. We suggested that to be the same person through time was to have the same self-awareness. We can use this idea, together with the criteria for personal identity we discussed, to draw out some practical implications.

Cloning

Cloning is the creation of a living organism that is genetically identical (or almost genetically identical) to another living organism. Scientists have cloned a wide variety of species, including cattle, sheep, mice, goats, pigs, cats and dogs. As of March 2008, in human beings, only human embryos can be cloned.

Scientists hope to be able to make an embryo clone of an adult human being. This involves taking the DNA from one of the patient's cells, and putting it into a human egg cell that has had its nucleus removed. The cell is multiplied in culture to form the embryo. The point of doing this is to develop 'stem cells'. Stem cells have the potential to become any type of cell – brain, heart, liver, bone; and they are able to replicate themselves in the right conditions. Because the embryo is a clone of an adult, these cells will be genetically identical to the adult's cells, which means they can be transplanted into the adult safely. This may help lead to cures for diseases such as Alzheimer's and Parkinson's.

Suppose scientists figured out how to clone a human being, that is, they clone an embryo from an adult, implant the embryo in a woman's uterus, and a baby is born – what are the implications for personal identity?

None. The relation between the 'original' person and the 'clone' is similar to the relation between twins. And twins are two distinct people. They are distinct animals, they each have their own body and their own brain, they each have their own self-awareness and first-person perspective, they each have their own psychological connectedness and continuity, and if souls exist, they each have their own souls. The creation of a *genetic* duplicate is not the creation of a *personal* duplicate. Even if the clone was a *duplicate* of the person (not just their genetic code), it would be a duplicate and not the re-creation of the *same* person.

> Explain and illustrate the implications of cloning for personal identity.

Brain damage

Brain damage, however, may affect personal identity. If personal identity through time requires having enough of the same brain, functioning enough to support psychological continuity or self-awareness, then severe brain damage could cause a person to cease to exist, even though the organism or animal continues to exist. Brain damage that leads to a permanent coma or 'persistent vegetative state' would be an example of this. If, however, the animal or soul theory of personal identity is right, then the person continues to exist (because the animal or soul does), but without psychological continuity or self-awareness.

> Can brain damage change who a person is?

Body alterations

On all the theories of personal identity we have looked at, alterations to one's body does not change the person one is (although, of course, it might involve a change in personality, for example, as an effect of becoming disabled). Alterations to one's body do not affect one's first-person perspective, one's psychological continuity, one's soul or one's brain. If the body alterations are massive – having multiple organ transplants and loss or changes of limb – then we may say that this (new) body is no longer the same animal as it was before. In this case, the animal theory would say it was not the same person.

Etc.

These examples give us a way to think about other cases. On the first-person perspective, psychological continuity and soul theories, physical effects on their own make no difference to personal identity. The physical effects need to have important psychological consequences. This is true on the brain theory as well. The continuity of the brain is important because of its close connection to the person's psychology. The animal theory, however, allows much greater importance to physical effects independent of psychological effects, as we need to judge whether we can say the same animal has continued to exist.

> Discuss which theory of personal identity handles the implications of medical technology best.

Key points • • •

- Descartes argues that he is a soul – something that thinks and does not depend on the body.
- Locke objects that if we swap memories between two souls, each person would have a new soul, not new memories.
- Reincarnation does not necessarily support the view that persons are souls. Reincarnation could be psychological continuity without souls.
- Reid objects that memory can't be the criterion of personal identity, because to explain what a memory is, we must assume personal identity.
- The 'best candidate' theory says that whoever is the most psychologically continuous with a previous person is that person.
- Hume agrees that psychological continuity is not personal identity – but argues that personal identity is an illusion.
- Many philosophers think identity is intrinsic – it depends *only* on the relations between the two things thought to be identical.
- The psychological continuity theory faces the duplication problem. The soul theory and physical continuity theories can solve it. They both deny that a process that can 'duplicate' a person, for example, teletransportation, can

preserve personal identity. The new person doesn't have the old person's soul or body.

- The animal theory solves two problems facing the view that personal identity is psychological and brain continuity together: that aliens without brains can be persons, and that I am the same person as a baby that didn't have a mind.

- However, no theory is without objections, so perhaps there are no necessary and sufficient conditions for personal identity – it is unanalysable.

SUMMARY

In this chapter, we have looked at three questions about persons:

1. What are the characteristics associated with personhood?

2. What is a person?

3. What secures our personal identity through time?

In our discussion of these questions, we have looked at the following issues:

1. What are the characteristics associated with being a person? What are the relations between these characteristics? Are some necessary pre-conditions for others, for example, is language a pre-condition for being reflective on one's experiences?

2. Is any characteristic, for example, self-awareness, necessary and/or sufficient for being a person?

3. Is the concept of 'person' primitive?

4. Is a person a soul?

5. Are all humans persons?

6. To what extent do animals have the characteristics associated with person-hood? Are some animals persons? Do any have a first-person perspective?

7. Do computers have any of the characteristics associated with personhood?

8. Is psychological continuity a necessary or sufficient condition for being a person?

9. What is the problem of duplication? How can it be solved?
10. Does personal identity matter, or is survival more important?
11. Is being the same animal necessary or sufficient for being the same person?
12. Is the continuity of a functioning brain necessary or sufficient for being the same person?
13. Can any independent necessary and sufficient conditions be given for personal identity, or is it unanalysable?
14. What are the implications for personal identity of cloning, brain damage or body alterations?

AN INTRODUCTION TO PHILOSOPHY 2

Section 1: Knowledge of the external world

In this chapter, we will look at three theories of how we gain knowledge of the external world through perception: direct realism, representative realism and idealism. We will look at the strengths and weaknesses of each. By the end of the chapter, you should be able to demonstrate a good understanding of the three theories, and be able to analyse and evaluate several arguments for and against each one.

SYLLABUS CHECKLIST

The AQA AS syllabus for this chapter is:

Realism

✔ What are the immediate objects of perception? Do physical objects have the properties we perceive in them? Is the common-sense view naive? Do sceptical arguments cast doubt on the common-sense view?

✔ The secondary qualities thesis: does this establish that only the primary qualities of objects are objectively real? Characteristics of primary and secondary qualities.

Representative realism

✔ Do sceptical arguments establish the sense-data theory? Examples of sceptical arguments: illusion, perceptual variation, science-inspired arguments, time lags. Differences between sense-data and physical objects.

✔ Could we know of a relation between sense-data and physical objects? Could the existence of the external world be a hypothesis?

Idealism

✔ Should physical objects be regarded as collections of ideas/sense-data? Are there good reasons for accepting idealism, for example, solving the problem of material substance, consistency with empiricism, no linking problem?

✔ Inherent difficulties with idealism: problem of unperceived objects, availability of simpler, more systematic alternatives and confusion in the use of the term 'idea'.

epistemology

epistemology is the study (-ology) of knowledge (episteme) and related concepts, including belief, justification, certainty. It looks at the possibility and sources of knowledge.

We might have other kinds of experience, for example, religious experiences, but we won't be talking about them here. This is not because they are less important, or not a source of knowledge – they may or may not be. This is examined in A2 Unit 3.5 Philosophy of Religion.

INTRODUCTION

As we saw in Unit 1.1 REASON AND EXPERIENCE (p. 6), central to the branch of philosophy called **epistemology** are the questions 'What do we know? What *can* we know? How do we know what we know?' As we saw, the two main answers to this last question are 'reason' and 'experience'. In this chapter, we will focus on 'experience' and on the question 'How are human beings "hooked up" to the world?'. So our question is, 'What can sense experience tell us about the world outside our minds?'. Sense experiences are those given to us by our senses – sight, hearing, smell, taste, touch and bodily sensations. We want to know whether sense experience shows that there is a world of physical objects that exists outside and independently of our minds – the world 'external' to our minds; and if it does, what is the best account of how we *perceive* it?

'Physical objects' are the ordinary, everyday things – tables, books, our own bodies, plants – which common sense says we perceive through our senses (philosophers usually focus on vision, partly because it is our 'dominant' sense). We could also call them 'material' objects because, we think, they are made of matter – whatever that is! But is matter the final analysis of what they are made of? Perhaps 'physical objects' is better, because physics is the science that studies what they are, ultimately, made up of.

I. Realism

What do we perceive? Direct and representative realism

Theories of perception can be divided into camps by how they answer the question 'What do we perceive when we perceive physical objects?' Realists claim that physical objects exist as things that are independent of our minds and of our perceptions of them. Idealists argue that physical objects, in the sense that realists think of them as independent of our minds, don't exist at all. The only things we perceive, the only things that exist, are mental; so what we think of as physical objects are actually particular sorts of ideas (p. 209).

Direct realism is the natural starting point for theories of perception. Common sense suggests that physical objects exist independently of our minds. The theory of evolution suggests that matter existed before minds existed. For billions of years, there were no minds to experience the world; but it existed nevertheless. Direct realists claim that we perceive the physical objects themselves. When we are perceiving the world, it certainly seems to us that we are directly perceiving physical objects that exist independently of our minds.

A little reflection suggests that what we perceive isn't quite the same as what is 'out there'. For example, if you put your thumb up against the moon, it looks like your thumb is larger than the moon, but it isn't. If you move away from a table, you don't think the table itself gets smaller, even though it looks smaller. Or again, if you look at a red rose in sodium street lights, it looks grey, but the rose itself hasn't changed. If you half-submerge a straight stick in water and look at it from the side, it looks bent; but it isn't. So *what* we perceive in all these cases isn't the world as it is; but we are still perceiving the world – the moon, the rose, the stick – in some way (see Figures 6.1 and 6.2).

We can put this thought in the form of a question. When we perceive physical objects, do we perceive them 'directly' and as they actually are, or do we perceive them 'indirectly', in virtue of some representation in our minds? Direct realism claims that the *immediate object* of perception is the physical

What is epistemology? What is the common-sense idea of a physical object?

Theories of perception are theories of what and how we can know through sense experience. The philosophical theory that knowledge comes from (sense) experience is called **empiricism** (for a more precise definition and discussion, see REASON AND EXPERIENCE, p. 10). In discussing the knowledge sense experience gives us, we are discussing the issue that is the heart of empiricism.

David Hume made this argument in *An Enquiry Concerning Human Understanding*, § XII

Figure 6.1
A giraffe and a bridge.

Figure 6.2
Thermometer in liquid.

Give your own example that supports the view that what we 'see' is not what is 'out there'.

object itself. We don't perceive it in virtue of perceiving something else that 'mediates' between our minds and the physical object. Representative realists say that we perceive them 'indirectly'; what we perceive 'directly' is a 'representation', a mental image, that exists in our minds but which represents the physical object. The physical object is perceived 'via' this representation. The representation is an 'appearance'; philosophers have called it a **sense-datum**. We will look at REPRESENTATIVE REALISM later (p. 205f.), when I'll also talk more about the differences between sense-data and physical objects. We'll focus first on direct realism.

Do physical objects have the properties we perceive them to have?

Is direct realism naive?

If what we perceive is the physical object, then it would seem to follow that the physical object has all the properties we perceive in it. So, I see a brown and black desk, rectangular, about 1.5m long, smelling faintly of factory chemicals. Are all these properties of the desk? Do physical objects have all the properties they appear to have?

This is a question about the distinction between appearance and reality. Obviously, much of the time, we talk as though things are just as they seem. But the three earlier examples – of your thumb and the moon, of the rose under sodium light, of the stick in water – show that we also distinguish between appearance and reality. And when we do so, then it seems that physical objects do not have exactly the properties they appear to have.

Does this show that direct realism is wrong? Direct realism has sometimes been called 'naive realism', because it seems to take the world at face value. Is it 'naive' in taking physical objects to exist just exactly as we experience them?

Distance and size

First, the thumb and the moon. Does your thumb really look *bigger* than the moon? Or is it rather that the moon looks *further away*? The way our visual system works, it is difficult to separate properties of size from properties of distance. How big something looks, in the usual sense of that phrase, depends on how far away it looks. Something which only takes up a small part of the visual field might actually look huge and very distant.

Direct realists say that you directly perceive the physical object; but this doesn't mean that *every* aspect of your perceptual experience is determined by the properties of the physical object itself. For example, in this case, there is also the relative property of its distance from you. We experience both the size of the object and its distance. (The experience – distant things taking up less of the visual field – is also determined by facts about light and our visual system. But these facts aren't themselves *part* of the experience – we don't experience them.) So, to explain your thumb and the moon, we don't need to say that you are immediately perceiving sense-data, which are different from physical objects. You are directly perceiving physical objects, but you are directly perceiving their distance as well as their size.

We might object that we do not *experience* distance. Rather, the object does look small but, because we know about distance and size, we *judge* it to be large and far away. When we don't know how large something is, we can sometimes wrongly judge it to be small and close, rather than large and distant, or vice-versa. This shows that we don't experience distance directly, and there is a distinction between how big it seems and how big it is. To account for this, we need sense-data.

Think of looking at a skyscraper from a distance – does the skyscraper *look* small?

Explain the debate in your own words. Which position is stronger, direct or representative realism?

Illusions

When we look at the stick half-submerged in water, we see a bent stick. But the stick isn't bent. So *what is*? We see *something* bent, but it isn't the stick. So it must be a sense-datum. We have a mental image of a bent stick; the stick in the image is bent. But that means that we don't see the real stick directly; we see it indirectly, via sense-data. So direct realism is false, and representative realism must be right.

We must admit that in cases of illusion, we do not see the object as it is. The stick isn't really bent. So the object doesn't have the property that it appears to have. In Development, we will look at two answers direct realists have given (p. 217).

The secondary quality thesis

We have looked at the examples of your thumb and the moon, and of the bent stick. These dealt with the properties of size and shape. But what about the rose looking grey, rather than red, under sodium lighting? If direct realism is right to argue that physical objects have the properties of size and shape, is it also right to think that they have colour or smell as well?

This question is about a distinction between 'primary qualities' and 'secondary qualities', which was developed during the rise of modern science. In the first instance, we can think of this as a distinction between properties that science says objects have – size, shape, motion – and properties that depend upon particular ways of perceiving objects. Colour, by definition, is something that is experienced in vision. The work that scientists such as Newton, Descartes and Galileo did on light laid the foundations for our modern theory of colour as wavelengths of the electromagnetic field we experience as light. Science, therefore, was beginning to develop an explanation for colour. And likewise, it has developed theories of sound, smell, taste and other secondary properties. But these theories – that colour is frequency of electromagnetic radiation, that smell and taste are chemical compounds – suggest that the world as we experience it through our senses and the world as science describes it are quite different. We experience all the wonderful properties of the senses; the world 'as it is in itself', as described by science, is 'particles in motion' and empty space.

Do these secondary properties exist 'in the object' or 'in the mind' of the perceiver? Direct realists have to say that objects really are coloured. However, Hume thought that modern science and philosophy had shown that secondary qualities exist only in the mind. Objects aren't coloured; instead, we could say, their parts have certain properties of size and motion and so on, causing them to emit or reflect wavelengths of light (which is a type of vibration, not itself a colour). It is not until we turn to human experience – something mental – that we need the concept of colour, that we come across 'colour experience'.

In his discussion of primary and secondary qualities, Locke claims that the 'ideas' (the sense impressions) of primary qualities – our sense-data of shape, size, motion and so on – 'resemble' the primary qualities that the object we are perceiving has. However, the sense impressions of secondary qualities – our sense-data of colour, smell and so on – don't resemble the object at all. The experience of seeing red, for example, just isn't like detecting a vibration – yet it is. This shows, he argues, that we don't perceive the object 'immediately'. We

> Discuss the relation between the concepts 'wavelength of light' and 'colour'.

do so via our sense-data of the object, which resemble it in regard to its primary qualities, but not in regard to secondary qualities.

Key points • • •

- Both direct and representative realists claim that physical objects exist as things that are independent of our minds and of our perceptions of them.
- Direct realism claims that when we perceive physical objects, we perceive them 'directly'. Representative realism claims that we perceive them 'indirectly', in virtue of mental representations of them, 'sense-data'.
- If direct realism is right, then it seems that physical objects should have the properties we perceive them to have.
- However, this doesn't mean every aspect of perceptual experience is fixed by the properties of the object. When looking at a large object in the distance, we might say it looks small (so it doesn't have the property it appears to have). But we could equally say that it looks like a large object far away. Do we *see* this or do we *judge* it?
- Illusions, however, depend on a gap between appearance and reality. What we see, for example, a bent stick, does not exist as we see it.
- An argument from science also suggests a gap between appearance and reality. It suggests that properties such as colour and smell exist in the mind; objects only have size, shape, motion and so on – colour, for instance, is a wavelength of light.

II. Representative realism

Arguments in favour of representative realism can begin as objections to direct realism. We looked at three examples of the way in which what we see isn't quite the same as the physical objects themselves: your thumb looking larger than the moon, a red rose looking grey in sodium lighting, and a straight stick looking bent when half-submerged in water. Representative realists argue that they have a good explanation of this. There is a distinction between how the world is and how we perceive the world to be, but it still makes sense to say we perceive *the world*. We perceive it 'indirectly'. What is immediately present to our consciousness, what we perceive 'directly', is a representation of the world, a sense-datum.

> 1. What does Locke mean by resemblance? Can you think of an objection to his theory?
> 2. Explain and illustrate the distinction between primary and secondary qualities.

> Representative realism claims two things: that we perceive a world of physical objects external to our minds; but that we do so indirectly, via perceiving sense-data that represent these objects.

Cases of hallucination support the case for sense-data still further. If I hallucinate seeing an elephant, there is nothing in the world that I am seeing *as* an elephant. So what is it that looks like an elephant? It can only be something mental, viz. the sense-datum of an elephant.

If the rose looks grey, but it isn't, what is it that we are seeing that *is* grey? If the stick isn't bent, then what is it that is bent? Representative realists say it is the sense-datum of the rose that is grey, the sense-datum of the stick that is bent. Sense-data, then, are mental things which are the way we perceive them to be. They are 'appearances'. When we are perceiving the world, we perceive it via the sense-data that represent objects in the world. This representation can be accurate or inaccurate in certain ways.

Sense-data and physical objects

It is worth taking a moment just to list the essential characteristics of sense-data in contrast to physical objects. These essential properties feature importantly in the argument which we have just seen, that sense-data are needed to explain perception, and also in the objections that will be raised to sense-data.

Sense-data are mental things – they exist as part of the mind. Physical objects, by contrast, exist physically. It is perhaps unclear what it means to say that something exists 'mentally' – is the mind a thing? We don't need to settle that here. The important point is that sense-data have at least these three important properties that physical objects do not:

1. Sense-data are 'private'. No one else can experience *your* sense-data. They are the particular sense-data they are, by definition, as part of your consciousness. By contrast, physical objects are 'public'. One and the same table can be experienced by different people.
2. Sense-data only exist while they are being experienced. An experience must be experienced by someone to exist at all. A physical object, such as a table, can exist when no one experiences it.
3. Sense-data are exactly as they seem. As we said above, they are 'appearances'. There is no further reality to an appearance than how it appears. (Otherwise, you would have to ask whether you perceived the appearance as it appears or as it really is!) Physical objects can appear differently from how they really are (for example, the stick in water). They have a reality which is not defined by appearance.

Discuss the contrast between physical objects and sense-data. Try to put the distinction in your own words.

These, at least, are the traditional contrasts between physical objects and sense-data. When we look at IDEALISM (p. 209f.), we will see the contrasts being challenged.

From illusion to a theory of perception

In cases in which the world isn't the way we perceive it to be, it looks like we need to say we perceive sense-data. But, argue representative realists, there is really no difference between these cases and cases in which the world *is* the way we perceive it to be. If someone didn't know that straight sticks look bent in water, when he looked at such a stick, it would seem to him as though he was looking at a *bent stick*. And when you are in the grip of a hallucination, you don't know you are hallucinating. You can't tell, just by how it seems, whether you are perceiving an illusion, perceiving the world the way it really is, or hallucinating. But then, if we are perceiving sense-data in the cases of illusion and hallucination, yet subjectively we can't tell the difference between these cases and cases in which we perceive the world as it is, we should say we are perceiving sense-data in every case. We can't tell the difference is because we see the *same thing* in both cases, viz. sense-data. And likewise in hallucinations: why is it that we can describe both a hallucination, for example, of an elephant, and a perception of an elephant in exactly the same way unless they have something in common? So we don't just perceive sense-data in these cases of illusion and hallucination; we *always* perceive sense-data. In **veridical** perception, we perceive the world 'in virtue of' perceiving sense-data.

Could we know of a relation between sense-data and physical objects?

If we don't directly perceive physical objects, but only sense-data, how is it that we can think about a world 'beyond' sense-data? On what grounds is representative realism realist? Can we know what the world of physical objects is really like? In fact, can we know that it even exists?

We could argue that we know what the world is like, and that it exists, because sense-data resemble the world in primary qualities, but not secondary qualities. But both Hume and Berkeley disagree. Berkeley pointed out that Locke was wrong to say that the appearance resembles the object in its primary qualities, but not in its secondary. For example, circles do not *look circular* when viewed from an angle, they *look oval* (see Figure 6.3). So the lack of resemblance applies to both primary and secondary properties. There is no more constancy in one than the other.

veridical
'veridical' means accurate, not mistaken, telling or showing the truth.

Analyse and assess the argument from illusion to representative realism.

Figure 6.3
Circular objects from obtuse angles.

? Why can't we compare sense-data and physical objects? If we can't, why does this matter?

Since we only ever experience sense-data 'immediately', if there were no physical objects, how would we know? It wouldn't seem any different if our sensations were caused by a computer; or were not caused at all, but just 'happened'.

Compare the strengths and weaknesses of direct and representative realism.

Second, Berkeley argued, you can't say that two things resemble each other unless you can compare them. But you can never compare the physical object to the sense-data, since you only ever perceive sense-data immediately. We can't say that physical objects have *any* of the qualities we perceive, including size and shape, because the only basis for doing so is our experience of the sense-data. We don't know that physical objects have size and shape unless we know our sense-data resemble them; but we don't know whether our sense-data resemble them unless we can say they have size and shape!

To reply to these objections, representative realists dropped the idea of 'resemblance' in favour of 'representation'. They emphasise the other part of Locke's theory, that sense-data are *caused by* physical objects; and this causation is very detailed and systematic. Yes, if you turn a penny, it looks circular, then increasingly oval, then flat (from the side). But all of these sense-data represent the penny because they are very systematically related to it. We can explain representation in terms of this complex causation. What remains central to representative realism is that we perceive the world via sense-data.

But, Hume argues, how can we even know that physical objects exist, and cause our sense-data? From the sense-data themselves, how can we tell what, if anything, causes them? We can't: all that perceptual experience gives us is the sense-data, not any connection between sense-data and physical objects. In order to know that physical objects cause our sense-data, we first have to know that physical objects exist. But the only access we have to physical objects is through our sense-data. So, in fact, we cannot know that a world of physical objects exists independently of our sense-data. At best, then, saying that physical objects exist is a *hypothesis*, a theory to explain our sense-data.

Key points • • •

- Representative realism claims to explain illusions and hallucinations. When we see a stick that looks bent but isn't, what we see that is bent is the sense-datum of the stick. When we hallucinate, we see only sense-data.
- However, we can't tell the difference between an illusion and perceiving the world as it is just from the experience we have. Since we are perceiving sense-data in the case of illusion, we should infer that we always perceive sense-data.
- Sense-data are private (by definition belonging to someone's consciousness); they only exist while they are being experienced; and they are exactly

as they seem. Physical objects are public, exist when not being perceived, and can be different from how they appear.

- Locke argued that sense-data resembled the world in primary qualities, but not in secondary qualities. Berkeley argued that this is not true, and that we can't judge whether two things resemble each other unless we can compare them – but we can't compare the world and sense-data if we only ever perceive sense-data directly. Representative realists abandoned resemblance in favour of representation.

- In fact, how do we know physical objects exist at all? We cannot know what causes sense-data if all we experience are sense-data.

III. Idealism

Are physical objects collections of ideas?

We will concentrate on the idealism of Bishop Berkeley. He rejects the existence of physical objects, as they are usually thought of. Whatever we think they are, our idea is that a physical object is something that is *mind-independent*. All forms of idealism claim that reality is, in some important sense, dependent on minds. Berkeley claims that the ordinary objects of perception – tables, chairs, trees and so on – are dependent on minds. They must be perceived in order to exist. The only things that exist, then, are minds (that perceive) and what minds perceive. Therefore, nothing exists that is independent of mind.

esse est percipi (aut percipere)
to be is to be perceived (or to perceive).

So idealism claims that what we think of as physical objects are bundles of ideas that we have come to associate with each other because they 'are observed to accompany each other'. Does this make sense, and why does Berkeley argue for this conclusion? A central reason is that we can't make proper sense of the idea of a physical object, he claims.

We have seen an argument from science to suggest that secondary qualities are subjective (p. 204). But in his objections to representative realism, Berkeley argued that primary qualities don't resemble objects any more than secondary qualities do (p. 207). They can be just as subjective, for example, the apparent shape of something changes from different angles. So you and I could be looking at a penny, and you see something circular and I see something oval.

This suggests that what we perceive (at least directly) are sense-data. And, of course, sense-data can't exist without being perceived. Could there be an experience of colour that was no one's experience? No; colours, sounds, smells, and shapes and sizes, says Berkeley, all depend on being perceived to exist at all. What we perceive when we perceive 'physical objects' are all ideas; and ideas can't exist without minds.

This doesn't yet show that physical objects *themselves* are ideas, only that we can only perceive them via ideas. But, Berkeley says, when we perceive physical objects, everything we perceive is either a primary or a secondary quality. We don't perceive anything *in addition* to its primary and secondary qualities. But if both primary and secondary qualities are mind-dependent, then nothing that we perceive is left to exist independently of the mind.

If we say, as realists do, that there is the physical object 'itself', its 'substance' – well, what do we mean by this? How do we gain knowledge of its existence? We certainly don't perceive it – as just argued. In fact, can we even form a coherent idea of what we mean by the physical object 'itself' independently of all the

Look at this table (Figure 6.4). Notice the difference between looking at it in black and white, and how it would look in colour. Now try to picture it without its solidity (Figure 6.5). Now try to picture it without its shape (Figure 6.6). Berkeley argues we always perceive the qualities of physical objects, and, as a result, we can't even make sense of what a physical object independent of its qualities is. Since its qualities are all mind-dependent, there is nothing left of a physical object to be mind-independent.

Figure 6.4 Partially completed jigsaw on table.

Figure 6.5 Table.

Figure 6.6

qualities we perceive? Berkeley argues that we can't. So all that is left – what we *must* mean by 'physical object' – is that bundle of ideas which we perceive.

Two good reasons for idealism

Berkeley's idealism is very counter-intuitive. Berkeley realised this, and many of his arguments, some of which we have already discussed, are objections to representative and direct realism. If realism doesn't work, perhaps idealism is the answer. Berkeley's claim that there is nothing to physical objects apart from ideas is certainly odd, but, he says, it should be welcome upon reflection. Here are two good reasons for thinking that idealism solves the problems that realism throws up. (A third will be discussed in Development, p. 228.)

> Discuss the concept of 'substance'. Can we experience anything apart from properties?

The linking problem

As well as not making sense, realism also leads to **scepticism**. How is that we can connect up our experiences to something 'beyond' them – which, following the objection just made, we can't even describe or understand? How can we know that ideas really do represent (and represent accurately) something that exists completely independently of them? Idealism solves the problem of scepticism, because there is no need to 'link' the ideas we perceive to something else (physical objects). Ideas don't *represent* physical objects, they *are* physical objects. The possibility of a world quite different from what we experience just doesn't arise. In experiencing ideas, we are experiencing the world.

Empiricism

Berkeley also argues that idealism is more consistent than realism with a commitment to empiricism. The hypothesis that there is a physical world, quite independent of our experience of it, is not something we can verify through experience. We have no experience of substance, only of primary and secondary qualities. Worse still, the hypothesis of physical 'substance' is not one that is even *suggested* by experience. If we pay close attention to experience, we are led to the claim that all there is (all we can say there is) is what we can experience, and what we experience are ideas.

> What does Berkeley mean by claiming that empiricism leads to idealism?

Difficulties with idealism

We've seen how idealism can emerge from the problems of realism, indeed Berkeley argues, from common sense. But it is no improvement on realism if it faces objections that are just as powerful as those facing realism.

Is realism a simpler alternative to idealism?

First, what causes perceptions? Without physical objects, what explains why we perceive what we do? There are three options: ideas, my mind and another mind. But ideas themselves don't cause anything, says Berkeley, they are completely passive. Second, perception is quite different to imagining; we are more passive – the sensations just occur to us, and we can't control them. From this difference between (voluntary) imagination and (involuntary) perception, we can rule out my mind. So they must be caused by another mind. When you think of the complexity and systematicity of our perceptions, Berkeley argues, that mind must be God.

If this seems **ad hoc**, Berkeley argues that it is at least no worse than invoking physical objects. Realism claims to be able to explain perception by appealing to something outside our minds, physical objects, that cause our experiences. But Berkeley argues that physical objects provide no explanation at all. No one has been able to say *how* it is that physical objects give rise to ideas (even if we can say now how physical objects affect processes in the brain, we still have no explanation of how any of this causes an experience). So how our experiences come about remains a mystery.

A second objection: if ordinary ('physical') objects are really ideas, how can I distinguish between my 'ideas', just part of my mind, and 'real things', part of the world beyond my mind? Berkeley replies by again pointing out the distinction between perception and imagination. In fact, Berkeley has three criteria for an idea being (part of) an object of perception, rather than *just* my mind: the idea is not voluntary; the idea forms part of the order of nature, the coherent set of ideas that we experience as reality; and the idea is caused by (or part of – see below) the mind of God.

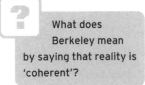

Discuss the difference between perception and imagination.

Is it simpler to say that God causes my sensations or that physical objects do?

What does Berkeley mean by saying that reality is 'coherent'?

Unperceived objects

Berkeley has answers for the objections so far. But the claim that realism is a simpler theory than idealism is supported by a further objection: If 'to be is to be perceived' for ordinary objects, that entails that when they are not being perceived, they do not exist. So if I leave a room, and no one else is in it, then everything in the room ceases to exist! This is very counter-intuitive. The objection was put in the form of a limerick:

> There was a young man who said God
> must find it exceedingly odd
> when He finds that the tree
> continues to be
> when no one's about in the Quad.

Berkeley provides two different answers in different books. His first reply is this: what the word 'exists' means when applied to an ordinary object of perception is that it is *or can be* perceived. 'The table exists' means the table is being perceived, or would be perceived if in the presence of some mind.

However, this reply conflicts with 'to be is to be perceived', which entails not that the table *does* exist if it were perceived, but rather that it *would* exist if it were perceived. So tables do pop in and out of existence. But should we worry about this, as long as they do so with complete regularity? We might reply that we shouldn't *worry* but this hardly seems as plausible as the idea that physical objects exist independently of our minds.

Berkeley's second, and more consistent, reply is summarised in the second part of the limerick:

> Dear Sir, your astonishment's odd.
> I'm always about in the Quad,
> And that's why the tree
> continues to be
> Since observed by, yours faithfully, God.

According to this response, God does not only *cause* our ideas of perception. What we perceive exists *in* the mind of God. But this is also problematic: *our* ideas of perception couldn't be part of a divine mind, which can't have the sorts of sensations we have. Second, ordinary objects change and go out of existence,

> So what if things did cease to exist when no one was looking? What then?

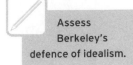

Assess Berkeley's defence of idealism.

but God's mind is said to be unchanging and eternal. But Berkeley may respond that God's ideas which correspond to ordinary objects are not ones God thinks, but what God *wills* us to experience: 'things . . . may properly be said to begin their existence . . . when God decreed they should become perceptible to intelligent creatures'.

Key points • • •

- Idealism claims that all that exists are minds and ideas.
- Berkeley rejects the view that what we think of as physical objects are mind-independent. In fact, they are collections of ideas.
- Everything we perceive is either a primary or a secondary quality. Berkeley objects to direct realism that secondary qualities are subjective, so we don't perceive physical objects directly. He then objects to representative realism that primary qualities are equally subjective. Since both are mind-dependent, everything we perceive is mind-dependent.
- Idealism solves the objection to representative realism that we cannot know how the world is. In experiencing ideas, we are experiencing the world.
- Berkeley also argues that empiricism supports idealism, for we have no experience of anything except ideas.
- To explain why we perceive anything, Berkeley must invoke the existence of God. Ideas do not cause their own perception, and I do not cause (imagine) what I perceive. So what I perceive must be caused by another mind, viz. God.
- We can distinguish between my ideas and the ideas that make up 'real things' by the facts the latter are not voluntary and they are part of a coherent order of nature.
- If to be is to be perceived, 'physical' objects go out of existence when not being perceived. Berkeley can ask whether this matters, if it happens with complete regularity; or he can say that to be is to be perceived or to be able to be perceived in the presence of a mind; or he can say that God always perceives everything.

DEVELOPMENT

Situating the question

In this discussion, there is a basic assumption we need to notice. It is that the issue is framed in terms of *minds* and *bodies* (physical objects). Knowledge is usually understood as a state of mind; and knowledge of physical objects is, according to common sense, knowledge of what exists 'outside' the mind. So the question is whether physical objects really do exist 'outside' our minds, that is, independently of them, whether we can know this, and if we can, then how we know about them. Before reading this chapter so far, the answers to these questions may have seemed obvious. Now, they may be less obvious, and I hope you think the questions really are worth thinking about!

What is not being questioned is that we can know what is *inside* our minds. How do you know that you are thinking what you are thinking? How do you know that you are feeling pain when you are? The answer, whatever it is, won't be 'through the senses'. So we aren't concerned with it. Assume that we do know what we are conscious of – the experience or the thought itself. The question is whether, and how, this can give us knowledge of physical objects.

The question of whether physical objects exist (or what it means to say that they exist) is actually a question in **metaphysics**, not epistemology. Metaphysics is the branch of philosophy that asks questions about the fundamental nature of reality. *Meta-* means above, beyond, or after; physics enquires into the physical structure of reality – but there may be more to reality than that, and physics might use concepts, such as causation, that it can't explain. One question in metaphysics is 'What exists?' (this question leads to the study of what exists, called **ontology**). So this chapter deals with both epistemology (how do we know?) and some metaphysics (what exists?).

> How does metaphysics differ from epistemology? What metaphysical questions have been raised in the INTRODUCTION?

ontology
ontology is the study (-ology) of what exists or 'being' (ont).

I. Realism

Is direct realism naive? II

Direct realists claim that we perceive the world directly, not via sense-data. It doesn't understand sense experiences as mental *things*. Of course, in perceiving the world, we experience it. But we shouldn't say that we perceive the world in virtue of perceiving sense-data. If we want to say we 'have experiences' of the world, we shouldn't say we *perceive* the experience; we *have* it, thereby perceiving the object. Or better still, experiences aren't 'things'; we *experience*, and in virtue of experiencing, we perceive the object. We do not perceive a mental thing.

Over the last thirty years, many philosophers have come to think some form of direct realism is defensible. It can give answers that are quite sophisticated to the challenges we have seen.

Going further: the content of sense experience

One argument for direct realism comes from considering how we describe what we see. Try to describe what you see. Of course, you would usually do so by referring to physical objects: 'I see a desk, covered with pens and paper, and a plant'. But if you perceived the world via sense-data, the immediate 'content' of what you perceive is mental. So try to describe your experience in terms of sense-data, without referring to any physical objects? For example, you could talk about 'coloured patches' standing in spatial relations (above, below, left, right, etc.) to each other. However, it turns out that this is virtually impossible for any normal scene. What shape is that coloured patch on the left? – well, 'plant-shaped'! But 'plant' refers to a physical object. So our way of describing sense-data is dependent on concepts of physical objects. We can't give an account of what we experience without referring to physical objects.

Direct realists argue that this shows that our epistemic 'access' to physical objects is direct. If we immediately perceived sense-data, we should be able to describe them in themselves, as coloured patches, without using concepts that refer to physical objects. But we can't. We can't make sense of sense-data, without relying on physical objects. So we can't use sense-data to explain our experience of physical objects.

Here's a parallel example: if you want to explain how a light bulb works, you need to refer to electricity. If you then tried to explain electricity just as 'it's what makes light bulbs work', you wouldn't have explained anything: 'light bulbs work by the stuff that makes light bulbs work'! So you need an *independent* explanation of electricity. It's the same with sense-data and physical objects. Suppose you explain your perception of the physical objects you see in terms of sense-data. You then need an *independent* account of the sense-data you are experiencing. But this is what you can't have – you can't describe the sense-data without referring to the physical objects. This at least suggests that what we experience are physical objects, not sense-data.

Illusions

We left the discussion of illusion as an objection to direct realism (p. 203). How can direct realists reply to the case of the straight stick that looks bent because it is half-submerged in water?

The first reply from direct realism *accepts* that if something looks bent, then something is bent; and since the stick isn't, I am seeing a sense-datum. But this doesn't make representative realism true as a general theory of perception. The reason is that cases of illusion and of veridical perception are quite different. In illusions, I see a sense-datum, but in veridical perception, I see physical objects. So direct realism is true for normal perception.

This view says if it looks to me as if something is F (a stick is bent) then *either* there is something that is F that I see *or* it is, for me, just *as if* there is something that is F. In the first case, I see the world as it is; in the second case, I see sense-data. But just because I see sense-data in cases of illusion doesn't mean I see sense-data, rather than the world, in cases of veridical perception. Illusions and veridical perception are two completely different kinds of mental state. (Of course, they can seem exactly the same to the person who experiences an illusion without knowing it; but that doesn't prove that they *are* the same.)

The second explanation *rejects* the claim that if it looks to me as if something is F, then there is something that is F. When the stick in water looks bent, there is nothing that *is* bent. Instead, the *stick* has the property of *looking bent* when half-submerged in water. The property of 'looking bent' is a distinct property from 'being bent'. It is a relational property, a property the stick has in relation to being seen by us. But because it is a property the *stick* has, we don't need to say that sense-data exist. There is a real difference between the property 'being straight' and the property 'looking straight'. Usually, of course, something looks straight when it is straight. But the two properties can come apart, and

An either/or claim is called a disjunction, so this theory is called 'disjunctivism'.

Analyse the two types of direct realism. Which is more persuasive?

something can look bent when it is straight. So, physical objects don't always have the properties they appear to have, but that doesn't make direct realism false.

Going further: what exists in a hallucination?

In the case of hallucinations, there is no physical object that 'looks' a certain way, because there is no physical object at all! However, following the lead of disjunctivists, all direct realists argue that we can't generalise from hallucinations to perception generally, that is, we can't use hallucinations to argue that we always perceive sense-data. Just because they seem similar subjectively doesn't mean the same thing (seeing sense-data) is going on. Hallucination and perception are different types of mental state, because in hallucination, the person isn't connected up to the world.

But this doesn't tell us what we *do* see in cases of hallucination. Disjunctivists can say that in hallucinations, as in illusions, we perceive sense-data. The other direct realists can't. However, they can compare cases of hallucination with *thoughts* about objects that don't exist. For example, I can think that unicorns are white; but unicorns don't exist. What do I think is white when I think 'a unicorn is white'? Just the unicorn – which doesn't exist. Suppose now I hallucinate seeing a white unicorn. What have I seen that is white? Again, just the unicorn; no physical object 'looks white' or 'looks like a unicorn' in this hallucination. Whatever explains how unicorns can be white without existing will also explain hallucinations of white unicorns.

An objection to this is that it is one thing to *think about* unicorns, and quite another to think you are *seeing* a unicorn. In the hallucination, it seems you are confronted, in your consciousness, with an example of something white. The experience is quite different from thinking about something white. Again, the defenders of sense-data will say, in a hallucination of something white, something must *be* white; in a thought of something white, nothing needs to be white. And this difference arises from how different it is to have a hallucination from having a thought.

What is the difference between thinking and hallucinating?

Has direct realism shown that we do not need sense-data to explain perceptual experience?

The secondary quality thesis II

The distinction between primary and secondary qualities also posed a challenge to direct realism. Part of its response is to try to understand the distinction more fully.

The distinction is most famously associated with John Locke's *An Essay concerning Human Understanding*, though Descartes, Galileo and others all defended it in some form. For Locke, primary qualities are those properties of an object that are not related by definition to perceivers. The primary qualities are size, shape, motion, number and solidity. We might say that the object has these properties 'in and of itself'. Primary qualities, Locke says, are 'inseparable' from a physical object, whatever changes it goes through. For example, physical objects always have *some* shape and size. These properties don't depend, either conceptually or for their existence, on whether and how the object is perceived.

By contrast, secondary qualities are related to perceivers by definition. As we saw, colour, by definition, is something that is experienced in vision. So it is a property that an object can have only in relation to its being seen by someone. The other secondary qualities are temperature, smell, taste and sound. Secondary qualities aren't possessed by all physical objects, for example, plain glass doesn't have a colour or a smell. And they aren't even possessed by the same physical object at different times, for example, glass is made from sand, and sand does have colour. So sand loses its colour completely when it is made into glass.

But do secondary qualities exist in the mind? Locke's 'official' theory is that secondary qualities are properties of the object that are related to its being perceived by us. Secondary qualities 'are nothing in the objects themselves but powers to produce various sensations in us'. Here Locke identifies the secondary quality with the *power of the object*. He goes on to argue that this power should be understood in terms of primary properties of the object's 'most minute parts', or as we would now put it, in terms of its atomic and molecular structure. As we suggested, secondary qualities can be causally explained in terms of primary properties.

Direct realists can use this definition to resist Hume's argument (p. 204) that colours only exist in experience. The argument confuses the relation between secondary qualities and experience: secondary qualities are powers in the physical object *to produce* certain experiences in us. Direct realists say that when we perceive secondary qualities, for example, colours, we still perceive the objects but *as they appear to us*. Just as a stick can have the property of 'looking

> If you study A2 Unit 4.2 *Descartes' Meditations,* you'll find he has a famous argument about wax that supports this distinction.

> *Essay on Human Understanding,* I. viii. 10

> **?**
> How does this definition differ from the one first suggested (p. 204)?

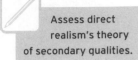

Assess direct realism's theory of secondary qualities.

bent' under certain conditions, it can have the property of 'looking brown'. In fact, direct realists argue, to *be* brown is to look brown to normal perceivers under normal conditions. So secondary qualities are no less real, no less part of the external world, than primary qualities; it is just that they are a different *type* of property, one defined in terms of how we perceive the world.

A further objection: perceptual variation

But some philosophers, following an argument in Plato's *Theaetetus*, have argued that there is another contrast we can draw between primary and secondary qualities, which supports the view that secondary qualities exist in the mind. Plato argues that 'heat' *isn't* a real property of an object, since what is hot to one person is not to another. By contrast, we might think that 'being two feet long' *is* a property of an object, since this doesn't vary from one person to another. Locke also gives this argument, undermining his own 'official' theory. Likewise, some philosophers, including Bishop Berkeley in his *Principles of Knowledge*, claim that secondary qualities vary from person to person. For example, the sea may look blue to me and green to you; an apple might taste sweet to me and sour to you. But the sea can't be both blue and green; an apple can't be both sweet and sour. So we shouldn't say that secondary qualities are properties *of the object*. What shade of colour is *it* – how you see it or how I see it? Secondary qualities, they conclude, only *exist* in the mind of the perceiver, whereas primary qualities exist independently of the perceiver. Primary qualities are objective, but secondary qualities are subjective. It must be, then, that we don't perceive the object directly, that some of the properties we perceive are actually properties of the sensations that occur in each of our minds.

Direct realists could insist that whether the sea is blue or green depends on whether it looks blue or green to normal perceivers under normal conditions. But in this example, it is hard, perhaps impossible, to say who and what conditions will count as 'normal'. And in the case of the apple, taste in general seems to differ from one person to another. Direct realists could say that the taste is still a power in the object to create experiences, but that this power creates different experiences in each of us. So the apple is sweet-to-me and sour-to-you; the apple *really is* both of these – so we both perceive the apple when we taste it, not sense-data.

Is this answer persuasive? Is it simpler to say we don't perceive the object as *it* is, that is, we don't perceive the object directly, but in virtue of sense-data?

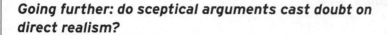

Going further: do sceptical arguments cast doubt on direct realism?

The two arguments we looked at earlier – from size/distance and from illusion – and the argument from perceptual variation we just looked at, can all be considered 'sceptical' arguments.

Scepticism can pose a challenge to realism in general, that is, to the claim that we can know there are physical objects existing independently of our minds. In the two examples we looked at, people can easily make mistakes, thinking something is small and close when it is distant and large; or not realising that they are seeing an illusion and, worse yet, a hallucination. The sceptic asks how we can tell we are not making such a mistake right now. If a hallucination *looks* just the same as seeing something veridically, how can we tell the difference? If we can't tell the difference, how do we know that we are seeing veridically? If I don't know I'm seeing a table, rather than experiencing a hallucination, then surely I don't know that *there is* a table in front of me.

This isn't a problem just for direct realism, but for all theories of perception (even idealism!). But some theories might give better answers than others. We can note that the direct realist can say that even if it is true that we can't tell the difference subjectively between veridical perception and hallucination, they are completely different mental states. Veridical perception can give us knowledge because in it, we are 'hooked up' to the world.

Scepticism can challenge direct realism more specifically, though. Direct realism tends to think of physical objects having the properties, including secondary qualities, we perceive them having. So I might say that I know the apple is sour. But the argument from perceptual variation challenges the certainty of my claims about taste (or any other secondary quality). Is 'the apple is sour' something I can *know* if people's sense of taste differs? If perceptual variation doesn't show that direct realism is false, then perhaps it at least shows that we can't have knowledge about secondary qualities.

In response, direct realism can appeal to 'normal conditions' again. Under normal conditions, if we are normal observers, yes, we disagree, but within a small range of variation. So I can confidently say, and know, that my shirt is blue, even if I can't know as certainly that it is cyan rather than aquamarine.

Arguments or views are 'sceptical' if they seek to challenge what we (think we) can know. Scepticism is discussed in detail in A2 Unit 3.3 Epistemology and Metaphysics.

To say any more, we would need to discuss how sceptical challenges can be replied to, which isn't covered until A2.

Key points • • •

- All direct realists claim that, *when we perceive the world veridically*, we perceive the world directly, not via sense-data.
- Disjunctivists claim that in illusions and hallucinations we do perceive sense-data, but argue that we cannot generalise from these cases to veridical perception.
- Other direct realists argue that in illusion, nothing *is* the way it looks to you. Rather, the physical object has the property of *looking* a certain way. Cases of hallucination are more difficult. They still argue that *nothing* is the way it looks, for example, nothing *is* white when you hallucinate a unicorn, just as nothing *is* a unicorn when you think of a unicorn. You simply have the visual experience of white.
- Direct realism argues that secondary qualities do not 'exist in the mind', but are properties that physical objects have, viz. the power to cause certain perceptual experiences. To be red is to look red to normal perceivers in normal light.
- But then how do we explain that different people have different perceptual experiences? Must we say that the apple has two properties, 'sour-to-you' and 'sweet-to-me'? But we can object that these are subjective properties of the experience, not properties in the object.
- Scepticism raises the question of how we can know there are physical objects at all; but this is a challenge to all theories of perception.

II. Representative realism

Do sceptical arguments establish sense-data?

Perceptual variation

The argument from perceptual variation, presented as an objection to direct realism, is equally an argument in favour of representative realism. We perceive (at least) secondary qualities, such as colour, temperature and taste differently. The air can feel warm to me, but cool to you. This can be explained if these qualities are not part of the objects we perceive, but part of our perceptions of them. The air 'itself' is neither warm nor cool (though its heat can be measured physically in calories), but only feels warm or cool. So how we perceive the air is not how it is itself. How warm it feels is part of our representation of the air. So we must perceive the air via sense-data, and secondary qualities are aspects of sense-data.

In fact, you can run the argument from perceptual variation with primary qualities as well. If you look at a circle straight on, it looks circular. But if I'm looking at it from an angle, it looks elliptical. We see it differently, but it doesn't change. So we must perceive it via sense-data; your sense-data look circular, mine look elliptical. As we saw in COULD WE KNOW OF A RELATION BETWEEN SENSE-DATA AND PHYSICAL OBJECTS? (p. 207), this causes trouble for representative realism: how do we know what the world beyond our experience is really like? The argument from perceptual variation begins by supporting representative realism, but turns into an objection to it.

> Assess the implications of the argument from perceptual variation for realist theories of perception.

Secondary qualities: the argument from science

The objection to direct realism from secondary qualities is also an argument in favour of representative realism. The difference between how we experience the world – coloured, smelly and so on – and how science says the world is – particles in motion – this difference, representative realism argues, shows that we do not experience physical objects directly, but via sense-data. If we experienced the world directly, then we would experience physical objects the way that science describes them.

We have seen one response from direct realism above (p. 219). A complementary objection to this argument from secondary qualities is this: the argument seems to be that physical objects don't have the properties (secondary qualities) we experience them to have. So what we experience (directly) can't be physical objects, but must be sense data. But this is a confusion. Is representative realism suggesting that physical objects aren't 'really' coloured? Or don't 'really' have a smell? This misinterprets what it means to say that something is coloured or smells. To say that the table is brown is *not* to say that it must be composed of microscopic particles which are also brown. It is to say that the table looks brown to normal observers under normal conditions. The sub-atomic particles that make up a table don't have to be brown for the table to be brown!

So, the representative realist suggests that because there is a difference between how science describes physical objects and how we experience them this shows that we don't experience physical objects directly. The direct realist

> If the representative realist says that physical objects aren't really coloured, then it seems that *sense-data must be*. But does it make sense to say that sense-data – which are a kind of idea – literally have colour? Or smell? We will return to this below.

says this doesn't follow: science explains *what it is* for physical objects to have the properties we perceive them to have; it doesn't mean that they don't have these properties. But to this, the representative realist can reply that what science explains is what it is *for us to perceive* these properties; and the explanation – that these perceptions are caused by 'particles in motion' – shows that the properties are part of our perceptual experiences, part of the mind, not part of the object.

Time lag

A different argument from science relates to time lags. It takes time for light waves, or sound waves, or smells, to get from physical objects to our sense organs. For example, it takes 8 minutes for light from the sun to reach the Earth. If you look at the sun (not a good idea unless it's an eclipse!), you are actually seeing it as it was 8 minutes ago. For example, if it blew up, you would see it normally for 8 minutes after it had blown up – it wouldn't even exist anymore, and you'd still see it! Therefore, we could argue, you aren't seeing it directly.

Does this show, however, that what you perceive is actually sense-data? It's hard to see why. The 'image' you see of the sun is *physical*, that is, carried in light waves. The light waves exist during those 8 minutes – it is not as though the light from the sun immediately causes sense-data, but your sense-data are delayed by 8 minutes! So *if* you see the sun indirectly, then it is because you see light waves directly.

This isn't the conclusion representative realism was after. The argument from time lags seems to show that we perceive the physical medium by which we detect physical objects (light waves, sound waves, chemicals for smell and taste), not that we perceive sense-data. However, it does suggest that we don't perceive *physical objects* directly.

But, direct realism can reply, this is a confusion. What science tells us here is *how* we perceive (we perceive visually by detecting light waves, we perceive aurally by detecting sound waves and so on). It doesn't tell us *what* we perceive. Compare these two pairs of questions: 1. 'Can you see table?' and 'Can you see the light reflecting from the table?'; 2. 'Can you see the lake?' and 'Can you see the light reflecting off the lake?'.

In (1) there is no difference in *what* one is supposed to see. To 'see' the light the table reflects is just to see the table. In fact, you cannot *see* the light itself; only the table. To see light, rather than to see by means of light, requires special conditions. (2) picks these out; you turn your attention to something different in response to the two questions. So, direct realism can argue, we don't perceive light waves directly and physical objects indirectly. Light waves are part of the story of how we see physical objects.

But surely the time lag means we see the physical object as it was a moment before, not as it is now. This means that if we see it, we see it in the past – so we see into the past?! Well, perhaps so. We always experience the world as it was a moment ago. A strange, but not impossible, conclusion.

> Assess whether arguments from the science of perception support any particular philosophical theory of perception.

Going further: sense-data are impossible

When we try to get clear on exactly what sense-data are, and what properties they are said to have, the concept can become more confused instead of less. Locke seems to claim that sense-data have the very properties that the objects they represent do. So a sense-datum of a yellow square is itself square and yellow. The object 'in itself' is square, so the sense-datum and the object resemble each other; but the object 'in itself' isn't yellow, so the sense-datum doesn't resemble it. But how can sense-data be *literally* square or yellow? A sense-datum isn't in space, it doesn't take up space, so how can it be square? And how can something mental actually *be* yellow? Ideas and experiences can't really be coloured. As mental things, sense-data can't resemble what the physical objects represent at all.

This is a very strong objection to the argument that representative realism used to argue for the existence of sense-data. If the rose looks grey, it said, there must be something that *is* grey. But, the objection claims, how can anything mental actually *be* grey? Certainly, something is *represented as* looking grey. But that 'something' that is represented as grey is *the rose* itself.

Representative realists point out a difficulty with this objection. If the rose isn't grey, and there is no sense-datum which is grey, how is it possible that I *see* a (rose-shaped) patch of grey? Surely it is true that if I see grey, then something must be grey. If it isn't the rose, then it *must* be something mental.

There is a second objection that sense-data just don't make sense. Sense-data are said to be exactly how they seem; they are appearances. So it seems that my sense-data can't have properties that I am not aware of. But consider looking at a scattered pile of matches on the table, I don't know how many. How many matches are there in my sense-datum? Is it the same number as on the table? But then why don't I know how many matches there are if my sense-data are exactly as they appear? Alternatively, since I don't know how many matches there are, we could say that there are an 'indeterminate' number of matches in my sense-datum. But how can we say there are a number of matches in my sense-datum, but that that number is not 52 or 54 or 49; it is an 'indeterminate number'? There is no such number as an 'indeterminate number'!

> Explain the argument that sense-data cannot exist.

Could we know of a relation between sense-data and physical objects? II

As we have seen, many representative realists claim that secondary qualities are subjective, and only primary qualities are real. But Berkeley argued that we cannot form a conception of a physical object that has primary properties alone. For example, we can't conceive of something as merely having size and shape, it must have colour as well (try imagining a shape of no colour). However, Locke agrees that we can't conceive of something as merely having size and shape. But rather than colour, Locke argues the other property we need is solidity, which is a primary property. We can have a coherent conception of something as simply extended and solid without having any further secondary qualities. Colour is not necessary – just ask any blind person!

Hume, meanwhile, says that while everyone accepts that secondary qualities do not properly belong to physical objects, but are 'in the mind', we have no reason to suppose that the same is not true of primary qualities. These are equally derived from our senses, and all that we are given in experience is the sense-data themselves. Perhaps nothing in the object resembles squareness, just as nothing resembles redness. Perhaps our experiences of both are caused by something quite different. Going just on sense-data, how could we know? As Berkeley argued (p. 208), you can't know that two things resemble each other unless you can compare them, and we can't compare sense-data and physical objects.

Representative realists respond to both these objections, that we can't know what physical objects are like or whether they exist, by saying they misunderstand sense-data. The objections wrongly assume sense-data 'come between' us and the world. In fact, we perceive the *world via* sense-data, which are the 'medium' by which we perceive the world. Sense-data don't get in the way of perceiving the world. They are *how* we perceive the world. They don't block our access to the world, they mediate it. The world is still what we perceive; and so it is not a hypothesis.

But what of the fact that sense-data differ from the physical objects they represent (think of the bent stick again)? Doesn't this show that sense-data come between us and the world? No, replies representative realism; this is all explicable in terms of physical objects, and their effects on us, and *only* in these terms. In other words, in order to properly explain illusions, secondary qualities, perceptual variation, and all the rest, we need *both* sense-data and physical objects.

> Compare: we describe the world using words. But words don't get in the way of describing the world. We couldn't describe the world without them!

> Assess representative realism.

Key points • • •

- Representative realists often argue that the world has only primary qualities 'in itself', but we perceive it as having secondary qualities. This is another way in which what we perceive is different from how the world is 'in itself'. So we perceive the world indirectly.
- Another argument is that what we perceive is no longer how the world is, because it takes time for us to perceive physical objects. However, this does not show that we perceive (mental) sense-data instead.
- Two objections claim that sense-data can't exist. First, as mental objects, they can't have colour, size or other properties that we think physical objects have. Second, they seem to be indeterminate – but nothing that exists can be literally indeterminate.
- Berkeley objects that the idea of a world with just primary qualities makes no sense, for example, something that has size and shape must also have colour (a secondary quality). Locke argues that something that has size and shape must also have solidity, a primary quality, so a world of just primary qualities does make sense.
- To the objection that if all we perceive are sense-data, we cannot know about the physical world, representative realists reply that this wrongly assumes we *don't* perceive the world, only sense-data. But the theory claims we *do* perceive the world, only indirectly.

III. Idealism

A third good reason for idealism: substance

In our earlier discussion, we identified two good reasons for idealism (p. 211). The second argued that experience gives us no idea of 'substance' – we experience only primary and secondary properties. But we need the idea of substance to argue that physical objects are independent of minds. Locke argued that primary and secondary properties belonged to the physical object; the properties are 'held together' or 'united' by its substance – matter. We need the concept to account for properties being held together to make 'one' thing (a chair, a dog, etc.). And we need it to claim that physical objects can exist unperceived – a substance is, by definition, something that does not depend on something else to exist. It is because physical objects have substance that they can exist unperceived. But what is substance (what is matter?) apart from its properties? Once you list all the properties of a table, what is left which is the 'substance' of the table? Locke saw the point, and accepted that substance was unknowable. So a realist view of physical objects involves a mystery.

Berkeley's idealism solves the need for talking about the substance of physical objects: they are nothing more than the ideas we perceive, existing together as a bundle. He objected that we didn't really know what we were talking about, or even if we were talking sense, in talking about substance. He has argued that what we experience when we experience qualities – primary or secondary – are ideas; and ideas only exist in the mind. It doesn't make sense to say a pain exists unless someone feels, or that a colour exists unless someone sees it. Nor does it make sense to say a shape exists unless someone sees or feels it. What is the shape 'square' except what we see or feel? We can only make sense of it as our experience of square.

Locke and other realists can respond that primary qualities are not dependent upon being perceived, and in this way, we can make sense of physical objects existing unperceived. The table is still 1.5m long, even when no one is looking. (If direct realists are right, then it is also brown when no one is looking; Locke might be more inclined to say that they still reflect wavelengths of light when no one is looking.)

But this, to Berkeley, makes no sense. Locke argues that the squareness of a physical object (unlike what makes it look red) *resembles* what we see. But nothing resembles an idea, says Berkeley, except another idea. What do we mean when we say that the shape of the table 'resembles' the shape we see?

How can squareness resemble the idea of squareness? The *only* idea of shape we have is the one we see (or feel). So, he concludes, it makes no sense to say that primary qualities – any more than pain or colour – exist in physical objects when they are not being perceived.

If this is right, then when substance exists unperceived, it exists without any qualities at all. And this, Berkeley says, is quite literally inconceivable. While realism is tied to saying that substance exists, idealism gets rid of it.

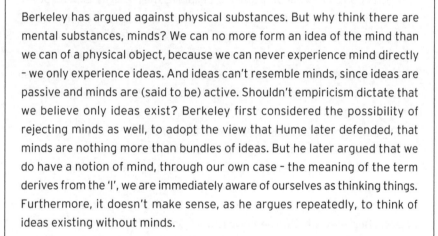

Analyse and explain Berkeley's argument against physical substance.

Going further: do minds exist?

Berkeley has argued against physical substances. But why think there are mental substances, minds? We can no more form an idea of the mind than we can of a physical object, because we can never experience mind directly – we only experience ideas. And ideas can't resemble minds, since ideas are passive and minds are (said to be) active. Shouldn't empiricism dictate that we believe only ideas exist? Berkeley first considered the possibility of rejecting minds as well, to adopt the view that Hume later defended, that minds are nothing more than bundles of ideas. But he later argued that we do have a notion of mind, through our own case - the meaning of the term derives from the 'I', we are immediately aware of ourselves as thinking things. Furthermore, it doesn't make sense, as he argues repeatedly, to think of ideas existing without minds.

Difficulties with idealism II

Illusions

Berkeley has argued that we can tell the difference between imagination and perception by voluntariness and regularity (p. 212). But what about misperceptions and illusions? Misperceptions are no more voluntary than perceptions, and can be perfectly regular and natural: a stick looks bent half-submerged in water, red looks grey under yellow light and so on. Is the stick both bent and not bent? Berkeley's response is that we aren't misperceiving – the stick is bent when half-submerged. However, this is misleading if we infer that the stick would be bent

Compare and contrast the idealist and the direct realist explanations of illusions.

when pulled out of the water. So we shouldn't *say* 'the stick is bent', since this means it would remain so under normal conditions; the intuitive thing to say is that 'the stick looks bent' – and this is correct, it does look bent.

Going further: simplicity again

We have seen how Berkeley's position can be *consistent*, but we may still not think that his position is really *plausible*. The hypothesis that there are physical objects that are independent of our minds seems *simpler* than the claim that God causes our perceptions. It explains the passivity of perception, the distinction between an idea in my mind and what is real, the nature of illusions and mistakes, the continued existence of physical objects when we aren't perceiving them, all very well. And we can challenge Berkeley's claim that empiricism leads to idealism: arguably, we *do* experience physical objects – either directly or via representations – but we certainly have *no* sensory experience of God.

To press the point, think about scientific investigation of physical objects. For instance, when we open up the body of an animal, we discover – we see for the first time – its heart, lungs, stomach and so on. Did they not exist before we saw them? If they didn't, how did the animal pump blood, breathe or digest food?! But if they did exist, is that because God perceived them? No, says Berkeley: what we perceive is what God *wills* us to perceive (p. 214).

Furthermore, Berkeley says that ideas can't cause anything – and the heart, lungs, stomach are collections of ideas. If physical objects are ideas, and ideas don't cause anything, then physical objects don't cause anything. So the animal's organs don't *cause* it to stay alive. Instead, Berkeley says, it is only minds that cause things – so *everything* in the natural world is actually caused by God. Of course, we can *say* that the heart pumps blood or the stomach digests food – but it is not strictly true. We should 'think with the learned, and speak with the vulgar'. Science therefore doesn't discover causal relations; it only discovers *regularities*, such as – if you open up an animal, you will discover its organs; an animal whose organs don't work dies; and so on.

Again, we can object that this shows that idealism is a much more complicated account of perception than realism.

Critically discuss the objection that idealism cannot explain experience as well as realism.

A confusion about 'ideas'

It can be easy to think that idealism entails that physical objects are completely *subjective*, that is, that they depend on our perceiving them to exist at all. After all, if they are ideas, and ideas don't exist except in minds, then physical objects must depend on our minds to exist. But this doesn't follow: Berkeley is a 'realist' *about ideas* of physical objects, in this sense: the ideas that make up physical objects are independent of our minds – we can't imagine up a physical object or change its properties by will (see DIFFICULTIES WITH IDEALISM, p. 212). So although they are composed of ideas, they are just as independent of our minds as if they were mind-independent in the way that direct and representative realists say they are. Yet, as ideas, they depend on a mind. But it is not our minds they depend on, it is God's.

But can Berkeley make this reply? A final objection to Berkeley's idealism is that it is confused in its use of 'ideas', at least when it comes to saying whether something is the 'same' idea or not. The objection goes like this:

1. Ideas exist in the mind.
2. So when I perceive the table, the ideas I perceive (which comprise the table) exist in my mind. They are, after all, *my* perceptions.
3. But that means the table I perceive must exist in *my* mind.
4. You cannot experience my ideas. So you cannot see the very same table I see.
5. At best, you will experience a similar table, perhaps even an exact twin. While you might see something *qualitatively* identical, you won't see the *numerically* identical table.

> Explain and illustrate the distinction between numerical and qualitative identity.

Berkeley replies that we see the same table in the sense of 'exactly resembling'. We might say, likewise, that if you and I both think of ice cream, we have the same idea. But, of course, there are two ideas in this case – one that exists in your mind, and one that exists in my mind. 'The same idea' is used ambiguously (with more than one meaning), because we can count ideas by their content ('table', 'ice cream') or we can count them by whose idea it is (your thought of ice cream, my thought of ice cream).

But this reply runs counter to common sense. Surely you and I can look at the same (numerically the same) table. Realism, of course, says we can; the table is a physical object, publicly accessible and independent of either of our minds.

Berkeley then has a further, two-part response. First, representative realism faces the same problem – you experience your sense-data of the table, I experience mine, so we don't experience the same thing. But representative realism can say that we do, viz. we both experience one and the same table via our different sense-data. But then Berkeley says, he can say the same regarding the idea of the table in *God's* mind; we both experience the table that is in or caused by God's mind.

However, this causes a further problem: how can the ideas that I perceive when I perceive the table exist *both* in God's mind and in mine? They must exist in mine because *I* am perceiving them. So all we can say is that my ideas *resemble* God's. But, in fact, we saw the problem that ideas of physical objects don't exist in God's mind in anything like the way they exist in mine. The solution was that God wills me to experience the ideas of the table. But then if God wills you to experience them as well, once again, we don't perceive the *very same* table (set of ideas), but each perceive the set of ideas God wills us to perceive.

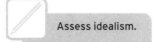

Assess idealism.

Key points • • •

- The idea of mind-independent objects doesn't make sense: if we argue that physical objects are substances, we have no conception of this independent of its properties.
- Since physical objects, being ideas, don't cause perceptions, Berkeley argues that God does.
- Regular illusions are part of the order of nature, but to mark the fact that the perception is not 'normal', we say that what we see 'looks' a certain way rather than 'is' a certain way.
- We can object that idealism is over-complicated. It has to posit the existence of God, of which we have no sensory experience. It has to reinterpret what happens when we first see the 'inside' of a physical object, and reject the view that physical objects can have effects.
- Idealism is unclear on the identity of 'ideas'. When we perceive the 'same' physical object, do we perceive one and the same idea or just exactly similar ones? Is the idea we perceive one and the same as the idea in the mind of God?

SUMMARY

In this chapter, we have considered three theories of how we know about the external world of physical objects:

1. Direct realism: we directly perceive physical objects, which exist independently of the mind.

2. Representative realism: we perceive physical objects, which exist independently of the mind, indirectly via sense-data.

3. Idealism: we directly perceive 'physical objects', but these do not exist independently of the mind – they are collections of ideas.

In our discussion and evaluation of these theories, we have looked at the following issues:

1. Do physical objects have the properties we perceive them to have?

2. What do we perceive in an illusion or hallucination?

3. What are primary and secondary qualities? Is there a valid distinction between them? Do secondary qualities exist 'in the mind' while primary qualities exist 'in the object'?

4. How do we explain variations between what people perceive?

5. Do the arguments from illusion, secondary qualities, or perceptual variation support the existence of sense-data?

6. Do scientific theories of perception provide support for any particular philosophical theory of perception?

7. Can we coherently describe our perceptual experiences without presupposing the existence of physical objects?

8. Is the concept of sense-data coherent?

9. If we perceive only sense-data directly, can we know anything about physical objects? How do sense-data relate us to physical objects?

10. Can we form a coherent idea of physical objects existing independently of the mind? Do we have any experience that supports this idea?

11. Do physical objects cease to exist when unperceived?

12. Can idealism satisfactorily distinguish between ideas that form 'reality' (physical objects) and subjective ideas?

13. Is realism or idealism a better (simpler) explanation of perceptual experience?

7

UNIT 2 AN INTRODUCTION TO PHILOSOPHY 2

Section 2: Tolerance

In this chapter, we discuss a number of issues about tolerance, including what tolerance is and how it relates to liberalism and pluralism; what arguments support tolerance, and whether a tolerant society is a good thing; what it takes to be a tolerant individual and whether tolerant people must be liberals; whether a liberal society can tolerate an illiberal or intolerant culture; and whether tolerance should be extended to minority religions, lifestyles and cultural practices. By the end of the chapter, you should be able to analyse and evaluate a number of arguments related to each issue.

SYLLABUS CHECKLIST ✔

The AQA AS syllabus for this chapter is:

The tolerant society

✔ Tolerance and the ideal of a liberal democracy: tolerance as the virtue of a pluralist democracy. Whether tolerant societies should be neutral with regard to conceptions of the good life; whether a culture which encourages tolerance, civility and respect for others should be nurtured.

✔ Arguments for tolerance: fallibility; the fact that coercion is ineffective; the threat posed by strife; the value of autonomy; the value of diversity.

The tolerant individual

✔ What characteristics do tolerant individuals possess? Is individual rationality and autonomy the basis for tolerance or is cultural membership the basis of rational and autonomous choice?

✔ Does tolerance merely imply that we leave other individuals alone to think and do as they please or does it also require us to do or say nothing to offend others?

Tensions and applications

✔ Should a liberal society tolerate a minority culture that doesn't respect its values? Could a liberal society nourish a particular culture and make judgements about the relative worth of diverse lifestyles without becoming intolerant? Does tolerance foster critical faculties and new ideas or does it create false needs and 'repressive desublimation'?

✔ Tolerance and religion: should we tolerate the beliefs, practices, lifestyle and laws of religious minorities? Tolerance and social difference: should we tolerate unpopular lifestyles and cultural expressions?

INTRODUCTION

What is tolerance?

This introductory section aims to provide a working understanding of the concept of tolerance with which we can then tackle the issues raised in the syllabus.

Weak and strong senses of 'tolerance'

Let us start with an obvious point – that tolerance requires difference. We can only tolerate practices, or values, or beliefs of other people when these differ from our own. It doesn't make sense to talk of 'tolerating' what we agree with. In everyday language, we say someone is tolerant if they are happy to let other people live as they choose – 'live and let live'. But we can respond to what is different in a variety of ways.

1. Someone can *not care* how other people live – this doesn't sound like tolerance; or
2. they can *not object* to how other people live – this is a weak sense of 'tolerance'; it is weak because if they don't mind, how are they 'being tolerant'?; or
3. in a stronger sense of 'tolerance', the fact that the other person's view is different *matters* to them – because their own views, for example, in religion or morality, matter to them.

In the strong sense of tolerance, we only tolerate what is different and important to us. Take the example of vegetarians who disapprove of eating meat. They oppose meat-eating. Vegetarians who don't try to rid the world of meat-eaters tolerate the practice of eating meat. But meat-eaters for whom eating meat is not a moral issue, who aren't *opposed* to vegetarianism (though they don't want it imposed on them), *don't tolerate* vegetarians. They simply don't mind them.

To *tolerate* is not, for instance, to welcome or embrace; it suggests that what is tolerated is problematic somehow. If the difference of view does matter, a person stands in opposition to the different practice or value. This opposition may mean we want to suppress it, but toleration means that we do not try to do so. From now on, we shall talk of tolerance meaning 'in the strong sense'.

> Throughout this chapter, I shall talk of tolerating 'views'. By this, I will mean beliefs, values and practices.

> We will discuss this further in WHAT CHARACTERISTICS DO TOLERANT INDIVIDUALS POSSESS? II (p. 261).

> Explain and illustrate the difference between the weak and strong senses of tolerance.

Opposition

If tolerance involves opposition, what kind of opposition? Is mere dislike enough? Suppose I dislike instant coffee, and would like it to be banned to stop people offering it to me; am I being tolerant by not lobbying for it to be banned? This seems to trivialise the idea of tolerance. But, on the other hand, suppose how your friend dresses annoys or embarrasses you, but you remain good friends and don't try to change them – is this tolerance?

If tolerance is just about dislike, then a racist who simply doesn't like people of other colours, but who doesn't act on his racism, is tolerant. This doesn't sound right; isn't a tolerant person *not* a racist in the first place? The racist sounds more self-controlled than tolerant. Is this true of the embarassed friend as well?

Perhaps tolerance depends not on mere dislike, but disapproval. What we merely like and dislike we take to be a question of taste, something which can quite legitimately differ from one person to another, and which we can't support by giving objective reasons and arguments. If I like turnips and you don't, neither of us is *wrong* about whether turnips taste nice. But disapproval is, or should be, based on reasons. Disapproval is based on thinking that one's view is *justified*, while the different view is not; it is not simply a question of taste. This explains the way differences of view *matter* to us.

> Explain and illustrate the difference between dislike and disapproval.

The value of tolerance

So tolerance is a matter of refraining from acting on one's disapproval of another practice or value. Why should we think tolerance is a good thing? What is wrong, we might think, should not be tolerated; we don't tolerate murder or theft. Yet we take tolerance to have a positive moral or political value.

So we should say that tolerance requires more than mere self-restraint in the face of one's disapproval. Tolerance must be based on reasons of morality or politics to be tolerance.

> We will look at these reasons in ARGUMENTS FOR TOLERANCE (pp. 242f. and 251f.).

Two final points

In concluding our analysis, we should make explicit two further conditions that have been implicit in the discussion. Because tolerance involves restraint, the person must take themselves to be able to *do* something about the practices or values they oppose. In other words, they must have some *power*; we cannot tolerate that which we cannot influence – we can only resign ourselves to it. Second, and obviously, in tolerance, a person refrains from exercising this power.

> What is tolerance? What issues does an attempt to define tolerance raise?

Key points • • •

- Tolerance in the weak sense is not minding different beliefs, values and practices. Tolerance in the strong sense involves opposing such different views.

- The opposition involved in tolerance is (usually) disapproval, not mere dislike.
- Tolerance is not acting on one's opposition to another belief, value or practice, even though one has some power to influence or suppress it, because one believes there is some political or moral reason for restraint.

I. The tolerant society

Tolerance and the ideal of a liberal democracy

Liberal democracy

Liberalism is the political view that claims liberty is the central, most important political value. In the history of ideas, liberals have argued that human beings are 'naturally' free, and so any restraint on their liberty needs to be justified. That means that the state – with its powers to pass and enforce laws that limit liberty – needs to be justified. Most liberals also argue that while some restrictions on liberty can be justified, *extensive* restrictions cannot. A liberal society, then, is one in which citizens have a large degree of individual liberty.

As discussed in Unit 1.2 WHY SHOULD I BE GOVERNED? (pp. 53f. and 75f.), the most common answer – certainly the most common liberal answer – to how to justify the state is some form of democracy. The theory is that through democracy we can be governed but also be free – because we have consented to being governed (or if 'consent' is too strong, at least, we have some say in the matter).

But a liberal will not be happy with *any* form of democracy. Democracies can pass laws that restrict individual liberty when they should not. A *liberal* democracy recognises the individual's right to liberty, and other rights that are based on the importance of liberty. These rights – whether enshrined in a constitution or just in the political culture – restrict what laws the government can pass.

A very influential argument for liberalism comes from J.S. Mill. He argues that 'the dealings of society with the individual' should be regulated by 'one simple principle', known as the Liberty or Harm Principle: 'The only purpose for which power can be rightfully exercised over any member of a civilized community, against his will, is to prevent harm to others . . . Over himself, over his own body and mind, the individual is sovereign.'

Mill thinks liberty should be very extensive, as extensive as possible, without giving us the freedom to harm other people. Mill wants to protect individual freedom in three key areas:

> What is the relation between democracy and liberalism?

> *On Liberty*, studied in A2 Unit 4.2.

> *On Liberty*, pp. 68-9.

> How does Mill's Harm Principle protect individual liberty?

Mill's work marks the beginning of the modern idea of toleration. Before Mill, discussion of toleration was limited to whether *religious* differences should be tolerated or not.

1. Freedom of thought, which covers *all* areas of belief – factual, religious, moral, and so on.
2. Freedom in how we live our lives.
3. Freedom to unite with others for any purpose to which we agree.

THE TYRANNY OF THE MAJORITY

In the days of monarchy, there was a threat of tyranny from the monarch. Many people felt that threat diminished with democracy. Democracy is rule of the people by the people; and the rulers express the will of the people.

But Mill remained concerned. 'The people' who rule are not the same 'people' who are ruled, even when the rulers express the will of 'the people', because within any society, there will be majorities and minorities. The rulers express the will of the majority, not the will of all people within society. We need to protect the minority from a 'tyranny of the majority'.

The majority might exercise power over individuals through the processes of democratic government, that is, eventually through the *physical* enforcement of laws by the police. A democratic government could pass a law forbidding people to practice a particular form of religious belief, if that is what the majority of people in society wanted. A different example: homosexual practices (at least between men) was a criminal offence in the UK until 1967. And it was not until 2003, that the US Supreme Court ruled that individual states could not criminalise homosexual practices.

Explain how 'tyranny' is still possible in a democracy.

On Liberty, p. 63

The majority also has a tendency to impose its ideas and practices ('what we do/think around here') as rules of conduct on everyone, so that people who don't abide by them suffer social consequences. This can be worse than political oppression, says Mill, because 'it leaves fewer means of escape, penetrating much more deeply into the details of life, and enslaving the soul itself'. It is a kind of *psychological* coercion.

Think of the disapproval of other religious practices, of other cultures' traditions, of homosexuality, even though they are legal. Think how such attitudes are communicated in the press. These feelings of approval and disapproval, when they become 'public opinion', affect how people think and what they do; they are not free to think, feel and experiment with life as they please, knowing it will incur the disapproval of others.

Explain and illustrate the two forms of tyranny of the majority.

A liberal democracy, for Mill, is more than a democracy; it is a democracy in which individual freedoms are protected against legislation and social opinion.

The place of tolerance

Upholding individual liberty is going to require tolerance, that is, it is going to require refraining – both in legislation and in the way social opinion is formed and expressed – from acting on opposition to the views of others in such a way that would suppress or interfere with those views. In particular, it will involve tolerance of the majority, which has the social and political power to act on this opposition.

Because liberalism extends liberty very widely, then tolerance will also need to extend widely. This is a trait of liberalism: it aims to tolerate as much as possible. Mill says that we may 'argue, entreat, remonstrate' with other people; but we are not to exercise power over them in our opposition to their views.

> Explain why tolerance is important to a liberal democracy.

Tolerance as the virtue of a pluralist democracy

A pluralist society is one in which there are different views on questions of politics, morality, religion and what it is to lead a good and meaningful life. Many liberal philosophers argue that disagreements, opposition, and conflicts of ideas and practices are an *inevitable and permanent* part of human society. Even if one tries to get rid of them by force, in the use of that force, there is still a conflict. While many conflicts can be resolved by political means, conflicts about what to think, how to live, how society is best organised, or how to achieve salvation, cannot.

We can respond to pluralism by trying to force everyone to agree with us – either by changing people's minds, or simply by killing or forcing out of the country those who disagree. Historically, this has been a common response. The thought that everyone must become a Christian or a Muslim or a communist, or at least, must lead a life that is in accordance with the rules and values of Christianity, Islam, or communism, has inspired a great deal of political and social conflict.

If pluralism is permanent, the only alternative to force is tolerance. If we are not to act to suppress or interfere with those practices and values with which we disagree, we must tolerate them. Of course, as Mill notes, we can still try to persuade other people of our point of view. But either we use force or we do not. If we do not, then this is tolerance.

> Explain why pluralism requires tolerance.

So tolerance becomes the virtue that characterises a pluralist liberal democracy. Without it, such a society is not possible.

Arguments for tolerance

Tolerance has not universally been thought to be a good thing. Communists argued that it avoids real social change that will improve people's lives. Conservatives argued that it is morally spineless. Religious thinkers condemn it as leading to the damnation, since people need moral guidance.

These criticisms demonstrate one of the *paradoxes* of tolerance. If tolerance involves not acting on your opposition to a view you think is wrong, why should we be tolerant? Shouldn't we condemn what is wrong and seek to correct it? To solve the paradox, we need independent arguments that show how it can be right to tolerate what we think is wrong.

There are two others. One – the paradox of the tolerant racist – is discussed in WHAT CHARACTERISTICS DO TOLERANT INDIVIDUALS POSSESS? (p. 246f.); the other – the paradox of tolerating the intolerant – is discussed in LIBERALISM AND THE LIMITS OF TOLERANCE (p. 248f.).

The threat posed by strife

If disagreement and opposition are part of human life, then the only alternative to tolerance is conflict. This conflict won't be resolved – we cannot settle matters of belief and value by force. Such ongoing conflict or 'strife' threatens the survival of society.

To avoid strife, we need tolerance. We must find some way of agreeing to live with our differences. Liberalism, on this view, is a *modus vivendi* – a way of living, based on avoiding the very serious harms of conflict, fear and humiliation.

In THE STATE OF NATURE, Ch. 2, p. 68, we discuss two different responses to this threat – the absolutism of Hobbes and the liberalism of Locke.

We can object that this is not tolerance, but resignation. This is mistaken. If we are merely resigned, we think that, if only we *could* impose the right beliefs and values on others, things would be better. We think that liberalism is the second-best option really. Thinking like this fails to understand that even if one view comes to dominate, there will be people who suffer from its intolerance. Tolerance is not a fall-back virtue, the result of failing to achieve something ideal. Instead, *the ideal is dangerous*. Pluralism should be encouraged so that we avoid a totalitarian society that tries to control people's beliefs and values.

Outline and illustrate the argument from strife.

Fallibility

Someone who is fallible is someone who fails sometimes. We are all fallible, not just individuals, but also governments and societies. The argument from fallibility claims that we do not always know the truth about morality and religion, even when we think we do.

Mill gave a famous argument from fallibility in favour of freedom of speech. Since freedom of speech requires people to tolerate points of view they disagree with, we can use it as an argument for tolerance. His argument appeals to the value of truth, and he sums it up as follows:

First, if any opinion is compelled to silence, that opinion may, for aught we can certainly know, be true. To deny this is to assume our own infallibility.

Second, though the silenced opinion be an error, it may, and very commonly does, contain a portion of the truth; and since the general or prevailing opinion on any subject is rarely or never the whole truth, it is only by the collision of adverse opinions that the remainder of the truth has any chance of being supplied.

We must distinguish between certainty and truth. Confidence that our view is correct, and that some other view is mistaken, cannot justify suppressing the expression of that view, because we may be wrong. To allow the truth to be known, we must be tolerant.

But what about, for example, the belief that racism is wrong? Surely we may claim enough knowledge, and confidence in it, to justify censoring certain expressions of opinion. Why should we tolerate what we know is wrong?

Mill's response is that if we can have such certainty, this can only rest on the freedom of expression itself. To develop and defend our points of view, to correct our opinions and weigh their value, we need free discussion. And so we will need to tolerate the expression of differing beliefs and values.

We can, however, question Mill's assumption that freedom of speech will enable us to discover the truth better than (selective) censorship. Compare allowing racist speech to banning it. Which will lead to fewer people making the mistake of thinking racism is right? If we allow it, the emotional arguments appealing to vested interests ('they come over here, taking our jobs . . .') may persuade some people. If we ban it, then they won't hear these arguments, and so will be less likely to form a false belief. Or so we can argue. Mill assumes that people are rational; perhaps they aren't.

So if we don't tolerate certain beliefs and values, we are assuming infallibility – which could deprive people of the truth; if we do tolerate these beliefs and values, then we risk the truth being lost again. In this case, the argument from fallibility is not enough to give us a good reason to be tolerant.

We need to distinguish the argument for tolerance from fallibility from two closely related arguments: the argument from subjectivism (p. 251) and the argument from reasonable disagreement (p. 252).

On Liberty, pp. 115-16

Outline and discuss Mill's argument from fallibility.

'Autonomy' is from the Latin for self-rule: 'auto' means self and 'nomos' means rule or law.

On Liberty, p. 72

This is discussed in Ch. 5, THE CHARACTERISTICS ASSOCIATED WITH PERSONHOOD (p. 167) and ARE NON-HUMAN ANIMALS OR MACHINES PERSONS? (p. 185)

On Liberty, p. 120

This is discussed further in WHETHER A CULTURE WHICH ENCOURAGES TOLERANCE SHOULD BE NURTURED (p. 257).

Explain Mill's argument that autonomy is necessary for happiness.

The value of autonomy

AUTONOMY AND HAPPINESS

Autonomy is acting on 'rules' one gives oneself, as opposed to obeying other people's rules. Mill argues that '[t]he only freedom which deserves the name is that of pursuing our own good in our own way'. Because of its connection to liberty, autonomy is a core value for liberalism.

We can argue that it must also be a core value for any creature that is autonomous. To be autonomous is to be able to reflect on and evaluate one's desires, beliefs and values. We don't just act, we choose how to act, we choose which goals to adopt, and we reflect on the reasons for our beliefs. In these ways, we can shape ourselves and our lives; and if we shape ourselves according to our own values, we express our individuality.

Mill argues that 'the free development of individuality is one of the leading essentials of well-being'. Leading our own lives in our own way, making our own choices expresses and develops our thoughts, feelings and imagination – who we are as individuals. We will only get pleasure from this if we think, imagine and choose how to act for ourselves. So to be happy, we need to be autonomous.

If people are autonomous, they are going to express different beliefs and values. To enable this, we must be tolerant.

But does autonomy lead to happiness? We can argue that if people are left without any moral guidance, they will not be happy and they will make bad choices. Mill assumes that people learn from their own and others' mistakes, that autonomy contributes to happiness because people discover what really is good for them. But we can doubt this. People may not be equally capable of making good decisions. Those that aren't need firm social expectations to enable them to lead good lives.

AUTONOMY, EQUALITY AND RESPECT

Rather than see autonomy as valuable because it contributes to happiness, we can argue that it is valuable in its own right. It makes human life valuable. We can guide our lives according to what we value. Without autonomy, we cannot be praised or blamed – unless we choose what we do, we aren't responsible. So autonomy is a prerequisite for morality.

It may be true that some humans are better at making good choices than others. But we can argue that the *state* should treat people as equals, as autonomous equals. Even if this is a fiction, it is better than the state treating people as though they are not autonomous.

The value of autonomy requires that we respect the autonomy of other people. This requires that we respect their ability to make choices, adopt values and form beliefs. It does not require that we respect the actual choices, values and beliefs they have, but we do have to tolerate them as exercises of the person's autonomy. To be intolerant of others is not to respect their autonomy.

We can object that autonomy is only valuable if we use it to make *good* choices and adopt the *right* values. After all, suppose that someone can only choose between equally meaningless options. Where is the value in their having a choice at all? The value of having the power to shape oneself depends on the values one chooses to adopt. So if people choose the wrong values, does the fact that they make this choice on its own matter very much? If it doesn't, then to argue that we should be tolerant, we need to appeal not just to autonomy, but also to what people do with it.

> Assess the argument from autonomy.

Key points • • •

- Mill argued that a liberal democracy must avoid the tyranny of the majority in legislation and social opinion. Tolerance of different, especially minority, views is therefore an important part of liberalism.
- Many liberals argue that opposition between ideas and practices is inevitable and permanent. The only alternative to violent conflict in a pluralist society is tolerance.
- This forms the first argument for tolerance – that it is necessary to avoid strife. Any attempt to impose one view on everyone will lead to suffering and conflict.
- Mill argues that to suppress different views is to claim that we are infallible in knowing what is right; and only through a conflict of ideas can we discover what is true.
- Mill also argues that autonomy is necessary for happiness. Autonomy is needed for us to develop as individuals, and this self-expression is central to happiness. We can object that people need moral guidance, and autonomy will lead to unhappiness and bad choices.
- Even if it leads to some unhappiness, autonomy is valuable in its own right and so must be respected. This means being tolerant of the views of others, as these views are exercises of their autonomy. We can object that autonomy is only valuable if it leads to good choices.

II. The tolerant individual

What characteristics do tolerant individuals possess?

We concluded the discussion WHAT IS TOLERANCE? (p. 238) by saying tolerance (in the strong sense) involves not acting on one's disapproval of a practice or value that one opposes. This definition still allows that racists can be tolerant. Racists have offered arguments for racism, for example, it is wrong to treat different races equally, because some races are inferior to others (and this claim is then backed up by some theory or other). So racism can *disapprove* of racial equality. There are three ways in which we could develop our definition of tolerance so that racists are not tolerant, even if they don't act on their racism.

Responsible judgement

We make many value judgements without really thinking about them, without trying to justify them or understand other views. However, when we are reflective and still maintain our commitment to our own position, then our opposition to others is 'responsible'. To be tolerant, we can say, our opposition must be responsible in this sense. Because a lot of prejudice is uninformed and irre-sponsible, most prejudiced people will not count as tolerant.

    However, this allows that a thoughtful racist, or to change the example, someone who has thought carefully about homosexuality, but remains opposed to it on religious grounds, can count as tolerant.

    This sounds right *in a way*. We may still want to claim that the person is prejudiced, but they are clearly not 'merely' prejudiced. Yet we may still want to say that their view is itself intolerant.

> **?** What is 'responsible' judgement? Does it preclude racism?

> Reasonableness helps to explain the link between the weak and strong senses of tolerance (p. 237). A tolerant person does not mind or oppose different views that they have no good reason to oppose. When they do oppose other views, their opposition is not unreasonable.

Reasonableness

So perhaps, to be tolerant, a person's opposition must be 'reasonable' in the sense that it does not rest on irrational prejudice and hatred. Of course, respon-sible judgement will often uncover these irrational sources. But we need to add this condition, because even when people think about their beliefs and values, they are sometimes unable to see their irrational basis. What is needed is not that the person refrains from acting on their opposition to views, but that their beliefs and values themselves change.

One obvious difficulty with this suggestion is finding an account of what is 'reasonable', and being able to discover when disapproval rests on irrational prejudice. People are very good at 'rationalising', giving reasons for their beliefs or values that do not depend on those reasons at all.

Could racism be reasonable?

Tolerance as a virtue

In not trying to suppress those of whom they disapprove, racists are acting in a tolerant way. But this is not enough to say that they are genuinely tolerant. We can distinguish between tolerant *behaviour* and tolerance as a *virtue*.

With any virtue, we can act in accordance with the virtue but without being virtuous. For example, you can make a 'generous' donation to charity but without being a generous person – if the reason you made the donation was to impress someone. So someone can act in a 'tolerant' way without being what we would want to call a tolerant person.

We need to look at the *kinds of reason* a tolerant person gives for being tolerant. The racist who simply doesn't want to get into trouble with the law, or thinks that the time is not yet right to expel all other races from the country, is not tolerant. The truly tolerant person thinks it is *right* – for moral or political reasons – not to act on their opposition to the views of others; and this is why they restrain themselves. *Why* it is right to be tolerant, people may disagree about. As examples of the relevant types of reason, we may think of respect for others (moral) or a commitment to live peacefully with others (political).

Explain and illustrate the difference between acting tolerantly and being tolerant.

Comparing accounts

If someone is genuinely tolerant, do we also need to say that their opposition must be responsible? Perhaps not. We needed to appeal to that condition to characterise 'tolerant' behaviour when the person wasn't tolerant. But if the person is motivated by moral or political reasons to restrain themselves, then perhaps that is enough to say that they are tolerant even if their opposition is not 'responsible'. There are, after all, many positions that we oppose but have not had the time to investigate and understand (very few people understand all the world's major religions) but we are disposed not to try to suppress them.

If this is right, then what is wrong with prejudice is not so much that it is irresponsible – though this is not a good thing! – but that the prejudiced person rarely accepts moral or political reasons for not acting on their prejudice. Prejudice usually undermines the ability to recognise reasons for tolerance, at least in this case. For example, suppose respect for others is a reason for tolerance. Prejudice involves a lack of respect for others; so the prejudiced person will not restrain their actions on the basis of respect.

So the tolerant individual refrains from acting on their opposition to other people's views on the grounds that they thinks it is morally or politically right to refrain.

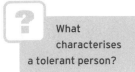

What characterises a tolerant person?

Key points • • •

- If tolerance is just refraining from acting on one's disapproval of other views, then racists can be tolerant.
- Perhaps tolerance also involves 'responsible' judgement, based on an attempt to understand other views and justify one's own.
- Alternatively, we can argue that a tolerant person's opposition to other views must be 'reasonable', not based on irrational prejudice or hatred.
- We can distinguish tolerant behaviour from the virtue of tolerance. To be tolerant, someone must act tolerantly because they believe it is morally or politically right.

III. Tensions and applications

Liberalism and the limits of tolerance

The syllabus asks 'Should a liberal society tolerate a minority culture that doesn't respect its values?' and 'Could a liberal society nourish a particular culture and make judgements about the relative worth of diverse lifestyles without becoming intolerant?'. Both questions point towards paradoxes in tolerance, and we'll take them in turn.

Tolerating the intolerant

Suppose a minority culture rejects the values of autonomy and tolerance. For pragmatic reasons, it does not attempt to enforce its views on others outside

It is worth noting that the direction of tolerance is from the society, that is, the majority, towards the minority. This follows from the view that tolerance involves not acting on the power one has to suppress different views (p. 238). The majority, but not the minority, has this power.

it. However, it actively maintains the cultural community: it brings social sanctions against its own members that dispute its views. Perhaps some conservative Islamic communities in the UK are an example.

Suppose further that in rejecting the exercise of individual autonomy and rationality, and subjecting both to the authority of tradition, the culture refuses to acknowledge that other points of view could be true. It does not display tolerance in that, if it *were* the culture of the majority, it would advocate legal or social sanctions against those who held these other points of view. Should a liberal society tolerate such a culture?

If the reason for tolerance is to respect autonomy, why would we tolerate a view that did not respect autonomy? Let's put the point another way. If we are tolerant, we increase autonomy – more people are able to live their own lives in their own way. But a view that rejects autonomy seeks to get people to live their lives in a way it prescribes. So do we increase autonomy more by *not* tolerating this view?

Consider how children are raised. The conservative culture wants to raise its children to adopt traditional views. A liberal culture wants children to be raised in a way that allows them to reflect on, evaluate and choose their views so they become autonomous. If the conservative culture is tolerated, then people raised within that culture may not be as autonomous as they would be if the culture was not tolerated.

On the other hand, being part of a conservative culture can be an expression of autonomy, an expression of living life as one thinks it should be lived. Not to tolerate the culture would mean this conservative way of living was no longer available in society. But the arguments from autonomy and fallibility mean that a liberal society should *not* undermine other ways of living. If a liberal society could only tolerate cultures that accept liberal values, how would this be tolerance at all?

However, there will be practical limits to the nature of the tolerance extended to the culture. The beliefs and values of the culture can be tolerated without contradiction. However, since the society is liberal, individuals will have certain rights that protect them against harm (Mill's Harm Principle, p. 239). If the culture's *practices* violates those rights, for example, by using force against members of the community, then a liberal society cannot tolerate those practices.

This reveals a paradox in tolerance: tolerance is only really needed when the beliefs and values to be tolerated are *intolerant* or *intolerable*. If two otherwise different moral points of view agree that autonomy must be respected, little tolerance is needed, because underlying the opposition of views is agreement. Tolerance becomes much more necessary when one side rejects the very values that tolerance is based upon.

Can intolerance of intolerant views increase autonomy?

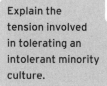

Explain the tension involved in tolerating an intolerant minority culture.

The impossibility of tolerance?

Describing certain beliefs and values as intolerant has, historically, often been the result of intolerance, misunderstanding and prejudice. If every attempt to draw a line between what can be tolerated and what cannot is an act of *intolerance*, then tolerance ends before it begins. Defining the limits of tolerance is an expression of intolerance.

This argument rests on a confusion between two meanings of 'intolerant'. Views which are intolerant deny that tolerance is valuable. The attempt to draw a distinction between these views and others is not intolerant in this sense. To argue that intolerant views cannot be tolerated is not to deny that tolerance is valuable. (Even then there is no need to say that beliefs and values can't be tolerated, only that certain practices cannot.) This 'intolerance' is quite different from the intolerance of a view that tries to impose a specific way of living on people.

We can object that to make *any* value judgement about different cultures is intolerant. Tolerance involves recognising that there are different standards of value in different cultures (or lifestyles). If a liberal society nourishes and supports a culture based on individual autonomy, then it displays intolerance towards different standards of value.

The difficulty with this argument is that we lose any general reason to be tolerant – because the arguments for tolerance all invoke value judgements. To say that one *should* be tolerant is itself a value judgement, one that rejects intolerance. It compares different standards of value (tolerant and intolerant ones), and sides with tolerance. And if we think tolerance is right, then why is it? Well, we have seen the values that support tolerance, and they are values that liberalism endorses.

Making value judgements is, in any case, not itself intolerant. In WHAT IS TOLERANCE? (p. 237), we argued that tolerance requires opposition. Value judgements express this opposition. Intolerance is not opposition, but acting on this opposition in a way that suppresses the view one disagrees with.

We can still object that in a liberal society, it may be harder to live according to a way of life that promotes submission to tradition than a way of life which is based on individual rationality and choice. Tolerance would seem to advantage those views that accept autonomy over views that do not. We can argue that this result shows that tolerance isn't really possible. We return to this issue in TOLERANCE AND NEUTRALITY, p. 255.

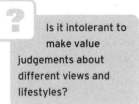

Explain the difference between an intolerant view and not tolerating intolerant views.

Is it intolerant to make value judgements about different views and lifestyles?

Can we tolerate the intolerant? What paradoxes does this create for tolerance?

Key points • • •

- Some minority cultures reject liberal values of autonomy and tolerance. This leads to a paradox: if the culture is tolerated, the values of tolerance may be undermined; if the culture is not tolerated, tolerance does not extend beyond views that support it – which doesn't seem tolerant.
- Distinguishing between tolerant and intolerant views itself may be thought to be intolerant, since it involves value judgements. But this is a mistake – unless there is opposition, expressed by value judgements, there is no tolerance. And there is a difference between an intolerant view and not tolerating intolerance.

DEVELOPMENT

I. The tolerant society

Arguments for tolerance II

Variations on fallibilism

SUBJECTIVISM

Many people believe that there are no right answers when it comes to morality. Morality is subjective, a reflection of our personal feelings or choices. This is often offered as an argument for tolerance. If my values differ from yours, but values are subjective, then who are you to tell me that my morality is wrong? Subjectivism implies tolerance, many people claim, because no one can correct anyone else. To be intolerant is to assume that your values are the right values – but there are no 'right' values.

> Subjectivism is discussed in THE DENIAL OF MORAL TRUTH, A2 Unit 3.4 Moral Philosophy.

Whether subjectivism is true or not, *it doesn't support tolerance*. Tolerance is itself a moral value. 'You ought to tolerate other people's values, because there are no objective moral values' is self-contradictory. We only *ought* to be tolerant if tolerance is a good thing. So, turning the tables, who are you to tell someone else to be tolerant? If tolerance is one of your values, what right do you have to impose it on other people?

Tolerance means not acting on one's disapproval of other people's values. So it will conflict with some other values the person has (or there would be no disapproval). So we need *reasons* to be tolerant, for example, the value of autonomy. But if these values are also subjective, how can we justify the demand to be tolerant to other people?

If we want to argue that we ought to be tolerant, we should not argue that moral values are subjective. At least some moral values – such as tolerance, respect, autonomy – need to be objective if we want to justify tolerance.

ARGUMENT FROM REASONABLENESS

John Rawls argues that disagreement and opposition is 'the natural outcome of the activities of human reason under enduring free institutions', which is why it is inevitable and permanent (p. 241). Equally rational and open-minded people come to different judgements because of 'the burdens of judgement':

1. That empirical evidence relevant to some issues can be complex and hard to assess.
2. That even if we agree about what is relevant, we can disagree about the importance of each factor.
3. That our concepts are vague and need to be interpreted.
4. That the way we weigh up evidence and values is shaped by our whole life experience.
5. That there are different *kinds* of values for and against a particular point of view, which makes it hard to weigh them up.

Rawls argues that all reasonable people accept the burdens of judgement. As a result, we don't treat other people's differing views as a result of their being irrational; people can disagree *reasonably*. And so we should be tolerant – at least of all reasonable disagreement.

That coercion is ineffective

In 1689, John Locke wrote a famous defence of religious tolerance. He argued that it was irrational to attempt to impose particular religious beliefs. The state can only force people to *do* things; it can't make people *believe* things. Religious faith is a form of belief, and belief can't be forced. Of course, the state can force people to go through certain religious practices, such as going to church. But this is pointless, if the aim is to save people's souls, because religious practice without religious belief is worthless; to be saved, someone must have religious

Assess the claim that we should be tolerant because values are subjective.

Political Liberalism, p. xxiv

It is important to note that, like Mill, Rawls is not a sceptic or a subjectivist. There is truth, but it is hard to know what it is.

Explain the argument from reasonableness.

A Letter Concerning Toleration

beliefs. Attempting to coerce someone into a particular religion is completely ineffective, so it is irrational to try. Being intolerant in this way is irrational.

Just as you can't coerce religious belief, you can't coerce moral beliefs either. You cannot force someone to have the 'right' moral values, so there is no point trying. And if you are aiming for a more harmonious society in which people don't disagree about such matters, force won't achieve that either. People will continue to disagree even if they can't express their disagreement, and their resentment at oppression will threaten to destabilise society.

OBJECTIONS

We can challenge this argument on three grounds.

First, Locke assumes that the point of persecuting or outlawing people with different religious beliefs is to get them to change their beliefs. But intolerance may not have this aim. If it aims to kill people with offensive views, or just to prevent them from acting on their views, then coercion is *not* ineffective. And it may create a more harmonious society by driving people out of society (this is the aim of those who argue that different races should live separately).

Second, is it true that beliefs cannot be brought about by force? You cannot simply *choose* to believe something. But beliefs can be *indirectly* influenced. For instance, beliefs respond to our experience. Legislation could restrict our experience of the world and of ideas, for example, by banning certain books, making it illegal to teach particular points of view, and restricting access to public sources of information.

Third, we can object that even if Locke is right and intolerance is irrational, this is not what is wrong with intolerance. This is the wrong reason for condemning intolerance. When intolerance is wrong, it is wrong because of its effects on the people suffering it, not because intolerant people are irrational.

The value of diversity

As people 'pursue their own good in their own way', they conduct what Mill calls 'experiments of living'. They discover what works in life and what doesn't, what leads to their good and what detracts from it. To limit these experiments will be a mistake for a variety of reasons. First, to impose a way of life on someone else is to assume infallibility about what is good; but our moral values might not be right – there might be better ways to live, which we have yet to discover. 'Genius' can introduce new good ideas into society. Second, misguided ways of

> Explain the argument that intolerance is irrational because coercion is ineffective.

> The techniques of brainwashing only work for a time. Once the person returns to normal conditions of living, they often shed the beliefs and values adopted under pressure. So brainwashing has to be constant to be effective.

> Assess the claim that using force to try to change religious or moral beliefs is irrational.

> *On Liberty*, Ch. 3

life may still contain some partial insight; so even if we are mostly right in what we believe is good, generally bad ways of living may still reveal something we don't know or haven't thought of. For example, we may have too narrow a range of experience. Third, diversity encourages people to *think* about how they live, because they are challenged by alternatives. This creates a context in which they seek to improve their lives. Finally, different people need different conditions in order to develop: one size does not fit all. For all these reasons, diversity will lead to better ways of living, to social progress, to greater happiness. But diversity requires tolerance.

A diverse and tolerant society will have other valuable features, argues Mill. The constantly bubbling up of ideas and new ways of doing things will lead to a creativity and energy in society as a whole. It will be constantly progressing and will display confidence and vigour in its pursuit of ways to make life better. By contrast, societies that are not tolerant will stagnate. What is new is always something that has to be tolerated at first – it is rarely welcomed straight away. So in an intolerant society, few genuinely new ways of doing things will appear or be accepted.

Outline and illustrate the argument from diversity.

These issues are discussed further in WHETHER A CULTURE WHICH ENCOURAGES TOLERANCE SHOULD BE NURTURED, p. 257.

Discuss the value of diversity.

OBJECTIONS

We can make similar objections to this argument that we made to Mill's argument from fallibility (p. 242). First, is Mill right to think that allowing diversity will help people find *better* ways of living, ones that will make them happy? Mill is assuming that people learn from their and others' mistakes, so that diversity will lead to knowledge of what is truly good. But in the time since Mill wrote, we can argue that there has been greater diversity – the development of pluralistic societies – but no great increase in happiness or good living. Is individuality in the sense of pursuing our own good in our own way such a good thing? Or would people be happier with strong social guidance on how to live?

Second, is Mill right to think that if we limit diversity, society won't discover new ways of living and new values? 'Genius' has not flourished under liberal societies alone. For example, the rule of Frederick the Great of Prussia in the eighteenth century was a dictatorship, but during his rule, there was great artistic invention. Would a lack of diversity really contribute to a lack of social progress and development?

Tolerance and neutrality

Someone's 'conception of the good life' is their view of how to live. It is not necessarily explicit or systematic. It includes their ideas about morality and religion, perhaps also ideas about progress, human nature and society. If a society adopted some particular conception, then its structures and laws would reflect and promote the way of life of that conception, and the kinds of reasons given for passing laws would appeal to the values of that conception of the good. For example, in a theocracy, laws are passed on the basis of being in accordance with the will and commands of God, as a particular religion represents these (as in Islam's sharia law).

The ARGUMENTS FOR TOLERANCE from fallibilism (p. 242), reasonableness (p. 252), autonomy (p. 244) and diversity (p. 253) all suggest that imposing one's conception of the good life on other people is wrong. From these arguments, we might conclude that for a society to be tolerant, it must be 'neutral' between conceptions of the good life.

John Rawls has defended neutrality. Because of the burdens of reason (see p. 252), a tolerant society will not exercise power, for example, through legal or social sanctions, except by appealing to reasons that everyone reasonable can accept. To enforce a value or policy on the basis of reasons that depend on your own particular conception of the good, reasons that others would reasonably reject, is to be intolerant. To be neutral, social structures and laws must not favour one conception of the good over another.

Rawls faces three challenges. First, we may argue that to be tolerant, a society need not be neutral. Second, we can argue that neutrality is inconsistent with the values of tolerance. Third, we may argue that neutrality is not itself a neutral ideal.

The tolerant society need not be neutral

A tolerant society, we can argue, is one that does not exercise a tyranny of the majority (see p. 240). This doesn't mean that there isn't a majority view on morality, religion, etc., but that it is not imposed. A tolerant society can adopt a particular conception of the good, as long as its laws still allow for the *private* pursuit of conceptions of the good that are different. An intolerant society tries to get citizens to live – not just in public life, but throughout their lives – in accordance with its conception of the good.

> Individuals, of course, will not be neutral – we each have our conceptions of the good. This does not make an individual intolerant, as long as they don't try to impose that conception on others.

> Explain what neutrality is. Why does Rawls think tolerance requires neutrality?

> This is sometimes called a 'permission' conception of tolerance – views are allowed to exist within a society that, on the whole, disagrees with them.

?
Is protecting the private pursuit of one's conception of the good life enough for a tolerant society?

But we can object that this is not enough. Tolerance requires greater recognition and equality, and the state should be responsive to all conceptions of the good equally. In practice, this is only possible if it is neutral. For example, as Rawls argues, laws are passed on the basis of reasons that everyone can accept. No particular conception of the good enters into public life.

Neutrality is inconsistent with the values of tolerance

The Morality of Freedom, Ch. 5, Ch. 14

Joseph Raz argues that the point of tolerance is to respect and encourage autonomy. However, neutrality undermines autonomy, because people will not be able to pursue certain ways of living if society is completely neutral. Some conceptions of the good, or rather, the possibility of living according to those conceptions, will be unable to sustain themselves without support from society. For example, for many people, art forms part of a good life, and a life without art would be very impoverished. In the UK, there is strong government support for the arts – museums are kept free by government subsidy, there are many government awards for new artists and for organising exhibitions. Without this support, many people think, art would suffer terribly, and fewer people would be able to enjoy art. But if society was *neutral* between conceptions of the good that involve art and those that don't, it could not support art.

Raz concludes that the state should preserve a range of valuable options for individuals to choose between. Without valuable options, the value of autonomy diminishes. Of course, options may only appear valuable within certain conceptions of the good, and so in this sense, society cannot remain neutral between conceptions of the good.

We can object that this is not to abandon neutrality – society is just ensuring that conceptions of the good are preserved. If it would do this for any conception of the good, then surely it remains neutral.

But this overlooks the point that society must appeal to *values that not everyone shares*, while neutrality requires that laws are based on reasons every reasonable person can accept.

Assess the claim that society cannot support art while remaining neutral.

Going further: neutrality is not neutral

Neutrality will not appeal to everyone. Not every conception of the good accepts the restriction of giving only neutral reasons in support of legislation. However, Rawls argues that every *reasonable* conception of the good accepts the project of basing society on 'reasonable agreement'.

But this seems to require accepting the values of justifying power to individuals, of equality, and of reason. Unless a conception of the good ranks freedom more important than truth, say, why should its believers acquiesce to giving only reasons all can accept rather than reasons based in their conception of the good? To say they should is not neutrality.

Furthermore, to say that conceptions of the good that don't accept these values are 'unreasonable' is itself unreasonable. Rawls defends his idea of what is reasonable in terms of the burdens of judgement. But the burdens of judgement allow us to say that ideas of freedom, equality and reasonableness are themselves contentious. Rawls' idea of the reasonable will appeal only to those who are already reasonable *by its standards* – but this standard can be (reasonably?) contested. So Rawls' idea of neutrality is not itself neutral.

This doesn't entail that society can't be tolerant, only that we shouldn't understand tolerance in terms of neutrality.

For example, fundamentalists could argue that it is reasonable to believe that an individual's reason is weak and sinful (e.g. used in the service of pride and self-interest, and so should not be trusted.

Can neutrality be defended as an ideal that is neutral between (reasonable) conceptions of the good?

Whether a culture which encourages tolerance should be nurtured

The ARGUMENTS FOR TOLERANCE (pp. 242f. and 251f.) all support the view that a tolerant society should be encouraged. For example, tolerance is necessary to avoid conflict; tolerance enables a society to avoid error and gain the truth; tolerance acknowledges the burdens of judgement and so respects the reasonableness of other people; tolerance allows people to pursue their own good in their own way, which will lead to happiness; tolerance respects the value of autonomy; tolerance encourages diversity, which helps us discover better ways to live, encourages us to think how to live and leads to social progress.

However, to reach the judgement that a tolerant society should be encouraged, we need to look at two questions: 'Is tolerance necessary for society to realise these values?' and 'What are the objections to tolerance – could it produce bad results?'. We then need to weigh the bad against the good.

We have already questioned whether tolerance is the best means to securing the truth; whether people become happier as society grows more tolerant; whether the value of autonomy depends on being able to make the right choices, which may be less likely without moral guidance; whether the burdens of judgement support tolerance; and whether genius and new ideas only emerge under conditions of tolerance and diversity.

Review and assess these arguments and objections.

Devlin's argument

Lord Devlin argued that preserving and enforcing common moral values is part of the government's business, and that failing to do so would lead to the disintegration of society. It is worth giving the argument in his own words:

> [A]n established morality is as necessary as good government to the welfare of society. Societies disintegrate from within more frequently than they are broken up by external pressures. There is disintegration when no common morality is observed and history shows that the loosening of moral bonds is often the first stage of disintegration, so that society is justified in taking the same steps to preserve its moral code as it does to preserve its government and other essential institutions.
>
> The suppression of vice is as much the law's business as the suppression of subversive activities; it is no more possible to define a sphere of private morality than it is to define one of private subversive activity. It is wrong to talk of private morality . . . You may argue that if a man's sins affect only himself it cannot be the concern of society. If he chooses to get drunk every night in the privacy of his own home, is anyone except himself the worse for it? But suppose a quarter or a half of the population got drunk every night, what sort of society would it be? You cannot set a theoretical limit to the number of people who can get drunk before society is entitled to legislate against drunkenness.

'Morals and Criminal Law'

In outline, Devlin argues that

1. Morality is essential to the welfare of society.
2. Morality is social, not private.

3. It is the business of government to look after the welfare of society.
4. So it is legitimate for government to pass laws on the basis of preserving moral values.

This, of course, means not tolerating practices, and perhaps discouraging beliefs, that are in conflict with these moral values.

Devlin's argument points to the importance of social cohesion. The only argument for tolerance that took account of this value was the threat from strife (p. 242). And we can use that argument to respond to Devlin – if we follow his recommendations, society faces the threat of conflict from people who have different moral values. But Devlin can respond: if we follow his recommendations, there won't *be* (many) people who have different moral values. There will be a common moral code that everyone in society recognises as legitimate.

Objections

Devlin appeals to moral *agreement*, not to moral *truth*. Mill would respond that in Devlin's society, we will not get at the truth about morality and correct our mistakes. Social morality may well need to change, as it might be inhibiting individual and social welfare.

We can also object that 'the welfare of society' is not a value to be protected at any cost. Perhaps society's morality shouldn't be enforced if it infringes people's autonomy. Or, following Rawls, we can argue that the common morality that should be encouraged is one of tolerance.

But we can question the assumption of the arguments for tolerance that people are equal, reasonable and autonomous. If they are not, treating them as such can only lead to misery and social breakdown. People need strong moral guidance, they need to be told the difference between right and wrong, between what is acceptable and what is not, or they will not be happy.

> Explain and illustrate the claim that tolerance could undermine social cohesion.

> Devlin was arguing against the legalisation of homosexuality between consenting adults. Has this law led to the disintegration of social morality or society itself? Or is social morality better because it no longer condemns homosexuals?

> Should a culture which encourages tolerance be nurtured?

Going further: civility and respect

The syllabus asks 'whether a society which encourages tolerance, civility and respect for others should be nurtured'. This seems to assume that tolerance, civility and respect go together. But perhaps civility and respect stem from a strong common morality, not tolerance.

This is the 'permission' conception of tolerance discussed on p. xxx.

New Oxford Dictionary of English

? Does a society that encourages tolerance also encourage civility and respect?

One interpretation of respect is linked to tolerance, viz. that respect is respect for autonomy and the results of the burdens of judgement. People should be allowed to form their own views and shape their lives as they see fit. We respect this by not trying to force our views on them.

But we can respect other people while also arguing for a common, public moral code. We can allow and respect freedom of conscience, but argue that minority views cannot expect to have any impact on society. Or again, we may respectfully ask (and then require) people with particular views to leave the society. Neither of these conceptions of respect lead to tolerance.

Civility is 'formal politeness and courtesy in behaviour and speech'. A racist can state their views politely, so civility doesn't mean tolerance. And encouraging civility might involve showing intolerance towards people who are impolite and discourteous. However, a tolerant person recognises the moral or political value of tolerance, and so will be motivated to treat other people with civility.

Key points • • •

- Subjectivism does not support tolerance. If moral values are subjective, then tolerance, and the values that support tolerance, are not objectively good.
- Rawls argues that the burdens of judgement mean that people will disagree on important issues. Reasonable people recognise this, and will be tolerant of these disagreements.
- Locke argued that it is irrational to use force to try to change religious (and we can add, moral) beliefs. Beliefs cannot be forced, and religious practice without belief is pointless.
- We can object that force is not irrational if the aim is not to change people's minds but to destroy or drive out other views; and that beliefs can be indirectly influenced, so controlling experience is not irrational.
- Mill argues that diversity, 'experiments of living', is valuable for introducing new ideas into society, creating more thoughtful citizens, and promoting social progress.
- We can object that diversity may not lead to happiness, as people need strong moral guidance, and that diversity is not required for new ideas and social progress.

- Rawls argues that the state should be neutral between competing conceptions of the good, only passing legislation on grounds that all reasonable people can accept.
- We can object that the state may adopt the majority conception of the good, as long as it allows the private pursuit of different conceptions; that in order to preserve some conceptions of the good, it must pass laws on the basis of values that some may reject; and that Rawls' ideas of neutrality and reasonableness are not values all (reasonable?) conceptions of the good may accept.
- Whether tolerance should be nurtured depends on the balance between the arguments for tolerance and objections to them. Devlin adds the argument that a common morality is necessary for social cohesion.
- We can object that moral truth is a better aim than moral agreement and that autonomy is more important than social cohesion. The question remains whether the arguments from tolerance are right to suppose that treating people as equal, reasonable and autonomous is best.
- Tolerance encourages respect for others' autonomy and civility. However, both respect and civility may be possible without tolerance.

II. The tolerant individual

What characteristics do tolerant individuals possess? II

Going further: strong and weak tolerance again

In WHAT IS TOLERANCE? (p. 236), we drew a distinction between tolerance in the weak sense (not minding different views) and in the strong sense (opposing but restraining oneself). In WHAT CHARACTERISTICS DO TOLERANT INDIVIDUALS POSSESS? (p. 247), we argued that tolerance is not restraint for any reason, but involves thinking it is *right* to restrain oneself in this way. This leads to a puzzle: if someone believes it is *right* to restrain themselves, do they remain motivated to suppress others' views? Does a *really* tolerant person *accept*, rather than oppose, different views? This takes us back towards weak tolerance. On the one hand, to be tolerant a person must oppose the other view; on the other, a tolerant person accepts other views.

We can resolve this tension by getting clearer on what we mean by 'accept'. A person's commitment to their own view involves the thought that they are not mistaken. A commitment involves the rejection of alternatives; to this extent, there is opposition. And of course, they will argue for and defend their position. But if the reasons for tolerance are strong in their minds, their opposition may motivate them to do *no more* than this. *Some* tension between the reasons for toleration and the reasons that support their views may remain; and this is why they require tolerance. But in a very tolerant person, the level of mental conflict may not be great.

This explains why we sometimes think that a tolerant person 'does not mind' different practices, even though we also think that they must oppose them in some way. Tolerance, when it is most developed, does not just *restrain* one from acting on motivations stemming from opposition; as a commitment itself, it supplies motivations of its own which can, to an extent, undermine the original motivations that need restraining.

? In what sense does a tolerant person accept views that oppose their own?

Individual rationality and autonomy, and cultural membership

Does a tolerant person have to be a liberal? Or is tolerance possible for people with strong moral or religious views, for example, religious fundamentalists? If a fundamentalist can accept of the ARGUMENTS FOR TOLERANCE (pp. 242f. and 251f.), then fundamentalists can be tolerant.

The wording of the syllabus is unclear at this point. The following interpretation of the issue was confirmed, though only verbally, with a senior examiner.

We will focus just on whether illiberal religious fundamentalists could be tolerant. There can be liberal religious fundamentalists, viz. those that believe God

continued

TOLERANT ILLIBERALS
A fundamentalist is unlikely to accept the argument from fallibilism (p. 242). Acknowledging doubt over whether what they believe is really the word of God is not a trait of fundamentalists. Nor is the argument from diversity (p. 253) likely to appeal – the best way to live is discovered through a sacred text or tradition, not through experiments of living. And fundamentalism understands morality to be objective, not subjective (p. 251).

However, Locke's argument (p. 252) that coercion is ineffective at changing people's religious beliefs may well be a ground for tolerance. Fundamentalists usually aim at others coming to share their religious beliefs, but they may also believe that using social or legal sanctions will not achieve this. They may also believe, with Locke, that religious belief is only of value if it is arrived at freely.

Finally, they may believe that there are moral restrictions on what one may do to bring others to believe – many religions show a respect for freedom of thought.

On the other hand, fundamentalists may be more concerned that people behave in accordance with God's law. It is the *practices*, rather than the beliefs, of others they want to change. In this case, Locke's argument is beside the point.

This leaves the arguments from reasonableness (p. 252), developed further in the discussion on neutrality (p. 255), and from strife (p. 242). These both present *political* reasons for tolerance. If we wish to live together peacefully, and we cannot demonstrate, through reason and argument, that views different from ours are mistaken, then tolerance is necessary.

Many religions have traditions that support this line of thought – that spiritual knowledge is difficult, that individuals must find their own way to God through experience (while paying attention to tradition), and that a peaceful society is part of God's plan for human beings. However, fundamentalists often think that what is morally required is clear; that individuals cannot be left to discover the truth for themselves, but need to be told; and (often) that human reason is both weak and sinful, which is why the truth lies in revelation.

If reasonableness is unpersuasive, the argument from strife still stands. Fundamentalists (and others with strong moral and religious views) can draw a distinction between an *ideal* society – in which the laws of God or morality are reflected in society's laws – and the kind of society we can realistically expect. If an attempt to transform society as it is into an ideal society would lead to conflict and suffering, for example, because of pluralism, they may advocate tolerance. This position remains distinct from liberalism, because it retains the view that an ideal society would be one in which a particular conception of the good is enshrined in law.

endowed human beings with freedom, reason and autonomy, and gave everyone the duty to respect these qualities. However, it is unusual for a fundamentalist to value autonomy higher than all other moral values.

Can fundamentalists be tolerant?

CULTURAL MEMBERSHIP AND INTOLERANT LIBERALS

In a liberal society, with its emphasis on autonomy, reasonableness and toler-ance, attempting to impose one conception of the good on others will not succeed. If this is the reason a fundamentalist is tolerant, must they be part of a liberal culture in order to be tolerant? Suppose they live in a society in which God's law is, or can be made, the basis of law, for example, if society adopts Islam's sharia law. Can someone who is part of such a society be a tolerant individual?

Just because someone lives under sharia law does not mean that they approve of it. They may, on the grounds of tolerance, advocate that it is repealed precisely because it is one conception of the good. But what of someone who approves of the rule of sharia law, living in a culture that also approves?

Whether someone is tolerant depends on how they respond to those who disagree with them. If someone approves of a culture that imposes its conception of the good on its members by social and legal sanctions, whether or not they accept this conception, then that individual cannot be called tolerant.

In LIBERALISM AND THE LIMITS OF TOLERANCE (p. 248), we noted that for all of us, our identity is partly defined by the culture to which we belong. In a liberal society, united by a particular understanding of individual autonomy that contrasts it with tradition, liberals struggle with how to respond to practices that appear not to respect individual autonomy, and cannot understand how individuals who take part in such practices could do so autonomously. Three contemporary examples: arranged marriages; in Islam, women wearing clothing that signifies and protects modesty (whether it is the headscarf or the burkha); and female circumcision. If a liberal argues that we should outlaw all such practices, this could be argued to be an intolerant response. Tolerance would recommend allowing such practices to exist where individuals choose to continue them.

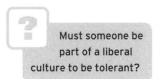

Must someone be part of a liberal culture to be tolerant?

Tolerance, leaving others alone, and offence

Tolerance does not involve 'leaving others alone to think and do as they please', as the syllabus suggests. For example, Mill says that we can still argue, entreat and remonstrate with people who seem to live in a way that we think is damaging them. We must, however, not attempt by any other means than persuasion to prevent them from leading their lives as they see fit.

Will a tolerant person try to avoid being offensive? Tolerance involves respect for the other. And giving offence is often considered a mark of lack of respect. Not all tolerance, of course, is motivated by respect (we have seen other arguments). However, if a tolerant person is tolerant because they believe it is right to respect other points of view, then they will be motivated to avoid offending others.

There will, however, be a limit to this. Suppose someone believes that homosexuality is an unnatural perversion. They may take offence at anyone simply declaring support for homosexuality. Does this mean a tolerant person shouldn't declare such support? No, because it is *intolerant* to require people not to express their views. So while a tolerant person will avoid *unnecessary* offence, out of respect, they need not give up expressing views which may cause offence to others.

Key points • • •

- A tolerant person believes it is right to be tolerant. This undermines their motivation to suppress other views. In this sense, they accept other views, even while, in their commitment to their own views, they remain opposed to other views.
- Fundamentalists are unlikely to accept the arguments for tolerance from fallibilism, diversity and subjectivism. They may accept Locke's argument that coercion is ineffective, if their aim is to change people's religious beliefs; but they may reject this if their aim is only to change people's practices. They may or may not accept the arguments from reasonableness and from strife, especially if they are part of a liberal society.
- Someone who approves of the state imposing a particular conception of the good on all citizens, regardless of whether they accept it, cannot be called tolerant. However, this is a challenge to liberals as well, who may find it difficult to accept certain traditional cultural practices as expressions of autonomy.
- Tolerance does not require us to leave others alone, in that we may argue with them to try to change their minds. A tolerant person will try to avoid giving offence unnecessarily, but need not refrain from expressing their views.

III. Tensions and applications

Tolerance and a liberal culture

In LIBERALISM AND THE LIMITS OF TOLERANCE (p. 248f.), we discussed the liberal response to a culture that rejects its values. And in TOLERANCE AND NEUTRALITY (p. 255f.), we noted that not all conceptions of the good will accept neutrality. Many religious conceptions will not – to live according to the laws of God is a duty that extends throughout life, not something to be relegated to one's private life, they may argue.

Or again, Rawls requires that laws are justified on grounds that everyone can accept. But some conceptions of the good argue that our individual powers

> We can add that attempting to draw a line between the public and private is also problematic because it is unclear that even liberalism can respect it. Think of all the laws and institutions that relate to the family.

of reason are too weak to support this kind of individualism, and place more emphasis on accepting a tradition. And yet a tolerant society is one that refuses to allow people to impose their conceptions of the good on others.

How can a society support both liberalism and tolerance? By basing social and legal sanctions on values that support tolerance. In a sense, this imposes a (minimal) conception of the good, one that recognises tolerance and the values that support it, on people who do not accept this.

What makes a society tolerant is not neutrality, but the response of the society to 'unreasonable' views and the people who hold them. To actively discourage unreasonable views strays too far from tolerance, a case of intolerant liberalism. Yet the unreasonable view cannot extend into the public sphere in a way that would suppress other views. So a tolerant society must attempt to contain unreasonable views, to prevent them from undermining what consensus of the reasonable exists.

For example, to maintain a commitment to reasonableness and tolerance in society, Rawls insists that children are taught their rights, in particular freedom of conscience, that they understand the importance of the division between public reasonableness and private conceptions of the good. He recognises that this could well undermine unreasonable conceptions of the good over time, but if the values of individual autonomy and reasonableness are upheld, this may be an inevitable consequence.

> **?** Could a liberal society nourish a liberal culture without being intolerant?

Tolerance, critical faculties and false needs

New ideas and critical faculties

In his argument from diversity (p. 253), Mill argued that tolerance will encourage new ideas to be introduced into society and it will encourage people to think about their lives more reflectively, thus developing their critical faculties. New ideas require an atmosphere of tolerance, because people can be tempted to dismiss what is new out of hand. Tolerance enables people to develop new ideas without fear of being immediately rejected, and it allows new ideas to spread through society.

With the constant challenge of new ideas, we will be required to think, to reflect, not only on the new ideas, but also on the views we already hold. To take another view seriously demands that we justify our own view against it. An intolerant society involves the rejection of other points of view without thought. Tolerance creates an atmosphere in which people are required to think.

Explain Mill's argument that tolerance encourages new ideas and critical faculties.

False needs and repressive desublimation

The terms 'false needs' and 'repressive desublimation' come from a discussion by Herbert Marcuse of the state of 'advanced industrial society'. He argued that technological progress, instead of leading to greater freedom, has created less freedom. It is, however, 'a comfortable, smooth, reasonable, democratic unfreedom'. People are kept happy by rising standards of living and economic progress, which society manages very well. It is a paradoxical situation, people are happy but not free.

One-Dimensional Man, esp. Ch. 1 and Ch. 3

Why not free? Because every aspect of society is understood in terms of means-end rationality, where the 'end' is more technological and economic progress. 'Independence of thought, autonomy, and the right to political opposition are being deprived of their basic critical function in a society which seems increasingly capable of satisfying the needs of individuals through the way in which it is organized.' We have lost an inner dimension to ourselves, the rational reflection that rejects how things are. Because we are happy, it seems unreasonable to reject and attack the structure and organisation of society that has made us happy. We are becoming unable to think differently.

Society, then, comes to define what we need in terms of what will contribute to progress: 'social controls exact the . . . need for the production and consumption of waste; . . . the need for maintaining such deceptive liberties as free competition at administered prices, a free press which censors itself, free choice between brands and gadgets'. 'Most of the prevailing needs to relax, to have fun, to behave and consume in accordance with the advertisements, to love and hate what others love and hate' are *false needs*. We feel we need these things, but the sense of needing them is a product of a society seeking only technological and economic progress.

Explain the concept of a 'false need'.

Going further: repressive desublimation

As a result, there are so few 'experiments of living' that really seek to strike out; those that do – that look 'dangerous' or really 'different' – are held up as *images to be consumed*, not as challenges to the system of consumption. Mass communication blends art, politics, religion and philosophy with *commercials*. Everything becomes a commodity, and this deprives it of its meaning as an alternative to the life of consumption.

'Higher' culture was critical of society, alien, opposite, transcendent. So it drew our attention to what society was not, to other possibilities for how to find meaning in life. This made us unhappy, but we were *conscious* of the gap between reality and possibility. The gap was bad, but the consciousness was good and necessary for social change. Now we don't understand higher culture in this challenging way, but as a taste or image, something to be bought and sold, discarded as the fashion passes. Its truth has been replaced by technological, economic, means-end rationality. We don't see it as an *alternative* to this way of thinking, as an argument for some things being valuable for their own sake. We have lost our consciousness of how things might be different.

Despite this, we have become more satisfied. Marcuse calls this 'repressive desublimation'. 'Higher' culture derives its motivation and its energy, according to Freud and Marcuse, from our drives, in particular our sexual drives. Because it is socially unacceptable to have sex wherever, however, whenever we want, this energy is redirected into forms of creativity. The frustration, however, emerges once again in the challenge to society from higher culture. So in sublimation, we remain conscious of society's repression of our drives.

As higher culture has become commodified, we have gained more satisfaction, from both technological and economic progress, but also from sexuality. Sexuality is much more free, more daring and uninhibited than it used to be, but also, therefore, *much more limited* – it expresses itself just as sex, not as creativity. This is 'desublimation', but it is still repressive, creating false needs and undermining our ability to think. The system makes us happy, why conduct an 'experiment in living'? The satisfaction we get weakens the rationality of protesting against society.

His theory draws on the ideas of Sigmund Freud.

Explain repressive desublimation.

How does tolerance fit into all this? In fact, *at no point* does Marcuse say that tolerance contributes to the problem. The system may, however, generate something we may *mistake* for tolerance. As society absorbs all the challenges to it, what emerges is 'a harmonizing pluralism, where the most contradictory works and truths peacefully coexist in indifference'. Peaceful coexistence sounds like tolerance, but technological progress has produced *indifference*. Everyone signs up to economic progress, jobs, some form of capitalism; what does it matter what else they think?

This is not tolerance, but the inability to *take seriously* critical challenges to society. So a genuinely tolerant society – one in which autonomy is encouraged, real difference can flourish, many lifestyles are genuinely possible – will not create false needs and repressive desublimation. Perhaps our society is not genuinely tolerant, but an imitation, a fake.

I think Mill would sympathise with much of this, as he too wanted to free thought and action from the tyranny of public opinion. Despite Mill's argument from diversity, says Marcuse, 'Under the conditions of a rising standard of living, non-conformity with the system itself appears to be socially useless'. We need to find new forms of freedom, freedom from the economy, freedom from politics we can't control, freedom of thought from the influence of mass communication, the abolition of 'public opinion'.

> **?** Does a tolerant society encourage critical thinking or is tolerance part of repressive desublimation?

Tolerance and religion

The arguments for tolerance suggest we should tolerate a variety of religious lifestyles and practices. It is necessary to avoid strife (p. 242); we are fallible about religious truth (p. 242); if we were to be intolerant with the aim of converting people to a different religion, this is irrational (p. 252); religious allegiance is an expression of individual autonomy (p. 244); a diversity of lifestyles (among them religious lifestyles) may introduce new good ideas into society (p. 253; and accepting the burdens of reason leads us to recognise that a variety of religious beliefs can be reasonable (p. 252).

Against these arguments, we can argue that tolerance will not help us discover religious truth or better ways of living, while intolerance may help us preserve them (p. 242). We can also put forward a variation of Lord Devlin's argument (p. 258): tolerating a variety of religious lifestyles and practices may contribute to the disintegration of society. These practices may be at odds with society's common morality, they may require exceptions to be made in the application of laws.

> An example: the law requires that animals are knocked unconscious before being slaughtered – except for Jewish and Muslim slaughterhouses, as Jewish and Muslim law requires that the animal is conscious.

We have also seen the limits of tolerance: it would be difficult for a liberal society to tolerate those practices (and laws) that would undermine autonomy. However, where individuals autonomously submit to these laws, then it would be intolerant to force them not to. So if a Jew *chooses* to have a legal case heard and decided in a Jewish court, under Jewish law, it would be intolerant to prevent this. On the other hand, if Jewish law violated the rights of the individual under society's law, it is hard to see how a liberal society could allow Jewish law to be used.

Tolerance and social difference

Should we tolerate unpopular lifestyles and expressions of culture? Again, we can cite the arguments for tolerance that would support a positive answer: it is necessary to avoid strife (p. 242); we are fallible about the best way to live (p. 242); a choice of lifestyle is an expression of individual autonomy (p. 244); a diversity of lifestyles and cultures may introduce new good ideas into society (p. 253); and accepting the burdens of reason leads us to recognise that a variety of lifestyles can be reasonable (p. 252).

And again, against these arguments, we can argue that tolerance will not help us discover better ways of living, while intolerance may help us preserve them (p. 242). We can argue that: tolerating a variety of lifestyles and cultural practices may contribute to the disintegration of society (p. 258). These practices may be at odds with society's common morality. The traditions and customs of the majority, embodied in their culture and lifestyles, are what holds society together. Encouraging people to define their 'own' lifestyles will only lead to a breakdown in the bonds of society.

Key points • • •

- A society can foster liberalism without intolerance by basing legal and social sanctions on the values that support tolerance. Those views that do not support these values can be contained, but should not be actively discouraged through sanctions.
- Mill's argument from diversity suggests that tolerance will encourage new ideas and also the development of critical faculties.
- Marcuse argues that technological and economic progress, while making

Should we tolerate the beliefs, practices, lifestyles and laws of religious minorities? Discuss the question in relation to each of beliefs, practices, lifestyles and laws separately. Do you arrive at the same answer for each?

Assess the claim that unpopular lifestyles should not be tolerated.

Are there important differences between justifying the tolerance of religion and the tolerance of lifestyles?

people happy, has created false needs and an inability to think independently and critically.

- It has also caused repressive desublimation, in which the critical challenge of 'higher' culture has been undermined through commercialisation, and the creative energy of sublimation has been released in more overt sexuality.
- Because the challenge of new ideas has been subverted, society adopts a 'harmonising pluralism' of indifference. This can be confused for tolerance.
- The many arguments for tolerance, and objections to them, discussed throughout the chapter, can be applied to the question of whether and to what extent we should tolerate minority religions and unpopular lifestyles.

SUMMARY

In this chapter, we have looked at three issues:

1. The tolerant society.

2. The tolerant individual.

3. Tensions and applications.

In discussing these issues, we looked at the following questions:

1. What is tolerance? Does it require an opposition between different views?

2. In what sense is tolerance the virtue of liberal, pluralist societies?

3. What are the arguments for tolerance? What values support it?

4. Is tolerance necessary for the discovery of the truth or for social progress?

5. What are the characteristics of a tolerant individual? What is the difference between tolerant behaviour and the virtue of tolerance?

6. Can people who are not liberals be tolerant?

7. Should we tolerate the intolerant?

8. Is it possible to draw a distinction between tolerance and intolerance without being intolerant?

9. Can a liberal culture be encouraged without becoming intolerant?

10. Should a tolerant society be neutral between competing conceptions of the good?

11. Does tolerance undermine social cohesion?

12. Is tolerance a characteristic of a society of false needs and repressive desublimation?

UNIT 2 **AN INTRODUCTION TO PHILOSOPHY 2**

Section 3: The value of art

In this chapter, we look at three answers to the question of why we value art: because, in some way, it represents the world and informs us; or because it has a special 'artistic' quality that produces a particular kind of aesthetic pleasure; or because it expresses and elicits emotions. We will look at the strengths and weaknesses of each. By the end of the chapter, you should be able to demonstrate a good understanding of the three answers, and be able to analyse and evaluate several arguments for and against each one.

SYLLABUS CHECKLIST

The AQA AS syllabus for this chapter is:

We value art because it informs us

✔ Good art should illuminate our experience, reveal 'truths', articulate a 'vision', be epiphanic, portray authentically or at least imitate or represent its subject convincingly or faithfully.

✔ How is art supposed to stand for reality? Are all arts equally concerned with representing? What could we mean by 'truth' in art? Even if art informs us, is that why we value it as art? Is art especially informative?

We value art because of its expressive quality

✔ Good art is moving or otherwise captures a mood or feeling. We describe and appraise it using an affective vocabulary. But how can psychological ascriptions normally attributed to persons apply to works of art? Are such descriptions merely metaphorical?

✔ Is it really the artists' self-expression we value, or are our own responses occasioned by the art the focus of our appreciation?

We value art because of its particular 'artistic' quality

✔ Good art is good because it affords a peculiar aesthetic enjoyment of 'form': balance, structure, proportion, harmony, wholeness, 'significant form'.

✔ Is the notion of 'form' clear? As a matter of fact, are there recognisable formal universals displayed in art? Even if 'form' matters is it the 'essence' of art qua art? Does formalism neglect the place art has in the hurly-burly of human life?

INTRODUCTION

Introductory remarks

What is art v. the value of art

In most introductions to the philosophy of art, the question discussed is 'What is art?'. Our focus, by contrast, is why we value art. The two questions should be kept distinct. But they are related, because we value works of art because of what it is about them that makes them 'art'. So in the course of the discussion, we will look at claims about what art is, but always and only in the context of trying to discover why we value art. We assume that we have enough of an idea of what counts as art to be able to discuss why we value it.

As a result, we will not discuss some famous theories about what works count as 'art' because they do not help us with our question. For example, the

'Institutional theory' argues that something is an artwork because someone, on behalf of the social institution called the 'art world', has said that this work can be appreciated as a work of art. Another theory says that something is an artwork if it has been seriously intended to be regarded as an artwork. But neither of these theories say what is valuable about art – so we set them aside.

Valuing art

Another question we shall not discuss is whether the value of art is subjective. Following the syllabus, we are assuming that we value art. We can argue this is a development from natural, universal human responses, which we can call 'aesthetic'. From a very young age, children display responses of delight in music; in how we dress and decorate our homes, we all respond with like or dislike to colours and combinations of colours. The judgements of whether something 'works' or doesn't, are valuable to us, and we guide our decisions by them constantly.

> The word 'aesthetic' comes from the Greek *aisthesis*, meaning 'perception' or 'sensation'.

Furthermore, we have a very important ability, apparently unique among animals, to see meaningful shapes 'in' natural phenomena – such as seeing a face in a cloud, in the bark of a tree, or in marks on a wall. This ability expresses and stimulates our imaginative interactions with what we experience and underpins our ability to create and interpret (visual) art.

Our question is what is *the* value of art, and we shall discuss each answer, at first, as though it were the *only* answer to the question. But why should we assume that we value art for *just one reason*? We will see that each of our three answers has something to contribute. It may also be that different types of art are valued in different ways and that, at different periods in history, different ways of valuing art have been dominant.

Engaging with the argument

The other philosophical issues in this book do not assume much particular prior knowledge. But it is not possible to discuss art unless one knows something about works of art. In particular, many arguments are made by reference to individual works of art.

In producing this book, we decided not to include photos of the artworks referred to. They are only useful if they are high-quality colour reproductions,

www.routledge.com/
alevel/philosophy.

On thinking about art:
when confronted with a
work that doesn't seem
like art at all, it is
worth asking why the
artist may have
thought that making
that artwork at that
time would be a good
idea, or even the *only*
way to make art.

which would make the book much more expensive. Instead, we have put weblinks to all the works numbered in **bold** on the companion website. To follow the argument fully, you need to look at and think about the artworks used as examples.

Because paintings are most readily available on the internet and it is easier and cheaper to look at a picture than download a music track or go to a play, most of my examples are paintings. Of course, it is better to see a work of art in the original than on the internet. For this reason, I have – as far as possible – chosen examples that are held by art galleries in the UK (the National Gallery and the Tate galleries).

In discussing the three answers on the syllabus, I have swapped around sections on expressiveness and on a special artistic quality, so that the discussion of valuing art for its artistic quality occurs now in section II and the discussion of expressiveness occurs in section III.

I. We value art because it informs us

Good art should portray authentically

The value of representation

The desire to make pictures of the world goes back tens of thousands of years. **1** The caves of Lascaux contain over 2,000 paintings, some dating from 30,000 years ago. Today, we put photos up on websites for other people to see. Human beings have a drive to represent the world and a desire to see these representations.

The most common starting point for understanding a painting is to think about what it is a painting *of*. We often praise a picture for the way in which it has managed to capture a scene. **2** Constable's *The Hay Wain* (1821) is so true to nature, you can almost see the clouds moving across the sky. We praise a bust for its likeness to the person it represents, such as **3** Oscar Nemon's depiction of *Churchill* (c. 1955). We praise a play, such as Arthur Miller's *Death of a Salesman*, for being true to life.

Paintings represent objects in such a way that we can see the object *in* the painting. If we don't know who or what the painting is a painting of, then it loses its point. Knowing that a painting is of **4** *King Henry VIII* (c. 1536; after Hans Holbein the Younger) makes a difference to what we think about it. **5**

Heda's *Still Life with a Lobster* (1650–9) is impressive in its accuracy and complexity. If a painting claims to represent some object, but we just can't see the object in the painting, then the painting has failed as a painting.

All this supports the claim that the ability to portray objects or situations authentically is one we value. We can point out, further, that artists spend many years developing and perfecting techniques that enable them to gain this ability. To portray a character convincingly, actors may even temporarily live life the way the character would (in *Marathon Man*, whenever there was a scene in which his character was breathless from running, Dustin Hoffman would run half a mile to become breathless before filming the scene). The artists, then, are clearly attempting to get the audience to *recognise* what is being depicted in the artwork.

That art should represent authentically also explains why certain real events, such as the Holocaust, or objects, such as bodies mutilated by torture, can seem 'off-limits' for art. The horror, terror, wrongness of the original event or object stops the work from becoming art. An attempt to turn real-life horror into art can seem tasteless and disrespectful.

> Outline and illustrate two reasons to think good art should portray authentically.

How is art supposed to stand for reality?

IMITATION AND COPYING

What is the relation between an artwork and what the artwork is of? Plato argued that art is an imitation or a copy of reality.

We first need to remind ourselves of his **metaphysics**. Plato argued that the ultimate reality is the Forms. Particular things, what we detect with our senses, are a kind of 'copy' of the Forms. The Form of Beauty is perfect beauty. All beautiful things are beautiful because they 'share' or 'participate' in the Form. But none do so perfectly – nothing we experience with our senses is ever perfectly beautiful. So we can say that particular things are a kind of imperfect 'copy' of the Forms.

> We discussed Plato's theory of the Forms in ARE ALL CLAIMS ABOUT WHAT EXISTS ULTIMATELY GROUNDED IN AND JUSTIFIED BY SENSE DATA? II (Ch. 1, p. 29).

Plato argued that art copies particular things. He gives the example of a bed. There is the perfect Form of a bed; then, as a kind of copy of that, a carpenter makes a bed; a painting of a bed is a copy of the carpenter's bed.

> *Republic*, Book X

Whether or not particular things are copies of the Forms, is all art an imitation or copy of particular things? In any literal sense, we can argue it is not. Imitation first. To paint a facial expression is not to imitate a facial expression. We do not confuse a painting of a facial expression for a real face; nor do pictures try to fool us into thinking that we are looking at reality, not a picture. Actors

An exception is *trompe l'oeil* paintings, such as **6** Pere Borrell del Caso, *Escaping Criticism* (1874). (*Trompe l'oeil* is French for 'trick the eye'.) But even here, we only enjoy the painting when we cease to be fooled.

CONCEPTUAL SCHEMES AND THEIR PHILOSOPHICAL IMPLICATIONS (pp. 21 and 40)

Discuss the claim that art does not imitate or copy reality.

do not imitate the characters they play, they 'become' them temporarily. If they had to imitate them, how could they discover what the character 'really' does, so as to imitate it?

Copying does no better. First, copying presupposes there is an original to copy. Second, the success of a copy is judged by the degree to which it accurately resembles the original. Neither seems to be true of art.

In Ch. 1, we discussed the idea that experience is interpreted by concepts. There is no real 'experience' before this process of interpretation. If this is right, then artists cannot 'copy' from the world, because no experience of the world is prior to interpretation. What we see is conditioned by the concepts we have.

We can object that there is still better or worse resemblance between a painting and what it is of. A painting with red grass and a green sky does not resemble the world as well as a painting with green grass and a blue sky. Nevertheless, we can argue that even when an artwork resembles reality and resemblance is captured by an artwork, there isn't always some particular scene or situation the artist had in mind before they completed the work; they may invent it as they go. And so they cannot be copying from the world.

More importantly, we can argue that a good copy is not the same as good art. First, in art, resemblance is often besides the point. Compare two sunsets, **7** Vernet's *A Landscape at Sunset* (1773) and **8** Turner's *The Scarlet Sunset* (1830–40). The styles are quite different; in making a comparison, is accuracy or the degree of *resemblance* to a sunset the point? Both involve stylistic interpretations of a sunset. Or again, consider **9** Picasso's *The Three Dancers* (1925). Its lack of resemblance does not detract at all from its power. If resemblance was the main reason we value art, then wouldn't a photograph always be a better work of art than a painting? Second, copying does not involve the creative imagination as good art does. For example, a good *forgery* is a good copy, but that does not make it a good work of art (or a work of art at all).

All these points can be made about the visual arts, in which there is at least the possibility that the artist is copying from reality. But what about music or poetry or literature? In these cases, there is simply nothing the artist could be copying from.

REPRESENTATION

Perhaps, then, to say that good art should portray authentically is to say simply that it should represent reality, where this is not taken to mean imitate, copy or even resemble. This avoids the objections above, but can we say what representation means, beyond the idea that there is something the artwork is *of* or *about*? We won't have understood why we value art unless we can say something more specific.

There is this: we can point out that to understand a work of art, we need to master a system of conventions or symbols. For example, in medieval and Renaissance art, St Paul is always represented with a book and sword, as in **10** Cima de Conegliano's *The Virgin and Child with Saint Paul and Saint Francis* (c. 1508–30); saints are always represented with haloes, as in **11** *The Wilton Diptych* (1395–9). These conventions, and many others, help us to understand the painting. Art uses the system of conventions to represent, just as language does. But is this enough to save the theory?

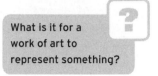

What is it for a work of art to represent something?

Are all arts equally concerned with representing?

If there are works of art that do not represent, then the claim that we value art because it represents the world must be false. At least, this cannot be the only reason we value art; and perhaps it will not even be the main reason. And there clearly are artworks that are not representational.

Within painting, there is abstract art, such as **12** Karel Appel, *Untitled* (1960). However, we can respond that this is representational. The painting is itself two-dimensional, but in what is represented, some shapes are *in front of* others. In other words, three-dimensional space is represented. This is an important point – representation in its most general sense does not need to be representation of anything recognisable in the world.

However, some abstract art does not even represent three-dimensional space (**13** Barnett Newman, *Adam* (1951–2)). Second, this response doesn't help the claim that good art should portray authentically, because in cases of representing abstract three-dimensional spaces, no thing is represented, so we cannot talk about 'authentic' representation.

In music (not set to words or actions), the lack of representation is obvious – a sequence of sounds does not describe or try to describe anything else. It also shows that a system of conventions is not the same as representation. Classical music has a very large number of conventions – the idea of a 'key', acceptable key changes, which instruments are used, the organisation of movements within a piece, and so on – but for all that, it doesn't represent anything.

We can reply that we can read something into music, that it reminds us of this or that. But we cannot say that it *represents* this or that unless it was part of the artist's intention for it to represent in this way.

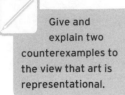

Give and explain two counterexamples to the view that art is representational.

Could we say that a piece of music represents a mood or an emotion? But while Beethoven's *Symphony No. 7* is a very joyful piece, we don't say it *represents* joy. Emotions can't be seen the way the Virgin Mary can be seen in **11** *The Wilton Diptych*; they can't be heard the way sounds can. It is more accurate to say that emotion or mood is expressed rather than represented.

Even if art informs us, is that why we value it as art?

Plato uses his theory of art as copying to criticise art. If art is just representation, valued for what it represents, why would we look at art rather than at the world? Anyone can create images, Plato says – just carry a mirror around and you can make an image of anything in the world! For Plato, the Forms are reality, particular objects are a poor substitute, and art is a poor substitute for particular objects. As a copy of a copy, art is inferior indeed. If we want to be informed, we should turn to philosophy and the Forms, not art.

We can add a second criticism to this: if we valued art for what it represented, then we would value a forgery as much as the original artwork, because it would convey the same information. But we don't, so there must be some other reason we value art.

We can reply that in saying we value representation, we don't need to say that we value a painting for *what* it represents. Instead, we value it *as* a representation. For example, we enjoy imitations even when we do not enjoy what is imitated. While someone's walk may be ungainly, an imitation of their walk may be amusing. Likewise, in art, we enjoy the skill involved, the choice of what to represent, how it is represented, and so on. But this reply takes us away from the idea that we value art because it informs us, and points to the activity of *imagination*, both of the artist and of the viewer.

Finally, focusing on how we are informed by art makes our appreciation of art too intellectual. We would always need to get the resemblance, the allusion, the message. But our response to art is much more than this. In particular, it involves our emotions.

Discuss the claim that good art portrays authentically.

Key points • • •

- We have a natural desire to make and look at representations. We praise art that is true to nature or to life, or that resembles what it is of.

- Artists work hard to develop techniques for depicting objects and situations accurately or authentically.
- Plato argued that art imitates particular objects, as particular objects imitate the Forms.
- But art does not literally imitate reality. Nor does it copy it. First, all perceptual experience involves interpretation – there is nothing independent to copy. Second, good art need not be a good copy.
- We could still argue that good art represents reality well. But then we need an account of 'representation'; and in any case, not all art represents anything at all.
- If we valued art for what it represents, why not just look at what is represented? If we value it as a representation, this suggests we value it not just because it informs us, but because of its imaginative qualities.
- Finally, concentrating just on how it may inform us overlooks the emotional nature of our response to art.

II. We value art because of its particular 'artistic' quality

Good art affords an aesthetic enjoyment of 'form'

Aesthetic enjoyment

We do not respond to works of art in the same way as we would if we were seeing what is represented. For example, in a play, if there is a murder, we don't try to call the police. In response to **14** Caravaggio's *Salome receives the head of St John the Baptist* (1607–10), we do not vomit as we might if confronted with a real severed head. In fact, we are capable of enjoying the painting whereas we could never enjoy the reality.

Immanuel Kant argues that there is a special kind of pleasure that goes with enjoying works of art, which explains why we value art. Aesthetic pleasure is distinct from getting pleasure from what we like or from what is morally good. It is 'disinterested' in a variety of ways.

First, whether what is represented exists is irrelevant. We enjoy simply contemplating it. Second, approving of what is represented is irrelevant to our enjoyment, as in **14** Caravaggio's *Salome*. Third, whether what is represented is something we want or could use is irrelevant. Finally, the pleasure taken in

Critique of Judgment

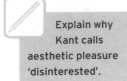

Explain why Kant calls aesthetic pleasure 'disinterested'.

the artwork is not itself the satisfaction of any independent desire or practical interest. For instance, being pleased at owning a painting is not aesthetic pleasure; nor is being pleased that it will make money; nor is being pleased that a play criticises someone disliked.

'PSYCHIC DISTANCE'

This has led some thinkers to suggest that the right attitude to take towards artworks involves 'psychic distance', indicating the fact that the attitude doesn't involve our personal interests and that we are aware we are experiencing a representation, not reality.

However, the phrase is unfortunate. First, it is misleading if we think of psychic distance as a 'scale' (more or less distant). Someone who calls the police when watching Shakespeare's *Macbeth* is not less psychically distant than someone who is motivated to, but resists doing so. To treat the play as reality *at all* is not to have adopted an aesthetic attitude.

Second, it suggests that we aren't moved emotionally (it reminds us of the term 'emotionally distant'). But aesthetic responses can be emotionally powerful.

Third, we can object that there is no special aesthetic *attitude*. Instead, we simply pay attention to the aesthetic *features* of an artwork. The reason this seems like a distinct attitude is that we are not able to direct our attention in this way when it is distracted by other, more practical concerns. (When faced with a charging lion, you don't admire the beauty of its mane.) But in fact, we can argue, aesthetic attention is not a matter of *how* we look but *what* we are concentrating on.

Discuss the concept of 'psychic distance'.

PLEASURE AND VALUE

We need not say that Kant's account of aesthetic pleasure as disinterested involves 'psychic distance' as a special attitude of attention. But we might still object that it is not the answer to why we value art.

First, we can object that other emotional responses, apart from aesthetic pleasure, are part of our response to art. Second, we can object that we value more than just the individual pleasure that art brings. For example, we value its emotional expressiveness (see p. 287). Third, neither a description of the attitude nor of aesthetic pleasure tells us what we *are* aware of, what *gives* us pleasure, in experiencing artworks.

We can suggest a reply to the third objection. Kant and other philosophers who emphasise the importance of a special aesthetic enjoyment argue that what we respond to in artworks is *form*.

Explain and illustrate the claim that we value art for the aesthetic pleasure it gives us.

Form

There are many non-aesthetic descriptions we can give of any artwork. We may describe the shapes and the colours in a painting. We can note the rhymes, meter and alliteration of a poem. Of a piece of music, we can list the key it is in, how many movements it has, the pace of each, the motifs and when they appear and reappear. In a novel, we may talk of the structure of the plot.

In aesthetic judgements, we say that a work is balanced, harmonious, well-rounded or feels complete (for example, **15** Leonardo Da Vinci's *The Virgin of the Rocks* (c. 1491–1508)). In sculpture and architecture in particular, we will say that it is well-proportioned (**16** Palladio's *Villa Capra* (1566–71)) or flows dynamically (**17** Brancusi's *Fish* (1926)). In ballet, we talk of the elegance and grace of the dancers' bodies, both individually and in arrangement together. In each case, we pick out *relations between non-aesthetic features*. We are talking about the form of the work.

In aesthetic response and pleasure, Kant argued, we respond to the formal properties (the properties of form) of a work. What we value, then, about a work of art is its form, which is its 'particular aesthetic quality'.

This position was also famously defended by Clive Bell. He argued that accuracy of representation is not the point in art (see p. 278). It must therefore be something else about the artwork, viz. its formal qualities, how the artist has manipulated (for painting) colour and shape. In **18** Cezanne's *Hillside in Provence* (1890–2), the view is not realistic, in the sense of 'an accurate portrayal', but this is irrelevant. What captures us is the way he has put colours together to produce the effect that elicits from us an aesthetic response.

Bell argued that because form is the object of aesthetic appreciation, everything we need to take into account is there in the work of art. We do not consider what it is meant to represent, why the artist made it, or the culture in which and for which it was made.

The view that form is what we value avoids a number of the objections we made against representation. For example, every artwork has formal qualities, but not every artwork represents something. Formal qualities are properties of the representation (the artwork), not what is represented – this explains how we can be interested in a painting but not in what it is a painting of.

We may object that form does not distinguish art from what is not art, so it cannot be what we value about art. We can respond that while everything, in a sense, has *some* form, what is distinctive about art is that it explores, develops and manipulates formal qualities just for the sake of contemplating them. Many

Explain the relation between aesthetic pleasure and form.

Art

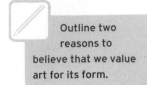

Outline two reasons to believe that we value art for its form.

artists spend their careers attempting to discover and present a perfection of form, and a great deal of both art theory and criticism has been written on the techniques of creating good form.

Criticisms of formalism

Is the notion of 'form' clear?

A first objection to formalism is that the central concept of 'form' is unclear. If we want to defend the value of an artwork, we cannot simply say 'look at its form'. Even to say that it is elegant is unclear – are all elegant artworks elegant in the same way? We need to illustrate the formal description (elegant, balanced, etc.) by what is *specific* in *this* work of art. Until we have done that, our praise remains vague. It seemed a strength of the account that all artworks have 'form'. But without application to specific cases, this gives us no idea of what we value.

Second, to say that we respond to just the form of a painting is very implausible. To ignore what it represents, as Bell suggests, would undermine our response. That a painting is a portrait (that is, that it represents a person) and of *this* person (**4** *King Henry VIII*) forms part of our understanding of it. The same goes for the importance of facial expressions, as in **19** Rembrandt's *Self-portrait at the age of 63* (1669), and of knowing the story that a painting represents, as in **20** Velazquez's *Christ in the House of Martha and Mary* (1618) (the story is to be found in the gospel of Luke, Ch. 10). Furthermore, we cannot begin to understand certain works of art, such as **21** Duchamp's infamous *Fountain* (1917), without knowing the context in which they were made. Even for Cezanne (Bell's chosen example), it was important that he was true to life, that he captured the natural scene and its mood, though not through direct resemblance.

Third, for the vast majority of representational paintings, it is impossible for us to experience the form in isolation – we do so via representation. For example, it is almost impossible to describe shapes, as in a portrait, without saying what they are shapes *of* (eyes, nose, chin), and it is impossible to see them just as shapes in formal relation to each other.

A similar argument was made in Is DIRECT REALISM NAIVE II? (Ch. 6, p. 216) by direct realism against representative realism.

Formalism is perhaps most persuasive in the case of music, when there is no issue of representation. The sounds by themselves are clearly not what we value, it is their arrangement. Our aesthetic appreciation of music is therefore an appreciation of the form.

But even here we should not overgeneralise. Many people have thought that music in some way expresses emotions (see p. 287), and that this is what gives us pleasure. And when music is accompanied by words or actions (as in opera), and the music works with the words and drama to represent or express something.

Can we say clearly what it is that we value in valuing the form of an artwork?

Are there recognisable formal universals displayed in art?

Bell thought that for us to talk meaningfully about art, there needed to be something universal across all works of art. But it doesn't look like the same formal qualities are displayed throughout art. Even when we might use the same word, such as 'elegant', of a painting, a poem, or a ballet, it is difficult to say what these different 'elegances' have in common. And we don't always value particular qualities each time they appear. So, for example, a painting might be elegant yet it would have been better if it had been 'rougher', for example, because the subject matter requires it. It is 'too elegant'.

But we can reply that there do not need to be universal formal qualities. The only universal is 'form' itself, but – like colour – there are many, many ways in which artworks can display good form. Yet we can still say that we value form, because in each case we are basing our judgements on the relations between features of the work.

But we can press the objection by appealing to the point above – that the general idea of 'form' is doing almost no work. Until we have applied it to the *particular* artwork and demonstrated how *this* work has good form, we have not clarified the claim that the work is valuable because of its form.

Is 'good form' the same thing in each artwork?

Even if 'form' matters, is it the 'essence' of art qua art?

We suggested (p. 280) that it is not what is represented, but something about the painting as a representation that engages our imagination and emotions that we value. We can argue that the same is true of form. It is not form, but what form expresses or enables, that we respond to in art.

To support this claim, note that we cannot move from aesthetic descriptions of a work's formal qualities (elegance, balance, etc.) to a judgement of whether it is *any good*, that is, whether we value it. Unity can be tedious, harmony can be mindless. So we need to go beyond form, as we need to go beyond representation, to find what makes art valuable.

Discuss the view that good art affords an aesthetic enjoyment of form.

Key points • • •

- Kant argues that aesthetic enjoyment is disinterested. Whether what is represented exists is irrelevant, as is whether we approve, like or can use it. Any desire satisfied by the artwork, except through contemplating it, is also irrelevant.
- Does this involve a special aesthetic attitude of psychic distance? We can argue the term is misleading in suggesting a 'scale' and a lack of emotion. We can also argue there is no special aesthetic attitude, only attention to aesthetic features.
- We can object that aesthetic enjoyment is not the only value of art – we have other emotional responses and we value expressiveness.
- The form of an artwork is the relations between its non-aesthetic features. Kant and Bell argue that aesthetic pleasure derives from contemplating form.
- Bell argued that only form matters; representation is completely irrelevant. The importance of form explains the fact that we can be interested in a painting but not in what it represents; and the fact that many artists seek to perfect form.
- Even if there are no universal formal properties across art, formalism can argue that all good art displays good form.
- We can object that 'form' as such is unclear, and has to be explained in the case of each artwork individually. Furthermore, we cannot experience or describe form separately from representation.
- We can object that form is not enough to account for why we value art, because we cannot infer from a description of form as to whether a work is any good.

III. We value art because of its expressive quality

Good art is moving or captures a mood or feeling

Emotion in art

Representationalism and formalism, we can argue, miss the psychological dimension of art. There are two sides to this. First, in making a work of art, artists are expressing themselves, especially their emotions, not necessarily directly, but in some way. This is true even of the most abstract works. In his work, for example, **22** *Composition C (No. III) with Red, Yellow and Blue* (1935), Piet Mondrian said he was trying to express the spiritual sublime.

Second, we are emotionally moved in response to art. We could argue that there is a special, aesthetic emotion that arises in us. But this can seem too narrow. Just as art can express any number of feelings, so it can arouse different feelings. Perhaps, then, we can say that there is a special aesthetic way of experiencing emotions, one that takes into account the 'disinterested' nature of aesthetic response, for example, maybe we feel them 'in imagination'. For example, Wordsworth talked of poetry as 'emotion recollected in tranquillity'.

We can argue that this account improves on the two above. First, as we've already argued (p. 280), it is more accurate to say that artworks *express* emotion than that they *represent* emotion. Of course, emotions can be represented. But we need to distinguish between the emotion represented in a painting and the emotion expressed by a painting, as in **23** Jan Steen's *The Effects of Intemperance* (1663–5). All the characters are in drunken merriment, but the painting as a whole serves as a warning. We are interested in the emotions expressed by the work as a whole.

But, second, this doesn't make representation irrelevant, because there is a close connection between what is represented, how it is represented and the feelings expressed, as clearly shown in **24** Grünewald's *The Crucifixion* (c. 1502). The tortured body of Christ and the sickly greens and yellows combine to express horror and pathos. However, what is represented need not be something we could actually encounter for the work to express and generate powerful feelings, as in **25** Francis Bacon's *Three Studies for Figures at the Base of a Crucifixion* (c. 1944).

Third, non-representational art can equally express or evoke feelings, for example, through its form. In **26** Mark Rothko's *Red on Maroon* (1959), the pulsating edges, the lack of saturation in the colour, the smears in the red are unsettling, yet the way in which the red rectangle sinks gently into the darker background at the bottom is comforting. In music, we find rhythms, pace and key echo our emotional experiences – a 'lively' pace in a major key can have the energy and optimism of joy, a slow pace in a minor key can express sadness.

Furthermore, our understanding of what the artist was expressing is increased by looking at the context in which the work was created, including the personal life of the artist, the tradition in which they worked, the innovations in

This is discussed further in AESTHETIC EMOTION? (p. 306).

expression they made, and the broader culture context (as in **21** Duchamp's *Fountain*). Trying to see the work as the original audience would have seen it, with the ideas and expectations of their time, further deepens our response.

The Russian novelist and critic Leo Tolstoy defended a version of this theory about the value of art. It is not just that the art expresses the artist and evokes emotions in the audience; it is that it *connects* the two: 'Art is a human activity consisting in this, that one man consciously by means of certain external signs, hands onto others feelings he has lived through, and that others are infected by those feelings and also experience them'. The value of art doesn't lie in the pleasure of individuals, taken as individuals. We are, Tolstoy argued, social creatures, and art connects us to each other. The audience comes to share the artist's psychological state, establishing a bond between them. We may add that, as the audience comes to share the same psychological state as each other, a bond is also established between members of the audience.

Discussion and development

As expressed so far, this theory is open to a number of objections.

First, a work of art can't be just about transmitting feeling – in that case, anything that transmitted the feeling from artist to audience would serve as well. But artworks are not replaceable in this way.

We can reply that nothing else *could* convey exactly this feeling, as nothing else expresses exactly this feeling. A central claim of expressivism is that the feeling is not something that takes a precise form *before* the work is completed. The artist is not 'copying' from a feeling to the work. Instead, in creating the work they are working out the feeling more precisely. The artist makes the work 'just so', a task that is demanding in its detail. 'Infection is only obtained when an artist finds those infinitely minute degrees of which a work of art consists', says Tolstoy. Hence nothing else could take its place as an expression of this feeling.

But, second, it is simply false that the artist needs to experience the emotions that they are trying to arouse in the audience. A composer commissioned to write a rousing, patriotic piece may not feel patriotism. This is true, but they do need to be acquainted with emotions well enough to create an imaginative expression of what will arouse those feelings.

Third, we can object that it is too restrictive to talk just of 'mood' or 'feeling'. What is expressed is not just emotion. This misses out the intellectual aspects of art, the *ideas* that the artist is expressing. We can argue, then, that

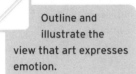

What is Art?

Outline and illustrate the view that art expresses emotion.

Discuss the relation between the emotions of the artist, those expressed in the work, and those aroused in the audience.

it would be better to talk of good art as expressing a vision rather than a feeling or mood.

We can reply that this misses the important second half of the theory, that good art should be *moving*. In other words, the vision cannot be just intellectual; it must touch us emotionally, and for it to do this, we can argue, it must also be an expression of emotion.

Fourth, we can argue that the audience need not come to *share* the artist's feelings or attitudes. For example, Marat was a controversial political figure who advocated the guillotining of many of his political opponents after the French Revolution and was assassinated in his bath. In **27** *The Death of Marat* (1793), Jacques-Louis David, who shared Marat's political views, portrays Marat sympathetically, as a martyr. In responding to his painting aesthetically, we need not come to share these feelings about Marat or his death. We should accept this, but can reply that to engage with a work, we nevertheless need to try to see it from the perspective that is expressed by it.

Finally, we may object that the theory has not yet explained what is *distinctive* about emotional expression in art and our emotional responses to art.

> We discuss this idea of vision in GOOD ART SHOULD ILLUMINATE OUR EXPERIENCE OR REVEAL 'TRUTHS' (p. 292).

> Discuss the claim that art transmits emotions from the artist to the audience.

Collingwood

The philosopher R.C. Collingwood provides an answer to this last point by developing the point mentioned in response to the first objection above. A work of art is not an outpouring of emotion or an attempt to deliberately arouse emotions, he argued. It is, instead, a clarification of emotion. It is pure expression for its own sake, and the emotion expressed is not known until the work is complete. Art is not 'the conscious working-out of means to the achievement of a conscious purpose', but what the completed work expresses unfolds in the process of creation. It invites an exercise of imagination in the audience to recreate this emotion for themselves.

> *The Principles of Art*

When talking about what an artwork expresses, it would be a mistake to think this was conscious to the mind of the artist as they worked. While the artist may have certain conscious 'intentions', much more of their psychology goes into the work than this. In particular, their unconscious mental states, emotions, vision and experience of the world, can play a large role. An artist can be surprised by their own product. Nevertheless, when they view the work, they sense it has expressed something for them.

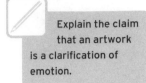

Explain the claim that an artwork is a clarification of emotion.

Collingwood argues that 'art proper' is not an expression of emotion for any purpose or entertainment. As such, it should be distinguished from art as entertainment, where the purpose is to *arouse and discharge* particular emotions in the audience. Horror films are a clear example of this, where the aim is that the audience feels (enjoyably) terrified. Art proper should also be distinguished from art as 'magic', where the purpose is to *arouse and direct* particular emotions, such as patriotism or, in religious art, devotion to God.

Objections to Collingwood

We can object that the theory turns the audience into an artist – they must imaginatively reconstruct the emotion of the artist, to discover the precise emotion expressed in the work. This seems implausible, and in fact, Collingwood accepts that it is, at best, only partially successful. But we can reply that art can *communicate*, not just arouse, emotion – if not by imaginative reconstruction, then how?

Second, does all art express emotion? Some conceptual art, for instance, expresses an idea; many artefacts, such as vases or rugs, may be beautiful without expressing any feeling; and what of 'nice' music, pleasant to listen to, but expressing nothing in particular? Collingwood's response is to say that none of this is art proper. We can object that this threatens to make his account circular: 'What do we value about art? Emotional expression. What about art that isn't expressive? It isn't art.' If what *counts* as art is that which is emotionally expressive, then *of course* emotional expression will be what we value. But this isn't a complete account of what we value if we try to include as art everything that has usually been seen as art.

Third, many things that are emotionally expressive, like saying 'I love you', are not art. It must be, then, that there is something else about art that we value or we cannot explain why we value it *as art*. Collingwood would respond that art proper does not seek to arouse emotion directly, as these other expressions would. But again, we can object that much religious art, such as **28** Bellini's *The Dead Christ supported by Angels* (1465–70), was painted to help arouse religious experience and emotions. People clearly have valued art for this function. To exclude it completely seems arbitrary. So, again, what distinguishes art from other expressions of emotion? We can reply that it is the attempt to clarify precisely a feeling that is unclear.

Finally, on this view, whether something is a work of art depends entirely on its origins in the state of mind of the artist. If it is a working-out, a clarification or articulation of their feeling, then it is art; otherwise, it is not. Is this right? Are not other issues of form and success in representation also relevant?

> Explain and illustrate two objections to the view that we value art because it expresses and arouses emotion.

Key points • • •

- In making works of art, artists express themselves, especially their emotions. In experiencing art, we are emotionally moved.
- The emotions expressed by a work of art are distinct from those (if any) represented by it. Our interest is in the emotions expressed.
- This account can explain the importance of representation and form – they help express feeling. It also explains why knowing the background to an artwork is useful – it helps us understand what the artist is expressing.
- Tolstoy argued the value of art is not just in expression and arousal, but in the connection between the artist and audience that is created.
- Works of art aren't replaceable. An artwork is a precise expression of a feeling that is not fully formed or clear to the artist before the work is complete. This is what makes the expression of emotion in art distinctive.
- In some cases, artists do not need to experience the very emotion they want to arouse, but they do need to be acquainted with them.
- More than just emotion can be expressed; but we can argue that good art should always be moving, so cannot be just intellectual.
- The audience needn't come to share the artist's emotions, but to understand the work, they need to try to see it from the perspective that it expresses.
- Talking of what the artist expresses is not talking of what was conscious to the artist or what they consciously intended. Much of their psychology goes into the creation of the work.
- We can object that not all art expresses emotion. So what do we value in these works of art?
- Not everything that expresses emotion is art, so what is distinctive about art? Collingwood argues that art does not try to arouse emotion directly, but we can object that, for example, religious art, does. A better defence is that art tries to clarify precisely feelings that are initially unclear.
- Is this the only criterion for art, or do matters of representation and form count as well?

DEVELOPMENT

I. We value art because it informs us

Good art should illuminate our experience or reveal 'truths'

The artist's vision

In our previous discussion, we rejected the idea that the value of art lay in its ability to portray authentically (p. 278f.). Yet we might say that art is in some way *about* reality if it conveys some kind of 'knowledge' or 'truth'. For example, **29** Picasso's *Guernica* (1937) shows us the horror and awfulness of war. This is the 'message' that people come away with.

We objected (p. 288) that to say art expresses only emotion is too narrow. Think again of **24** Grünewald's *The Crucifixion*. The crucifixion of Christ has a huge symbolic meaning in the Christian understanding of God, human life and our place in the universe. Grünewald is not simply evoking sorrow and anguish, but a religious message as well. What an artwork informs us of, then, is a vision of the world.

This version of the view that we value art because it informs us avoids many of the objections raised against the previous version. First, the issues about imitating or copying from what is seen become irrelevant. The artist is not seeking to replicate or resemble what we perceive. When they use representation, they use it to express a deeper sense of reality, something that tells us not (or not merely) what we can see but what we experience in a fuller sense.

Second, we can accept the distinction between what the work represents explicitly and what it expresses. Artists use representation to convey their vision. This also explains the difference between valuing what is represented and valuing the artwork as a representation of it.

Third, we can distinguish between the value of an original artwork and that of a forgery. A forgery does not express the forger's vision; it is not made as an expression of an insight or a truth that the artist searches for and works out in the making of the work. What the forgery will look like (if it is good) is fixed from the outset.

That art expresses a vision is also shown by our criticism of art that has 'lost touch'. The work of an artist can lose its force over time if they fall into certain habits; their vision is no longer 'fresh' and what they express seems dull or facile. Or again, a work may try to capture and express an important event, but we say that it fails because it is not 'true to' the real significance of what happened; the artist's vision is faulty.

Compare and contrast the claims that good art portrays authentically and that it expresses a vision.

Going further: what could we mean by 'truth' in art?

What do we mean of the artist's vision, and what does it inform us of? We can start by thinking about idealisation. **30** Palma Vecchio's *A Blonde Woman* (c. 1520) is not a portrait of any particular woman, but an expression of the ideal woman, or the ideal of 'woman' – as Palma Vecchio imagines it. Many Renaissance artists consciously sought to represent what was ideal. Talk of idealisation reminds us of Plato's theory of the Forms. In idealisation, art is not copying particular objects, as Plato thought, it is 'copying' the Forms. Alternatively, we can argue that nothing is copied because the ideal, or more generally the vision, does not exist precisely prior to the completion of the artwork. The ideal or vision is clarified and made more precise as the work develops.

Plato thought the Forms are ultimate reality, and knowledge of the Forms knowledge of the deepest truths. To 'copy' or express them would therefore express truth. Even if we don't accept Plato's idea of the Forms, the model of idealisation helps us understand one way in which art might express a truth. That *this* is ideal is an expression of human judgement. So understanding something as an expression of an ideal contributes to self-understanding. Or again, an ideal may illuminate our experience, for example, by operating as a standard against which we measure experience.

See GOOD ART IS MOVING OR CAPTURES A MOOD OR FEELING (p. 289).

See ARE ALL CLAIMS ABOUT WHAT EXISTS ULTIMATELY GROUNDED IN AND JUSTIFIED BY SENSE DATA? II (Ch. 1, p. 29).

A different way art may express 'truth' is through the attention it pays to the ordinary. 'Look', a painting can say; look at how *individual*, how *unique* objects that we take for granted really are. This intensity of vision is found in Van Gogh's work, such as **31** *Van Gogh's Chair* (1888). The artist sees what we overlook in everyday life, and expresses the truth that everything is precisely itself and nothing else, to be valued for its unique existence.

Novels can contribute to self-understanding and illuminate experience in other ways. A good novelist can portray the different points of view of different characters; the novel therefore may help us to understand how other people think and feel (as long as we don't confuse real people with

Explain and illustrate the view that good art reveals truths.

fictional characters!). The novelist may portray the experience of someone very different from us in a sympathetic light and so lead us to understand the world in a different light. They may also describe universal human experiences, such as getting older and the different views someone takes of their younger self over time; and so we may come to understand ourselves better.

Even if art informs us, is that why we value it as art? II

We can object that not all art expresses a vision or truth or even tries to. It is difficult to say of much music that it expresses a vision, rather than simply emotion. And there is art that is made simply to be enjoyed, and nothing more. Examples include pleasant, entertaining music and artefacts such as vases and rugs.

Second, in our previous discussion (p. 280), we objected that this view of the value of art was too intellectual. We can repeat that objection here if we say that the vision of the artist is valuable because it informs us rather than, say, because of its expressive qualities.

Third, the idea of vision – particularly if we say that the vision develops as the artwork is created – does not always involve an understanding of how the world is already. We are therefore not learning something *about* the world independently of what is being expressed in the artwork. There is not always a message to take away into life more generally. In many cases, the vision is there just be to enjoyed and contemplated. 'Information', then, is the wrong model.

Finally, emphasising information also misses what is distinctive about art as art. A work of theology can express a religious view of the crucifixion. But it is not art and is not valued as art. So, again, it is the expressive qualities – both how the vision is expressed and the emotional qualities of the vision – that we value in art. The vision must move us, and it is being moved that is part of what we value.

Assess the claim that we value art because it informs us.

Key points • • •

- The view that good art expresses a vision or reveals truths improves on the claim that it portrays authentically. The artist is not necessarily trying to resemble what we see; there is a distinction between what is explicitly represented and what is expressed; and we can explain why a forgery is not as valuable as an original.
- We criticise art if its vision is 'faulty' in some way.
- Art can reveal truths through portraying idealisations, which can tell us about the object idealised and about ourselves; through drawing our attention to the uniqueness of what we experience; and through helping us understand other people and ourselves.
- We can object that not all art expresses a vision or truth.
- We can also object that this view of why we value art is too intellectual, that the model of art conveying 'information' is wrong and doesn't express what is distinctive about art.

II. We value art because of its particular 'artistic' quality

Good art affords an aesthetic enjoyment of 'form' II

We need to take further the suggestion, made at the end of our discussion of AESTHETIC ENJOYMENT (p. 281), that aesthetic pleasure is related to form.

Kant on 'free play'

We discussed Kant's theory of sensory experience in Ch. 1. He argues that until experience is organised by concepts, it remains unintelligible, meaningless, a confused buzz. Our most basic concepts, which Kant calls 'categories', enable us to experience an objective world of physical objects. However, we obviously have many more concepts than these. The production and application of concepts is the work of what Kant calls the 'understanding'. However, the organisation of stimuli is the work of the 'imagination'. In normal perception, the understanding dominates, in that the way stimuli are organised is constrained

CONCEPTUAL SCHEMES
AND THEIR
PHILOSOPHICAL
IMPLICATIONS II (p. 41f.).

by the concepts we apply. So, for example, as I walk through a wood, I see the trees, their branches moving gently in the wind. But if I free my imagination up from applying the concept of 'tree', I can start to see the trees as persons, their branches as arms. I give my imagination a degree of 'free play', though still guided by the shapes of the trees.

Something like this happens in the aesthetic response, argues Kant. Because we are disinterested, we can ignore the question of what something 'really' is. There is no need to constrain our experience by particular concepts. Our imagination has free play in how it organises what we see, our understanding has free play in creating new concepts (why stop at persons, why not invent a new type of creature out of the trees?). Good art enables us to do this; it stimulates us to free our imagination and understanding and just enjoy making representations. Aesthetic enjoyment, we might argue (going beyond Kant), celebrates freedom and the possibility of refreshing our minds, our creative powers, what is at the very heart of our experience of anything. It is a form of spiritual renewal.

This freedom, Kant says, is enabled by the form of what we experience. For instance, a beautiful object seems as though it were made to be looked at. There is a feeling of perfect match between the powers and nature of our senses and the object itself. This can't be produced just by what Kant calls the 'matter' of the representations, in vision, colours, in hearing, sounds. It must be produced by the way in which the matter is organised, that is, the form: 'The colours which give brilliancy to the sketch are part of the charm. They may no doubt, in their own way, enliven the object for sensation, but make it really worth looking at and beautiful they cannot.'

Because his account draws on the disinterested nature of the aesthetic attitude and the structure of the mind, we can argue that it has this advantage over expressivism: it justifies aesthetic judgements as *objective*. Aesthetic judgements rely on nothing particular in me – no interest or experience of mine. If they depended on specific emotions, wouldn't these vary from person to person and make the judgements subjective? According to Kant, everyone who responds to the object in the right way, that is, disinterestedly and to its form, should make the same aesthetic judgement about it.

Outline the idea of 'free play' of imagination and understanding.

Critique of Judgment, § 14

Explain Kant's account of the relation between form and aesthetic pleasure.

Going further: Bell on significant form

Bell argues that it is not form per se that we respond to, but what he calls 'significant form'. After all, everything has *some* form or other. But not all form is significant form, which, in painting, is a matter of lines, shapes and colours in certain relations. Only art can have significant form, and significant form is what all good art has. As we saw previously (p. 283), representation is irrelevant for Bell. His one concession is the representation of three-dimensional space – what is represented as behind and what in front. Otherwise, he argues, to appreciate art we need no knowledge of life or the emotions.

We have seen objections to many of these claims (p. 284f.), and won't repeat them here. Our concern is to develop Bell's account of the relation between the aesthetic attitude and significant form.

What is significant form? First, we can only know it, says Bell, through what he calls 'aesthetic emotion'. He agrees with the objection (p. 285) that we cannot infer something's value from its form; but that is because not all form is significant form. It is only when we feel aesthetic emotion that we know we are in the presence of significant form; it is not something we can infer any other way.

Second, in significant form, we get a glimpse of the world as it is, though not directly (Bell admits this claim is very speculative). The artist looks at the world without concern for associations or the function of things; they are interested only in the pure form of things. This vision produces an emotion in the artist, and they express this emotion through the significant form of the artwork. Significant form has the power to move us, to create the aesthetic emotion in us, because it is the expression of the artist's emotion.

This sounds similar to expressivism, but Bell argues that we should not look for expression of emotion in art or seek to respond to this. We should focus on significant form; that is the way in which aesthetic emotion will be invoked in us.

Bell develops the account just in relation to visual art (and painting specifically), but believes it is possible to extend it to other types of art.

Explain Bell's theory of significant form.

Criticisms of formalism II

Even if 'form' matters, is it the 'essence' of art qua art? II

Kant's and Bell's theories of how form connects with aesthetic emotion enables us to think further about the importance of form.

We may object that Bell's account of significant form and aesthetic emotion is unclear. First, his description of significant form – lines, shapes and colours in a certain relation – is in fact a description only of *form*. So Bell hasn't established what is being talked about. Second, he then says that we detect significant form by aesthetic emotion, but his definition of aesthetic emotion is what we feel in the presence of significant form! This is circular, so if we do not understand significant form or aesthetic emotion, his account doesn't help at all.

Bell can reply that it is impossible to identify the value of an artwork except through our intuitive response to it. The criticism that we cannot *infer* value from formal qualities is right. We must experience the work; and in our experience of it, we discover its value.

But at least, we may ask, what is 'significant form' significant of? It signifies the expression of the artist's emotions in response to their glimpse of the pure form of reality. This makes the value of form depend on the value of the emotion expressed, rather than being valuable in its own right. Bell's formalism becomes expressivism.

Kant provides us with an independent theory of how form matters, and gives us an account of what it is to experience aesthetic pleasure. But he faces three objections alongside Bell.

First, we may object that a perfect forgery would have the same form (or significant form) as the original; yet we value the original more. Bell replies that a perfect forgery is not possible, and so any forgery would not have the significant form of the original. The minute differences between the two would be felt immediately. And the reason a perfect forgery is not possible is because it is created in a different state of mind; it is not an expression of the emotion of an artist who experiences pure form. But in this response, Bell again relies on expressivism.

Second, we argued in EMOTION IN ART (p. 287) that the value of art does not reside just in the pleasure of individuals. Yet Kant's theory would make it so. We can argue that art communicates and expresses a vision or emotion. This social, communicative function of art is lost in Kant's theory of aesthetic pleasure as the value of art.

> Outline two objections to the claim that significant form is the value of art.

Finally, both Kant and Bell are ready to reject works that do not have the right form. We can question these judgements.

For Kant, colour can only add 'charm'. But first, a work of art such as **32** Yves Klein's *IKB 79* (1959) consists of just one colour – but what a colour it is (the colour, says Klein, expresses 'pure space')! Second, Kant has failed to notice how the use of colour is intrinsic to form, as **33** Titian's *Bacchus and Ariadne* (1520–3) demonstrates. The relation of the blue and brown, both spatially and as complementary colours, structures the painting.

Bell, on the other hand, argued that works that don't produce 'aesthetic emotion' aren't in fact art. They are either descriptive – simply conveying anecdotes or ideas – or cause emotions directly (not through significant form). As a result, he rejects a great deal of art as of secondary value. We may suspect, then, that formalism is not an account of what we do value but of what formalists say we *should* value.

> Discuss the claim that aesthetic enjoyment is always a response to the form of an artwork.

Does formalism neglect the place art has in life?

The syllabus raises this final point about formalism. Formalism threatens to detach art from the rest of life completely by its emphasis on attending just to form, on a completely original and distinct aesthetic response, on the irrelevance of what is represented and its relation to our interests and concerns. Against formalism, we have argued for the importance of context and what the artist is trying to express, in interpreting the work (p. 287). Creating art is part of the lives of artists, and those lives are lived under certain cultural conditions, in certain relationships to other people, and they witness important historical events. Other people commission artworks, from private portraits to public statues to religious altarpieces. Most of us simply experience artworks, and while the experience of finding a moment of tranquillity and reflection, detached from the rest of our lives, is an important reason we seek out art, we have also argued that art can contribute to self-understanding and illuminate our experience of life more generally (p. 293). Furthermore, Tolstoy argued that art serves a social function, bonding artist and audience in a common understanding or experience (p. 288).

In all these ways, art is closely tied into life. That formalists have been willing to reject much of art because it was, for them, closely tied to life through representation or emotion, should make us suspicious that it is not a complete account of why we value art.

> Assess the claim that we value art because it produces an aesthetic enjoyment of form.

Key points • • •

- Kant argues that in aesthetic response, our imagination has 'free play', in not having to bring what we experience under fixed concepts, and our understanding is free to invent new ones. Aesthetic pleasure is enjoying making representations.
- Good art stimulates this through its form.
- Bell argues that it is not form, but significant form, that produces 'aesthetic emotion'. We can only tell when an artwork has significant form by feeling aesthetic emotion when we experience it.
- Significant form is the expression of the emotion aroused in the artist who experiences the pure form of things. Because it is an expression of emotion, it is able to arouse emotion.
- We can object that Bell's account of significant form and aesthetic emotion is unclear and circular. Bell can respond that it must be so; significant form can't be analysed.
- We can also object that a forgery would have the same form (and significant form) as an original, yet we don't value it as much. Bell replies that a perfect forgery is impossible because it is not created in the same state of mind as the original was.
- We can argue that the value of art does not rest just in individual pleasure, but also in the communicative function of art, which Kant overlooks.
- Formalists reject as (good) art works that don't meet their theory of form. We can object that formalism is therefore not a theory of what we actually value.
- In emphasising form, a distinct aesthetic response, the irrelevance of representation and cultural context, formalism threatens to cut art off from life.

III. We value art because of its expressive quality

Good art is moving or captures a mood or feeling II

Croce: the expressive function of art

The Aesthetic as the Science of Expression and of the Linguistic in General

Benedetto Croce developed the ideas of Kant into a form of expressivism. Like Kant, he argued that we must organise stimuli in order to create experience of the world that is intelligible (representations). The artist does the same thing. However, unlike Kant, Croce argued that receiving orderless stimuli is frustrating and painful, so we want to organise it, which we do by imposing a form. He pointed to the sense of frustration we can all have at not being able to find the right words to express ourselves, a frustration artists also feel when they can't quite complete a painting or identify the right chord sequence. It is central to art that one solution after another is tried and rejected in the attempt to find exactly the 'right' expression of what the artist has a sense of. When the right expression is found, aesthetic pleasure follows. Our representations are also expressions.

Croce agrees with Tolstoy and Collingwood that when art expresses emotion, then, this is not simply letting out an emotion, but searching for precisely the right outlet. For this, the artist must be in control of their emotion. When the expression seems 'just right', it enables self-understanding: 'this is how I feel'. To grasp what is expressed, the audience must recreate the expression in themselves. This insight is gained directly, intuitively, not through inference from an analysis of the features of the work, although a great knowledge of the context of the work and what it represents can help us come to understand what is expressed. Only after we have grasped what is expressed can we analyse how each part of the work contributes towards this effect. For Croce, the whole is greater than the sum of its parts.

> Croce thought that *all* representations are expressions, and there is no determinate reality prior to our representations. In this he defended a form of IDEALISM (Ch. 6, p. 209).

> Compare and contrast Croce's and Collingwood's theories of expression in art.

Objections

Going further: art and the artist's state of mind

In our previous discussion, our last objection (p. 290) was that expressivism seems to place all the value of art in the state of mind of the artist. There is a way in which the artwork is really in the mind, in what the artist seeks to express and its imaginative articulation. Both Croce and Collingwood suggest as much – works of art are fundamentally mental, though expressed in physical form. The product is secondary to the mental process of working through what is expressed.

But this, we can object, is wrong in at least two ways. First, on this view, it is what the artist is trying to express that makes an artwork successful as art or not. But a work can be good art even if it doesn't express what the artist intended.

In reply, we could agree that the intention of the artist is not the criteria for the success or value of the work, but it is crucial for interpretation. But this gives way too quickly. We made the point in discussing Collingwood (p. 289) that we should not confuse what the artist expressed with what they *intended* to express. In trying to discover what the artist expressed, we aren't trying to recreate what *went on* in the artist's mind when they were creating the work. Their intention may change in response to how the work develops and much of what they are doing may be unconscious to them. References to the artist's 'intention' should be understood in the broadest possible way to include all the psychological states that contributed to them making the artwork exactly as they did, though perhaps with special emphasis on the feelings being made precise. On this view, given that the artist's intention develops with the creation of the work, what they intend to express *is* what makes the artwork good, if they succeed in expressing it. (We can then add that a good artist is one who succeeds in expressing what they are trying to express.)

Second, to say works of art are mental runs against our aesthetic experience, which is so strongly directed by the product itself. This is less true in literature, which is the case used by Croce and Collingwood to support their case. But we should not generalise, as they did, from literature to other types of art such as painting and sculpture, where our visual experience of what (*physical* thing) we are *looking* at is so dominant.

Given the way in which neither what the artist seeks to express nor its expression exists clearly in the mind of the artist before the artwork is complete, this suggests that Croce and Collingwood are wrong to separate and contrast the mental and physical aspects of the work of art. The artwork is not purely physical, because it has been created throughout by a process of thought. On the other hand, that process of thought was not possible except through expression in a physical form. This is shown by the fact that the artist tries and rejects many physical forms (paint marks, chords in sound, words on a page, and so on) in developing the expression of their sense of the emotion (or vision) that needs to be expressed. And they do not get the sense of the right solution until they *see* it (or hear it).

Discuss the relation between what the artist seeks to express and the artwork.

IS ART EXPRESSION?

We previously objected (p. 290) that expression cannot be what we value about art because not all art is expression and not all expression is art. We can now reply using Croce's idea of finding exactly the right solution to express what we want to. Music that is pleasant to listen to but expresses 'nothing in particular', as we put it, does in fact still express something. It expresses the composer's idea of how pleasant music should sound. At any number of points in the composition, different notes could have been written, different themes developed. The composer chose what they chose because it was precisely the right thing at the right time. That such judgements are not always challenging does not change the fact that they are *of the same kind* as the judgements made by a great artist in a masterpiece.

This response has two important consequences. First, it moves away from the view that what is expressed in a work of art is always mainly emotional. The more general view is that the artist expresses a 'vision', even if that vision is only of how pleasant music should sound.

Second, the response erases any sharp line between what is art and what is not art, because we *all* make this kind of aesthetic judgement – when we are getting dressed, decorating our houses, or putting together a play list for a party. But then what is it about art that we value? One reply is that it is a matter of degree. In the art we value most, what is expressed may be profound and very difficult to express, yet the solution found is adequate to it.

> Assess the claim that art is expressive.

How can psychological ascriptions apply to works of art?

When describing the expressive nature of works of art, we frequently use emotional terms, such as 'sad', 'melancholic', 'cheerful', 'peaceful' and so on.

For example, **34** Schedoni's *The Holy Family with the Virgin teaching the Child to Read* (c. 1615) is intimate, calm and conveys contentment. But these are words for psychological properties – people are sad, calm or content. A painting can't literally be sad – it won't burst into tears or mope around! So what do we mean when we describe paintings in this way?

Are we describing what the painting is of? For example, Jesus and his parents look intimate, calm and content. But we noted earlier (p. 286) that we need to distinguish the emotions represented by an artwork and the emotion expressed by the artwork, as in **23** Steen's *The Effects of Intemperance*. Are we then describing how the painting makes *us* feel looking at it? But then shouldn't we say that the painting is 'saddening', not 'sad', and 'calming', not 'calm'?

> In this section, we discuss only psychological ascriptions specifically related to what the artwork expresses. However, we also say that an artwork is pretentious or sensitive or insightful. This type of psychological ascription is discussed in the next section (p. 307).

Expression as metaphor

Explain and illustrate the claim that ascribing psychological properties to artworks is metaphorical.

One response is to say that, literally speaking, we should. To say that a painting is 'sad' is a metaphor, a figure of speech in which the word used does not apply literally. In literature and poetry, writers create new, unfamiliar metaphors, as in Philip Larkin's poem 'Toads' that begins 'Why should I let the toad *work*/Squat on my life?'. But we use metaphor all the time, as in 'life is a journey', 'their marriage has broken down'. These are mundane metaphors, so familiar we often don't even recognise that they are metaphors. Talking about paintings as 'sad' etc. is another example of this.

Since paintings can't literally be sad, it seems uncontentious to say that describing them this way is metaphorical. But this doesn't help us understand the expressive nature of art. It is one thing to *apply a word* metaphorically, another to *experience an object* in those terms. While we say 'their marriage has broken down' and wonder what might 'fix' it, we don't actually experience marriage as a type of machine; to say that someone is a rat is not to actually *see* them as a rat (that would be an insane hallucination). But we can argue that our *experience* of a painting is affected, shot-through with the sadness we say it expresses. We don't just say it is sad, we *see* it as 'sad' (in a metaphorical sense).

We can reply that to 'experience' a painting as sad, etc. is *nothing more than* to metaphorically apply this psychological term to it. But if this is right, then to 'experience' a painting as sad is quite different from seeing the marks of paint as the Virgin Mary (see p. 280). Seeing-as is a genuine form of perception; but what we can call 'expressive perception' – experiencing what the painting expresses – is not a genuine form of perception at all. Instead, we see the painting (and see in it what it represents) and then, separately and as a consequence, apply the metaphor to it. And this doesn't seem true to aesthetic experience. We *see* the sadness *in* the painting.

Discuss the claim that psychological descriptions of paintings are *merely* metaphorical.

Second, we say paintings are depressing, not depressed, disturbing rather than disturbed. (The right-hand panel of **35** Hieronymus Bosch's *The Garden of Earthly Delights* (1500–5) is a good example of a disturbing painting.) This is not a metaphorical use of the same term we apply to people. Yet there is no fundamental difference in the way the painting expresses the relevant emotion when we say it is disturbing or sad. So expression is not to be explained *just* by the metaphorical application of a psychological term. What do metaphorical and non-metaphorical emotional descriptions have in common?

Going further: expression, effect and intention

One answer to this last question is that artworks arouse the emotion in the audience. To say the painting is disturbing is to say that we are disturbed; to say that it is sad is to say that we are saddened.

But this is too simple. First, someone might be saddened by **34** Schedoni's *Holy Family* as it reminds them of the loss of intimacy in their own family. That a painting merely *causes* an emotion is not enough to say that it *expresses* that emotion. The person won't say that the *painting* is sad merely because it causes them to be sad. On their own, the emotions caused in me are too subjective to ascribe any expressive property to the painting. Second, to explain what we mean by 'it is a sad painting' just by its effect on the audience ignores the fact that the painting is an expression of the artist.

We can take account of both points by referring to the artist's intention. An artwork is expressive because the artist is expressing themselves (emotions or vision) in it. The artist creates the work as it is *so that* people respond to it in a particular way. T.S. Eliot argues, 'The only way of expressing emotion in the form of art is by finding an "objective correlative"; in other words, a set of objects, a situation, a chain of events which shall be the formula of that *particular* emotion; such that when the external facts, which must terminate in sensory experience, are given, the emotion is immediately evoked'. When experienced 'correctly', the work causes the same feelings as those that caused the artist to create it (or, if the audience doesn't come to share the same feelings, at least they gain an understanding of the feelings the artist expresses).

This supports the claim that talk of the expressive properties of artworks is not merely metaphorical, but relates to how we *experience* the artwork. In creating the painting, the artist repeatedly looks at it, just as the audience will. They work on it until what they experience when looking at it is what they feel they are trying to express.

We can argue, then, that to say a painting is 'sad' is not just to say that we come to feel sad when we look at it, but also that this is the effect that the artist intended, this is the feeling the artist sought to express in painting the picture as they did. Furthermore, this feeling is not merely caused by looking at the painting, it impacts on how we experience it perceptually.

As above, 'intention' should be taken very broadly to cover all the psychological states that cause the artist to create the work just as it is.

'Hamlet and His Problems'

How can psychological ascriptions apply to works of art?

Aesthetic emotion?

To say that good art moves us refers to the emotions evoked in the audience. But understanding this emotional affect is problematic once we say that there is not just one, special 'aesthetic emotion' (or aesthetic pleasure) we experience in front of all good works of art. For example, if the account of expression given above is correct, then there is a way in which a sad painting makes us feel sad.

But in what way? It doesn't make us feel sad in the same way as receiving bad news. When we feel sad in everyday life, there is normally something about which we feel sad. What do we feel sad *about* when looking at a sad painting? Nothing in particular; or if there is something it is something personal in our lives, and the painting doesn't express sadness about that. Furthermore, feeling sad in real life won't make us feel happy, but we can enjoy how we feel in response to a sad painting.

So does a sad painting make us feel sad in a 'disinterested' way? Is there a special 'aesthetic' sadness? Perhaps it isn't quite right to say we feel sad; rather, we *imagine* feeling sad. We could argue that the artwork represents an object (a sunset – **7** and **8**) or situation (the crucifixion – **24**) that would arouse emotion in real life, and invites us to imagine how we would feel if we came face to face with it. But this is too superficial. In **15** Da Vinci, *The Virgin of the Rocks*, it is not (just?) the situation but the way it has been expressed that creates the emotional response. In any case, this explanation can only work for artwork that is representative. What of abstract art (**26** Rothko's *Red on Maroon*) or conceptual art (**21** Duchamp's *Fountain*) or music? So we don't respond by imagining what we would feel in a situation in real life.

Another answer is that we use our imagination to retrieve what it is that the artist is expressing. The 'aesthetic' way in which we feel relates to the way the artist expresses the emotion in the painting. This is different from how we experience and express emotion in daily life. An artwork is not an outpouring of emotion, as the artist must be able to work with the emotion to find the precise expression (see p. 289). So, as Wordsworth said, it involves emotion 'recollected in tranquillity'. Furthermore, what the artwork expresses is not a direct emotional response to any event. It is more general, as expressing oneself in art is part of a way of living. If we experience a version of what the artist has expressed, then this explains many of the differences between emotions in response to art and emotions in response to everyday life.

Lyrical Ballads, Introduction

? How should we understand emotional expression in art?

Do we value the artists' self-expression or our responses?

We argued above that to talk of what an artwork expresses is not to talk just of what we feel in response to it (p. 303). This would be too subjective and doesn't take account of what the artist sought to express. Therefore, if we value art for its expressive quality, then it cannot be just our responses to it that we value.

However, to say that we value just the artist's self-expression, and not our responses, is also implausible. That we enjoy art and that it can illuminate our experience are both clearly aspects of art's value to us.

The account of expression above connects the artist's self-expression and our responses as two sides of the same coin. We seek to experience what the artist has tried to express; the artist tries to find exactly the expression that will enable us to do this. In valuing expression, we value both what the artist has to express – the vision and feelings – and our own responses to this, including the work of imagination required of us to achieve it, the emotions evoked and the effects of the experience.

> Discuss the claim that valuing the artist's self-expression and valuing our responses are two sides of the same coin.

'The intentional fallacy'

Versions of all three of our answers to why we value art make reference to what the artist 'intended' to represent or express in order to understand an artwork. But any attempt to refer to the artist's state of mind in this way faces an important objection known as 'the intentional fallacy'.

The objection makes two points. First, it contrasts the public, accessible nature of the artwork, something we can all experience; and the private nature of the mind – each of us knows our own mental states 'first-hand', in a way that no one else can. From the artwork, we cannot infer the state of mind of the artist. We cannot know what the artist intended when creating the artwork. Second, it emphasises the distinction between the artwork and the artist's mind. These are distinct things; it is the artwork we respond to and should be thinking about, not the mind of the artist. For both reasons, the artist's intention is irrelevant to our interpretation and aesthetic response to the work. If this is right, then we cannot value art for the artist's self-expression, since we cannot know this. To disagree is to commit the intentional **fallacy**.

To come to know about the artist's mind, we would need to study the artist, that is, engage in biography. Or if we think we do know of some intention the artist had when making the artwork, then we need to check this by finding

> Wimsatt and Beardley, 'The intentional fallacy'

> This contrast is discussed in SUBSTANCE DUALISM, A2 Unit 3.1 Philosophy of Mind.

evidence of it in the artwork itself – in which case, again, we don't need to refer to the artist, but can study just the artwork on its own. The objection concludes that in making judgements about an artwork – interpreting it or valuing it – we should do it entirely on its own merits (the 'internal evidence', that is, the evidence present in the artwork itself) and not in terms of the psychological or social background which contributed to its creation (the 'external evidence').

In support of the objection, we can point to the distinction we make between applying certain psychological properties to the work and applying them to the artist. So we might say that the work is elegant, without saying the artist is elegant. To say a work is sad is not to say that the artist is sad (to express sadness in the work, they need to recollect sadness, not be sad). The psychological descriptions of an artwork don't derive from the psychological properties of the artist, they stand alone.

Since we respond to an artwork without knowing the mind of the artist, it cannot be the artist's state of mind that we value, but what the artwork evokes in us. The value of art must therefore lie in our responses.

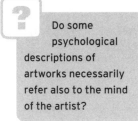

Outline and illustrate the 'intentional fallacy'.

OBJECTION

The distinction between the artwork and the artist's mind is an important one. But we can respond that it does not mean that we cannot refer to the mind of the artist *at all* in interpreting and valuing an artwork. We should note that *some* descriptions of an artwork only make sense if we apply them to the artist as well, for example, 'perceptive', 'sensitive', 'mature', 'courageous' or 'pretentious'. An artwork can't be perceptive in its own right; rather, we mean that it demonstrates an insight of the artist's, which they have then expressed in and through the artwork.

Do some psychological descriptions of artworks necessarily refer also to the mind of the artist?

But surely, we can reply, someone might create, say, a pretentious artwork without being a pretentious person. This is right, but isn't an objection. To say an artwork is pretentious is to say that the artist displays this quality *in this artwork*, on this occasion, not that they are generally a pretentious person. Likewise with perceptive, sensitive, mature and so on. We can therefore argue that we can value art for its expression of the artist's mind. The 'intentional fallacy' is not a fallacy at all.

Going further: the artist's mind in the artwork

If the artist only displays a quality in the artwork, then we can still distinguish between the work and the artist's mind. In literature, for instance, a man can write a novel from the first-person perspective of someone completely different, for example, a little girl. This is a kind of imitation or impersonation. Likewise, an actor can portray someone with completely different qualities to themselves. We can generalise: from the artwork we can infer the psychological properties of the person 'imitated', but this still tells us nothing about the artist themselves.

This argument is confused. First, while a novelist may write a novel to seem as if a little girl had written it, to say that an artwork is pretentious is *not* to say that the artist has successfully created the artwork *to seem as if* someone pretentious created it. To call an artwork pretentious is a criticism; to say that the artist successfully imitates someone pretentious in creating it can be praise, as this is difficult and may require great insight into how a pretentious person would think and create.

Second, the argument contradicts itself. It refers to the intentions of the artist while saying that we cannot do this. When a male novelist writes from the perspective of a girl, we can know that he *intends* this effect because we know he is not a girl. It is relevant to our assessment of the novel that we know this. Suppose we didn't know who the author was – we didn't know whether it was a little girl or an adult, male writer. Then, for example, we could not judge whether the effect is successful, whether the author has insight into the mind of a little girl or not, and so on. The same issue arises for whether an artwork is ironic or satirical. It is only satirical if the artist intends it to be. But if we do not know this, we may *mistakenly* take the point of view it expresses seriously. To say the artist imitates someone pretentious in making the artwork likewise requires us to refer to the intentions of the artist; an imitation is only an imitation if it is intended. So making the judgement that a work has its psychological properties because the artist imitated a person with those properties requires us to refer to the intentions of the artist – which is just what the argument says we can't do.

Third, some psychological properties cannot be imitated successfully by someone who doesn't have them. Someone who is not perceptive cannot successfully imitate being perceptive; someone who is immature cannot

Explain and discuss the idea that an artist may imitate someone else in creating an artwork.

successfully imitate maturity. So a perceptive and mature artwork must be created by a perceptive and mature artist. Again, to say this is not to say that the artist is perceptive and mature throughout all aspects of their lives. The distinction we need to observe is not between the artwork and the artist's mind, but between those psychological properties of the artist displayed in the artwork and the psychological properties that characterise the artist as a person generally. An artist may only be mature or perceptive *when creating art*, and a mess in the rest of their life.

This last point has an important implication, viz. that the best or even the only evidence that an artist is mature, perceptive etc. is their art. So the argument against the intentional fallacy is right to say that we need to find evidence of any intention in the artwork. But it is wrong to say that other sources of information, for example, biography, are irrelevant, as these can help us to see the intention expressed in the work.

It is worth emphasising a final time that in interpreting and valuing a work for what it expresses does not attempt to establish what went on consciously in the artist's mind. Expression is formed by much more than this. First, there are unconscious mental states that contribute to the process. Second, various happy accidents in making the work may lead the artist to adapt the picture. Third, as they respond to the work in creating it, they may alter their intention. Precisely what the work will be is not fixed in advance.

For these reasons, what the artist *says* the work expresses does not have special authority. What they say may only reflect what they are conscious of, while the artwork may express psychological properties of which they are not conscious. The artist may be more perceptive in creating the work than in interpreting it themselves! Their ability to express themselves in art does not mean they are equally able to express themselves in descriptions of art.

> Assess the view that we value art because of its expressive quality.

Key points • • •

- Croce argued that the artist seeks exactly the right expression of what they have a sense of. Finding the right representation, imposing a form on unorganised stimuli, is a relief and emotional expression.

- To grasp what an artwork expresses, the audience must recreate the expression in themselves. This is intuitive, and cannot be done just by analysing the work.
- We can object that what makes an artwork successful is not just the intention of the artist. We can reply that, if we take intention widely and not something fixed and conscious before the artwork is completed, then the intention, and the success of its expression, is what makes an artwork good.
- Croce and Collingwood make an artwork essentially mental. We should reject this, given the close interaction between the mind and the physical artwork in its creation.
- We can argue that all art expresses at least the artist's idea of what that work should be like.
- This view erases any sharp line between what is art and what is not, as we all make similar aesthetic judgements. What distinguishes art is just a matter of degree.
- To say a painting is sad is metaphorical. But we do not merely apply the word metaphorically, we experience the painting in light of it.
- When we ascribe psychological properties to paintings, perhaps we mean that they evoke these properties in the audience. We can object to this that what the painting expresses is not merely what it causes. Instead, the emotion expressed is the one the artist expresses in it and intends the audience to feel when viewing it.
- We don't feel sad in any normal sense when looking at a sad painting. But this is because the artist doesn't express normal sadness in the normal way when creating the work. The emotion is 'recollected in tranquillity' and is not about any specific event.
- This view entails that we value the artist's self-expression and our responses as two sides of the same coin.
- We can object that any attempt to relate the artwork to the intention of the artist commits the intentional fallacy. We cannot know the artist's intention, and it is, in any case, distinct from the artwork.
- We can respond that we have to refer to the artist's intention to interpret the work, and that many psychological descriptions of the work presuppose this. However, the work itself can be the best evidence of what the artist's intentions were.
- What an artist says a work expresses does not define what the work expresses. They may be unconscious of what is expressed or not able to put it into words.

SUMMARY

In this chapter, we have discussed three answers to the question 'Why do we value art?':

1. Because it informs us.

2. Because of its particular 'artistic' quality of form.

3. Because of its expressive quality.

In our discussion, we have looked at the following issues:

1. Should good art portray authentically? Do we value art for this reason?

2. What is the relation between art and the reality it represents?

3. How can art express or reveal truths?

4. What is aesthetic enjoyment? How does it relate to form?

5. What is the concept of 'form' or 'significant form'?

6. Is 'form' or 'significant form' all that we respond to and value about art?

7. What is the place of art in relation to life?

8. Does all art express emotions?

9. How does art express emotions or other psychological states?

10. Is it a fallacy to try to interpret art in terms of the artist's intention?

11. Should good art express emotions and move us emotionally?

UNIT 2 **AN INTRODUCTION TO PHILOSOPHY 2**

9

Section 4: God and the world

In this chapter we discuss three distinct issues. The first, the argument from design, uses the apparent order and purpose of nature to infer the existence of God. The second, the problem of evil, uses the existence of evil to infer that God, at least an all-loving and all-powerful God, does not exist. The third is about what it is to hold religious beliefs, about what it means to think that 'God exists'. By the end of this chapter, you should be able to discuss these issues, explaining and evaluating different positions on each of them, and give reasons supporting each position.

SYLLABUS CHECKLIST

The AQA AS syllabus for this chapter is:

The argument from design

✔ Arguments for design based on apparent order and purpose and challenges to those arguments.
✔ Arguments from design (analogy, the inadequacies of naturalistic explanations) and challenges to those arguments.

The problem of evil

✔ That the existence of evil counts against the existence of an all loving and all powerful God. Moral and natural evil and their relation to one another.

✔   Attempts to reconcile the evil we perceive with the existence of God
     (the free will defence, the best of all possible worlds, soul making
     and the afterlife).

The religious point of view

✔   Consideration of the claim that the world can accommodate different
     perspectives ('seeing-as').
✔   The status of the religious hypothesis; is it a 'hypothesis' at all?
     Consideration of the claim that religious 'belief' mirrors the feelings,
     attitudes and commitments of the religious rather than facts about
     the world.

INTRODUCTION

A note on referring to God: as in Ch. 4 THE IDEA OF GOD, I have adopted the traditional personal pronoun 'he' in referring to God. There are two reasons for this: first, the conception of God that is discussed in the syllabus is personal, so the impersonal 'it' sounds awkward. Second, English unfortunately has only two personal pronouns, 'he' and 'she', both gendered. If God exists, I don't believe that God is gendered in either way. My use of 'he' is purely to avoid the awkwardness of alternating 'he' and 'she' and of using 's/he'.

I. The argument from design

Arguments for design

A common human response to the world around us is amazement. Two things in particular are sources of fascination – the stars in the sky and life. The grandeur of a star-filled night, the vastness of the universe, inspires a sense of awe. The complexity and intricacy of living creatures fills us with wonder. As philosophers, we should first of all be amazed that we can understand the world *at all*. It could have been a complete shambles, nothing constant, no laws of nature, no means by which our reason could try to explain it. But what we find is order, constancy, predictability throughout, and in living creatures, different parts working together and the creature as a whole fitting neatly into its environment.

Life

When we talk about parts of a living creature, we often refer to their *purpose*: the heart is *for* pumping blood, the eye is *for* seeing, and so on. In fact, this is central to understanding the organ in question. You don't really know what an eye is unless you know that it is the organ of sight. And we explain parts of the eye in terms of their contribution to the purpose of the eye. So the lens focuses light onto the retina, the muscles attached to the lens change its thickness so that it can focus light onto the retina, and so on. Without this bit (the lens) or that bit (the retina), the eye wouldn't work properly.

The way in which living things work, which requires a huge coordination of lots of tiny bits, each doing their specific job, is amazingly complex. This coordination, the detail and intricacy of interrelations between parts, suggests planning – a plan that follows a purpose (of making a living creature, making an organ that enables the creature to see, etc.). Acting on a plan guided by a purpose is *design*. It's as if someone had it in mind that the eye should see, and put the bits together to ensure that it could. The way living creatures are suggests that they are designed – designed to be alive, with organs designed to keep them alive.

If living creatures are designed, then as a matter of definition, there must be a designer. You can't have design without a designer. This is the next step in an argument for the existence of God, which we will look at in ARGUMENTS FROM DESIGN (p. 317).

> The Greek word for this idea of 'purpose' or 'end' or 'what is aimed at' is *telos*. Arguments for the existence of God that invoke purpose or design are therefore also called teleological arguments.

> Explain and illustrate the inference from purpose to design.

EVOLUTION BY NATURAL SELECTION

Is the fact that we are amazingly complex, and our organs and many parts serve the purpose of keeping us alive, enough for us to say that living creatures are designed? The appearance of design in nature clearly requires *some* explanation. But what is the best explanation?

Darwin's theory of evolution by natural selection provides an excellent account of how the *appearance* of design could come about without anything being designed. Millions of alterations randomly take place. Most disappear without a trace. But a trait that *coincidentally* helps a creature to survive and reproduce, to function well, slowly spreads, because that creature and its descendents reproduce more. So more and more creatures end up with it. It's not that the feature is 'selected' *in order for* the creature to live better and so reproduce more. Instead, the feature simply *causes* the creature to reproduce more, so its descendents also have that feature and they reproduce more and so on. What appears to be designed is actually just evidence of good *functioning*.

One very small change is followed by another. Over time, this can lead to great complexity. In the end, then, creatures appear to be designed when they are in fact the product of coincidence. So we don't need to say that living things are actually designed (which would require the existence of a designer). This is a better explanation because it is simpler. We aren't inferring the existence of something we can't be sure exists.

Explain how evolution by natural selection undermines the argument for design.

The 'fine tuning' argument

Darwinism is sometimes thought to eliminate the question of design in nature. But we can ask 'How is evolution by natural selection possible?'. It didn't have to be possible – perhaps the universe could have been organised in such a way that evolution and life would be impossible. So the appearance of design needs a further explanation. For example, perhaps God set up the universe so that life evolves by natural selection.

This argument has been given support by recent work in cosmology – the study of the 'cosmos' or universe as a whole. Cosmologists have argued that the conditions needed for life to come into existence are incredibly improbable. As far as we understand, life needs planets; and planets need stars. But the universe needn't have contained stars. In fact, if anything about the beginnings of the universe (the Big Bang) or the laws of nature were different by the smallest amount, stars wouldn't exist. For example, the Big Bang was an explosion of matter-energy. Logically speaking, it could have been bigger, it could have been smaller – either more or less matter or more or less force of explosion. But for stars to be able to form, the initial strength of the explosion in the Big Bang had to be precise to one part in 10^{60} – it couldn't vary by more than 0.0000000000 00000000000000000000000000000000000000000001 *per cent*. That's as precise as hitting a one-inch target at the other side of the observable universe! And that's just for stars to form. For life to form on planets is *even more* improbable, because so many more laws are involved. Because it is so unlikely, the fact that everything is exactly adjusted so life can exist seems a staggering coincidence.

What could explain this? Science can't tell us *why* the Big Bang was exactly the size it was or *why* the laws of nature are the way they are. It can only tell us that this is how it is. One obvious explanation, then, is that the Big Bang, the properties of matter-energy, the laws of nature, were all designed to allow life to evolve. If they were designed, then instead of it being a massive coincidence that life could evolve, it becomes inevitable.

Outline and illustrate the fine tuning argument for design.

Arguments from design

We have so far given arguments *for* evidence of design in nature. Arguments *from* design start from this evidence of design and infer the existence of a *designer*, a mind that can order things for a purpose. The most famous of these is the argument from analogy.

The argument from analogy

David Hume expresses the argument like this:

Dialogues on Natural Religion, Part II

> The curious adapting of means to ends, through all nature, resembles exactly, though it much exceeds, the productions of human contrivance; of human design, thought, wisdom, and intelligence. Since, therefore, the effects resemble each other, we are led to infer, by all the rules of analogy, that the causes also resemble; and that the Author of Nature is somewhat similar to the mind of man, though possessed of much larger faculties, proportioned to the grandeur of the work which he has executed.

Hume is saying that nature is *like* human inventions in the way it displays purpose (the adaptation of means to ends, for example, the arrangement of the parts of the eye to see, of the heart to pump blood), so it must have a similar cause to human inventions, viz. a mind that intended to create such design. Similar effects have similar causes.

Explain the argument from analogy.

OBJECTIONS

However, Hume argues strongly against the analogy. First, he questions its strength. A watch is a typical example of something designed and made by humans. But living creatures aren't really like watches in all sorts of ways. For example, watches aren't alive and they don't reproduce. So the 'effects' – watches, living creatures – aren't all that similar, so we can't infer a similar cause. Likewise, the universe is not at all like a watch. So again, because the effects aren't very alike, we can't infer similar causes.

Second, even if the analogy between effects was better, inferring a similar cause would be dubious. Human beings are a fairly recent species living on a small planet on one of billions of galaxies. We can't reliably generalise from our very limited and finite experience to the cause of the universe as a whole. As Hume says, 'why select so minute, so weak, so bounded a principle as the reason and design of animals is found to be upon this planet' as a model for something that could set laws of nature?!

Third, as we have already seen, there could be other explanations of apparent design. Hume suggests the idea that if the universe is infinitely old, then over time, all possible combinations of matter will occur randomly. This suggestion isn't very good, because we know that the universe began around 13.8 billion years ago, and we know that matter doesn't organise itself randomly, but follows very particular laws of nature. But Hume's point is that if there *are* different explanations of the apparent design of the universe, then we can't infer that the cause is a designer.

IS THE DESIGNER GOD?

The argument from design is intended as an argument for the existence of God. However, as well as attacking the analogy, Hume also points out that even if we could infer the existence of a designer of the universe, it is an *extra step* to argue that the designer is God. And, because we are relying on analogy, this extra step also faces difficulties.

Let's take the analogy between human inventions and the universe further. First, we should note that, in the human case, the designer is not always also the creator. Someone who designs a car may not also build it. So we can't infer that the designer of the universe also created the universe. But God is said to be the creator of the universe; so we can't infer that the designer is God.

Second, the scale of the design reflects the *powers* of the designer. Watches aren't infinite, and neither are the minds that make them. But the universe isn't infinite either. So we can't infer that the designer is infinite, only that whoever designed the universe has sufficient power and intelligence to do that. But God is said to be infinite.

Third, we think that the *quality* of what is designed reflects the abilities of the designer. Designers need to be trained, and at first their designs will be poor

> With life, this is evolution. We don't know what might explain the universe, but then, that's the situation we were in about life before Darwin developed his theory.

> Discuss whether we can use an analogy between the appearance of design in nature and human inventions to infer that the universe has a designer.

and could be improved. We can argue that, if the purpose of the universe was life, this universe shows examples of poor design, for example, volcanoes and tsunamis that wipe out life. Perhaps we should infer that the designer of this universe was not fully skilled, but made mistakes. But God is said not to make mistakes.

Some of Hume's points can be debated. But the overall message is clear: if we rest the argument from design completely on analogy, then the argument faces many problems. What philosophers have done since Hume is to remove the appeal to analogy. In DEVELOPMENT (p. 333), we will see how to infer the existence of God from design without relying on analogy.

This idea is discussed further in THE PROBLEM OF EVIL (p. 320f.).

Assess the argument from analogy for the existence of God.

Key points • • •

- Arguments for design use the order and apparent purpose of natural things to infer that they are designed.
- While living creatures are incredibly complex, Darwin's theory of evolution by natural selection explains how they can appear designed without being designed.
- The 'fine tuning' argument points out that the universe must have very precise properties for life to evolve. It suggests that science cannot explain why the universe should be so improbably organised; however, if it is designed, that would explain it.
- Arguments from design use the evidence of design to infer the existence of a divine designer.
- One form uses analogy: artefacts created by humans exhibit purpose and order, and so do natural things. From purpose and order in artefacts, we infer that the artefact was designed. As natural things are similar, in exhibiting design, we may infer a similar cause, an intelligent mind, explains their design.
- Hume objected that the analogy is weak – natural things aren't very like human artefacts – and that we cannot infer similar causes from similar effects, because there are many other possible causes of the apparent design in natural things.
- Hume also objected that we can't infer the designer is God. If similar effects have similar causes, then the designer is imperfect and finite, because natural things appear to be imperfect and finite.

II. The problem of evil

The argument

In THE DIVINE ATTRIBUTES (Ch. 4, p. 125f.), we saw that God is traditionally understood to be perfectly good, omnipotent and omniscient. The existence of evil causes problems for this definition. If God is good, then he has the desire to eliminate evil. If God is omnipotent, then God is able to eliminate evil. If God is omniscient, then God knows that evil exists and knows how to eliminate it. But if God wants to eliminate evil and can eliminate evil, then why does evil exist? We can conclude that since evil exists, God – at least an omnipotent, good God – does not exist.

We can express this in terms of love. If you love someone, you don't want them to suffer, and you will do what you can to prevent them from suffering. If God is all-loving, then he would prevent us from suffering if he could. Evil causes us to suffer, so if God is all-loving and all-powerful, he would prevent evil. Since evil exists, either God does not exist or God is not all-loving and all-powerful.

The logical problem

There are two interpretations of this argument. One version, called the logical problem of evil, claims that the mere existence of evil is logically incompatible with the existence of an omnipotent, good God. It understands the argument **deductively**.

For the existence of evil to be logically incompatible with the existence of God, we have to suppose that being good, God has the desire to eliminate *all* evil. But this isn't true if some evil is *necessary for a greater good*. For example, unless we felt pain, we could never learn endurance; or again, what would love be like without sadness when we lose someone we love? But, as the old proverb says, ''Tis better to have loved and lost, than never to have loved at all'. So some evil is actually necessary to make the world as good a place as it is.

A variation of this argument is that we could not *appreciate* what is good, and so would not desire it as we do, unless we experienced evil to contrast it with. So being good, God does not desire to eliminate all evil. So the mere existence of evil is not logically incompatible with the existence of God.

Outline the logical problem of evil as a deductive argument, numbering the premises.

Explain and illustrate one challenge to the logical problem of evil.

The evidential problem

The evidential problem of evil claims that the *amount and distribution* of evil that exists is good evidence that an omnipotent, good God does not exist. It understands the argument **inductively**: the way evil actually exists is good evidence for thinking that God does not exist. For example, children can die of terrible diseases or they can be brutally treated. Animals can suffer in natural disasters such as drought. This seems exactly the kind of thing an omnipotent, good God would want to eradicate. Evil is unfairly distributed, and even if it is necessary for certain goods, is *so much* evil necessary? It is this version of the problem we will discuss.

> Compare and contrast the evidential and logical problems of evil.

Moral and natural evil

To understand the argument, we need to be clear on what 'evil' means in this context. 'Evil' usually refers to morally wrong actions or motives of human beings. So we say that Hitler was evil in trying to eradicate the Jews or that ethnic cleansing is an evil policy. This is 'moral evil'.

But this isn't the only kind of evil the problem of evil is talking about. There is also 'natural evil', which refers to suffering caused by natural events and processes, for example, the suffering caused by earthquakes, illness, the predation of animals on each other, and so on.

The two types of evil are distinct. What people choose to do to each other is not usually the result of natural events. Sometimes it is: famine may drive people to stealing and killing; but this is the exception. And natural events are not usually the result of what people choose to do. Again, sometimes they are – the results of global warming could be an example. But nothing people did caused the tsunami in the Indian Ocean on 26 December 2004 (which killed hundreds of thousands of people).

> We will see an argument below that challenges this claim.

We need to keep both types of evil in mind when we look at responses to the problem of evil. In particular, some responses may solve the problem of moral evil, but don't answer the problem of natural evil.

> Explain and illustrate the difference between moral and natural evil.

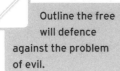

A theodicy is an argument which tries to make evil compatible with the existence of an omnipotent, good God.

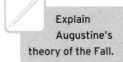

Outline the free will defence against the problem of evil.

The free will defence

Perhaps the most famous theodicy is the free will defence. It argues that evil is the result of our free will. God gave us free will, as something that is very good. It is better to have a universe with free will than without. Being morally imperfect, however, we do not always use our free will for good, but sometimes bring about evil. But God cannot *make* people with free will act for good. Given how good free will is, it is still better that we have free will and sometimes use it to bring about evil than that we don't have free will at all.

We can object that the argument only deals with moral evil, evil that *we bring about*, through our choices. It doesn't account for natural evil at all. There are two replies to this. First, we could argue that natural evil is the result of an evil supernatural being, such as the Devil. The traditional story goes that the Devil was an angel, created by God, endowed with free will. But he rebelled against God, and since then has sought to bring evil into the world. Natural evil is the effects of his actions, so it is moral evil. The second reply comes from St Augustine.

Augustine's argument

Augustine argues that natural evil is a result of the moral evil of human beings. He claims that the choice of Adam and Eve to disobey God led to 'The Fall'. The Fall was a *metaphysical* change, altering nature, human beings and the relationship between them: there is enmity between human beings and animals, giving birth causes pain, we must work hard to survive (Genesis 3:15–19). Nature and human nature are 'out of sorts'. So all evil, natural evil as well as moral evil, was caused by human free choice.

A first objection is that the Fall was not an actual event in human history. If it didn't happen, and if, for instance, animals were suffering long before human beings even existed, then free will can't be the cause of natural evil. Many Christians now understand the Fall as an important myth about the relationship between human beings, nature and God. But this means that we cannot claim the Fall is *literally responsible* for all natural evil.

A second objection is that, if it were true, it seems *grossly unfair*. Why should animals and children suffer as a result of a choice made by two people a very long time ago? It is not just to punish children for what their parents do; if your dad steals something, it isn't right that *you* get sent to prison! So how could a good God make the evil chosen by two people lead to such terrible consequences for so many other people? Surely it didn't *have* to be this way, and a good God wouldn't allow it.

> Discuss the claim that natural evil is the result of moral evil.

Soul-making

A different theodicy develops the idea we saw in response to the logical problem of evil (p. 320), that some evil is necessary for good. It argues that evil is necessary for us to become good people, for us to grow morally and spiritually. Virtues are impossible unless there is evil to respond to and correct. For example, we can't be courageous unless there is *real* danger, we can't be benevolent unless people have needs, we can't learn forgiveness unless people treat us wrongly, and so on. Through struggles and suffering with natural disasters, with illness, with the actions of other people, we mature and develop spiritually. So both natural and moral evil are necessary. We can understand this world, then, as a place of 'soul-making'.

> This argument is based on the ideas of the second-century thinker Irenaeus, and has been recently defended by John Hick.

Because God is good, he wants us to become good, and so he wants a world in which this is possible. It turns out that such a world must contain evil. And so the existence of evil is compatible with the existence of a loving, all-powerful God.

> Outline and illustrate the soul-making theodicy.

Objections

A first objection asks why God couldn't create us virtuous. Why do we need to *become* good? Hick replies that someone who has become good through confronting and dealing with evil 'is good in a richer and more valuable sense' than someone who is simply created good. In a phrase, no pain, no (real) gain.

A second, much stronger, objection notes that *all* evil is only justified by this argument if *all* evil leads to spiritual growth. But this doesn't seem plausible at all. Many people suffer terribly in a way that breaks their spirit, for example, children who never recover from being abused; others suffer at the end of their lives when there is little time to develop further; people die prematurely, before they have a chance of spiritual growth; people who need to grow spiritually don't suffer much at all; others who are already leading good and mature lives suffer a great deal. If the point of evil is that people become morally good, the *distribution* of evil doesn't seem to support this purpose.

Discuss one objection to the claim that evil, as it occurs in this world, is compatible with the existence of an all-powerful, all-loving God.

A third objection is that this theodicy only deals with the suffering of beings who can grow spiritually. It doesn't deal at all with the suffering of animals. One possible response is that animals have souls too, and can grow spiritually, but many religious traditions deny this.

Key points • • •

- The problem of evil: if God is good, then he has the desire to eliminate evil. If God is omnipotent, then God is able to eliminate evil. Evil exists, so an omnipotent, good God does not.
- The logical problem: the existence of evil is incompatible with the existence of an omnipotent, good God. This is implausible, since some evil must exist for certain goods to be possible.
- The evidential problem: the amount and distribution of evil makes the existence of an omnipotent, good God very unlikely.
- 'Evil' means moral and natural evil. Moral evil is that caused by beings with free will. Natural evil is suffering caused by natural processes, for example, drought and predation.
- The free will defence argues that evil is the result of our choices, and that it is justified by free will, which is good. This can be extended to cover natural evil if natural evil is the result of moral evil by the Devil or by human beings.
- Augustine argues that natural evil is a result of the free choice of Adam and Eve. But this is implausible if the Fall is a myth. And if it were literally true, it is very unjust, so a good God would not allow it.
- The soul-making theodicy says that evil is necessary for moral and spiritual growth. But this doesn't justify all evil if only *some* evil leads to these goods. It also doesn't deal with animal suffering.

III. The religious point of view

Different perspectives ('seeing-as')

In our discussion so far, and in Chapter 4, we have talked about religious belief, such as the belief that God exists. The arguments about God's existence operate as though we don't actually *experience* God, that God is absent from our experience – which is why we need to prove his existence. For example, you would say you 'believe that' the book is red more naturally if you can't see it; otherwise, you would simply say that you can see it is red. So what about religious experience?

By 'religious experience' here, I don't mean some unusual or mystical experience of 'communing' with God, but something more ordinary: 'religious differs from non-religious experience, not as the awareness of a different world, but as a different way of experiencing the same world. Events which can be experienced as having a purely natural significance are experienced by the religious mind as having also and at the same time religious significance and as mediating the presence and activity of God'.

> John Hick, 'Rational Theistic Belief without Proofs'

Perceptual experiencing-as

Hick develops an analogy between perception and experience of God. He starts with the idea that perception is not simply registering what is 'out there' neutrally. In the Necker Cube, one set of lines can be seen in two different ways. We can also see patterns in natural objects, as when we see a face or a fish in a cloud. We don't just see, we 'see-as' or 'see-in'. We see the lines *as* a cube facing this way or that; we see a face *in* the cloud (we can also say we see the shape of the cloud *as* a face).

> 'Religious Faith as Experiencing-as'

> The Necker Cube: in Figure 9.1, which side of the cube faces out of the page? The cube can be seen facing down and to the left, or up and to the right.

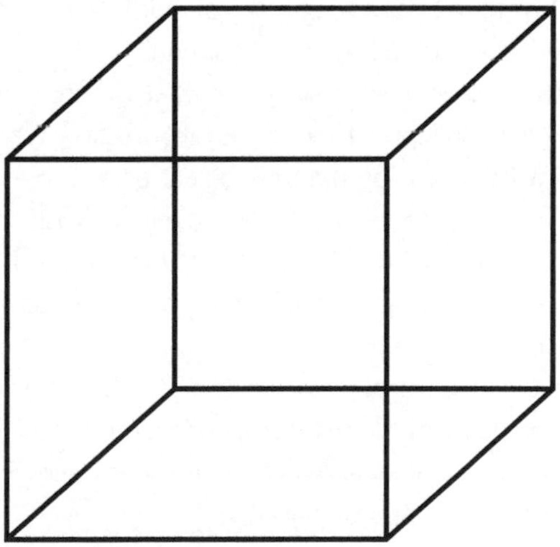

Figure 9.1 Necker Cube.

We discussed the relation between experience and concepts in Ch. 1, Do ALL IDEAS DERIVE FROM SENSE EXPERIENCE? II (p. 24) and CONCEPTUAL SCHEMES AND THEIR PHILOSOPHICAL IMPLICATIONS (p. 21).

We can argue that all seeing involves seeing-as. This is hard to accept at first. Do you see this book as a book? But consider what someone who has never seen a book, whose culture has no books, would experience. They wouldn't see the book *as* a book. For example, if they don't have the concept BOOK, they can't. And we can extend this idea from seeing to all experiencing – we hear a sound as bird-song, smell a smell as coffee, and so on. Perception, on this account, always involves *recognition* (or mis-recognition), bringing experience under a concept.

Sometimes, as with the Necker Cube, we can only see something as this *or* that, for example, we see the cube as facing one way *or* the other. But with other seeing-as, we can add layers of perceptual recognition – you can see the object in the sky as a bird and as a hawk and as a hawk hunting.

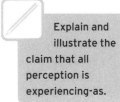

Explain and illustrate the claim that all perception is experiencing-as.

Religious experience

Hick then argues that religious experience is a kind of experiencing-as. The religious person experiences human life and history as an encounter with God, as well as an encounter with the physical world and other people. It is an *additional layer* of experiencing-as, a perspective on life and the world that the non-religious person doesn't have.

But is religious experience really analogous to perceptual experiencing-as? Or is it a *subjective projection* of religious meaning onto natural events? Hick accepts that there are disanalogies, for example, religious experience isn't sensory perception and we aren't perceiving types of object but the significance of events. But, he argues, there is an important continuity.

First, *all* perception involves making sense of what is perceived (through seeing-as, through applying concepts). Part of this involves how we respond to what we see. To see x as y – for example, this object as a fork – involves an appropriate response in how we are disposed to act in relation to it, for example, use it to eat with, not to write with. We shouldn't think, then, that we can contrast religious experience as a projection with 'neutral' perceptual experience. No experience is neutral.

Second, we don't just recognise objects, we recognise situations, as shown by our immediate appropriate responses to them. For example, seeing someone hanging off the edge of a cliff in fear initiates a *moral* response – of helping them. We recognise this a situation of moral significance.

Religious experience is a matter of recognising the religious significance of events or situations, for example, having a sense of God in the vastness or beauty of the natural world. This involves a change in how we are disposed to act; Hick argues that all religious experience disposes us to the 'service of God'. For Christians, this is indicated by Jesus' moral teaching. This response is not an optional extra – it is just as much part of experiencing human life and history as an encounter with God as using a fork to eat with is part of seeing it as a fork.

However, we can object that the analogy still doesn't work. While Hick is right that all recognition involves applying concepts to experience, we don't need to accept that all recognition is similar to perceptual recognition. If recognising the religious significance of a situation was analogous to recognising a fork, then we can ask 'Which sense do we use? Is there a "religious sense"? How does this religious sense detect religious significance (eyes detect light from the fork)?'. Hick doesn't suggest we can give answers to these questions.

Talk of 'recognition' or 'experiencing-as' in these contexts is not analogous to perception; it is *metaphorical*. So we shouldn't defend the claim that religious experience is experiencing the world as an encounter with God by analogy with perception.

The status of the religious 'hypothesis'

A 'hypothesis' is a proposal that needs to be tested (and confirmed or rejected) by experience. We use experience to infer its truth or falsehood; its truth is not something that we can experience directly. The 'religious hypothesis' is that 'God exists'. Is this a hypothesis?

When we test a scientific hypothesis, we look for experiences that will show that it is true or false. If 'God exists' is an **empirical** hypothesis, a statement of fact, then it must be possible to imagine the conditions under which we would say that it was not a fact. For example, the theory of evolution by natural selection is a hypothesis; if aliens came to Earth and demonstrated that they had planted 'fossils' (which actually they had made) for us to find, we would give up the theory. What would make us give up the claim that 'God exists'? We can argue that there are no tests of this kind, so 'God exists' is not a hypothesis.

Hick's argument leads us to the view that 'God exists' is not a 'hypothesis' for completely different reasons, viz. God's existence is experienced directly, in our experience of human life as an encounter with God. It is no more a hypothesis than the claim that 'this is a fork'.

But we can object that the same argument applies. Just as with hypotheses, when we talk of what we can experience directly, we can imagine situations in

Explain and illustrate Hick's claim that religious experience is continuous with perceptual experiencing-as.

Discuss the analogy between perceptual and religious experiencing-as.

Understanding the idea of God in this way was discussed in EXPLAINING THE IDEA OF 'GOD' AS A HUMAN CONSTRUCTION AND PROJECTION (Ch. 4, p. 134).

Could experiences of evil lead to this? They could, but they need not for many religious believers.

which we would withdraw our claim that 'this is an x'. The fork may be a hologram; or it could be a clever illusion, so that when we turn it around, we see it is not a fork at all, but a knife that has been painted; and so on. To be able to say 'this is a fork' *meaningfully*, we have to know what kinds of situation would lead us to say 'this is not a fork'. So if we say 'human life is an encounter with God', what kinds of experience would lead us to say, 'no, it was just an illusion, it isn't an encounter with God'? There is nothing that means one *has to* withdraw one's claim about encountering God. This suggests that 'God exists' is not something we know directly from experience.

However, we can object that this argument has a very limited view of meaning. It assumes that for 'God exists' to state a fact, we have to know how to test whether that fact is true or false against experience (and sensory experience at that). But we could argue that the meaning of 'God exists' is related to and secured by *making sense* of facts. For example, we could use the argument from design to infer that God's existence is the best explanation for the nature of the universe (or use the problem of evil to infer that God does not exist). In this case 'God exists' is a hypothesis, but not a *scientific* hypothesis, since we use philosophy, not science, to test it. What we mean by 'God exists' will be shown by these arguments.

Alternatively, we could understand how we make sense of experience as Hick does, and reject the idea that 'God exists' is a hypothesis. Philosophical arguments aren't the natural foundation of religious belief, so 'God exists' gains its meaning not from philosophical arguments but from how people experience human life.

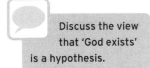

> Explain the argument that 'God exists' is not an empirical hypothesis.

> This is part of AYER'S VERIFICATION PRINCIPLE, which we discussed and rejected in Ch. 1, p. 34.

> Discuss the view that 'God exists' is a hypothesis.

Religious 'belief' mirrors attitudes rather than facts

The arguments so far still understand 'God exists' as a statement of *fact*. But we can challenge this. First, as we have already noted, if it is a statement of fact, it is peculiar in that we do not test it against empirical experience. Second, religious belief is clearly not purely intellectual. As Hick argues, if one experiences the world as an encounter with God, that involves a disposition to serve God. Third, people don't normally acquire religious beliefs by argument or testing evidence. Instead, they come to an understanding of the world that is expressed in values and a way of living. When someone converts to a religion, what changes isn't so much intellectual beliefs, but their *will*, what they value, how they choose to live. We can argue, then, that religious 'belief' is not really a genuine form of *belief* at all.

So what is it? To say it expresses 'feelings' is too shallow. Religion is not just about feeling, it is about ways of living. Every religion pays close attention to what people do and gives guidance on how to live. So we can say that religious 'beliefs' are expressions of attitude and commitment, attitudes towards other people, nature, oneself, human history and so on that put the world in a certain light and which support commitments to act in certain ways and to mature as a spiritual being. The core of accepting a religious faith, on this view, is the intention to follow the way of life prescribed by that religion.

This is not to say that we can turn any particular religious 'belief' on its own into a rule that guides action. Unlike moral beliefs, such as 'abortion is wrong', which are directed onto some specific action or policy, religious 'beliefs' always come together, a whole set of beliefs, and the set as a whole indicates a whole way of life.

> Explain and illustrate the view that religious 'belief' expresses attitudes rather than facts.

Objections

We can object that there is much more to religious 'beliefs' than a commitment to a way of life. What can we say about different religions that recommend similar ways of life? If commitment to a way of life is all that matters, then does it matter at all what one believes? Many religions have thought it does; some have even argued that how one lives is not the main point at all. Religious 'belief' is not the same as a general moral system. Furthermore, many Christians, for instance, would say that they live a certain way *because* God exists and showed us how to live. But if this answer only *expresses* the commitment to live a certain way then it doesn't answer the question *why* live that way. If religious 'belief' is just a commitment, what supports that commitment or is it arbitrary?

To answer these objections, we might add that religious beliefs relate to specific stories or myths. These stories differ in different religions, and they don't appear at all in purely moral systems. In Christianity, obviously the stories about Jesus' life and death are central. But then, doesn't this make religious belief about facts again? No, we can say, because the stories do not need to be believed to be true; they need to be believed *as stories*. The story is considered meaningful, rather than literally true, and it supports the commitment to a certain way of life.

This *might* explain the difference between religions and between religion and morality. But, we can still object, a story isn't the right kind of answer to 'Why live like that?'. Suppose a boy says that he wants to be a detective when he grows up, and to the question 'Why?', tells you a Sherlock Holmes story. This is fine. Now suppose a Christian, to the question 'Why love your enemy as yourself?' tells a story about Jesus. Is this a good answer? If all the stories about Jesus are false, and God doesn't exist, then it is not a command from God that we should try to live this way. So *why* should we? If religious 'beliefs' are just commitments to a way of life supported by stories, then they seem to be *subjective*. Many religious believers would not accept this interpretation of belief.

> **?** Does the view that religious 'belief' expresses attitudes make religion subjective?

Key points • • •

- Hick argues that religious experience is experience of human life *as* an encounter with God. Religious experiencing-as is analogous to perception, in which we experience things *as* books, bird-calls, the smell of coffee, and so on.
- We can object that, unlike perceptual experience, religious experience projects subjective meaning onto the natural world. Hick responds that no experience is 'neutral', but always involves interpretation and that we interpret and recognise events and situations just as we do objects.
- We can press the objection that religious experience is not analogous to perceptual experience, for example, there is no 'religious sense'.
- The religious 'hypothesis' that God exists is not really a hypothesis, because we do not test it against facts, as we test scientific hypotheses, to see if it is true or false. So 'God exists' cannot be a statement of fact.
- We can object that this argument rests on a narrow view of meaning. For instance, we can argue that 'God exists' makes sense (or doesn't make sense) of facts.
- Hick would argue that 'God exists' is not a hypothesis because we experience God directly in religious experience of the world.
- We can object that 'God exists' is not factual at all, but a reflection of the religious person's attitudes and commitments. To accept a set of religious 'beliefs' is to have the intention to follow that religion's way of life.
- We can object that this is too reductionist, that there is more to religious belief than adopting a way of life. We can also argue that religious people usually cite what they believe to support or justify their way of life, not simply to express it.

DEVELOPMENT

I. The argument from design

Arguments for design II

Paley and design-like properties

A famous argument for design was given by William Paley. He argues that if I found a stone lying in a field, and wondered how it came to be there, I might rightly think that, for all I knew, it had always been there. However, if I found a watch lying on the ground, I wouldn't feel the same answer was satisfactory. Examining it closely, I would infer it had a designer.

Now we know that watches have designers. But what is it about a watch *itself* that leads us to think it must have a designer? Paley spends a considerable time exploring this inference, and whether it is valid *in the case of the watch*. For example, would it undermine the inference if the watch sometimes went wrong, or if I'd never seen a watch being made? He is trying to identify exactly what it is about a watch that allows us to infer a designer. After all, in the case of a watch, this does seem a good inference. Watches don't just 'happen'. What properties of a watch are direct evidence of design?

Paley identifies the property of having an organisation of parts put together for a purpose as crucial. It is from this that we infer the watch has a designer – even if we know nothing about watchmakers. He then argues that we can make exactly the *same* argument in the case of natural things that exhibit that property. Natural things have the same property, so they too have a designer.

AN OBJECTION

Throughout the argument, Paley is relying on the idea that the sorts of properties he takes as evidence of design – in the case of the watch and of nature – cannot be produced by *natural means*, and so must be the result of a mind. In the case of the watch, this seems right – a watch *isn't* the kind of thing nature produces. So if we found a watch in a field, we would rightly wonder about its origin. However, natural things are precisely the sort of thing that nature *does* produce. We can't, then, argue that natural things cannot be produced by natural means, so must have been designed by a mind.

So what is the difference between natural things and watches? There is no question that natural things have *design-like* properties. Paley has established

Natural Theology, Ch. 1–3

It is often thought that Paley argues from analogy; but he is not arguing that natural things are *like* watches. He is arguing that watches have a property which supports the inference of a designer, and then argues that natural things have *exactly that property* as well.

Compare and contrast Paley's argument that natural things are designed with the argument from analogy.

this. The difficulty is that unlike watches, natural things don't show evidence of being *manufactured artefacts*. In this different context, their design-like properties aren't clearly good evidence for actually having been designed. Although we are making the same inference from design-like properties to a designer, the argument doesn't have the same force in the case of natural things. And as in our earlier discussion (p. 315), we can appeal to Darwinism to show that nature *can* produce design-like properties (though not manufactured artefacts).

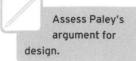

Assess Paley's argument for design.

Going further: 'intelligent design'

In the last twenty years, some thinkers have become dissatisfied with explanations of the complexity of living creatures in terms of evolution by natural selection. They have been struck by the 'irreducible complexity' of the systems and organs of living creatures. Michael Behe, a biochemist, defines irreducible complexity as 'a single system which is composed of several interacting parts that contribute to the basic function, and where the removal of any one of these parts causes the system to effectively cease functioning'. This property is precisely the one that Paley has argued is the basis for inferring a designer.

'Molecular machines'

As an example of such a situation, Behe describes the many parts (over forty) that work together to move the 'tail' that propels a certain bacterium. Behe argues that evolution couldn't produce such an organisation of parts. The reason is that, as we saw, evolution works by making small changes, accidentally, and one at a time. But until all the pieces are in place together, the tail wouldn't work. It's all or nothing. But evolution is bit by bit.

Like Paley, Behe argues that irreducible complexity is direct evidence of design. If a system won't work at all until all its parts are in place, then this suggests someone planned and organised the parts.

Explain and illustrate the argument from 'irreducible complexity'.

However, many evolutionary biologists reject this conclusion. First, Behe's argument assumes that each part in a system has always been that part in that system. But this isn't true in evolution. It often happens that a system, or its parts, having evolved to do one thing are 'co-opted' into doing something else. Some of the parts that move the bacterium's tail work as a kind of pump if taken alone. They may have had nothing at all to do with movement when they first evolved. They could have evolved as a pump, and later on some further accidental change meant they joined with some new part to move a tail.

Second, features that are initially minor improvements can become essential. Take lungs - very complex and without which we wouldn't survive. But they started out as relatively unimportant air bladders in fish (they help fish not sink to the sea floor, but not all fish have them, for example, sharks do not). They acquired a new function when fish made brief forays onto land, now operating to supply the fish with oxygen as well. Over time, developments in the air bladder served this new purpose, allowing for longer and longer trips out of water. Eventually they became lungs, and the fish ceased to be fish. Lungs didn't have to evolve all at once. So we can argue that evolution by natural selection can account for irreducible complexity.

Is any argument for design persuasive?

Arguments from design II

We ended the earlier discussion of ARGUMENTS FROM DESIGN (p. 317) wanting to avoid appealing to analogy when inferring the existence of a designer. We can do this by using the considerations about probability that we noted at the end of the earlier discussion of cosmology (p. 316). We said that cosmology supports the view that it is hugely improbable that the universe would have the right properties for life to evolve. But if God exists, we can explain this. So it is more probable that God exists and designed the universe for life than that the universe just randomly happened to have the right features for life. This is an **inductive** argument from probability for the existence of God.

Swinburne's argument

The argument only works if God is the only satisfactory way that we can explain the fact that the universe allows life to evolve. In other words, we need to ask whether God is the *best* explanation for this fact. For example, could we not give a scientific explanation? Richard Swinburne argues not. Science can't offer *any* satisfactory explanation, because science can't provide us with the right sort of answer to why the universe has the laws it has or the exact quantity of matter

*The Coherence of
Theism*, Ch. 8

it has. Science must *assume* the laws of nature in order to provide any explanations at all. It can't say where they come from or why they are the way they are, because all scientific explanations presuppose laws.

For example, science explains why water boils when you heat it in terms of the effect of heat on the properties of molecules. It explains these effects and these properties in terms of other laws and properties, atomic and sub-atomic ones. Some further explanation of these may be possible, but again, it will suppose other laws and properties. So at root, scientific laws are 'brute' – they have no explanation unless we can find some other kind of explanation for them.

We use another type of explanation all the time, viz. 'personal explanation'. We explain the products of human activity – this book, these sentences – in terms of a person. I'm writing things I *intend* to write. This sort of explanation explains an object or an event in terms of a person and their purposes. The hypothesis that God exists and intended life to evolve provides a personal explanation for why the universe is such that life can evolve.

However, we saw (p. 318) that Hume objected that even if you can show that the universe has a designer, you can't show that the designer is God, as we normally think of God. For example, this argument doesn't show that there is only one cause of the universe; nor does it show that that cause is perfect, omniscient, omnipotent, or cares about people. The argument only needs 'God' to be able to design the universe (and perhaps, put that design into effect). It doesn't say anything else about God.

> **Explain and illustrate the difference between scientific and personal explanation.**

Going further: best explanation

Swinburne's response is to accept this objection. The argument so far is only evidence for a designer, not evidence for the traditional theistic conception of God. However, he argues, the argument is about what is the *best explanation* for design; and God as we usually think of him remains the *best* explanation.

Swinburne says an explanation is good 'when the explanatory hypothesis [in this case, the existence of God and his intention for the universe to contain life] is simple and leads us with some probability to expect the data which we would not otherwise expect'. 'Simplicity' means not invoking more different kinds of thing than you need to; and not giving them more or more complex properties than they need for the explanation to work.

Simplicity requires that we shouldn't suppose that two possible causes exist when only one will do. Supposing there is more than one cause of the universe is a worse explanation, because it is not as simple. It is also simpler to suppose that the cause of the universe is itself uncaused, or we have a problem of regress. It is also simpler to suppose that God has infinite power and intelligence, or we would have to explain why God had just the amount of power and intelligence he has (enough to create the universe, but no more), that is, what limits God's power and intelligence.

(Swinburne adds infinite goodness to the properties of God, but we can question this - why does God need to be *good* in order to create the universe? This objection becomes more pressing when we consider THE PROBLEM OF EVIL, p. 320.)

Is God the simplest explanation of design in the universe?

The limits of explanation

If we explain design in terms of God, now we have to ask 'What explains God?' and this seems to be an even more puzzling question than 'What explains scientific laws?'. So from not being able to explain design in the universe, we end up not being able to explain something else. This is not progress.

Swinburne responds that it is progress, and that we do something similar all the time in science. Science will introduce an entity – like sub-atomic particles – in order to explain something, for example, explosions in a nuclear accelerator. However, these new entities now need explaining, and scientists don't yet know how to explain them. This is absolutely normal, and has happened repeatedly throughout the history of science. It *is* progress, because we have explained one more thing. So we can still say that God is a good explanation for scientific laws even if we can't explain God.

But if we will always have *something* we can't explain, why invoke God? Why not just say we can't explain scientific laws? Because scientific laws leave fewer things explained, and we should explain as much as we can. This is a principle of science and philosophy. If you give up on this, you give up on pursuing these forms of thought.

Discuss the claim that it is legitimate to introduce something you can't explain in order to explain something else.

Does the universe need explaining?

But do we need *any* explanation for why the universe appears designed? Some things that appear to be coincidence are in fact inevitable, for example, winning the lottery: it is very unlikely that you will win, but it is inevitable that *someone* will win. For whoever wins, that *they* won is a huge coincidence; but we don't need any special explanation for it (such as 'someone intended them to win, and rigged the lottery').

Suppose, then, that instead of just this universe, there are or have been millions of universes. Each had different scientific laws, and in most cases, the laws didn't allow the universe to continue to exist – as soon as it began, it ended. Others existed, but there was no life. It was inevitable, we might think, that given all the possible variations in scientific laws, a universe such as ours would exist, and therefore so would life. It doesn't need any special explanation – it had to happen.

But why *ours*? Well, it had to be ours because we wouldn't be here if it wasn't! Given that life *does* exist in it, *this* universe has to have the right scientific laws for life to exist. If it didn't, life wouldn't exist in it. There is nothing special about this universe, except that it has the right laws; just like there is nothing special about the ticket that wins the lottery.

But we can object that this response assumes the existence of *huge* numbers of other universes, which are completely inaccessible to us, and for which we have (virtually) no other evidence. Why should we assume that? The existence of God, by contrast, Swinburne argues, is simpler (just one God, not millions of universes) and is also supported by other evidence. So the existence of just one universe, designed by God, is a better explanation.

We can object, however, that we also have evidence *against* the existence of God, viz. THE PROBLEM OF EVIL (p. 320). At least we don't have evidence against the existence of other universes.

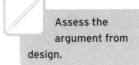

Explain the argument that the appearance of design in the universe needs no special explanation.

Swinburne argues that RELIGIOUS EXPERIENCE and MIRACLES, both studied in A2 Unit 3.5, are evidence for God's existence.

Assess the argument from design.

Key points • • •

- Paley tries to identify precisely what it is in human artefacts that supports the conclusion that they were designed. He then claims that these same properties exist in natural things, so the inference is equally valid.
- However, even if design-like properties exist in natural things, the inference to a designer is not supported, because natural objects are not like artefacts. Darwin's theory of evolution explains how nature can produce design-like properties.

- The argument from irreducible complexity says that evolution cannot produce an organisation of parts, all of which are needed for a system to perform its function. Many evolutionary biologists argue that it can.
- We can ask *why* nature is capable of producing apparently designed things, that is, what explains the laws of nature that enable this. As the chance of these laws occurring randomly is incredibly low, Swinburne argues that the best explanation is that God intended the evolution of apparently designed things.
- He argues that science cannot provide a satisfactory explanation of laws, since scientific explanations always presuppose laws. So we need a personal explanation.
- God is the simplest explanation of design, and so the best.
- However, chance could be a good explanation (or rather, no explanation is required): if there are or have been huge numbers of universes, the chance that one would have laws that enabled apparent design is much higher. However, this requires that many such other universes do or have existed, a claim for which we have little independent evidence.

II. The problem of evil

Going further: how good is free will?

We saw that it is central to the free will defence that free will is a great good (p. 322). It is better for God to have created a world in which beings with free will (us) cause evil than a world in which there is no free will and no evil. However, we can object that even if free will is a great good, that doesn't mean we should never interfere with it. If we see someone about to commit murder and do nothing about it, it is no defence to appeal to how wonderful it is that the murderer has free will. The existence and goodness of free will is compatible with interfering with it. So why doesn't God prevent evil actions?

We can reply that God would have to interfere *very often* to prevent all the evil we cause, and this would undermine our sense of free will. But perhaps that depends on how God interferes. Couldn't God arrange it that

These points are all the more powerful when we consider the free will of the Devil. We referred to the Devil to extend the free will defence to natural evil. But surely a world without the Devil, and so a world without natural evil, would be better than a world with the Devil and his free will. If this is right, then the free will defence cannot answer the problem of natural evil.

we would be *tempted* to harm one another, and believe that we were capable of doing so, but when it actually came to acting on such motives, a strong sense of conscience prevented us?

Second, God could have given us free will without giving us the power to commit terrible evil. Is free will, as it is now, such a good thing that its existence outweighs all the evil in the world? Wouldn't a limited kind of free will have been better? Richard Swinburne replies that the value of free will depends on what one can do with it. A world in which we couldn't harm each other would also be one in which we would have very little responsibility for each other's well-being. It would be a 'toy world'.

But does this follow? We could still have a world in which we could choose to greatly benefit each other or not. Or again, we could harm each other in more minor ways, but because of a strong conscience, feel terrible about it, so be less inclined to commit harm.

Assess the free will defence.

Soul-making II

We ended the earlier discussion of SOUL-MAKING (p. 323) with the objection that not all suffering leads to the being who is suffering growing morally and spiritually as a result. The suffering might break them or occur at the end of their lives; or if the being is an animal, it suffers but doesn't have a soul that can grow.

We can reply to this objection by rephrasing the argument that evil is necessary for spiritual growth. The argument should be taken generally. It is not that the suffering of the person necessarily or always helps that very person. For instance, it is in response to the suffering of *other people* that *we* grow.

We might still object that this doesn't always occur – there is still suffering that seems to lead to no good at all. Swinburne argues that this fact is also necessary for spiritual growth. If suffering was exactly matched to spiritual growth, and we could see and understand this in every case, then that would virtually be a proof of the existence of God!

Imagine such a world in which we knew on every occasion when someone suffered that it was for the best. We would need neither faith nor hope, both of which depend on uncertainty and unpredictability. But faith and hope are two central virtues, two ways in which souls grow spiritually. So for our souls to grow spiritually, it *must* look like the distribution and amount of evil are unfair or unjustified.

We can object that this remains unconvincing. Is *so much evil* distributed in *such* an unfair way *really* necessary for our souls to become morally and spiritually mature? Is it really impossible for goodness to grow in response to more minor evils? These questions press us towards the next approach to the problem of evil: is this really the best of all possible worlds?

The best of all possible worlds

One way of phrasing the problem of evil is to say that if God is all-loving and all-powerful, then he would make the best of all possible worlds for us to live in. This is clearly not the best of all possible worlds – the removal of many evils would make the world better. Therefore, an all-loving and all-powerful God does not exist.

One response is to argue that this *is* the best of all possible worlds. We have already seen indications of this: that the world is better with free will and evil than without either free will or evil, and we cannot have a world which has free will but not evil; or again, that the world is better with souls that develop morally and spiritually, but for this, evil is necessary.

We can also give a more general argument. It is easy to pick out some event or some feature of the world that we think the world would be better off without. If someone we know hadn't got cancer; if a particular type of parasite hadn't evolved; if Hitler had never got into power – the world would be a better place. However, we don't know what the consequences would be of removing these events or features from the world. We don't know the connections between these events and others. Removing these features or preventing these events may require all sorts of changes, which in the end would produce a worse world. Because we can't know this, we can't know that this *isn't* the best of all possible worlds.

The laws of nature

For example, the most obvious way we can imagine some single event changing is for God to intervene in what caused the event. For example, he could prevent Hitler's parents from meeting, or he could kill Hitler off by a freak lightning

Discuss the argument that evil must appear unjustified for us to grow spiritually.

Assess the soul-making theodicy.

Explain and illustrate the argument that evil does not show that this is not the best of all possible worlds.

strike. This would be a miracle – an intervention with events that are in accordance with the laws of nature. But the laws of nature are themselves a great good. For example, for free will to exist, for us to do anything at all, things need to happen in a regular way (chairs don't sprout wings, water quenches thirst, etc.). If events are going to happen in a regular way, then the world needs to be governed by natural laws. These laws will give rise to natural evil or to people who will commit moral evil. But this evil is justified because the alternative is a much worse world in which nothing takes place in a regular way.

OBJECTIONS

We can object that there would still be laws of nature if God intervened *sometimes*, to prevent the very worst evils from occurring. But once again, we can appeal to our ignorance of the effects if God miraculously prevented some event from happening or some feature of the world from existing. Suppose it is true, as the soul-making argument claims, that a certain amount of evil is necessary in the world for good souls to grow. Then while God could have prevented this evil or that evil, he would then have had to allow some *other* evil to occur, or there would not be enough total evil in the world for us to grow spiritually.

Second, how can this be the best of all possible worlds given the amount of suffering of animals, which does neither them nor us any good? One response is that for *us to exist*, given the laws of nature, many other sentient animals needed to exist as well. We have evolved from them, and we cannot know that if God had created a world without animals or a world in which animals didn't suffer (but we did – how?), that this would be a better world.

Finally, for this to justify evil, we must suppose that no *alternative set* of natural laws could lead to less natural evil. But this seems hard to believe. Is it *impossible* that there are no droughts? Is it *impossible* that animals all eat plants rather than each other? Is it *impossible* that cancer didn't exist? Surely there could be natural laws that meant these things never happened; and a good God would choose those laws that didn't lead to natural evil.

Do the laws of nature justify natural evil?

The standard for 'best possible world'

The problem of evil takes the happiness of creatures on Earth as the standard for judging whether the world could be better. But just as in THE ARGUMENT FROM ANALOGY (p. 318) we objected that we cannot take the intelligence of human beings as a model for the designer of the universe, so we can't take the happiness of human beings (and other animals we know about) as the standard for whether the universe is the best possible world. Suppose, for example, we expanded it just to 'the happiness of all beings capable of happiness and suffering'. We don't know what other beings exist in the universe, we don't know what supernatural beings, such as angels, exist as well. It might be that our unhappiness on Earth is very small in comparison with their happiness, and that to try to remove our unhappiness would lead to greater unhappiness overall.

Perhaps we can't know that this isn't the best of all possible worlds. We could still object that we have no good reason to think that it *is* the best of all possible worlds, and we have very good reason to think that it isn't.

> Assess the attempt to solve the problem of evil by claiming that this is or could be the best of all possible worlds.

Going further: the argument and the appeal to ignorance

The evidential problem of evil appeals to an intuition - that there is *no good reason* that *could* justify the amount and distribution of evil in the world. However, a religious believer may simply reply that we don't know this. It may be that all evil serves some higher purpose, but we simply don't, and perhaps can't, know what that purpose is or how evil serves it.

Yes, it may be, but then it may not be. This isn't enough to undermine the evidential problem of evil, because the argument isn't meant to be a *proof* that God doesn't exist. It only intends to show that it is very unlikely that God exists. So we should say this:

1. There is no good *that we know of* that could justify the evil that we see. Any higher good we can think of (such as free will or spiritual growth) could be obtained without God *having* to allow the evil that exists.
2. *Whatever* higher good evil is supposed to be necessary for, if it's anything we can think of already, it won't justify evil.
3. Therefore, evil can only be justified by a higher good that we are simply not familiar with.
4. It is *probable* that we know most goods.
5. So it is *probable* that there is no such higher good.

We often infer from what we know to what we don't know. For example, we constantly form beliefs about the future: the sun will rise tomorrow, chairs won't suddenly sprout wings, and so on. We do this because we think the future will be like the past. Inferring from 'nothing we know of will justify evil' to 'nothing will justify evil' is just the same.

When reasoning about what is *probable*, we don't usually allow the appeal to ignorance on its own. Instead, we need a *good reason* for thinking that *there is* some higher good that we don't know about. Suppose we have a revelation from God that everything is for the best. This won't really count, because if it is unlikely that God exists, it is unlikely that the revelation is genuine. But we don't know whether it is unlikely that God exists or not until we have solved the problem of evil.

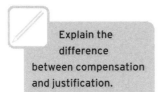

Can the problem of evil be avoided by appealing to our ignorance?

The afterlife

A final theodicy takes a completely different approach. It doesn't try to justify the evil that exists in this life by other aspects of this life (free will, spiritual growth, etc.). Instead, it appeals to an 'afterlife'. The idea is that if you suffer unjustly in this life, God will make it up to you in the next life. On balance, everyone will get what they deserve in the end.

This argument has not been popular with philosophers. The difficulty is that it does not offer a *moral justification* for evil. For example, if I hit you and then give you £20, was it alright for me to hit you? Would it be alright if I gave you £1000? No, there is just something wrong with this way of thinking. At best, the money is *compensation* for something I did wrong, it does not justify what I did. The same applies to thinking about evil. If God rewards those who deserve it by eternal life in heaven, this is at best a compensation for the unjust suffering they experienced in life. It does not make it morally good or justifiable that they suffered. A loving God would not act this way.

Furthermore, if we want to bring about something good, but know that it will harm someone innocent as a result, we should at least ask their permission. If they consent, then perhaps the act and the compensation we offer is morally justified. They have agreed with our plan, and accept the consequences. But to go ahead without informing or asking them is to *use* them as a means to our end. If God has brought about a world in which evil is unfairly distributed, but

Explain the difference between compensation and justification.

this is necessary for some greater good, God has used people as a means to that end – even if they receive compensation in the afterlife.

At best, the afterlife might make us care less about the evil we suffer. But it cannot seem to offer a moral justification for how an all-good God could allow such evil in the first place.

?

Could the promise of rewards in the afterlife solve the problem of evil?

Key points • • •

- Even if free will is a great good, this does not mean it should not be interfered with. We can argue that an all-loving, all-powerful God would prevent evil actions, or at least the most evil actions (including those of the Devil).

- To the objection that not all evil contributes to spiritual growth, we can argue that it must appear this way, or we would not develop the important virtues of faith and hope. We can reply that such virtues (and others) could still develop with less evil distributed less unfairly.

- The problem of evil supposes that the world could be made better by removing certain evils. We can reply that we do not know what else would change if those evils were removed. For all we know, this could be the best of all possible worlds.

- An example is provided by the laws of nature. We need these for free will, but they will inevitably lead to natural evil as well.

- We can object that God could nevertheless intervene with the laws of nature sometimes, that animals suffer needlessly, and that some alternative set of natural laws could lead to less suffering. But in each case, we may reply that we cannot know that these changes would not lead to some important good being lost.

- We can also argue that we cannot take the suffering of creatures of Earth as the criterion for whether this is the best of all possible worlds.

- We can object that this argument has given us no good reason to think that this *is* the best of all possible worlds.

- In general, we cannot appeal to ignorance to solve the evidential problem of evil. That argument claims that an all-loving, all-powerful God is improbable. We therefore need some reason to think that evil *is* justified, not just that it could be.

- We might argue that the afterlife will make up for the evil we suffer. However, this is just compensation, not a justification of evil. It would be morally wrong of God to allow evil to occur unjustly and then compensate us for it.

III. The religious point of view

Different perspectives ('seeing-as') II

We ended our previous discussion by objecting that Hick's idea of experiencing human life as an encounter with God was not analogous to perceptual 'seeing-as'. Rather, seeing-as was no more than a metaphor (p. 327). But what Hick wants to emphasise with the analogy is the contrast between something 'experiential' and beliefs that we form by argument or inference. To see something as a fork is to dispose us to use it to eat with; we don't infer we should use it this way. In the situation of the person hanging off the cliff, we don't infer that we should help, we see that help is needed. So, he argues, the religious person doesn't infer that God exists, but experiences life as an encounter with God. It is immediate, like perception, not inferred, like theoretical beliefs.

But we can object that with perception, we *all* experience the natural world. Religious experience is much less common and religious people come to different beliefs on the basis of their experience. If God was 'there' in the same way the natural world is 'there', we would all have the same religious experience, just as we have the same (or very similar) perceptual experience. So religious experience may *feel* immediate, but differences in religious experience suggest that actually it is inferred.

We can reply that this simplifies perceptual experience. People who are experts at recognising birds 'see' or 'hear' hawks, eagles, chuffs, woodcocks and so on; they don't have some perceptual experience we could all share and then 'infer' the species. Once one has *learned* to recognise an object, one recognises it immediately – but first one must learn. So, Hick argues, not everyone recognises events as an encounter with God. Furthermore, if God was as unmistakable as the natural world, this would completely change religious faith – for the worse. So God gave us 'cognitive freedom' in being able to recognise or not recognise life as an encounter with him. Once one has freely opened oneself to this perspective, then (as with recognising birds) the experience is immediate.

But could it not all be an illusion? After all, someone who is mad might experience the world in a way that shows that they are being persecuted

> **?** Is religious experience a form of experiencing-as or based on inference?

telepathically by aliens who want to conquer Earth. Hick responds that religious faith does not seem like a madness. The religious person gives no signs of psychological breakdown or an inability to function in the world. In fact, some religious teachers have a very high degree of psychological integration and maturity. So, as yet, we have no reason to think that experiencing the world religiously is irrational.

This is not meant to convince anyone of the existence of God. Hick is only arguing that experiencing the world in this way is legitimate; for someone who has this experience, it is rational for them to believe in God. Someone who doesn't have this experience is unaffected by the argument. They do not need arguments, but different experiences, a different perspective on the world.

What about the different religious beliefs that people hold? Either, in time, someone's experience of the world will make particular religious beliefs irrational and unsustainable – and perhaps, in the long run, just one religion will be justified by religious experience; or this won't happen, and no one religion will be better supported by religious experience than any other. In that case, we should argue that there are many ways of experiencing God.

> Explain and discuss the view that there are religious and non-religious perspectives on the world.

Religious 'belief', hypothesis and attitudes

In our previous discussion, we looked at the claim that 'God exists' doesn't operate like a statement of fact (p. 328). To deepen our understanding of the issue, we first need to think more about meaning.

Going further: Wittgenstein on language

Ludwig Wittgenstein argued that we cannot understand language without understanding the ways in which language is used and how it interacts with how we live and what we do. He attempted to illuminate the nature of language by comparing language to games. In particular, like games, language is an activity guided by rules - in games, rules governing what one can do, in language, rules governing meaning; and second, meaning is learned from the rules governing the use of the word/sentence, like 'pieces' in a game are understood by how they can be used.

> *Philosophical Investigations*

Meaning, then, is often a matter of how words are *used*. Appreciating this requires a distinction between *surface grammar* and *depth grammar*: words or sentences in one context describing *objects* or an *event* may be similar on the surface to ones that in another context do nothing of the sort, for example, 'the bus passes the bus stop', 'the peace of the Lord passes understanding'. To understand a particular 'piece' of language, one must look at how the language is used, as meaning is not given by the form of words alone.

When looking at how words are used, we need to look at the 'language game' – that bit of language and the rules it follows – which gives the words their meaning. (Wittgenstein lists as examples of language games asking, thanking, cursing, praying, greeting and so on.)

The idea of 'language games' emphasises the foundation of language in activity. Wittgenstein says that a language game is the speaking part of a 'form of life'. A form of life is far broader than any specific language game, it is the foundation out of which language games grow, the collection of cultural practices which embed language games.

> Explain and illustrate Wittgenstein's claim that the meaning of a word is its use.

> The very foundation is biology, and Wittgenstein often emphasises how our natural reactions form the basis for language games. (Think of talking about pain or colour or even responses to music.) But the biology is always taken up in a particular culture, and what is 'natural' is often only natural within a particular way of living as a human being. 'Human nature' involves both biology and culture.

Religious belief

So religious language must be understood as part of a religious life. Religious language contains the many different language games of praise and worship, prayer, miracles and so on; but it can also be understood as forming a game in its own right, governed by particular rules – those displayed in the analysis of its depth grammar. Wittgenstein argued that religious language has a depth grammar quite distinct from its surface grammar. Its surface grammar can look empirical, as though, like science, religious language is talking about things and events. This is misleading.

A central part of Wittgenstein's analysis is that 'God exists' is not a statement of fact. It is not about a *thing*, an *object* that exists as part of the world like natural objects do. It is not a claim about an entity at all. Of course, if it is not an empirical statement, then believing it is not an empirical belief: 'a religious belief could only be something like a passionate commitment to a system of reference. Hence, although it's a *belief*, it's really a way of living, or a way of assessing life. It's passionately seizing hold of *this* interpretation.' He argued

> *Culture and Value*, p. 64

that if we look at how the statement is *used*, what it *expresses* for people who believe it, we see that it is not used as a description, it is used to express a form of commitment.

This can be illustrated by talk of the Last Judgement. This is not a hypothesis about a possible future event; if it was, it would be utterly bizarre (what's the evidence? how is such a belief formed?). The Last Judgement is a 'picture', an understanding of life by which the believer is guided through life. Another example is provided by D.Z. Phillips, who defended and developed Wittgenstein's theory. He argues that if someone thinks that prayer is a means to obtaining something, they have misunderstood the nature of religion, and their belief has become superstition.

Religious language expresses an emotional attitude and understanding of life and a commitment to living life according to that understanding. It is not a description of the way the world is. Phillips argued that this means that God is not 'logically prior' to religion, some thing to which religion is a human response. Talk of God only makes sense within religious practices. To understand religious language is to understand the place of certain statements in the life of the believer and religious community. And the nature of religious faith and morality shows that these statements are not factual.

DISCUSSION

An important implication of the view that religious belief is not empirical, but mirrors attitudes and commitments, is that we can't criticise or support religious beliefs by using *evidence*. Religion cannot be criticised on the grounds that it is *not true* or highly *improbable*; for this presupposes that it makes factual claims, and it does not. So, for example, both the argument from design and the problem of evil are irrelevant as attempts to prove or disprove the existence of God. This, we might argue, cuts religious belief off from reason too severely.

However, Phillips points out that his view doesn't mean there are no grounds for accepting or rejecting religious belief. Religion is part of a form of human life: 'Religion has something to say about . . . birth, death, joy, misery, despair, hope, fortune, and misfortune.' If religious faith makes no sense in the light of such experiences, we will rightly reject it. The problem of evil could be relevant here. Not any set of attitudes and commitments makes sense.

But, as we noted in our previous discussion (p. 329), we can object that this interpretation of religious belief as not factual conflicts with how many believers think of God and their faith. Wittgenstein's account looks like a *reinterpretation* of religious belief, not an analysis of it. It also makes *what you believe* much less

Is talk of God talk of an entity? What are the similarities and differences?

'Religious beliefs and language games'

Outline Wittgenstein's account of religious language.

important, as religious faith is about how we live. Yet many religious believers who act in similar ways and hold similar values argue there is something distinctive and important about the different beliefs they hold. Furthermore, within the history of any religion, there have been heated arguments about how to interpret a particular doctrine (for example, in Christianity, the Incarnation), when it is very difficult to see how the different interpretations could make any impact on different ways of living. All this suggests that religious language is intended to be true, that is, fact-stating, and not just expressive.

We can argue that Wittgenstein was right to point to the expressive use of religious language. But he was wrong to think that because religious beliefs express attitudes, they cannot *also* be empirical. There is no reason to think that they cannot be *both*. After all, religious believers *do* think they are saying something factual when they say 'God exists'. It has this use.

> Assess the claim that religious 'belief' mirrors attitudes rather than facts.

Key points • • •

- Hick argues that religious belief isn't inferred by arguments and evidence, but based on direct experience of life as an encounter with God. Not everyone has this experience, as God has given us cognitive freedom. But for those who have it, it is as immediate as perceptual experience.
- We can object that it could be an illusory experience. Given the fact that religious people show no signs of breakdown or poor functioning, Hick argues that we have no reason to think it is.
- Wittgenstein argues that to understand what a word means, we must understand its use in the particular 'language game' in which it is employed. The surface grammar of sentences can be very different from their depth grammar. The foundations of language lie in our practices.
- He argues that religious belief is part of a distinctive language game. The depth grammar of religious language shows that God is not a thing that exists. Instead, talk of God is used to express a commitment to a particular way of living and to a framework for understanding and guiding life.
- If religious belief is not empirical, it can't be criticised or supported by empirical or philosophical reasoning. We can object that this cuts it off from reason too much. Phillips replies that faith still needs to 'make sense' of our experiences.
- But we may object that many religious believers think their faith is partly

empirical. Religious language can express attitudes *and* still refer to an independent divine reality.

SUMMARY

In this chapter, we have looked at three issues:

1. The argument from design.

2. The problem of evil.

3. The nature of the religious point of view and religious language.

In discussing these issues, we looked at the following questions:

1. Is the apparent purpose found in living creatures and the organisation of their parts evidence of design?

2. Does an analogy between human inventions and the natural world support the claim that there is a designer of the natural world?

3. What is the best explanation of the incredible improbability of the universe being able to support life?

4. If there is a designer of the natural world, is that designer God?

5. What is the problem of evil?

6. Does the existence of free will reconcile the existence of evil with the existence of an all-loving, all-powerful God?

7. Does the fact that we need to face evil in order to grow spiritually justify the amount and distribution of evil in the world?

8. Could this be the best of all possible worlds?

9. Does the existence of an afterlife solve the problem of evil?

10. Is religious experience analogous to perceptual experiencing-as?

11. Is 'God exists' a hypothesis?

12. Is 'God exists' meant as a statement of fact or an expression of an attitude or commitment?

10

AN INTRODUCTION TO PHILOSOPHY 2

Section 5: Free will and determinism

There are three central issues relating to free will and determinism. First, what is determinism? Second, is free will compatible with determinism? And third, what are the implications of determinism for moral responsibility and rationality? By the end of this chapter, you should be able to discuss these questions, explaining and evaluating different answers to each of them, and give reasons supporting each answer.

SYLLABUS CHECKLIST

The AQA AS syllabus for this chapter is:

What is determinism?

✔ Determinism is defined as the belief that a determinate set of conditions can only produce one possible outcome given fixed laws of nature; distinguished from fatalism, the religious notion of predestination and predictability. Chance as compatible with determinism.

✔ Determinism and human action. All human action as the inevitable result of environmental and hereditary factors. Human action as subject to natural laws. The experience of free will as an illusion.

What is free will?

✔ Free will as requiring indeterminism. The view that free will requires a gap in universal causality. Human decision making as occupying a special place outside of the natural order.

✔ Free will as compatible with determinism. Voluntary action as defined in terms of the type of cause from which it issues – soft determinism. Voluntary action as causally determined and yet distinguishable from psychologically or physically constrained action.

The implications of determinism

✔ Determinism as undermining moral responsibility. The implications of the view that 'ought' implies 'can'. The extent to which praise, blame and punishment can be meaningfully employed if determinism is true.

✔ Determinism as undermining rationality. The distinction between reasons and causes. The distinction between action and bodily movement.

INTRODUCTION

I. What is determinism?

Determinism defined

The syllabus defines determinism as 'the belief that a determinate set of conditions can only produce one possible outcome given fixed laws of nature'. Determinism is a view about causality. In its most common form, it holds, first, that every event – everything that happens or occurs – has a cause (universal causation). Second, it holds that given the total set of conditions under which the cause occurs, only one effect is possible (causal necessity). These views can plausibly claim to reflect our common-sense notion of causality, and they are strongly supported by the way natural science investigates the world.

Universal causation

Suppose there is water on the kitchen floor. We assume that there is a causal explanation of how the water got there, even if no one knows what it is. If the mess was not caused at all, then we would consider it a miracle. Suppose a pipe burst. So we say 'If the pipe had not burst, there would not be water on the kitchen floor'. Causes 'make a difference'.

Why think 'every event has a cause'? This isn't an empirical discovery, because we haven't discovered the cause of *every* event. However, as science has progressed, it has explained more and more events, so that we may believe that we *could* – in many cases, in practice, but *always in principle* – discover the cause of an event. 'Every event has a cause' is best understood as a *commitment* that we make. To think that some event has *no* cause would be to give up on trying to account for it by science at all. Universal causation is a commitment of science.

Again, laws of nature are universal – there is no part of the universe in which they don't apply. So every event – at least every *physical* event – falls under the laws of nature. So every physical event was caused in accordance with these laws.

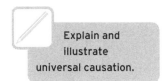
Explain and illustrate universal causation.

Causal necessity

'The burst pipe caused the kitchen floor to become wet' is about this one occasion. But we expect that on other occasions if pipes burst in the kitchen, the floor would be wet. Our idea of causality includes the idea of *regularity*, that the same cause will operate in the same way on different occasions. This allows us to formulate laws of nature.

If on another occasion, a pipe burst, but the floor remained dry, there must be something between that situation and our original one which is *different*. (For example, that the whole house is well below freezing, so that the water in the burst pipe is and remains ice – so it stays where it is, and the floor remains dry.) If the burst pipe caused the mess, then this licenses us to say that, if all other factors remain exactly the same, 'Were the pipe to burst, then there would be water on the kitchen floor'.

The idea of regularity leads to the stronger thought that, given this cause – in exactly this situation – only one outcome is *possible*. In a different situation, a burst pipe might not lead to water on the floor; but in this situation, not only does the burst pipe lead to a wet floor, but it *had* to. The situation determines a *unique* effect. This is the idea of *causal necessity*.

These two ideas – universal causation and causal necessity – give us determinism: a determinate set of conditions can only produce one possible outcome given fixed laws of nature.

Explain and illustrate causal necessity.

Determinism and human action

Physical determinism – determinism expressed in terms of physical causes and laws – provides the clearest, most persuasive example of determinism. But determinism is a completely general doctrine, which could be just as true of human beings, our choices and actions, as it is of physical objects.

Action and causation

If all causation is deterministic, then wherever we find causation, we find determinism. Are our actions caused? Intuitively, we say 'yes'; we explain our actions in terms of motivation, and it is natural to think of motivation as a kind of causation. Motivation – being moved – can feel like a psychological 'force', which is a causal idea; motivation makes things happen.

Notice that we use statements such as 'If he had wanted to learn, he wouldn't have thrown away his books', and 'If he were to want a drink, he would go to the kitchen' – expressing the kind of regularity involved in causation. The same motives produce the same actions, at least in similar situations. (If the action is different, then we appeal to different causes or situations.)

'But he might change his mind, and in an unpredictable way'. We discuss prediction later (p. 356).

We rely on this regularity all the time. We expect that others will, in their *voluntary* actions, act in very specific ways, for example, in taking goods to market, I expect others to come, to want to buy and so on. People's choices and actions are regular.

Determinism threatens free will like this: our actions are events. Therefore, they have causes. Given the causes they have, no action is possible other than what we actually do. If we couldn't do any other action, then we do not have free will, for example, to choose between doing different actions. The argument can be run at the level of choices as well: our choices are events, and so have causes. Given those causes, only one choice is possible. So we are not free to choose anything other than what we actually choose.

How does determinism threaten free will?

An important contrast

There is, however, a very important difference between action and physical (or 'natural') causation, between what we *do* and things that just *happen*. Take the example of crop circles. Some people explain them in terms of natural forces, such as whirlwinds or a peculiar magnetic phenomenon. Once we have established the cause and how it works, we have explained crop circles – end of story. It is quite different to explain them in terms of people deliberately creating them. After showing *that* someone created a crop circle, we can ask *why* they did, how successful they are in creating a particular design, and so on. Unlike natural events, actions don't just happen.

We can develop this idea by noting another distinction – between what we do and what happens to us. Compare deliberately pushing someone over and accidentally knocking them over, for example, because you trip. In both cases, your body moves in a particular way and has the same effect. But in one case, you do something, and you move your body, and in the other, something happens to you, and the movement of your body is imposed. When you do something, what you do is *intentional* – you intended it and brought it about. When something happens to you, what follows is not intentional – it just happened.

These two distinctions are the basis for a third contrast between action and natural causation. We are *responsible* for our actions, but natural causes are not responsible for their effects. For example, people who create crop circles can be blamed for destroying crops or praised for their creativity. If a crop circle is created by a whirlwind, the wind can't be praised or blamed.

But we can respond that we can make too much of these distinctions. After all, aren't our actions *natural* events?

> Outline and illustrate the distinction between action and 'natural' causation.

Human action as subject to natural laws

Physical laws

Physical determinism claims that determinism applies to all physical events. Our bodies are physical, so every event involving our bodies will be determined. This applies to our actions. Many actions involve moving one's body. Bodily movements are caused by events in the brain. For example, if I help an old lady across the road, immediately before I do this, my brain is in a particular state –

the chemicals and neural connections are all a particular way. The neurones fire, my muscles move. That brain state causes my bodily movements, which are part of my action of helping the old lady. According to determinism, given the 'determinate set of conditions' of my brain and the laws of nature, those bodily movements were the only possible outcome. If there was no other possible movement of my body at that time, there was no other action I could have done.

This applies to the state of my brain that caused those bodily movements. It, too, is physical, so it, too, is caused by some preceding physical state in accordance with the laws of nature. The state of my brain that caused my bodily movement of helping the old lady is causally determined by the state of my brain (and other aspects of the physical world) immediately before the decision. And that earlier state of my brain is determined by still earlier states of my brain and the world, and so on. So helping the old lady across the road was causally determined long before I actually performed the action.

This depends, of course, on human actions falling under natural laws, either the laws of physics, as bodies are physical objects, or neurophysiological laws. If so, then, says physical determinism, our actions and choices are determined *in the same way* that physical events are. Human beings are part of the natural, physical world, and so events involving human beings should be able to be explained in the same way as other events. If this wasn't true, the laws of physics wouldn't apply to human bodies and their movements! But science claims that the laws of nature apply throughout the universe.

> Explain how human actions fall under physical laws.

Psychological laws

We can run the same argument using psychology rather than physics and neurophysiology. Psychological determinism claims a person's psychology, their mental states and their experience, causally determines what they will choose to do. (Their mental states and experiences are in turn causally determined by previous mental states and by the physical world.) Our choices, then, have psychological causes. Given a determinate set of psychological conditions, and fixed psychological laws, only one choice is possible.

However, psychological determinism can make sense of the apparent difference between action and 'natural' causation. Explanations in terms of psychological causes – what someone believes and desires – are different from explanations in terms of physical causes. In physical explanation, we don't talk

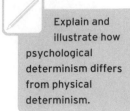

Explain and illustrate how psychological determinism differs from physical determinism.

about desiring and believing (the whirlwind doesn't *want* anything), so we don't talk about *intending* either.

We will discuss psychological determinism further in Development (p. 371), but it is worth noting that psychology has not so far discovered *any laws* linking choices (as effects) to other mental states (as causes). Given the complexity of people, the prospects for psychological determinism are not good.

Determinism distinguished from predictability

Scientists can get predictions wrong. But this is no objection to determinism. Determinism is not the claim that we can predict every event accurately; it claims that every event is predictable *in principle*. The reason we cannot and do not predict events accurately is because we do not know everything about the laws of nature nor about the 'determinate set of conditions' that leads to the effect. A being that did have this knowledge would be able to make completely accurate predictions.

This goes for choices as well. Determinism doesn't claim that anyone can come to know *all* a person's mental states and experiences so as to be able to predict what they do. But it maintains that *if* we had this knowledge, we could predict what they do.

We should also note that predictability doesn't entail determinism. For example, you may simply know that if you offer someone prawns or meat, they will choose meat because they don't like prawns. Similarly, you can predict that a friend of yours will help this old lady across the street, because he is a kind person, in a good mood, and has just said that this is what he will do. These examples don't show that choices are determined, even if they are predictable.

Key points • • •

- Determinism makes two claims: that every event has a cause (universal causation); and that given the total set of conditions under which the cause occurs, only one effect is possible (causal necessity).
- These claims can't be empirically proven, but can be understood as commitments of science.
- We can understand actions and choices as events. Therefore, according to

determinism, they have causes. In any situation, given those causes, only one action or choice is possible.

- However, there is an important distinction between actions and natural causation. We distinguish between what someone does and what just happens, and explain them differently. We also hold people responsible for their actions.
- Determinism argues that human actions are subject to natural laws – the laws of physics, neurophysiology, or psychology.
- Determinism does not mean that we can predict what happens. It means that if we could know everything about the cause and set of conditions, we could predict the effect. This applies as much to choices as anything else.

II. What is free will?

Free will as requiring indeterminism

Hard determinism and libertarianism

As we have presented the arguments for determinism, it looks as though if determinism is true, we have no free will. This position is 'incompatibilism'. It has two options, 'hard' determinism and 'libertarianism':

'Hard' determinism:

1. If determinism is true, we have no free will.
2. Determinism is true.
3. Therefore, we have no free will.

Libertarianism:

1. If determinism is true, we have no free will.
2a. We have free will.
3a. Therefore, determinism is false.

Libertarianism can be challenged by hard determinism (which rejects Premise 2a) or by 'compatibilism' (which rejects Premise 1). As we will discuss compatibilism later (see p. 359), in the following discussion, we will only look at the debate between libertarianism and hard determinism.

Libertarianism standardly claims that when we choose to act, we cause certain events (for example, movements of our body) to happen, but nothing causes us to cause these events. Our power to choose – the will – is not caused to decide one way or another. Of course, our choices could be influenced, but to be influenced is not to be caused.

We can understand these influences in two ways. First, our desires: these can sometimes feel like 'forces', pushing us to do something, for example, hunger. If we could not stand back from our desires and reflect on them, then what we did would be caused. And this is perhaps how it is for animals. For human beings, though, we are able to refrain from acting on our desires (within limits, anyway). So our desires become influences, but not determining causes. Second, when we act, we can give reasons for why we chose what we did. These reasons are also influences, but not causes. For example, 'I gave him the money because he needed it'. His need is my reason, but I chose freely to give him the money. A free will responds to reasons, but is not caused to choose by either reasons or desires.

As well as this argument about the nature of will, that we *feel* free is very important. We feel we could choose *this* or *that*, we could act or not act. Nothing forces us to choose one way or another.

See THE CHARACTERISTICS ASSOCIATED WITH PERSONHOOD (Ch. 5, p. 166).

We discuss THE DISTINCTION BETWEEN REASONS AND CAUSES on p. 386.

Outline libertarianism.

Objections

The hard determinist will argue that feeling free is not good evidence for free will. Suppose someone had brain tumour which repeatedly caused them to drink, but also caused them to feel this was a free choice. If we ask the person, they say they are choosing whenever they have a drink; yet when we remove the brain tumour, they stop drinking so much. It is possible, then, that our choices are caused yet they feel free.

A second objection is that if our choices are uncaused, then they must be random. Free will means being able to control what we choose. If our choices are random, then we don't have free will. We need our choices to be caused, because causation is what makes events ordered and regular.

Thomas Reid responded that our choices are caused, but that 'The cause of the volition is the man that willed it'. All events have causes. And making a decision is indeed an event. But libertarianism claims that *we* cause our choices. Because I am the cause of my choice, and nothing causes me to cause it, it is free.

See THE EXPERIENCE OF FREE WILL AS AN ILLUSION (p. 374).

'Letter to James Gregory' in *Philosophical Works*, p. 88

A second response rejects the claim that uncaused choices must be random. Causation is not the only account of order and regularity. Our choices are ordered and regular because they respond to reasons.

We could, however, argue that reasons influence choices by causing them. However, we could then argue that this kind of causation is not deterministic, and is not subject to the laws of nature. So our choices are free, not determined.

But to this we can object that we have no concept of causation without causal necessity. Hume says that if someone manages to define a cause without any necessary connexion to its effect, he will grant that libertarianism could be true.

An Enquiry Concerning Human Understanding, p. 159

But there is a further objection we can bring against libertarianism. There is no scientific evidence that when we make a choice, something happens that has no physical cause. For example, if I voluntarily raise my arm, neurones in my brain fire to contract my arm muscles. What causes the neurones to fire? According to libertarianism, *I* (not some physical event) am the cause of my choices, and so of the neurones firing. Yet nothing different appears to happen in the brain from the usual sequence of physical events.

We can respond that the evidence is not yet very good. We know very little about the brain and may not be able to tell when something different is happening. But this is still open to the objection that to say there is no (physical) cause is to fly in the face of the *project* of science, which is to discover physical causes.

Discuss the challenges facing libertarianism.

Compatibilism I: voluntary action as defined in terms of the type of cause from which it issues

Compatibilism is the view that determinism is not incompatible with free will, that is, even if determinism is true, we still have free will. Most compatibilists argue that incompatibilism (hard determinism and libertarianism) rests on a misunderstanding of free will.

A first form of compatibilism argues that to have free will is simply for one's choice to cause one's action. To do what you want to do is the essence of free will. So, for example, Hume says that free will is simply '*a power of acting or not acting, according to the determinations of the will*'. In other words, I act as I do because of what I chose to do. If I had chosen to act differently, then I would have acted differently.

An Enquiry Concerning Human Understanding, p. 159

This does not conflict with determinism. My action is caused by my choice. And my choice may in turn be caused by other events. So there is a causal story for my choice and action. And determinism agrees that if my choice had been different, then I would have acted differently (different cause, different effect).

But we can object that this is *too weak* a notion of free will. It is not enough to say that I *would* have acted differently *if* I had chosen differently. We also need to say that I *could* have chosen differently. Someone may choose to act as they do, but be motivated by a compulsion or addiction. For example, if I am addicted to smoking, there may be times when I feel I have to have a cigarette – I can't chose not to. Yet it would still be true, that *if* I did chose not to, then I wouldn't. But I'm not free to chose not to have a cigarette.

Another example: suppose that someone has inserted a chip into my brain and is able to cause me to choose to act in a particular way. It is true that *if* I had chosen differently, I would have acted differently. But I *couldn't* have chosen differently, because someone is controlling what I choose. In both examples, what I choose determines what I do, yet I could not choose anything else, so in what sense are my choices free?

> Explain the claim that I am free because if I had chosen differently, I would have acted differently. How does it differ from the claim that I am free because I could have chosen differently?

Compatibilism II: voluntary action as causally determined and yet distinguishable from psychologically or physically constrained action

A second form of compatibilism argues that it is a confusion to oppose free will and causation. The opposite of caused is *uncaused*; the opposite of free is *constrained*. *Events* are caused or uncaused, *actions* are free or constrained. So the opposite of a free action is not a caused event but a constrained action. Actions that are not constrained are free. The issue of causation is irrelevant.

Here are four cases of constraint that bring out the contrast with free action:

1. You trip and fall into someone, knocking them over. Your knocking them over is physically constrained, not something that you had any choice or control over.
2. Someone puts a gun to your head, and tells you to push someone over. You have a *kind* of choice here – you can push them or die. But your action is very constrained, by coercion, a psychological constraint.
3. You are addicted to heroin, and acting on the intense desire for it, you steal from a store to get the money to buy more. You hate your addiction and would chose to be without it if you could. Your action is driven by an addiction, so it is physically (and psychologically) constrained, and not free.

4. Kleptomania is the compulsion to steal, without needing to or profiting from it. If you were a kleptomaniac, you would want to steal things, even things that aren't much use to you. You may even want to not want to steal and try to resist stealing; but you don't (always) succeed. We could argue that being a kleptomaniac is a case of psychological compulsion.

These four cases all stand in contrast to what it is to act freely, to act without physical or psychological constraint. This, say compatibilists, is the contrast that matters to whether we are free.

Objections

The hard determinist argues that there is no real difference between free and constrained action. *All* action is similar to being a kleptomaniac or tripping and falling. The reason there is no relevant difference is that in both cases, the action is *caused*. All that changes is *how* the action is caused (whether the cause is gravity, a psychological condition or a series of events in the brain that we call 'choice').

Denying the distinction between free and constrained action is counter-intuitive. But we can ask whether the contrast is clear and reliable. If not, then perhaps free will is not so distinct from constraint, and the determinist isn't wrong after all.

To defend the distinction we can ask whether either threats or rational argument would change what the person does. If the action really is constrained, then they will not – the person can't change what they do. So, for instance, threatening someone who already has a gun to their head will change nothing, and arguing with someone who trips and knocks someone over will not prevent them from knocking someone over next time they trip.

But sometimes drug addicts respond to threats and arguments, and try harder to kick their habit. Perhaps kleptomaniacs would be deterred by greater security in stores. On the other hand, hardened criminals seem not to respond to either – does this mean that they are not free? Are they not responsible for their crimes?

A second way to defend the distinction is in terms of praise and blame. If we would blame someone for what they did, then they acted freely. If we would not – as in the cases above – then the action was constrained. But we can object that this gets things the wrong way around. It tries to define free will in terms

These cases develop the important contrast being what we do intentionally and what happens to us that we noted in DETERMINISM AND HUMAN ACTION (p. 354).

Explain and illustrate the claim that free action is action that is not constrained.

A different example: punish the idle, but not the stupid.

Discuss whether
we can say that
an action is free if it is
not constrained.

of praise and blame. But when is it right to blame someone? Can we say without referring to free will? Surely it is absurd to blame someone unless we already think that they *are* free. We can't first decide that it is right to blame them, and then conclude that therefore they must be free.

The hard determinist, then, will argue that there is no real distinction between free and constrained action. In that case, to oppose free and caused is not a confusion, so the challenge of determinism remains.

Key points • • •

- Incompatibilism claims that if determinism is true, we do not have free will. Hard determinists claim that determinism is true, so we don't have free will. Libertarians argue that we do have free will, so determinism is false.

- Libertarianism argues that when we choose, nothing causes us to choose as we do. Our choices can be influenced by desires and reasons, but these are not causes if we exercise our ability to choose.

- Libertarians often appeal to the fact that we feel free. Hard determinists argue that this is no evidence that we are free, but could be an illusion.

- We can object that if our choices are uncaused, they must be random. Libertarians can argue that we cause our choices (but nothing causes us to cause them), and that they are not random because they respond to reasons.

- However, libertarianism is committed to the view that some physical events have no physical cause that can be discovered by science.

- Compatibilism claims that even if determinism is true, we still have free will.

- One form argues that free will is simply the ability to do what you want. We can object that this is too weak – free will means not just that if I had chosen differently, I would have acted differently, but also that I could have chosen differently.

- A second form argues that we act freely when we act without constraint. The issue of causation is irrelevant.

- We can object that there is no real difference between free and constrained action, and that 'free' action is just like 'constrained' action in being causally determined.

III. The implications of determinism

Determinism as undermining moral responsibility

People are moral agents and so their actions can be held against the standards of morality. We react with attitudes of praise and blame. To rescue someone drowning receives praise; to steal someone's handbag receives blame. In holding people's actions against the standards of morality, we hold them to be morally responsible for what they do.

But how far does our idea of moral responsibility depend on the idea that someone *could have acted differently*? If you are blamed for what you did, then you ought to have done a different action. What if you couldn't? For example, if you are strapped to a chair and cannot free yourself, then you are not to blame if you do not help someone drowning. There is nothing you can do, so you are not morally responsible for failing to help. Whether we blame someone depends on whether we think they were able to act differently from how they in fact acted.

If it makes no sense to blame or praise someone when there was no other action they could have performed, then moral responsibility depends on free will. So if free will is undermined by determinism, so is moral responsibility. No one is responsible for natural events, such as earthquakes. But determinism claims that actions are just like natural events in that they are *all* causally determined. If we don't blame or praise people when there was nothing else they could do, we should never blame or praise people. In other words, no one is ever truly morally responsible for what they do. (The same argument can be run about our choices.)

How does determinism threaten to undermine moral responsibility?

The implications of the view that 'ought' implies 'can'

This argument turns on the principle that 'ought implies can'. If there is something that you ought to do, then you are able to do it. So if you ought to have acted differently (as we think when we blame someone), then you could have acted differently. If you could *not* have acted differently, as determinism argues, it makes no sense to say that you ought to have acted differently. And if it's not true that you ought to have acted differently, how are you to blame for what you did?

The libertarian about moral responsibility will argue that there is moral responsibility and determinism is false; the hard determinist line is that there is no moral responsibility – at least in the usual meaning of the phrase. Compatibilism about moral responsibility has three options:

1. It can accept that ought implies can and argue that there is a relevant sense in which a person could have acted differently, even though determinism is true, and so they are morally responsible.
2. It can argue that issues of determinism and 'ought implies can' are irrelevant to moral responsibility.
3. It can explicitly reject the 'ought implies can' principle, so the fact that a person cannot do anything else does not mean that they are not morally responsible for it.

In the next section, we look at an example of 1 and of 3. (An example of 2 is discussed in Development, p. 382.)

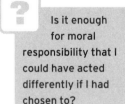

How does the principle 'ought implies can' relate to the question of moral responsibility?

The extent to which praise, blame and punishment can be meaningfully employed if determinism is true

Ought implies can

The first variety of compatibilism (COMPATIBILISM I, p. 359) argues that free will means that *if* they had chosen differently, they *would* have acted differently. This entails that they *could* have acted differently had they chosen differently. So even though determinism is true, they are morally responsible.

Is it enough for moral responsibility that I could have acted differently if I had chosen to?

We objected that this view of free will was too weak. Likewise, we can say that it is not enough for moral responsibility. We need to say not only that they could have acted differently if they *had* chosen differently, but also that they *could have* chosen differently. But determinism means that they could not have chosen differently.

Ought does not imply can

We can try to justify moral responsibility in terms of the benefits that come from our practice of holding people responsible for their choices and actions. We want more good actions and less bad ones. Our practices of praise (and reward) and blame (and punishment) have causal effects on people's behaviour. They enjoy praise and dislike blame, so they will tend towards doing more praise-worthy actions and fewer blameworthy ones. So even if determinism is true, and someone could not have done otherwise, we are justified in praising or blaming them, because people will perform more good actions if we do.

But is this really moral responsibility any more? On this defence, morality and moral responsibility have become no more than a system for classifying and controlling behaviour, like the rewards and punishments we use for training animals. But animals are not moral agents; if morality is no different from training animals, this is to give up the idea that people are morally responsible for what they do.

Can moral responsibility be justified in terms of the effects of our practice of praise and blame?

Determinism as undermining rationality

If determinism is true, and incompatible with free will, no one ever freely chooses to be a determinist. No one ever freely chooses to believe in free will either. To make a judgement, to form a belief, these are also actions – mental actions. If determinism is true, the beliefs we have are causally determined just as much as the actions we do.

This has a strange result. Suppose I believe that the theory of evolution is true. I have read books about evolution and arguments against evolution; I have been to museums and seen fossils; I have discussed the issue with creationists and scientists. On the basis of the evidence, I judge that the theory of evolution is true. But if determinism is true, I am causally determined to have this belief, so I do not have it because I freely judge that the theory of evolution is true. Instead, I cannot (or could not) believe otherwise.

If this is right, then I don't form the belief on the basis of reasons I consider. In fact, the whole idea of a reason seems to disappear. To give someone a reason to believe something, to show them evidence, is not to *cause* them to believe in a deterministic way. It is certainly not to force them to believe the way we can force them to fall over by pushing them. They can weigh up the evidence and make up their minds, we say. But this is causally determined, according to determinism.

Suppose we apply this result to beliefs about determinism. First, no one ever freely judges that determinism is true or false. Second, if you try to convince someone that determinism is true, you do not provide evidence that enables them to make up their minds. Either the argument you give will cause them to believe in determinism or it will not; if it does, this isn't because they judge that your reasons are convincing. Rather, they could not believe anything else. Which arguments cause people to believe in determinism may have nothing to do with whether the arguments are rational, and may be different for different people. So there are no good arguments for (or against) determinism, only arguments that cause people to believe in it and arguments that don't.

We can turn this into an objection: if determinism is true, there is no such thing as reasoning. However, the arguments for determinism show that there is such a thing as reasoning. Therefore determinism must be false.

In fact, this conclusion only follows if determinism is *incompatible* with judgement. Compatibilism will reject this, and so reject the conclusion. But the objection does apply to hard determinism, the position that claims that because determinism is true, we don't form beliefs freely on the basis of judgement.

> Explain and illustrate how determinism threatens to undermine rationality.

Key points • • •

- We normally think that we can only blame someone for what they did if they could have acted differently. Determinism claims that because our actions are causally determined, we cannot act in any way other than how we actually act.
- The principle 'ought implies can' says that you only ought to do what you can do. If you ought to have acted differently, you could have acted differently.
- One form of compatibilism about moral responsibility says that you could have acted differently, if you had chosen differently – so you can be morally responsible. We can object that moral responsibility also requires that you could have chosen differently.
- A second form argues that we should hold people morally responsible, even if they could not act differently, as this will lead to better consequences. We can object that this is not moral responsibility, praise and blame, but a system of training like that which we use for animals.
- Determinism entails that our beliefs are causally determined. This threatens to undermine rational judgement. We think that we form beliefs on the basis of reasons, but if we could not believe differently, reasons no longer seem relevant in the same way.
- We can object, then, that determinism implies that there is no such thing as reasoning. As this is obviously false, determinism must be false. However, a compatibilist may argue that determinism is compatible with rational judgement.

DEVELOPMENT

I. What is determinism?

Determinism developed

The state of the universe

In DETERMINISM DEFINED (p. 351), we said that in the same situation, the same cause (a burst pipe) must lead to the same effect (a wet floor), as long as the two situations were the same. But any number of things may disrupt the cause producing the effect: a meteor could land at the moment the pipe bursts, destroying the kitchen floor, a simultaneous explosion of gas could turn all the water into steam – so the burst pipe doesn't lead to a wet floor.

To defend the idea of causal necessity, we need to be able to say that there is only one possible outcome, given the cause. Given the possibilities just mentioned, how can we? We need to consider anything that *could* have an effect. How can we do this? The safest, and most complete, specification of the situation is *the entire state of the universe at that moment*. With the universe in that state (including the pipe bursting), the next state of the universe (including the wet floor) must follow, given the laws of nature.

We don't normally talk of 'the state of the universe'. But we need to get rid of 'other things being equal' – as long as we allow this, the effect isn't the only *possible* event. So to capture causal necessity, we can take into account all 'other things' – the entire state of the universe. From this state, only one state can be caused by it and will follow it. The past determines a unique future. Determinism, then, is the view that given the state of the universe and the laws of nature, only *one* unique state of the universe can occur next.

Explain causal necessity.

Causal chain

As the universe continues through time, so the events which are effects of earlier causes become causes of later effects. This gives us the idea of a *causal chain*. This event, G, was caused by an earlier event, F, which in turn was caused by an earlier event, E, and so on. So any event is determined by what caused it; its causes were determined by what caused them; and so on, back through time. So any event is determined by what happened in the *distant past*. The entire

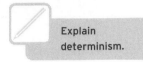

Explain determinism.

future of the universe was causally fixed from the first moment; from that first moment on, no other set of events than what has actually happened and will happen was physically possible. This is the very strongest statement of determinism.

Chance as compatible with determinism

If things happen by chance, does that make determinism false? What is 'chance' at one level can be explained at another level. For example, you might bump into an old friend 'by chance', that is, you hadn't arranged to meet. But if physical determinism is right, then this event was caused, in accordance with the laws of physics; and in that sense, it didn't happen by chance at all. But does chance operate at the physical level?

Chaos theory

Chaos theory is about how some complex systems, for example, the weather, work. Given 'same cause, same effect', we might expect that if we get the cause wrong by just a little bit, then our predictions of the effect will just be slightly wrong. But this isn't always true. A very small difference in the initial causal conditions can lead to a very big difference in effect; a popular – if unproven! – example is that a butterfly flapping its wings in Europe may lead to a storm in China.

The theory has been *misunderstood* to say that different effects can be produced by causes so similar as to be 'the same' – for all we can tell. But while we may not be able to specify the cause precisely enough to predict the effect accurately, chaos theory is completely deterministic: different effects require different causes; the effect is still predictable in principle (see p. 356), though not in practice; and given the *precise* cause (or causal chain), the effect must follow.

Does chaos theory threaten determinism?

Going further: quantum mechanics

Quantum mechanics is a theory about what happens at the sub-atomic level of physics. Many people believe that it is a *probabilistic* theory – that it can only say what will happen, for example, when a radioactive atom will 'decay', with a degree of probability. And probability is the degree of chance that something will happen.

However, we can argue that because the probabilities at the sub-atomic level are *fixed*, so at the level of our normal interactions with the world, events happen perfectly deterministically. Sub-atomic probabilities don't become chance at the macrophysical level.

However, one interpretation of quantum mechanics goes further than chance. It says that sub-atomic states are *not determinate*. A famous example (known as Heisenberg's Uncertainty Principle) is this: we cannot measure both the velocity and the position of an electron at one moment; if we measure how fast it is moving, we cannot tell exactly where it is; if we measure where it is, we cannot tell just how fast it is moving. Some physicists argue that we may say that the electron *does not have* a determinate velocity and position – it acquires one or the other when we measure it.

It is worth noting, however, that many physicists disagree with this interpretation and argue that what happens sub-atomically is fully determinate and determined (Schrödinger's equation shows that sub-atomic states change in a perfectly regular manner). Some argue that the apparent indeterminacy is just to do with our ability to make measurements. Some argue that there are 'hidden variables', causes we don't know about, and these cause events deterministically.

But even if the indeterminacy interpretation is right, this *still* isn't incompatible with determinism in this sense: determinism claims only that a *determinate* set of conditions will produce only one possible outcome. If sub-atomic states are not determinate, then determinism doesn't apply to sub-atomic states. So the same sub-atomic state may cause or be followed by a number of different possible outcomes on different occasions without conflicting with determinism.

We can object that the indeterminacy interpretation does undermine determinism. If sub-atomic states are indeterminate, then everything physical is indeterminate, because everything physical is ultimately composed of sub-atomic states. So determinism is false.

Discuss the implications of quantum mechanics for determinism.

Is determinism compatible with chance?

Determinism distinguished from fatalism and predestination

Fatalism

Determinism is not fatalism. Fatalism maintains that human choices and actions have no influence on future events. As a result, fatalism usually recommends some form of resignation, for example, there is no point trying to achieve one thing rather than another: *que sera sera* (whatever will be, will be).

There are two versions of fatalism. The first claims that no matter what we do, the eventual outcome will be the same. This appears in a story retold by Somerset Maugham (the narrator is Death):

> There was a merchant in Baghdad who sent his servant to market to buy provisions and in a little while the servant came back, white and trembling, and said, 'Master, just now when I was in the marketplace I was jostled by a woman in the crowd and when I turned I saw it was Death that jostled me. She looked at me and made a threatening gesture, now, lend me your horse, and I will ride away from this city and avoid my fate. I will go to Samara and there Death will not find me.'
>
> The merchant lent him his horse, and the servant mounted it, and he dug his spurs in its flanks and as fast as the horse could gallop he went. Then the merchant went down to the marketplace and he saw me standing in the crowd and he came to me and said, 'Why did you make a threatening gesture to my servant when you saw him this morning?'
>
> 'That was not a threatening gesture', I said, 'it was only a start of surprise. I was astonished to see him in Baghdad, for I had an appointment with him tonight in Samara.'

'The Appointment in Samara'

So, the fatalist moral: we may try to flee death, but will not escape; whatever we do, we end up dying exactly as 'fated' in advance.

But fatalism in this form allows that we can do, and choose to do, different actions; it simply maintains that these make no difference in the long run (the servant dies as fated). 'Were you to have done x instead of y', it would have made no difference, it says. By contrast, determinism allows that 'Were you to have done x instead of y', there could well have been a different result; different cause, different effect. But determinism maintains that you *could not* have done x instead of y (if it was y you did). Our actions are causally determined; and as such, no other action was possible.

The second version of fatalism claims that we cannot do anything other than what we actually do; for the future is already fixed; our actions cannot change this, since our actions are part of what is already fixed. While determinism maintains that our actions are fixed, it need not conclude that they make no difference: our actions will have effects, so a future with our actions is different from a future without them. Fatalism goes on that because the future is fixed, because we cannot do anything except we what do, we have no free will.

> What is fatalism? How does it differ from determinism?

Predestination

In its narrow and more common meaning, predestination is a religious doctrine that claims that God has already decided, even before people are born, who will be saved and who will be damned. Our own efforts to achieve salvation, therefore, are fruitless. There is no suggestion that we cannot choose or act other than how we actually do; only that it will make no difference to our salvation.

In a broader form, predestination is the view that everything that happens will happen according to the will of God – God intends everything to happen just as it does. This is a kind of 'divine determinism' if it is taken to suggest that we cannot do actions other than those we actually do, because we are powerless to do what God does not will. However, there are still clear differences, for example, the necessity of what happens follows from God's will, not the laws of nature.

> What is predestination? How does it differ from determinism?

All human action as the inevitable result of environmental and hereditary factors

In HUMAN ACTION AS SUBJECT TO NATURAL LAWS (p. 355), we briefly discussed psychological determinism. There are two types of causal factors that contribute to our psychology – nature (genetics) and nurture (environment). So one version of psychological determinism claims that given our genetics and our upbringing, we cannot do or choose anything other than what we do and choose.

In principle, there is no difference between the kind of arguments we can give for this view and the ones given for physical determinism. However, determinism on the basis of genetic and environmental factors is harder to establish.

> We are taking genetics and environmental factors *together* as the relevant causes that would determine human action. Therefore we don't need to consider the famous debate that asks whether it is nature *or* nurture which influences human psychology and action more.

Strong determinism

The strongest version is that every action we do is determined by our genetics + preceding environmental states and laws of psychology. If this was true, then we would be able to predict, in principle, exactly what someone was going to do, if only we knew all about their psychology and their genetic inheritance. But there is little evidence to support this.

First, psychology has discovered very few strict laws. Instead, it has 'rules of thumb' that help us understand people and statistical laws. On rules of thumb: we can say that if someone is thirsty, they will try to find a drink. But this is not always true. They may be fasting, they may be paranoid and think someone is trying to poison them and so on. We cannot list all the possible exceptions. So even with something as basic as thirst, there is not just one possible outcome. The outcome depends on the rest of the person's psychology. On statistical laws: psychologists can use experiments to find out what percentage of people will act in a certain way in a certain situation. But this doesn't support determinism, since each individual person may or may not act that way, and we can argue that this is because they can choose how to act.

Second, genes do not, on their own, determine a unique effect. They only ever have an effect through interaction with the environment. Someone may have a gene 'for' being tall, but how tall they become depends on their diet. Having a gene 'for' some trait only *increases your chances* of having that trait; it doesn't mean you will necessarily have it. This flexibility is very strong in the case of psychology. There may be some genetic dispositions to some traits of character, but we are also genetically disposed to be very responsive to our environment.

Finally, we have no laws that say someone from a particular background or who had a particular experience in the past will act in a particular way under certain situations. For example, 'people who had wealthy parents when growing up are interested in the arts'. Is this always true? No, even if a *high percentage* of people interested in the arts had wealthy parents rather than poor parents. In many cases, a person with wealthy parents is not interested in the arts and a person with poor parents is.

> **Explain the difference between laws of physics and 'laws' of psychology.**

> **Assess the claim that all human action is determined by environmental and hereditary factors.**

Weak determinism

A weaker form of determinism claims that the *patterns* of our actions are determined by our genetics and experiences. For example, though you love fattening foods, on any particular occasion, you might be able to choose to eat fruit rather than cake. But you may always struggle with choices about food because you feel low self-esteem. And you cannot simply 'choose' not to feel low self-esteem. So you cannot choose not to struggle with choices about food.

In this way, important aspects of our character are determined, and our character determines many of the actions that we choose to do. On the basis of knowing someone's character, we may well be able to predict what they are going to do.

But is our character *determined*, rather than just influenced, by past experience? People can reinforce or undermine the character traits they have by the choices they make.

And even if actions express someone's character, they are not, for that reason, unfree. People often seem to be most free, certainly most 'themselves', when they are acting in character. We do not have to act out of character to be free.

> If character is strongly influence by hereditary and environmental factors, do we lack free will?

Going further: limitation is not determinism

Given what we know about genetics and environment, it seems very likely that what someone chooses to do is *limited* by both. You cannot choose to become a neurosurgeon if you do not have the right skills or intelligence. You cannot choose to become a knight in shining armour, because society does not recognise this way of life any more. But we still make choices, even if we don't have many options to choose between. The debate between free will and determinism is about the *possibility* of choice, not about the *extent* of choice.

We can respond that this overlooks the issue of blame and moral responsibility. We use genetic and environmental explanations in two ways that conflict with thinking of people as free. First, we may appeal to someone's upbringing to argue that they shouldn't be blamed for what they did. Given their unhappy childhood, they were not responsible. Second, we sometimes explain social phenomena, for example, crime, in terms of social systems. The person, we say, is a product of the system, or a symptom of how society is getting something wrong. We need to change the system, for example, tackling inner city deprivation and creating employment opportunities, not blame the individual.

All this shows, we can respond, is the important and deep *influence* someone's environment may have on their choices. But it does not show that their choice was causally determined. Certain environmental conditions make choice difficult, others empower people. So we should change the environment to make it easier for people to make different choices. But this isn't determinism. Determinism would claim that *whatever* the environment, a person's choices are determined. Changing someone's environment wouldn't make them free, it would make them choose differently.

> Discuss the nature of the influence environmental and hereditary factors have on our actions.

The experience of free will as an illusion

If determinism is true and incompatible with free will, then we don't have free will. Yet, of course, we think we have free will because we have certain experiences of deliberating and choosing that feel or seem 'free'. When making a choice, it does not feel as if we have to do just one thing. It feels as if we *could* do any of several actions. But if we don't have free will, then this experience is an illusion. It may even be an unavoidable illusion. For example, believing that hard determinism is true does not remove the experience of making a choice.

How can this be? Could we be subject to an unavoidable illusion, or can we use our experience of free will to argue that determinism is wrong? Determinists can point out that there are *many* illusions that we suffer from, and that some of them are unavoidable. For example, there are unavoidable perceptual illusions. There are also 'cognitive illusions', such as the gambler's fallacy – if you roll a die repeatedly and don't get a '6', you can think that the chances of a 6 on the next throw are increased – 'it's got to come up'. But the chances haven't changed. The illusion that we have free will is like perceptual illusions, just a result of how our psychology works.

> Examples include a straight stick looking bent when half-submerged in water (see Ch. 6, p. 202) and the Müller-Lyer lines: Figure 10.1.

> Discuss the claim that the experience of free will is an illusion.

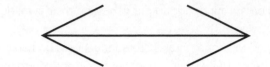

Figure 10.1
Müller-Lyer lines.

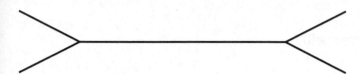

The top line looks shorter than the bottom but the lines are the same length.

Key points • • •

- To say that only one effect is possible, we must take into account the entire state of the universe at the time of the cause. So determinism is the view that given the state of the universe and the laws of nature, only *one* unique state of the universe can occur next.
- Because causes are effects of previous causes, any event is determined, through a chain of causes, by what happened in the distant past.
- Chaos theory does not work by chance, but by determinism. It only claims that a tiny difference in cause can lead to a very different effect.
- On one interpretation, quantum theory claims that sub-atomic states are indeterminate, and one state only follows another with a degree of probability. The determinist can challenge this interpretation of quantum theory, or argue that quantum indeterminacy doesn't undermine determinism at the macro-level.
- Fatalism claims that human actions have no influence on future events, which are 'fated' or fixed in advance. In one version, we can make choices, but can't avoid fate; on the other, we cannot do anything than what we end up doing.
- Predestination claims that we cannot influence our salvation through actions; or that, because God wills everything that occurs, we cannot change what occurs.
- The claim that all human action is determined by genetics and environment faces strong challenges: that we have no psychological laws that state what someone will do on any particular occasion, nor what they will do given a

certain environmental background; nor do our genes, on their own, determine our psychology.

- However, hereditary and environmental factors influence our characters, which influence our choices. But we can argue that this is not determinism.
- If determinism is true and incompatible with free will, the experience of free will is an illusion.

II. What is free will?

Human decision making as occupying a special place outside of the natural order

> Dualism claims the mind is separate from the body or brain. It is not a physical thing, but completely different. The view that persons are souls is a form of dualism, discussed in WHAT SECURES OUR PERSONAL IDENTITY THROUGH TIME? (Ch. 5, p. 188). SUBSTANCE DUALISM is discussed in A2 Unit 3.1, Philosophy of Mind.

In FREE WILL AS REQUIRING INDETERMINISM (p. 358), we said libertarianism is in conflict with the project of science. One way to defend libertarianism is in terms of dualism. We have free will because we are not completely physical, but have a non-physical mind. Making a choice is not a physical process. Because our will does not fall under the laws of nature, it can be free (if psychological determinism is false). Science only applies to physical causation, and free will is not a physical phenomenon.

According to dualism, then, making a choice is a non-physical cause which can have *physical effects* (such as events in the brain or movements of the body). First, this still challenges science, which aims to explain all physical events in terms of physical causes. Second, how can something non-physical cause something physical? To move your muscles, certain neurones in your brain need to 'fire' (send a signal). To do this, chemicals called neurotransmitters must move between neurones. To make anything physical move takes energy. Since your will is not physical, it does not have the physical energy needed to move neurotransmitters. Furthermore, if your neurotransmitters move without a physical cause, this breaks the Law of the Conservation of Energy, which says that the total quantity of matter/energy in the universe always remains the same. If your will causes your neurones to fire, this doesn't use up physical energy, but it does create movement, which is energy. So this creates new energy!

> Assess the claim that human decision making is not a natural process.

Free will requires a gap in universal causality

Our development of determinism in terms of 'states of the universe' (p. 367) allows us to restate incompatibilism more precisely. We can now say that free will requires that, given the state of the universe (past and present) and the laws of nature, there is *more than one way* the future may be in terms of what I do or choose next. Looking back on a decision, without *anything* being different in the entire history of the universe, I could have chosen differently and changed the direction of the future. But determinism says that the past state of the universe + the laws of nature determines a unique future state of the universe. So to have free will, I must either break the laws of nature or change the past. Since I can't do either, I don't have free will unless determinism is false.

> Explain and illustrate incompatibilism.

Free will and quantum theory

One interpretation of quantum theory claims that the sub-atomic world is indeterminate (see p. 369). Some philosophers argue that this means that causation cannot be deterministic. There are no deterministic sub-atomic causal laws, and all causal laws rest ultimately on sub-atomic causal laws (all physical events involve sub-atomic events). Because causation is not deterministic, then determinism is false.

> This view doesn't say that free will depends on a gap in causation, but that causation is not deterministic.

We can object, first, that this is not how scientists understand the relation between macro-level causal laws and sub-atomic indeterminacy. They are quite happy to say that causal laws at the macro-level (like burst pipes and wet floors) are deterministic.

Second, sub-atomic indeterminacy can't be enough for free will, since it applies to *everything* physical. What a billiard ball does next when struck would be just as indeterminate as what we do. So we will need some further account of what is needed for free will.

Finally, if sub-atomic uncertainty affects the macro-level, this would undermine agency. Your action would be random, undetermined by anything – including your choice. But we do choose how to act. Whatever secures this reliability between choice and action undermines the view that sub-atomic uncertainty gives us free will.

> Can quantum theory support the claim that we have free will?

Beyond Good and Evil,
§§ 21, 22, 36.
Nietzsche is studied in
A2 Unit 4.5.

Going further: Nietzsche on free will

Nietzsche argues that our understanding of both free will and determinism are mistaken. We should get rid of the ideas 'free will' and 'unfree will'. The only question is whether the will is strong or weak. First, the will is subject to causal forces and causal history. Those who argue for free will have a vain belief in their own powers. On the other hand, if someone thinks their will is causally constrained, this is just their inadequacy in imposing their will on the world and their inability to take responsibility for what they do. Neither position is honest or realistic.

Nietzsche then proposes a metaphysical theory that radically disagrees with science. First, he argues that there is no necessity in nature. There are no laws that physical things obey. This idea is no more than our *interpretation* of nature, the result of a desire for democracy and equality. Science is being driven by our moral values.

Second, the entirety of nature, all physical events, can be understood as expressions of will. Not our personal will, of course. Our sense of will is the will that underlies everything seen from the 'inside'. If there could be an inside sense to physical events, it would be the same, a sense of 'imposing' one's will, making something happen.

We can object that Nietzsche hasn't given us an argument for thinking his metaphysics is correct. But even if it is, he does not defend free will in any traditional form. There is no distinction in kind between me and a billiard ball, although my will might be more developed in some sense. This is as close to determinism as it is to free will, which is probably the position Nietzsche intended to defend.

?   Should we
replace the
debate about free will
with a debate about
strong and weak wills?

Free will as compatible with determinism

Frankfurt: second-order desires

'Freedom of the Will
and the Concept of a
Person'

Harry Frankfurt argues that in order to define and defend free will, we need to understand the will is complex. 'First-order' desires are desires to do or have certain things, for example, chocolate, seeing a film, etc. 'Second-order' desires are desires about first-order desires. For example, I may not like going to art galleries, but I may want to like going to art galleries. Or again, I may want a cigarette, but I may want not to want a cigarette.

What we *will* relates to desires that actually motivate us to do something. About anything that we will, we can have second-order desires. We can want the desire we are acting on to be what we will, or we can want it not to be. I can want to read philosophy, and this desire gets me to read philosophy, and I want this desire to be what I will. On the other hand, I can want a cigarette, and have one, but want my desire for a cigarette not to move me in this way.

In the second case, I am an unwilling smoker. But this is not a conflict between two first-order desires – the desire to smoke and the desire not to. It is a conflict between a first-order desire to smoke and the second-order desire that the desire to smoke not be my will. This gives the feeling that when I smoke, my will is not free. For my will to be free, I must be able to will what I want to will. Someone has free will if they can will what they want to will.

OBJECTIONS

First, what should we say of a drug addict who is happily an addict? He has the second-order desire that his addiction is his will. Is he free? Frankfurt can say 'yes', because he is willing what he wants to will. But Frankfurt can say 'no', because he is only free if he can *bring* his will into line with what he wants it to be. His addiction makes this impossible – he would continue to want drugs even if he didn't want to want them.

Second, does Frankfurt's view answer the challenge from determinism? When I want to will what I do, could I have wanted otherwise? On Frankfurt's definition, I can *will* otherwise, but this does not mean that I can change what I want to will. This might be determined, for example, by my character. Frankfurt can reply that this is true but irrelevant. Free will is about my *will* being free, that is, about what I will being responsive to what I want to will. Nothing more is required.

In THE CHARACTERISTICS ASSOCIATED WITH PERSONHOOD (Ch. 5, p. 186), we argued that the ability to evaluate what I want is central to being a person.

Frankfurt's view explains why just being able to *do* what I want isn't enough for free will, but his account still identifies free will with a particular kind of cause (see p. 359), viz. doing what I will when I want to will what I do. His view also provides us with a distinction between voluntary action and psychologically constrained action (see p. 360). When someone is not able to will what they want to will, then they are psychologically constrained.

Going further: free will and values

A third objection is that second-order desires are beside the point. We want first-order desires to be responsive to what we think we *should* want, that is, they should be responsive to our values and reasons for acting rather than just our desires. To choose freely is to choose according to one's values.

Explain and illustrate Frankfurt's theory of free will.

Fourth, even if Frankfurt accepts this amendment, it is still not enough for free will. If our choices and actions are responsive to our values and reasoning, if someone had provided us with a good reason not to act as we chose to act, we would have chosen differently. However, for free will, it must be true that I could have chosen otherwise - *in that very situation*. Frankfurt's account hasn't said how this is possible if determinism is true.

Frankfurt can reply that we are supposing that my choice depends on my values. Is the objection that I haven't chosen my values? But do we *choose* our values or our reasons for acting? Don't we rather respond to what is valuable? Where is the lack of freedom in that?

Regularity and necessity

A different defence of compatibilism argues that causation does not rule out free will, because there is no such thing as causal necessity. The determinist has misinterpreted the idea of regularity (see p. 352). Regularity does not entail necessity. Causes don't *compel* their effects. All we can say is that on each occasion, it is this one effect that occurs. To talk of causation is to talk of unbroken regularities, and so cause and effect are correlated. But we cannot, from this, draw any conclusions about necessity. Causation is about how things are, not how things must be.

Without causal necessity, it is not true that we *must* do whatever it is we do, or that we *could* not do anything else. What we choose is not compelled, and the motives on which we act don't *force* us to act as we do. It is not causation that threatens free will; it is causal necessity. If determinism is just the claim that every event has a cause, this is compatible with free will.

The hard determinist can respond that our concept of causation does involve necessity by pointing to the way science proceeds. In investigating the laws of nature, when we don't get the same effect in two cases we look for a difference that would explain this. Take 'Water boils at 100°C at sea level'. If we heat water, but it doesn't boil, we would think something about the situation was 'different' from what is specified by the law – perhaps the water isn't pure, perhaps we aren't at sea level, perhaps the water isn't yet 100°C. This demonstrates our commitment to the idea that water *must* boil at 100°C at sea level – it is the only possible effect (or the law is wrong).

Going further: 'other things being equal'

In DETERMINISM DEVELOPED (p. 367), we saw that our usual causal explanations depend upon 'other things being equal'. To defend causal necessity, and get rid of 'other things being equal', we introduced the idea of the entire state of the universe – from this state, only one state could be produced, in accordance with the laws of nature. But in order to understand causation, are we committed to eliminating 'other things being equal' in every case? It is not obvious that we are. Our causal explanations usually have a point, a purpose. They pick out what we consider *relevant* in the event. The 'other things being equal' clause helps us think about what *sorts* of other thing we need to 'control for' in establishing a cause (with water boiling: purity, height above sea level, etc.). This suggests that talking about 'the entire state of the universe' is not what we mean by 'other things being equal'.

If this is right, our idea of causation doesn't commit us to causal necessity – and so to determinism – in every case. Instead, we can argue that causal necessity is *a commitment in scientific investigation* – if there is a different effect, we continue looking for the difference in the cause. We can then argue that while this commitment is appropriate for natural science, it is *inappropriate* for other types of (causal) explanation, for example, in social science, psychology and accounts of what people do. These explanations don't look for or need exceptionless laws to work. When we explain why someone did something, we don't need to say that anyone in the same situation would do exactly the same thing.

So when doing natural science, we are committed to determinism, including causal necessity. When understanding and explaining people, we are not committed in this way, so we can allow that they have free will.

Is free will compatible with determinism?

Key points • • •

- Libertarians can argue that we have free will because the mind is not physical, and so the will is not causally determined.
- We can object that the claim that something non-physical (an act of will) can cause something physical (a bodily movement) contradicts science.
- One interpretation of quantum theory suggests that causation is not

deterministic. But this doesn't support free will, since the lack of determinism may only apply at the sub-atomic level; and even if nothing is determined, a billiard ball is as free as I am.

- Nietzsche rejects the free will debate and argues that nature is not causally determined, but is a matter of wills imposing themselves.

- Frankfurt argues that free will is the ability to will what one wants to will. We can object that this is not enough, as what we want to will may still be determined.

- We can also object that what we want to will is irrelevant, as free will requires that we will what we believe we should will. However, this still doesn't mean that I could have chosen otherwise in any situation. Frankfurt can respond that if our will reflects our values, that is enough.

- We can defend compatibilism by arguing that causation involves regularity, not necessity. However, scientific investigation demonstrates a commitment to causal necessity – that there *must* be some difference in the cause if the effects are different.

- We can respond that this is a commitment, not entailed by the concept of causation, and that it is appropriate for science, but not for explaining action.

III. The implications of determinism

The extent to which praise, blame and punishment can be meaningfully employed if determinism is true II

In our previous discussion (p. 364), we looked at two attempts to make sense of praise and blame, assuming determinism is true. Here are three more sophisticated theories.

Strawson: 'reactive attitudes'

'Freedom and Resentment'

Our practices of praise and blame are part of a *system of attitudes* that penetrates throughout our lives. These attitudes, which Peter Strawson calls 'reactive attitudes', include gratitude, resentment, forgiveness, love, hurt and many others: 'essentially natural human reactions to the good or ill will or indifference of others towards us'. They are responses to other people as moral agents; and they distinguish our interactions with people from our interactions with animals, computers and natural events.

Determinism wrongly associates not blaming someone when they couldn't do otherwise to not blaming a natural event. But the reason we don't blame someone because they couldn't avoid doing what they did, is quite different from the reason we don't blame computers or volcanoes, even though in both cases, the event was caused and unavoidable. Computers and volcanoes are not responsible because they are not responsible agents – *never* responsible. Not blaming someone on a particular occasion leaves intact our attitude to them as people – they are still responsible agents, even though they are not responsible for what happened. If we thought they were not responsible agents, for example, if they had a brain tumour or severe psychological illness, so that they cannot make choices at all, then our reactive attitudes towards them are replaced by an 'objective' attitude, the kind of attitude we take towards volcanoes and computers.

So, Strawson objects, if determinism implies that we should take the objective attitude towards *all* human actions, then it is saying the abnormal case is normal – which is self-contradictory. If we don't blame someone who is tied to a chair for not helping, this assumes that if they were able to help, but didn't, we could legitimately blame them. The usual reasons for not blaming someone depend on the normal cases in which blame is appropriate. Furthermore, the objective attitude would undermine all reactive attitudes, making all normal, personal human relationships impossible.

The hard determinist might respond that it is *rational* to take the objective attitude and *irrational* to have reactive attitudes. But what standard of rationality can we use here to make this judgement? The objective attitude is an intellectual, theoretical response to human behaviour, which determinism claims is supported by its theory of causation. However, to argue that this is the only attitude to take fails to take account of our experience of ourselves and others. It fails to see people as persons, part of a community of moral agents. Given this experience of ourselves and others, which we cannot abandon, the question of 'rationality' fails to arise: 'it is useless to ask whether it would not be rational for us to do what it is not in our nature to (be able to) do'. The complete absence of reactive attitudes is not humanly possible. And so the issue of moral responsibility is settled from *within* the perspective of reactive attitudes; we do not seek and we do not need an external justification. Determinism is irrelevant.

> Explain and illustrate the difference between reactive attitudes and the objective attitude.

> Is it irrational to have reactive attitudes?

OBJECTIONS

We can object that our reactive attitudes are only legitimate if people really are moral agents. In taking reactive attitudes for granted, Strawson has avoided the question of whether people are moral agents; he has assumed that we can legitimately treat them as such. But the hard determinist challenges this.

Second, Strawson claims that we cannot abandon reactive attitudes in favour of the objective attitude. But is this true? And even if it is, it does not show that we have moral responsibility, only that we cannot give up the idea (illusion?) that we have.

Third, Strawson argues that it is not rational to suggest we do something – abandon reactive attitudes – that we are not capable of. But this assumes that there is such a thing as choosing and acting, in this case whether or not to abandon reactive attitudes. But determinism challenges the assumption that we have any choices. Again, the response doesn't address the truth of the claim that determinism undermines moral responsibility.

> Assess the claim that reactive attitudes show that we can meaningfully talk of praise and blame even if determinism is true.

Moral responsibility and persons

> 'Responsibility for Self'

> This concept of a person was discussed in THE CHARACTERISTICS ASSOCIATED WITH PERSONHOOD (Ch. 5, p. 167).

Charles Taylor suggests a different way of defending moral responsibility. He argues that a person is a being who can raise the question 'Do I really want to be what I now am?' and evaluate the alternatives. When we evaluate how to be, we make our choices for reasons, but reasons are not themselves part of what we can choose. But this limitation doesn't undermine responsibility for ourselves, as we still *resolve* to be a certain way. Because it is in the very nature of a self to be able to raise the question of how to be and to resolve to be a particular way, we are responsible for ourselves. Because people are responsible in this way, it makes sense to praise and blame them. Determinism doesn't imply that we are not persons, so it is irrelevant to the question of moral responsibility.

Has Taylor has assumed free will in our resolution to be a certain way? If determinism is not compatible with free will, then resolving to be a certain way rather than another is an illusion. We can raise the question of how to be, but that does not mean that we are able to respond to the question as Taylor thinks we can. So we are not responsible for how we are.

> Discuss whether being able to change how you are as a person is enough for moral responsibility.

Taylor may respond that determinism does *not* show that we cannot respond to our thoughts about how to be. People do change how they are. As long as this remains true, then there is moral responsibility.

Going further: moral responsibility without being able to do otherwise

The challenge of determinism to moral responsibility is from the idea that we are not able to do otherwise (p. 363). Frankfurt argues that this is irrelevant. Suppose Smith wants Jones to perform a particular action, for example, make a donation to charity. If Jones decides to make the donation, there is nothing Smith needs to do and he does nothing; however, Smith has implanted a microchip in Jones' brain – if it looks like Jones will decide not to make the donation, Smith activates the chip, which causes Jones to decide to make the donation.

In this situation, there is no alternative for Jones – either he decides to make the donation 'on his own' or he is caused by the microchip to decide to make the donation. So he could not have chosen otherwise. Nevertheless, if he makes that decision *without* Smith activating the microchip, then he is morally responsible. (He is not morally responsible if Smith activates the microchip.) So what is important to moral responsibility is that the action is brought about by the person's *own* choices and desires.

But doesn't this assume that in the case in which Smith doesn't interfere, Jones *chooses* to make the donation? But was this choice an illusion, since only this action was possible? The hard determinist can reply that Jones *never* makes a choice – choice is dependent on free will, and there is no free will. So there is still no moral responsibility.

But we don't have to accept this. The example brings out the different relation someone can have to what they decide; it is this difference that moral responsibility picks up. Determinism doesn't do away with the difference between the case in which Jones comes to his decision without Smith's interference from the case in which Smith causes the decision. That difference is all that is needed for moral responsibility. The difference gives us the sense in which a decision is *mine* or not, quite independent of whether there is free will in the sense of being able to choose otherwise.

The determinist can insist that the distinction is some kind of illusion. Jones' decision is not 'his' in any sense that is strong enough for real moral responsibility; it is equally caused in every case, whether by Smith or some other process of natural causation.

'Alternate possibilities and moral responsibility'

Explain the claim that moral responsibility does not depend on being able to do otherwise.

Does moral responsibility require being able to do otherwise?

If determinism is true, can we meaningfully employ praise, blame and punishment?

The distinction between reasons and causes

In the discussions of Frankfurt's theory of free will (p. 378) and of Taylor's defence of moral responsibility (p. 384), we emphasised the idea of our choices being responsive to reasons. A final argument in favour of compatibilism develops the distinction between talking about causes, as determinism does, and talking about reasons, which we apply to choices and actions, and therefore to free will. We can argue that these two ways of talking are independent of each other, so determinism does not undermine free will. The argument develops a point made very early on (p. 354) that there is an important distinction between action and 'natural' causation.

The claim is this: to explain some occurrence as an action by giving the reasons why the person did it is logically different from explaining it as an effect of some (natural) cause.

1. Causes precede their effects in time. Reasons do not need to – if I give money to charity because it helps the needy, 'charity helps the needy' is not something that 'occurs' before I give money (it doesn't occur in time at all).
2. As the example of charity shows, reasons can cite purposes – 'in order to . . .'. But a causal explanation cannot cite a purpose.
3. Reasons can be 'good' or 'bad'. Not anything can be a (good) reason to act in a certain way: 'I hit him because his socks are purple.' But a cause cannot be good or bad in the same way. If the colour of his socks caused me to hit him, then it did; but it can't be a reason to hit him. Anything can be the cause of anything, logically speaking. This is not true of reasons.
4. If I say 'the cigarette caused the fire', this entails that there was a fire. However, if I say 'he intended to start a fire in order to keep warm', this doesn't entail that he actually started the fire. When we identify a cause, then the effect must exist. When we identify an intention or a reason, the action it is an intention or reason for does not have to have occurred.

> Outline and illustrate the distinction between reasons and causes.

The distinction between action and bodily movement

From these differences, we can argue that to identify some occurrence as an action and to identify it as an effect are logically independent. When we characterise something as an action, we talk of reasons and intentions. This depends on 'rules'. For example, to say that someone moved their queen and checkmated their opponent only makes sense in relation to the rules of chess. To say that someone got married requires us to understand marriage. To say that someone paid their bill implicitly refers to the rules that govern economic transactions.

None of these examples are *physical processes*. If you describe the physical causal sequence of someone moving a shaped piece of wood on a chequered board, you haven't said that they moved their queen. To say someone emitted the sounds that in English mean 'I do' is not to say they got married. To say someone made a series of ink marks on a piece of paper that they then put in a post box is not to say they paid their bill. We can only say what someone *did* if we don't talk at the level of bodily movements (or chemical exchanges in the brain) but at the level of social interactions.

Bodily movements are not actions, and actions cannot be reduced to bodily movements. What action a particular bodily movement serves depends on the context. Raising one's arm could be any number of actions – waving for help, making a bid at an auction, exercising. On the other hand, an action such as paying one's bill can involve many different kinds of bodily movement – writing (a cheque), typing (on a website), talking (over the phone).

> Outline and illustrate the distinction between actions and bodily movements.

The argument for compatibilism

The compatibilist can argue that the determinist is trying to reduce everything to the language of causes, to force us to talk about actions in terms of cause and effect. But we can't do this. Talking about actions is not reducible to talking about effects. As we noted in the discussion of 'OTHER THINGS BEING EQUAL' (p. 381), and have argued again here, if we talk about physical causes and effects, we lose sight of people and their actions. Having free will relates to people and their actions. So it is logically independent of determinism.

We can object that this leaves us with a puzzle. Even if the distinction between actions and bodily movements, reasons and causes, is right, this might not defend free will. Actions involve bodily movements, and the compatibilist accepts that the bodily movements are causally determined. But in that case, no other bodily movement is possible at a particular time from the one that occurred. If I raise my arm, then whether this is bidding, or waving, or exercising, I could not have not raised my arm. How, then, do I have free will? To become an argument for free will, perhaps the distinction between reasons and causes needs to be supplemented by other compatibilist accounts.

> Assess the claim that the distinction between reasons and causes makes determinism compatible with free will.

Key points • • •

- Strawson argues that we have reactive attitudes towards other people. We only adopt the objective attitude in abnormal cases. Hard determinism suggests reactive attitudes are irrational, and we should always adopt the objective attitude. But this makes the abnormal case normal and, in any case, is impossible for us to do. So determinism is irrelevant to moral responsibility.

- We can object that Strawson assumes that we *legitimately* have reactive attitudes towards others. But at best, he has shown that we cannot give up reactive attitudes, not that they are legitimate.

- Taylor argues that we can evaluate how we are as persons and respond by resolving to be a certain way. This makes us responsible for ourselves.

- We can object that resolving to be a certain way presupposes free will, which hard determinism argues we do not have.

- Frankfurt argues that we can be morally responsible without being able to do otherwise. We only need to act on our own desires and choices.

- We can object that if all our actions are caused, it makes no difference how they are caused.

- We can argue that reasons and causes are quite distinct, and so are actions and bodily movements. Talking about free will involves the language of reasons and actions, while determinism involves talking about causes and bodily movements. So determinism is irrelevant to free will.

- We can object that actions still involve bodily movements. If my body could not have moved otherwise, then in what sense is the action free?

SUMMARY

In this chapter, we have looked at the following questions:

1. What is determinism?

2. What is free will and is it compatible with determinism?

3. What are the implications of determinism for moral responsibility and rationality?

In our discussion of these questions, we have looked at the following issues:

1. What is determinism, and how is it distinct from predictability, fatalism and predestination?

2. Is determinism compatible with chance? Is there chance in the physical world?

3. Does our concept of causation involve the idea of causal necessity?

4. Is there a meaningful distinction between human action and the effect of a cause? Are reasons distinct from causes?

5. Do human actions fall under physical laws?

6. Are human actions determined by environmental and hereditary factors?

7. Is the experience of free will an illusion?

8. Are our choices caused?

9. Does human decision-making occupy a place outside the natural order?

10. Is free will simply being able to do what one wants to do? Is it being able to will what one wants to will?

11. Is the opposite of free action constrained action rather than caused effect?

12. Does determinism undermine rationality? If so, does this make the arguments for determinism incoherent?

13. Is it true that if we cannot do otherwise, then we are not morally responsible?

14. Can we meaningfully employ praise, blame and punishment if determinism is true?

11 PREPARING FOR THE EXAM

To get good exam results, you need to have a good sense of what the exam will be like and what the examiners are looking for, and to revise in a way that will help you prepare to answer the questions well. This probably sounds obvious, but, in fact, many students do not think about the exam itself, only about what questions might come up. There is a big difference. This chapter will provide you with some guidance on how to approach your exams in a way that will help get you the best results you can. It is divided into three sections: revision, understanding the question, and exam technique. Before continuing to read this chapter, it is worth looking back at the Introduction to see how exam questions are structured and what the Assessment Objectives are.

Throughout the chapter, I will highlight revision points and exam tips. You can find these collected together at the end of the chapter.

Revision: knowing what the examiners are looking for

There are lots of memory tricks for learning information for exams. This chapter isn't about those. Revision isn't just about learning information, but also about learning how to use that information well in the exam. Being able to do this isn't a question of memory, but of directed revision and concentration in the exam. If you've been doing the exercises throughout this book, then you have been putting into practice the advice I give below.

It may sound obvious, but in order to know how best to answer the exam questions, you need to think about how they are marked. The examiners mark your answers according to three principles, known as 'Assessment Objectives' (AOs). These are listed in the Introduction, on p. 3.

You can use these AOs to help guide your revision. AO1 (Knowledge and understanding) leads straight to the first revision point:

R1: Learn the arguments. Who said what? What terms and concepts did they use? How did they defend their positions?

This, you may think, is challenging enough! But this isn't enough. In displaying your knowledge, you need to show what is *relevant* to the question being asked. Knowing what is relevant is a special kind of knowledge, which involves thinking carefully about what you know about the theories in relation to the question asked. The best way to learn what is relevant is to practise answering questions, either exam questions or questions you make up for yourself or a friend. Try to make up questions that are similar to the exam questions, using the same 'key words' (I'll talk about these in the next section). Practising answering different questions on the same topic helps keep your knowledge flexible, because you have to think of just the right bit of information that will answer the question.

R2: Practise applying your knowledge by answering questions about it. The best questions to practise with are past exam questions, but you can also make up questions for yourself.

AO2 (Interpretation and analysis) means that your knowledge needs to be developed in a particular way. In philosophy, there is no easy, straightforward answer to 'What did he mean when he said . . .'. So in knowing and understanding arguments and issues, you need to be able to *interpret* them and defend your interpretation.

R3: Revise those aspects of the issue that are hard to understand. Practise arguing that they *can* be understood in more than one way, and why they *should* be understood to have the meaning you give them.

One aspect of interpretation is knowing what is relevant and what is not to the view you are discussing. From this point, what point follows next? Or again, what would be a relevant example? You can either remember good examples you have read, or create your own. In either case, you should know precisely what point the example is making. An irrelevant example demonstrates that you don't really know what you are talking about.

> R4: Prepare examples beforehand, rather than try to invent them in the exam. If you can use your own, that's great (you'll get extra marks if they are good). But they must be short and they must make the right point – so try them out on your friends and teachers first.

But this is only half of AO2. When interpreting someone, you also need to show what his arguments are and how they are supposed to work. This means being able to *analyse* an issue, finding its main claims and main arguments, and then breaking down the arguments down into premises and conclusions, and showing how the conclusion is supposed to follow from the premises.

> R5: Spend time identifying the main claims and arguments involved in each issue you have studied, putting arguments in your own words, stating clearly what the conclusion is and what the premises are. Point out or show how the reasoning is supposed to work.

What of AO3? How do you revise for 'assessment and evaluation'? This AO tests you on how well you can relate and compare arguments, how well you build an argument, deal with objections, and come to a supported conclusion. The best way to prepare for it is to spend time *thinking* about the arguments and issues. Thinking is quite different from knowing about. You might know Hume's arguments against rationalism, but you may never have stopped to really work out whether you think they are any good.

AO3 encourages you to do two things. One is to question what the argument actually shows – do the premises support the conclusion or some other point of view? The second is to relate a particular argument to other arguments and viewpoints on the issue, and in particular to reflect on whether the objections to an argument undermine it. Work through the arguments so that you understand for yourself the pros and cons of each viewpoint. As a minimum, be able to argue both for and against a particular view.

> R6: Think reflectively about the arguments and issues. Practise arguing for and against a particular view. Think about the place and importance of the arguments for the issue as a whole.

Finally, you need to be able to construct arguments, not just report them. This means that what you write should also take the form of premises and conclusion. The premises will be your judgements as you go along, in response to this view or that objection. These judgements need to add up to a conclusion. You shouldn't end your essay with a totally different point of view than your evaluations in the essay support. In other words, do the judgements you reach reflect the arguments you have presented?

This doesn't mean that you have to find one point of view on the issue and defend it. But if you can't come to a firm conclusion about which viewpoint is right, try to come to a firm conclusion about why the different points each seem right in their own way, and why it is difficult to choose. Philosophy is not about knowing the 'right answers', it is about understanding why an answer *might* be right and why it is difficult to know.

> R7: Think about how your judgements on the various arguments you have studied add up. Do they lead to one conclusion, one point of view being right? Or do you think arguments for and against one position are closely balanced?

These first seven revision points relate to taking in and understanding information. There are two more points that will help you organise the information, learn it better, and prepare you for answering exam questions.

A good way of organising your information is to create answer outlines or web-diagrams for particular issues. For example, from Unit 1.1 Reason and experience, you could create an outline or web-diagram for innate knowledge. Think about the essential points, and organise them, perhaps like this:

1. What is innate knowledge? Is there more than one interpretation?
2. Who argued against innate knowledge? What are the main arguments?
3. Who argued for innate knowledge? What knowledge did they say was innate? What arguments did they use?
4. What are the main strengths and weaknesses of the claim that there is innate knowledge?
5. What is your conclusion on the issue, and why?

With an outline like this, you should be able to answer any question that comes up on innate knowledge.

> R8: Create structured outlines or web-diagrams for particular issues. Try to cover all the main points.

Finally, once you've organised your notes into an outline or web-diagram, time yourself writing exam answers. Start by using your outline, relying on your memory to fill in the details. Then practise by memorising the outline as well, and doing it as though it were an actual exam. You might be surprised at how quickly the time goes by. You'll find that you need to be very focused – but this is what the examiners are looking for, answers that are thoughtful but to the point.

> R9: Practise writing timed answers. Use your notes at first, but then practise without them.

There is one more thing important to revision that I haven't yet talked about, which is how the structure of the questions and how the marks are awarded can help you to decide what to focus on. This is what we'll look at next.

Understanding the question: giving the examiners what they want

The key to doing well in an exam is understanding the question. I don't just mean understanding the *topic* of the question, such as 'empiricism' or 'free will'. Of course, this is very important. But you also need to understand what the question is asking you to *do*. And this is related, in a very strict way, to the three Assessment Objectives discussed earlier. This section is on how exam questions 'work'.

Key words

If you look at the examples of questions throughout this book, you will see that they start with different 'key words', such as 'explain', 'illustrate', 'outline', 'assess', 'discuss', 'consider' and 'evaluate'. Obeying these instructions is crucially important to getting a good mark. If you are asked to *explain* an argument and you argue that the argument is unpersuasive because . . . , then you will fail to gain marks. And the same is true if you are asked to assess a claim and you only describe and illustrate what the claim means.

In the exam, each question has two parts – the first uses one set of key words, the second uses a second set. The first set – 'explain', 'illustrate' and 'identify' – relate to AO1 (*knowledge and understanding*). You are being asked simply to say what the theories say in a way that is relevant to the question asked. All the marks available here are for AO1.

The second set – 'discuss', 'consider', 'assess' and 'evaluate' – relate to AO2 (*interpretation and analysis*) and AO3 (*assessment and evaluation*). You need to present an argument, explaining and illustrating it as you go along, which aims towards an answer to the question, showing why that particular answer is the best one.

The key to understanding what the question is asking, and so to getting a good mark, is to take notice of the key words.

Question structure and marks

Look at the sample questions in the Introduction (p. 4). Notice that the same key words always appear in the same parts of the question. This is because the marks given for each part of the question relate to a particular AO in a very strict way. All of the 15 points for part (a) are for AO1. There are 30 points for part (b): 3 for AO1, 18 for AO2, and 9 for AO3.

Why is this important? For the same reason that the key words are important. It tells you what you should be doing. If all the marks are for AO1 (knowledge and understanding), there is no point spending any time evaluating. And if there are 9 marks for AO3 (assessment and evaluation), then no matter how clearly you describe the theories and arguments, you cannot get a good mark for the question if you do not also evaluate them.

There is another reason this distribution of marks is important. It can help guide your revision. There are 45 marks available in total: 18 for AO1, 18 for AO2, and 9 for AO3. So you need to have a very firm grasp of the facts about ideas and arguments, and how to interpret and analyse them. However, you will find it difficult to get an 'A' or 'B' grade unless you also know how to evaluate them well.

Exam technique: getting the best result you can

If you've understood the question structure, and know what to expect in the exam, the exam will not seem so daunting. You'll have a good idea about how to proceed, and a sense of how the parts of the question are testing different aspects of your knowledge. This section gives you some tips on how to approach the questions when you are actually in the exam.

Exams are very exciting, whether in a good way or a bad way! It can be helpful, therefore, to take your time at the beginning, not to rush into your answers, but to plan your way. The tips I give below are roughly in the order that you might apply them when taking the exam. You might be surprised at the number of things it can be worth doing before you write anything at all.

If you have studied just two issues for Unit 1 and two issues for Unit 2, you have no choice about which questions to answer. If you have studied more than two issues in each unit, you need to decide carefully which question to answer, and this means reading the whole of each question before making your decision. You might find that although you know the answer to part (a), you aren't sure about part (b). If you don't read the whole question first, but just start your answer to part (a) straightaway, you could end up wishing you had answered the other question.

E1. Read through all the relevant questions before starting your answer. This will help you to decide which question you can answer best overall, taking into account all the parts.

Once you've decided which question to do, you need to think how long to spend on each part. Here the marks available for each part should be your guide. You have 90 minutes for the exam, and there are 90 marks available. So you've got one minute per mark. That means you should spend around 15 minutes on each part (a), and 30 minutes on each part (b). This isn't exact, and you may want to spend more time on the part (b) questions, which require more planning.

E2. The number of marks available for each part should be a rough guide to how long you spend on it. But allow a little extra time for the later parts and parts you find difficult.

Before you start to write your answer to any part, read the question again very closely. There are two things to look out for. First, notice the key words, and remind yourself what they are asking for. For example, the question might be 'Explain and illustrate what is meant by "power" in political concepts.' If you only explain, and do not provide examples, then you won't get full marks. Second, notice the precise phrasing of the question. For example, in part (b), it might say '"All ideas derive from the sense experiences which they copy." Discuss.' If you don't make any reference to the view that ideas are *copied* (not just derived generally) from experience, again, you won't get full marks.

   Because an exam is exciting (good or bad), many people have a tendency to notice only what the question is about, for example, empiricism or power. They don't notice the rest of the words in the question. But the question is never 'so tell me everything you know about empiricism'! *Every word counts*. Whether you are describing, outlining or evaluating, your answer should relate not just to the issue in general, but to the *specific words* of the question.

E3. Before starting your answer, read the questions again very closely. Take note of every word, and especially the 'key word' which tells you what to do.

You are now ready to start answering the question. But, especially with the longer answers (part (b)), many people find it is worth organising their thoughts first. What are you going to say, in what order? This is particularly important with questions that involve evaluation, since arguments require that you present ideas in a logical order. If you've memorised an outline or a web-diagram, quickly write it out at the beginning so that you note down all the points. It is very easy to forget something or to go off on a tangent once you are stuck into the arguments. Having an outline or web-diagram to work from will help you keep your answer relevant and structured. It will also remind you how much you still want to cover, so it can help you pace yourself better. However, you might discover, as you develop your answer, that parts of the outline or diagram are irrelevant or just don't fit. Don't worry – the outline is only there as a guide.

> E4. Before you start your answer, especially if it will be comparatively long, it can be worth writing out your outline or web-diagram first. This can help remind you of the key points you want to make, and the order in which you want to make them.

All the questions ask for examples at some point. Finding and using a good example is very important. Good examples are concise and relevant, and support your argument. But you need to explain why they support your argument. An example is an illustration, not an argument.

> E5. Keep your examples short and make sure they support the point you want to make. Always explain how they support your point.

Because philosophy is about the logical relationship of ideas, there are a number of rules of thumb about presentation. Here are four important ones.

E6. Four rules of thumb:

1. Don't use a 'technical term', like 'the state of nature' or 'the onto-logical argument', without saying what it means.
2. Describe a theory before evaluating it. (If you have described it in answer to a previous part, you don't need to describe it again.)
3. Keep related ideas together. If you have a thought later on, add a footnote indicating where in the answer you want it to be read.
4. Don't state the conclusion to an argument before you've discussed the argument, especially if you are going to present objections to that conclusion. You can state what the argument hopes to show, but don't state it *as* a conclusion.

For part (b), it is worth noting that evaluation is more than just presenting objections and responses side-by-side. Get the objections and the theory to 'talk' to each other, and try to come to some conclusion about which side is stronger. Finally, it is worth noting that one good discussion is worth more than many weak or superficial points, so choose two or three of the *most powerful* relevant objections, and discuss those in depth.

E7. Make sure your discussion is not just reporting a sequence of points of view, but presents objections and replies, and tries to reach a particular conclusion.

Finally, it is very easy to forget something, or say it in an unclear way. Leave time to check your answer at the end. You might find you can add a sentence here or there to connect two ideas together more clearly, or that some word is left undefined. These little things can make a big difference to the mark.

E8. Leave time to check your answer at the end. You may want to add a helpful sentence here and there.

Revision tips

R1: Learn the arguments. Who said what? What terms and concepts did they use? How did they defend their positions?

R2: Practise applying your knowledge by answering questions about it. The best questions to practise with are past exam questions, but you can also make up questions for yourself.

R3: Revise those aspects of the issue that are hard to understand. Practise arguing that they *can* be understood in more than one way, and why they *should* be understood to have the meaning you give them.

R4: Prepare examples beforehand, rather than try to invent them in the exam. If you can use your own, that's great (you'll get extra marks if they are good). But they must be short and they must make the right point – so try them out on your friends and teachers first.

R5: Spend time identifying the main claims and arguments involved in each issue you have studied, putting arguments in your own words, stating clearly what the conclusion is and what the premises are. Point out or show how the reasoning is supposed to work.

R6: Think reflectively about the arguments and issues. Practise arguing for and against a particular view. Think about the place and importance of the arguments for the issue as a whole.

R7: Think about how your judgements on the various arguments you have studied add up. Do they lead to one conclusion, one point of view being right? Or do you think arguments for and against one position are closely balanced?

R8: Create structured outlines or web-diagrams for particular issues. Try to cover all the main points.

R9: Practise writing timed answers. Use your notes at first, but then practise without them.

Exam tips

E1. Read through all the relevant questions before starting your answer. This will help you to decide which question you can answer best overall, taking into account all the parts.

E2. The number of marks available for each part should be a rough guide to how long you spend on it. But allow a little extra time for the later parts and parts you find difficult.

E3. Before starting your answer, read the question again very closely. Take note of every word, and especially the 'key word' which tells you what to do.

E4. Before you start your answer, especially if it will be comparatively long, it can be worth writing out your outline or web-diagram first. This can help remind you of the key points you want to make, and the order in which you want to make them.

E5. Keep your examples short and make sure they support the point you want to make. Always explain how they support your point.

E6. Four rules of thumb:

1. Don't use a 'technical term', like 'the state of nature' or 'the ontological argument', without saying what it means.
2. Describe a theory before evaluating it. (If you have described it in answer to a previous part, you don't need to describe it again.)
3. Keep related ideas together. If you have a thought later on, add a footnote indicating where in the answer you want it to be read.
4. Don't state the conclusion to an argument before you've discussed the argument, especially if you are going to present objections to that conclusion. You can state what the argument hopes to show, but don't state it *as* a conclusion.

E7. Make sure your discussion is not just reporting a sequence of points of view, but presents objections and replies, and tries to reach a particular conclusion.

E8. Leave time to check your answer at the end. You may want to add a helpful sentence here and there.

GLOSSARY

a posteriori – Knowledge of propositions that can only be known to be true or false through sense experience.

a priori – Knowledge of propositions that do not require (sense) experience to be known to be true or false.

ad hoc – A statement or a move in an argument that suits the purpose at hand but has no independent support.

analytic – An analytic proposition is true (or false) in virtue of the meanings of the words. For instance, 'a bachelor is an unmarried man' is analytically true, while 'a square has three sides' is analytically false.

argument – A reasoned inference from one set of claims – the premises – to another claim – the conclusion.

conditional – A proposition that takes the form of 'if . . ., then . . .'.

contingent – A proposition that could be either true or false, a state of affairs that may or may not hold, depending on how the world actually is.

deductive (deduction) – An argument whose conclusion is *logically entailed* by its premises, that is, if the premises are true, the conclusion *cannot* be false.

empirical – Relating to or deriving from experience, especially sense experience, but also including experimental scientific investigation.

empiricism – The theory that there can be no a priori knowledge of synthetic propositions about the world (outside my mind), that is, all a priori knowledge is of analytic propositions, while all knowledge of synthetic propositions must be checked against sense experience.

epistemology – The study ('-ology') of knowledge ('episteme') and related concepts, including belief, justification, certainty. It looks at the possibility and sources of knowledge.

fallacy – A pattern of poor reasoning. A fallacious argument or theory is one that is mistaken in some way.

inductive (induction) – An argument whose conclusion is *supported* by its premises, but is not logically entailed by them, that is, if the premises are true, the conclusion may be false, but this is unlikely (relative to the premises); one form of inductive argument is inference to the best explanation, that is, the conclusion presents the 'best explanation' for why the premises are true.

innate – Knowledge or ideas that are in some way present 'from birth'.

metaphysics – The branch of philosophy that enquires about the fundamental nature of reality.

necessary – A proposition that *must* be true (or if false, it must be false), a state of affairs that *must* hold.

necessary condition – The proposition P is a necessary condition for the proposition Q if the conditional 'If Q, then P' is true. If Q is true, then P must be true. So Q can only be true if P is true.

normative – Relating to 'norms', rules or reasons for conduct.

ontology – The study of (-ology) of what exists or 'being' (ont).

proposition – A declarative statement (or more accurately, what is claimed by a declarative statement), such as 'mice are mammals'; propositions can go after 'that' in 'I believe that . . .' and 'I know that . . .'.

rationalism – The theory that there can be a priori knowledge of synthetic propositions about the world (outside my mind); this knowledge is gained by reason without reliance on sense experience.

scepticism – The view that our usual justifications for claiming our beliefs amount to knowledge are inadequate, so we do not in fact have knowledge.

sense-data (singular **sense-datum**) – In perception, mental images or representations of what is perceived, 'bits' of experience; if they exist, they are the immediate objects of perception.

sufficient condition – The proposition P is a sufficient condition for the proposition Q if the conditional 'If P, then Q' is true. The truth of P is enough to ensure that Q is true.

synthetic – A proposition that is not analytic, but true or false depending on how the world is.

veridical – A proposition that is true or an experience that represents the world as it actually is.

INDEX BY SYLLABUS CONTENT

INDEX

Related titles from Routledge

The Basics of Essay Writing

Nigel Warburton

The ability to write a clear, well-argued essay is absolutely crucial for students working at every academic level. As the basis for coursework and the vast majority of written exams, the essay is unavoidably at the heart of modern education.

In *The Basics of Essay Writing* Nigel Warburton, bestselling author and experienced lecturer, provides all the guidance and advice you need to dramatically improve your essay-writing skills. The book opens with a discussion of why it is so important to write a good essay, and proceeds through a step-by-step exploration of exactly what you should consider to improve your essays and marks. Within, you will find help on how to:

- Focus on answering the question asked
- Research and plan your essay
- Build and sustain an argument
- Improve your writing style and tone

Written in the author's accomplished, student-friendly style, *The Basics of Essay Writing* is packed full of good advice and practical exercises. Students of all ages and in every subject area will find it an easy-to-use and indispensable aid to their studies.

ISBN: 978–0–415–43404–1 (pbk)

Available at all good bookshops
For ordering and further information please visit:
www.routledge.com